OUTDOOR LIFE DEER HUNTER'S YEARBOOK 1983

Outdoor Life Books, New York

Stackpole Books, Harrisburg, Pennsylvania

Published by

Outdoor Life Books
Times Mirror Magazines, Inc.
380 Madison Avenue
New York, NY 10017

Distributed to the trade by

Stackpole Books
Cameron and Kelker Streets
P.O. Box 1831
Harrisburg, PA 17105

ISSN 0734-2918

ISBN 0-943822-18-1

Manufactured in the United States of America

Contents

Preface

Welcome to the first *Outdoor Life Deer Hunter's Yearbook.* It begins an annual series designed to help you become a better deer hunter.

This book will broaden your knowledge of deer, guns, hunting, safety, and outdoor lore in general. And it will deepen your appreciation of the total hunting experience.

Of course, no book can teach you all there is to know about any subject, let alone deer hunting. But as you hunt alongside the experts here or "listen" as they expound on equipment and techniques – as well as on avoiding common mistakes – you'll find yourself getting better prepared for your days afield.

The book's 45 chapters were selected from recent issues of *Outdoor Life* and grouped into ten convenient sections. This arrangement lets you tackle subjects of keenest interest to you first.

You couldn't ask for a more highly qualified team of outdoor writers and photographers than you'll find represented here.

In Part 1, **Planning Your Hunt,** for instance, you get expert advice. Jim Carmichel, who has enjoyed dream hunts in 30 countries on six continents, tells how to go on your hunt of a lifetime. He covers everything from finding the right outfitter to getting the right gear and packing it properly. Norm Nelson, whose family has hunted deer for generations, tells how to make your own deer-hunting luck by using all your senses and by hunting smart. John Weiss, a writer-hunter known for his thorough reporting, refutes the claim that deer are color blind.

Jim Carmichel, *Outdoor Life*'s renowned gun expert, wrote all chapters in Part 2 (**Lowdown on Guns and Accessories**). The author of three gun books and the coauthor of 12, Jim draws from his vast background as engineer, competitive shooter, and master hunter when writing on subjects ranging from the components of deer cartridges to sighting-in a deer rifle.

In Part 3, **Going for Whitetails**, Gerald Almy calls forth his own experience and that of many veteran hunters. Then Byron Dalrymple, who has perhaps written more outdoor books than any other author, shares a wealth of lore in "A Lifetime of Whitetail Hunting." John O. Cartier, veteran field editor of *Outdoor Life* and the author of three outdoor books, explains how experts avoid making critical deer-hunting mistakes.

Samples of lore in Part 4, **Going for Mule Deer,** include "Work Hard for Big Muleys" by Bruce Brady, whose credentials include service as a licensed big-game guide, a state game-commission member, and an *Outdoor Life* editor-at-large. "The Trouble with Muleys," by writer-photographer Bill McRae, gives evidence why muleys are much tougher than many hunters have been led to believe. Jim Zumbo, wildlife and forest manager with a long list of magazine and book credits, interviews an immensely successful trophy hunter in "Nine Bucks for the Record."

The book's six other parts bulge with deer lore. Here's a sampling:

- **Outdoor Lore Can Make the Difference** (from selection of footgear to the latest scientific findings on what lost hunters ought to do).
- **Matters of Sportsmanship** (from a startling report on poaching to observations on the best way to start a new deer hunter).
- **Bowhunting: Basics and Fine Points** (heavily illustrated guide for serious bowhunters, plus related features).
- **The Spirit of the Hunt** (accounts of memorable hunts).

- **After Your Deer Is Down** (including step-by-step directions for field dressing your deer, by George Haas, *Outdoor Life* senior editor).
- **Big Bucks and the Records** (the Boone and Crockett and the Pope and Young records systems for trophy deer).

One thing you'll notice, though, if you read every chapter: In that great tradition of deer hunting, even the experts disagree on some points. As you advance toward expert status yourself, you'll encounter other experts in print and in the woods with whom *you'll* disagree. That's as it should be.

For now, we hope you'll enjoy this yearbook and find yourself referring to it often. But, again, it's not intended to be the last word (the next *Outdoor Life Deer Hunter's Yearbook* is already in the planning stages).

This first volume will add fundamentals and fine points to what you've gained from your own hunting. It will also provide fresh viewpoints with which to enter that annually renewing excitement we call deer hunting.

Good reading to you, and good hunting!

Chet Fish
Former Editor-in-Chief
Outdoor Life Magazine

OUTDOOR LIFE DEER HUNTER'S YEARBOOK

PART 1 PLANNING YOUR HUNT

How to Go on Your Hunt of a Lifetime

You've waited long enough. Now's the time to plan that hunt you've been dreaming about. Let's delay no longer. We'll start *right now* before prices go up yet again and the hills get even steeper.

What do you want to hunt? If you're an Easterner or Midwesterner, you may have your heart set on a hunt for mule deer. If you're a Westerner—even a Westerner with a great deal of hunting experience—you may find yourself with the desire the late great Jack O'Connor had late in his career. Despite all of Jack's vast hunting experience, he had never had the chance to take a good whitetail trophy. So a hunt for whitetail was high on his list until he achieved that goal.

Perhaps your hunt of a lifetime runs to thoughts of elk, grizzly, moose, pronghorn, or caribou.

What's that you say? You'd like to try for everything? That's a tall order. The days of the great combination hunts are mainly past. Mule deer and elk are still a likely combination, and you might even squeeze in a pronghorn on the same outing, but elk, grizzly, bighorn sheep, goat, deer and pronghorn on one trip? Not very likely. Staggered hunting seasons in most states rule out big combination bags, and some species have more or less isolated themselves in particular areas so that there is little overlapping of range. Some combinations that still work pretty well, though, are moose and grizzly in Alaska or British Columbia, Dall sheep and caribou in Alaska and the Yukon, and goat and moose in British Columbia.

If you have your heart set on just one species, say an elk, deciding where to go is easy, but if you are going for a combination you should decide which animal is most important to you and plan accordingly. Let's say you want to go to Alaska for grizzly and moose. In some areas there may be many very big moose but a shortage of bear. In another area your chances of getting a bear may be better, but the moose aren't so big. It's best to decide what you want most and build your plans around that particular animal. It simplifies your planning and makes for a better-organized hunt. It improves your relations with your outfitter. Most important, it greatly improves the chances that your hunt of a lifetime will result in the trophy of a lifetime.

Once you've decided on your principal trophy animal, the next step is to decide where and with whom you'd like to hunt. Successful big-game hunting, especially for the scarcer, more desirable species, requires a thorough knowledge of the area and a good understanding of the games' habits. You also need camps, equipment and wilderness transportation which may be 4 x 4 vehicles, horses or even aircraft. Since the hunter usually lacks one or more of these, the only realistic choice is usually a guided hunt, and in most instances this is the desirable alternative. Though it is possible to treat yourself to a do-it-yourself hunt in many major big-game areas, you must face the fact that competition with other hunters can be intense in public-domain areas, and the likelihood of success in such places is proportionately lower.

Licensed guides and outfitters in the Western states, Alaska and the Canadian provinces usually have an area assigned to them by the game department. This gives them exclusive or semi-exclusive use of that area for their clients. Semi-exclusive rights usually means that the outfitter's area is open to residents of the state or province but not to nonresidents or to other outfitters and their clients. Most of the areas assigned to licensed outfitters and guides are so remote and vast that there is lit-

Sighting a trophy, such as this muley, can owe less to luck than planning. *Photograph by Erwin A. Bauer*

tle chance you will see anyone when you're actually hunting, not even members of your own party. Licensed outfitters are very particular about an assigned area and go to considerable lengths to insure that it continues to produce quality trophies year after year.

Some bargain-price outfitters do not have assigned areas and may simply take you to a public-hunting area, which is probably overhunted. Beware! Some outfitters may actually own the lands they hunt, or they may lease hunting rights from the landowner. The hunting in these places is often very good, and this is especially true in New Mexico's high elk country.

But, you say, "Where do I find an outfitter?"

Turn to the back pages of Outdoor Life and you'll find dozens of outfitters listed along with a description of the game they hunt. In fact, you'll find so many guide services listed that you may become somewhat confused about where to begin. You can narrow the choice somewhat by selecting the region you prefer. If, for example, you've had your heart set on a hunt in the high country, you'll find listings under Mountain States. Your next step is to pick out a few outfitters who seem to offer what you are looking for and write for their brochures.

Time was when the typical guide was a scruffy-chinned cowpoke looking to pick up a few extra dollars between roundups, but those days have gone the way of the 60-day packtrip. Outfitting is real business these days and the typical guide is a professional. Don't be surprised then that the responses to your inquiries, rather than being penciled notes, are slick brochures with full-color pictures and a secretary-typed letter from the office manager.

Invariably the pictures show wonderful trophies that make you want to grab your rifle and jump on the next plane, but keep in mind that these are probably the best animals ever taken out of their camps. The outfitter is not necessarily trying to imply that all his clients get equally huge trophies, but by the same token he definitely wants to convince you that big animals do—or once did—live in his area. After all, he depends on his brochure to convince you that he's the guide you're looking for. So how do you decide which outfitter you want?

The best way to make this all-important decision is on the basis of personal recommendations. Don't hesitate to ask an outfitter for the names and addresses of past clients. Most outfitters keep an up-to-date list of addresses that they will send you, and most of these lists include telephone numbers. Ten or 15 references are usually provided, and if you start early you can contact all of them. Don't base your decision on only one or two.

Make sure that the reference list is up to date and pay particular attention to references from the season just past. They will give you the best idea of what to expect in the way of camp conditions and the availability of game. If a reference list is five years old or older, there might be reason for suspicion. In addition to questions about the quantity and quality of game in the outfitter's area, be sure to ask about the condition of the camp and the quality of food. Were the guides courteous and helpful? Were the horses docile, and did the tents leak? When you write past clients for their recommendations—or lack of recommendations—be sure to enclose a stamped, self-addressed envelope, and end your inquiry with this question, "Would you hunt with this outfitter again?"

You owe the outfitter something as well, and hopefully you'll be as honest with him as you expect him to be with you. For example, if you're afraid of horses don't wait until the first morning of the hunt to make your fears known. If you are in poor physical condition, say so and be sure he is aware of any other peculiarities or ailments that might affect your hunt. If you have special diet requirements most outfitters will happily cater to your needs if you give advance warning. Don't wait until you're at 14,000 feet and 40 miles from base camp to tell your guide that you exist on a diet of watercress and matzo balls.

You need a frank dialogue with the outfitter right from the beginning. A common cause of discord is a misunderstanding over the number of actual hunting days. Some hunters who sign up for a 10-day hunt are shocked to discover that they don't actually spend 10 days searching for game but instead use up two of the days packing to and from the hunting camp. The schedule varies with the outfitter, so be sure and ask how many actual hunting days you will have.

Also make sure how many other hunters will be in camp and whether or not each hunter will have his own guide or if you'll share a guide with another hunter. Too often hunters sign up for a guided big-game hunt with the notion that the party will consist of just himself and the guide plus a cook and wrangler in the uncharted wilderness. You can do it that way if you want to and if you can afford it, but don't be disappointed if you haven't asked and then discover that yours is not the only rifle in camp. Anyway, you probably won't see the other hunters during the day, and their company is pleasant at night.

One more thing. Don't be disappointed if the legendary Bronco Stetson, the outfitter with whom you booked, isn't your personal guide. He may not even be in camp. Your guide might be a pink-cheeked youngster fresh out of college, hardly your idea of what a wilderness guide should look like, but don't make snap judgments until you've seen him in action. He's probably very good at what he does or he wouldn't be there. After all, your name will be on next year's reference list, and the outfitter wants his clients to be happy.

Once you select your outfitter events begin to pick up speed, especially if you have booked for the upcoming season. (That's only one reason why it is a good idea to book at least 10 months in advance.) Several details need attention, not the least of which is applying for a license, especially if you wish to hunt in a state that has drawings or a lottery-type license-issuance system. Your outfitter will send the necessary application forms with the appropriate hunt areas already filled in, but it will be up to you to complete the form and submit it on time with the required fee. Usually the outfitter or his representative will be present at the drawing and will let you know immediately if your name has been drawn for a permit. These drawings are usually held well in advance of the coming season, so if you aren't successful there will be time to book a hunt in a state that has over-the-counter permit sales. Some states also issue special "landowner permits" that are often made available to an outfitter's clients, so inquire if such a permit can be had.

Once it is determined that you will be properly licensed to hunt in the outfitter's state and area, the outfitter will send you a hunt agreement which is, quite simply, a contract specifying the services to be provided by him and the payment he expects of you. Until now perhaps plans for your hunt have been progressing rather casually so it may be something of a shock to face the cold financial realities of big-game hunting. Perhaps most disturbing is the demand for a sizable deposit and the contract clause that specifies the deposit is nonrefundable if you cancel on short notice. For those of us accustomed to paying for what we get only after we get it, this is a big pill to get down, and it is worth explaining.

Keep in mind that the outfitter can guide hunts only within the open season set by the game commission in his state or province. Within that period, he must conduct his hunts on a very tight schedule. Once a hunter is booked, that particular slot is filled, and a non-paying cancellation could mean the difference between profit or loss for the whole season.

Most of the expenses of your hunt are incurred before you arrive. Your horse has to be paid for and fed. Your tent and saddle have to be bought and stored. Area fees to the state have to be paid, as do dozens of other related expenses. Your nonrefundable deposit is a guarantee that these expenses will be covered, even if you aren't there to reap the benefits. Even so, most outfitters are notoriously soft-hearted when it comes to cancellations. They try hard to fill your slot with another hunter so that at least part of your deposit can be refunded, or they apply the deposit to a hunt during the following season. Too many outfitters exist on the verge of bankruptcy simply because they are better guides and hunters than they are businessmen.

Another frequent cause of misunderstanding and hard feelings is the common practice among outfitters of quoting the cost of a guided hunt on a per-day basis. Let's say the cost of a 10-day hunt is $2,500. This sounds like a lot of money, so to ease the pain the client is told the hunt will cost $250 per day. This sometimes leads the client to believe that he is paying on a day-by-day basis. If he bags his trophy on the second day he says, "Thanks a lot. Here's the $500 I owe you for two days. I'm going home." A long discussion and a lot of ill will follows. Plan on paying the full price, stay the full time, and have the time of your life.

Once your deposit is paid and the dates are set, you know that you are really going and you'll get excited. I always do. You're like a five-year-old waiting for Christmas and the weeks roll by too slowly. But don't be lulled by what seems to be plenty of time to get ready. Too often hunters wait until the last couple of days to get ready only to find that they didn't allow enough time. Actually, getting ready for your big hunt is part of the fun, and your advance planning and preparation will have a lot to do with your comfort, efficiency and success.

You'll want some new hunting duds, of course, but don't make the common mistake of assuming that the western mountains, Alaska, British Columbia and the Yukon are frozen solid from the first of September until the end of June. Often first-time hunters step off the plane in Jackson Hole or White Horse bundled to the ears in hooded down jackets and felt-lined boots only to find balmy weather. Keep in mind that September, October and November are very changeable months. You may have warm sunny weather one day, a blizzard the next, and then more sun on the third day.

After fighting this kind of weather for quarter of a century I've decided that the sensible way to dress is in relatively thin layers. A thick down jacket is great if the temperature drops to zero but otherwise it will be too hot for hunting. Instead I wear a down vest and a light down jacket. Together they are as warm as a heavier jacket but I have the option of wearing one or both as the weather dictates.

My typical topside sub-freezing elk-hunting attire includes a long-sleeve waffle-weave cotton underwear top next to my skin (wool makes me itch). Over that I wear a heavy, all-wool shirt in a muted color. Next I wear a reversible down vest (Blaze Orange on one side) and over that a light down jacket which is Blaze Orange on one side and camouflage on the other.

The wisdom of layered dressing becomes apparent by midmorning when the sun is in full bloom or when you're climbing and working up a sweat. Just peel off the outer jacket and tuck it in a saddlebag or your day pack. The same for your vest if it gets even warmer. You'll find that the cotton undershirt doesn't get wet or clammy because the wool in the hunting shirt wicks the moisture away. Even when it's wet, wool will keep you warm. That's why there is no substitute for the real thing.

I wear a silk scarf around my neck. Don't laugh, it does wonders to keep my neck and chin warm and seals body heat inside my jacket. My pants are tightly woven wool whipcord over a lower unit of the waffle-weave cotton underwear. And I keep my pants up with old-fashioned fireman-type suspenders. Belts tend to bind and restrict movement, especially when you climb. I also wear pants about one size too big so waist and knees won't bind and grab. My socks are silk next to the skin for comfort and heavy wool next, to draw off moisture and for padding. My boots are always at least a year old. Don't go on your big hunt with new boots! If you need new boots, buy them in the spring and wear them often through the summer so they will be well broken in and tuned to your feet.

Everyone likes a cowboy hat, but don't overdo it. High crowns and wide brims get in the way and are always being knocked off when you ride through timber in the dark. Even if you are a good guy, never wear a white hat. It alarms the game. I wear a very soft felt hat with a low crown and a medium-wide brim that I keep turned down all around. This gives me extra good protection from sun, wind and rain. When the weather gets cold enough to nip my ears, I switch to an old-fashioned "toboggan" type wool cap or a "sheepherder" cap with ear flaps. Find out what the Blaze Orange requirements of the state or province are and abide by them. I like to have a Blaze Orange hatband with me so that if I change hats I can switch the band from hat to hat.

"He who travels light travels right" is an honored saying in the backwoods, but don't carry a good thing too far. It's always better to have a bit too much gear than not enough. I've made do with one parka, one wool shirt and pants, and a single set of long johns, but after the first week I got the feeling I'd been living with myself too long. Only when I'm backpacking into high sheep country do I try to get by with the clothes on my back. Otherwise, in addition to down jacket and vest, my clothing usually includes two wool shirts, one cotton shirt, one pair heavy wool pants, one pair lighter wool pants or perhaps a pair of jeans, one set of cotton waffle-weave two-piece underwear, and one two-piece set of cotton-and-wool underwear. I usually take three pairs of wool socks (so there'll always be a dry pair) and two pairs each of silk and cotton. Also two sets of light underwear and two cotton turtleneck shirts. Big cotton bandannas are worth their weight in gold, so take several. A lightweight, two-piece rain suit is always handy not just if it rains but also in case of snow, and a rain jacket is great protection in high winds. Get a soft green or camouflage color and, if you can manage the extra bucks, the "breatheable" fabrics are wonderful, especially if you are walking and climbing. Get a size large enough to fit over your down jacket with looseness to spare.

Often the cook tent is so hot and steamy that wearing a wool shirt in it is unbearable. That's why I like to change into light shirt and pants at the end of the day. Also take some light shoes for camp wear. Moccasins are OK, but the Maine type slip-ons with waterproof rubber bottoms are more convenient and practical, especially if there's snow. All the duds I've just described are in addition to your civilized traveling clothes and shoes, which can be left at the guide's headquarters until you get back.

A big-game hunt is no place to show off fancy luggage. Hard-case bags are hard to manage, harder to pack on a horse and invariably suffer considerable scuffing. Duffel bags are a lot better, not the old GI type duffel bag with its impossibly narrow mouth, but the big-zipper duffels that unfasten across three sides or at least across the top. They're cataloged by Bob Allen, Eddie Bauer, and L. L. Bean in a variety of sizes, and biggest is usually best.

I carry two duffels of about the same size, one packed with my sleeping bag, pillow, air or foam mattress and boots. The other is packed with clothes, starting with extra boots, camp shoes and raingear at the bottom and working up with softer pants, shirts and jackets. After everything is packed, I dig about halfway down and store my binoculars, spotting scope, ammo, film and extra camera lens where they will be well padded and best protected. The usual style toilet kit is too heavy and bulky, so leave yours at home and make for yourself what I call a miniature shaving-pac. By using a folding toothbrush, a plastic throw-away razor and small size containers of toothpaste, soap and deodorant I've managed to reduce weight and bulk to almost nothing. The aluminum boxes made for backpackers are great for packing this sort of gear, and you can get some other good ideas at your local hiking and backpack shop. Don't forget a couple of towels and washcloths. Take old ones.

If you wear glasses, you'll be smart to take along an extra pair, and if you're on prescription medicine be sure you have an ample supply. The aluminum hiker's boxes are great for these extras, and don't forget insect repellent if you're on an early season hunt. Take a couple of books. There's usually quite a bit of spare time, and it's nice to have some reading material to pass the time. Most outfitters have a medicine chest with dressings for blisters and cures for some other ailments, but a personal medical survival kit is a good idea.

In my daypack or saddlebags I also carry one of those reflective survival blankets that are the size of a pack of cigarettes, a compass, waterproof matches, a small flashlight and a few bars of high-energy candy.

You'll also need gloves. I always take three pair—one made of soft deerskin for riding, another lined for cold weather, and a pair or rubber or plastic-coated ones to wear when it's wet or snowing. I always carry two pair when it's cold, one pair inside my shirt where they are kept good and warm. When the pair I'm wearing gets cold, I swap with the warm ones. This way I always have a warm pair of gloves, and my hands are never cold.

Time was when traveling by air with rifles and ammo was no particular problem. Rather than risk my carefully zeroed rifle to the whims of baggage handlers and the hazards of the cargo hold I'd carry the gun on board and stash it in the seat beside me or give it to the pilot for safe keeping. Now, thanks to aircraft hijackers and subsequent federal regulations, you *must* check your rifle and ammo as baggage. This brings on all sorts of complications, and we've all heard horror stories about rifles damaged, lost or stolen in transit. Once you check your rifle in at the baggage counter, there's not much you can do but keep your fingers crossed and hope it arrives where and when you do. Over the years, though, I've learned a few tricks that seem to work.

First of all you cannot pack ammunition in your rifle case with your rifle. It must be packed separately. I like to carry about 40 rounds (in case the rifle must be re-zeroed) in the tough plastic boxes made by the MTM company. These are packed in my duffel. Also, and this is a particularly good idea, if I'm carrying a bolt-action rifle I remove the bolt and pack it in the duffel as well. If the rifle is stolen in transit, the thieves won't get a functioning gun. Most gunmakers insist that bolts be replaced at the factory, so if you alert them and give them the serial number, they'll be on the lookout in case your missing rifle is returned for a new bolt.

When you check your rifle at the baggage counter, the clerk may or may not ask you to open the case and demonstrate that the gun is unloaded. Have the key handy, not at the bottom of your duffel. Most airlines will not accept a gun that's packed only in a soft case. That's asking for trouble anyway. Some airlines, however, supply hard cases which you can rent for the duration of the flight with an option to buy. In any event, a hard-shell luggage-type gun case is a smart investment and a good one will last a lifetime.

Your baggage is automatically insured for $750 or thereabouts by most airlines, which is enough to cover the average scoped rifle. If you feel your rifle is worth more you can ask for additional insurance, which sells for four bits per hundred. For $5 you can thus get an additional $1,000 insurance. This is money well spent, and I've noticed that some airlines call ahead to your destination to announce that insured baggage is on the way. Your insured gun will often get special hand-carried treatment. If you have to make connections that involve a change of airlines, make sure that the insurance stays in effect. Some airlines do and some don't, and I try to avoid any airline that won't sell me continuing gun insurance for the duration (one way) of the trip. You can easily check this out with your travel agent or airlines representative.

If you're going on a horseback hunt, you'll need a saddle scabbard for your rifle. Check with your outfitter before buying one yourself. Most outfitters have a few to lend. And take lots of pictures. Not just of your trophy but *everything*. Take three times as much film as you think you'll need. If you don't have a good camera, get one and learn how to use it. The pictures you take will in time become the most treasured remembrance of your hunt of a lifetime. I think it's a good idea to take only transparencies because they can be used to make good color prints and can also be shown through a projector as well.

Don't forget your knife and a sharpening stone or hone. How about a pull-through rifle cleaning kit?

Part of your preparation for the hunt should be quite a lot of practice shooting. What's the use of going on a hunt of a lifetime only to miss the trophy of a lifetime?–***Jim Carmichel.***

Make Your Own Deer-Hunting Luck

My father got his 10-point whitetail buck last year before the season opened. No, he didn't poach it. The actual shooting was done on opening day. But good scouting before the opener "just about had that buck's liver in the pan," as my 79-year-old father put it.

The common denominator of all successful deer hunters is that they *know* the country they're hunting, whether it's muley rimrocks, whitetail haunts of farmbelt woodlots, Southern canebrakes, thick, second-growth forests of the lakes states and Northeast, or the Northwest blacktail's evergreen jungles. Those hunters don't rely on blind luck. They make their own luck by knowing in advance where the deer are and why.

In dad's case the formula was simple. His thoughtful, pre-season scouting revealed a set of buck tracks on a swampy, well-concealed runway not 100 yards from the family hunting cabin in Minnesota's north country. Next question—is this buster using that trail in daytime or only after dark? Many hunters don't realize it, but there are daytime trails and there are nighttime trails, and you'd better be able to sort out the two. More on this later.

Here's where the senior Nelson got clever. Two days running before season, he checked that trail in dim dawn. No fresh buck sign. He checked again shortly before noon. Fresh tracks, both days—the buck was using the trail after dawn. I suspect that after the second day's confirmation, my old man went back to the cabin and started peeling onions to go with the liver. On opening day the buck traveled that trail one more time, and it led to the meatpole behind the barn.

In open country mule deer can often be spotted at long range before the season opens. Try to locate their regular bedding and feeding areas.

Dad simply capitalized on the fact that deer tend to be creatures of habit. The main strategy of pre-season scouting is to learn what deer are doing and where in the area you plan to hunt. If you don't already know the lay of the land, better pick that up too. Like finding out where deer are, learning the physical layout of a hunting area is much better done before season than during it. Most of us don't have enough time to hunt in any event. Hitting a new area, sight unseen, means a great waste of hunting days just learning your way around.

For four generations my family has taken deer hunting seriously. One of the best hunters is my younger brother Al. Most of his whitetail hunting is done in less than 200 acres of brushy, second-growth forest and swamp around our cabin. That's not a big area. Despite his back-of-hand knowledge of the place, Al feels that a minimum of two days of pre-season scouting is needed every year before any meaningful hunting plans can be discussed. Investigating a totally new area of that mod-

This fine mule deer buck was shot in his bed early on opening day only because the hunter located his regular bed and did a catlike stalk.

est size would take at least twice as long.

What do we look for? Not deer. "Dry run" stillhunting for whitetails would be too time-consuming. Instead we look for deer sign—how much, how recent—tracks and scrapes made by bucks, recently used bedding areas, and signs of current browsing.

Though we know the area intimately, we check for any changes that have occurred, naturally or otherwise. Is the creek high enough this year to make the adjoining marshes too wet for good deer bedding? Farther downstream, did enough beavers escape spring trapping season to build dams that back water into the adjacent black ash swamp that our whitetails use heavily? Last year's prime runway may be zilch this year.

We look for new deer trails. For example, where a number of trees were cut for firewood two years ago a nice crop of aspen suckers and some dogwood is coming in—good deer foods. Are deer using it or still relying on annual summer vegetation? Any new feeding area naturally means a new set of deer trails connecting with whatever nearby bedding areas the deer consider safe and convenient.

These things apply to our area, but a similar checklist would be applicable to a lot of others. The key factors are whether deer are using your intended hunting place and *how*—feeding, bedding, or just passing through?

Brush-browsing by deer results in rough-cut ends of twigs or foliage, usually down low. If the twig ends are weathered, it's probably from feeding done last winter, meaning the area may not be in feeding use in the current early or mid-autumn period. But remember it for possible late-season or bad-weather conditions that might move deer back into this "winter feed" while the hunting season is still on. Other feeding signs can be ground scrapes where deer are rooting for mushrooms, fall fern shoots, or acorns.

Check the perimeters of croplands for signs of deer use. Such crops as alfalfa, cabbage, winter wheat, and corn attract deer. So do apple orchards, although this is often a late fall food for deer, possibly after hunting is closed for the year. Check out water sources too. With the exception of desert mule deer that get moisture from plants, other species need water.

The daily routine of a deer is no great mystery. It needs food, water, and cover. A deer needs cover for resting security, protected from enemies. What a deer likes is a bedding area that gives it a good chance to detect approaching predators, including man. This may be a ridge or knob for good surveillance, or it may be near a swamp where water and mud will make a predator's approach noisy. Bedding in thick brush or dense young timber also makes a quiet approach by an enemy unlikely.

While bedded, deer usually like to be concealed. Mule deer, which tend to be sharp-eyed, will sometimes bed in the open on an eminence, trading concealment in favor of better surveillance of the surrounding territory. However, both whitetails and blacktails don't depend that heavily on eyesight and prefer locations where they'll be well hidden, while still able to hear or possibly scent any approach.

So long as those requirements are met, deer can be surprisingly unchoosy about bedding areas. I remember one autumn at the family hunting camp when we hunted hard and had poor results. After the season, we found many deer beds in a swampy swale of thick alder bush and tall grass right behind the barn. Deer had been practically guarding camp for us while we were beating the brush far and wide.

Deer don't necessarily return to the same bedding areas day after day. Usually they have a number of alternative sites and choose one based on wind direction (to detect an approaching enemy) and weather conditions. If you have a good idea where deer are currently feeding, you can make book that the bedding area will be somewhere upwind. They won't travel any real distance crosswind or downwind. I've seen a whole herd of muleys stop, then turn 180° to head for a new bedding area when the wind shifted on them.

That's one of the best ways to get a shot at a mule deer if you are in fairly open country. Get up high if you can, and glass for deer, especially early in the morning and just before sundown. Once you have them located, you can stake out on their usual travel route or try to stalk a buck in his bed. That's hard to do, but it works sometimes.

The second factor of deer cover selection is protection against inclement weather. This includes hot sun, heavy rain, snow, wind, or just plain cold weather. There's no mystery in this. On a hot day, you'd pick a cool, shady place for a nap. So do deer. North sides of hills and ridges, cold pockets in swamps, or shaded timber are all likely warm-weather bedding places for deer in the fall when they're carrying maximum body fat and wearing their winter coats.

Although heavy rain or snow will cause deer to bed under low cover such as young evergreens, coastal blacktails are less predictable about this. Living in a very wet climate, blacktails are much more impervious to rain than are whitetails or muleys. In Northwest forests I've jumped blacktails in fairly open cover in downpours that would have had other deer curled up under the thickest evergreens available.

How far apart will feeding and bedding areas be? That depends on the lay of the land, availability of cover, and the kind of deer.

Deer tracks can be deceptive. Sometimes old tracks look very fresh, but if you find tracks during or after a snowfall the animal is nearby.

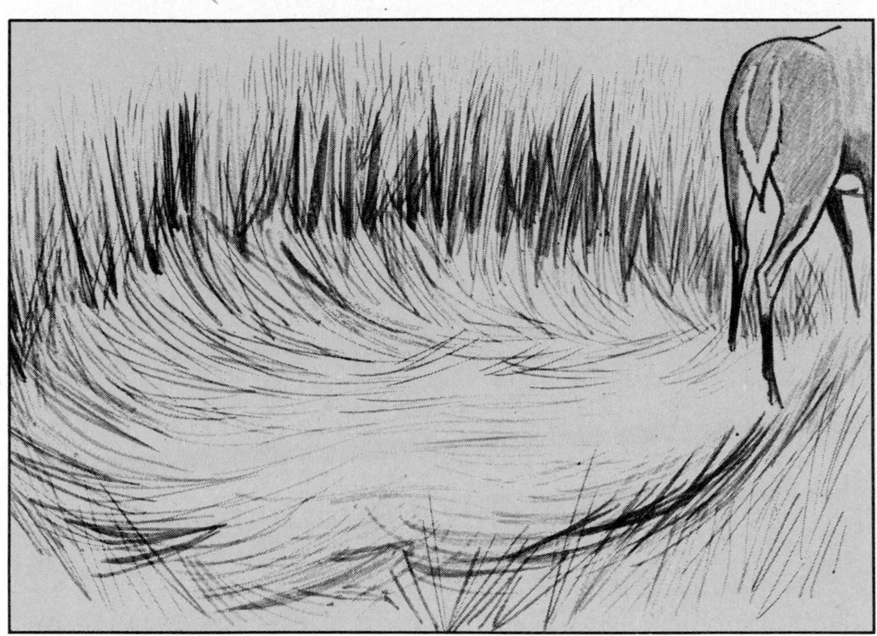

Finding deer beds is a hopeful sign. But if you can, use binoculars from a distance to determine whether or not the deer are still using them.

Whitetails and blacktails usually pick bedding areas pretty close to where they're feeding. Muleys, the long-distance commuters of the deer family, may have to range a couple of miles or more between an attractive valley alfalfa meadow and the nearest timbered or rimrocked hills offering bedding security. In the arid West's hard soils, tracked trails may be tough to find. Instead, look for strung-out patterns of deer droppings indicating regular travel.

Good trail sign also can be difficult to sort out in the thick, wet forests of the Northwest and South. Sometimes waist or chest-high undergrowth won't let you see your own boots let alone deer tracks. But established deer trails will still show up as narrow but discernible channels through tall grass, ferns, and other growth.

The more open the terrain the less deer rely on given trails. A whitetail or blacktail in typical, dense forest environment tends to stick to a trail or runway. A mule deer in more open country often uses a general route rather than a specific trail. He may travel regularly through a certain quarter-mile wide canyon between feeding and bedding areas. But exactly *where* he'll travel within that 400-plus yard canyon width may vary from one trip to the next, depending on factors such as wind direction and how security-conscious he is at the time. Such a canyon may have several alternative trails loosely defined. Pre-season scouting will show you these.

Some deer trails are primarily for after-dark travel, as cited earlier. You can waste days covering one of these and never see a deer. An example is a splendid deer trail running half a mile down the top of a fairly open aspen-birch ridge in my north country hunting area. This trail is so beaten down that you could ride a bike on it. But you'll never find a whitetail using it in daylight hours. In more than 70 years of family hunting, no one ever got a whitetail atop that ridge or, to my knowledge, ever saw a deer there in daylight.

However, we've taken a number of whitetails on trails on both sides of that ridge where the high ground blends into swamp cover. This is the kind of route habitual skulkers like whitetails and blacktails will take during the danger period of daylight. There's more trail cover and a very dense swamp literally one jump away if danger appears. Mule deer, which use distance rather than cover as a safeguard, have no compunctions about open, high-ground trails in daylight. But you'll rarely catch forest deer there after dawn.

Deer are lazy. Given an easy route and a tough one, they'll take the easy one, assuming it has at least some protective cover. The exception is when the animal is alarmed. Then he's likely to choose a brushy or steep escape

To attract does, bucks scrape a small area bare of vegetation and then urinate in it. If a scrape is fresh, it may pay to take a downwind stand.

route, hoping that danger can't catch up. So keep an eye open for little-used deer trails that seem to plunge illogically into thick cover or rough going. It's important to know some of these in hotspot hunting areas. A buck hard-pushed by a tight drive is likelier to use one of these than a main runway, and your standers had better be situated accordingly.

If you're scouting a large new area, orient yourself with map and compass and make notes on places where you see deer or find abundant deer sign.

In deer scouting much of the sign found will be from does and fawns. This is still significant to the mule-deer hunter, since muleys tend to travel in herds of both sexes. Over a 30-year span of hunting them from Wyoming to eastern Washington, I've got a number of decent mule bucks that were traveling with does and fawns many weeks before the rut. The biggest bucks, however, tend to be either loners or partners with other bucks before the rut.

For a bucks-only hunter of whitetails and blacktails, doe sign is not significant until close to the rut when bucks start taking interest in does. But if your season will coincide with the rut, pay lots of attention to signs of doe activity. You're going to find bucks in the same areas.

The pre-season hunting sleuth has the opportunity to learn a lot about buck activity. For starters, simply drive adjacent roads before daybreak. That last hour or two of darkness is a peak time for deer activity, thus worthwhile for a quickie buck census if you're lucky. Pay close attention to roads separating good crop areas from nearby timber or other bedding areas. Using big 7 x 50 night glasses, I've often picked up a buck crossing a field or clearing in the first, faint light of dawn. You're much less likely to find him exposed like that at daybreak.

Of course, track sign reveals bucks. Large, deeply imprinted, wider-span tracks (due to the buck's thicker body) are telltales of big bucks, although smaller males' tracks aren't easy to tell from does. If there's snow, a small-diameter urine hole in the trail indicates a buck—does make a wider spill.

Buck-rubbed trees aren't tactically important. Rubs only tell that there are male deer somewhere around, which was a safe assumption to begin with if the area has any deer population worth hunting. Studies of radio-tagged bucks show they don't habitually return to rubs.

Scrapes in the earth are another story. But neither muleys nor blacktails make scrapes as commonly as the whitetail buck, which is territorially much more aggressive than the other deer. I have seen surprisingly few scrapes and rubs in many years of scouting and hunting well-populated blacktail and mule-deer ranges. By contrast, even a fairly low-density whitetail population will produce scrapes galore. A lot of scrapes don't automatically mean that the area is overrun with bucks. One buck may paw out dozens of them in the fall.

The earthen scrape, anointed with the buck's urine, is his "at stud" advertisement. A doe ready to breed will urinate in a buck scrape, then wait nearby for the buck to come along on his patrol rounds of his scrapes.

How often a buck visits his scrapes depends on the size of his home territory. In turn, that depends on local deer population density. Lots of deer mean relatively small territories, so a buck may visit all his scrapes more than once a day at the peak of the rut. Fewer deer mean bigger territories for each buck, hence less frequent visitation of his scrapes.

Don't worry about positively defining an individual buck's scrape route. It may overlap into another buck's territory. Where several bucks' territories loosely overlap at the edges, it would take a radio-tagging study to sort out the players.

But that's not important. The big thing is that an area with plenty of large, fresh buck scrapes is going to be well worth the hunting effort. Close to or during the rut, well-sited trail watching (where more than one scrape can be covered by the hunter) is one of the surest ways to bag a buck. Sooner or later, the old boy that made those scrapes will come along to check them, unless he gets bushwhacked by another hunter. Heavy hunting pressure alone won't make the buck quit working his little trapline, although it may make him more cautious.

Worthwhile scouting requires some map work for reference and to take notes. The U.S. Geographic Survey maps are best for this since they show land forms and cover types. However, many of these are outdated for a given area—a forest on the map may have since been converted to farmland; new roads often exist that the older map doesn't show. Just to get an updated grasp of the land-use, let alone actual deer usage, preseason scouting is still essential.

Other map sources can be state or federal forest services, private timber companies, county auditors or county highway departments, and the Soil Conservation Service. Any chance at obtaining aerial photography (Soil Conservation or forestry people may have these on file) is worth taking. Even do-it-yourself, oblique-angle snapshots out the window of a light plane can be valuable scouting and hunting aids when enlarged to at least 8 x 10.

But nothing can substitute for on-the-ground reconnaissance of a potential hunting area by yourself and as many members of your hunting party as possible. Without that firsthand data, you're risking making drives in the wrong places, trail-watching the wrong trails, or wasting many hours painstakingly stillhunting in areas where there are no deer.

Naturally, the closer to hunting season that you can do your scouting the more relevant the information. Just remember that changing weather conditions may change deer usage patterns, often overnight. Cold, stormy weather will push deer from high country into low. Killing frosts will change deer diets from summer forage to winter browse, quite possibly meaning a change in feeding grounds and appropriate bedding areas too. Lots of hunting pressure will push deer out of easily accessible areas into farther-back or denser cover or higher, more rugged ground. But good advance scouting will give you an idea of where to hunt even when conditions and deer habits change abruptly. –*Norm Nelson.*

Deer Do See Color!

"Deer are completely color-blind. They live in a world of black, grays, and white."

That is typical of the declarations about deer vision that have found their way into sportsmen's magazines and books for the past 40 years. We have just learned it is not true. A whitetail deer's eyes do contain color-sensitive cones. The discovery is heralded as one of the major advances in animal biology.

Of course, how deer see and how they interpret what they see, have long been the bases for heated arguments in hunting camps. Are tree stands effective because deer don't expect danger from above, or is there some other reason? Are deer inactive on moonless nights because they can't see in pitch darkness?

Perhaps most importantly, such questions affect the colors of garments sportsmen should wear, especially the proved safety color variously known as hunter's orange, fluorescent orange, and the pigment's trade name Blaze Orange. In addition to making hunters far more visible to each other, does this safety color also make them more noticeable to the deer?

I've always encouraged the use of hunter's orange, but I've had many very different experiences in which deer seemed to exhibit definite reactions to it and other colors. At other times the critters seemed entirely unaware or unconcerned with color.

Minnesota's 1979 deer season was a prime example. I was sitting in a tree stand, so a deer would not see me unless it looked up, and I was careful not to make any noise. A light breeze was blowing directly into my face, so any deer that approached along the trail I was watching wasn't going to detect my scent. I was wearing a fluorescent orange coat and hat and black gloves, gray trousers, and brown boots.

About midmorning an eight-point buck stepped from a thicket of birch whips into a clearing. He was scuffling the leaves in search of the season's last remnants of green clover. With each step he briefly raised his head to ensure that the route ahead wasn't dangerous. The buck was about 60 yards away when he looked squarely in my direction. It wasn't that the animal looked up. He was far enough away to have me in his field vision when he looked forward.

I remained like a statue, confident my outline was well broken by the branches surrounding my stand. Nevertheless, the deer snapped to attention and craned his head from one side to the other. He obviously was *seeing* something alarming. He snorted, about-faced and, white banner waving astern, loped away in the direction from which he had just come. I was lucky. Thirty yards of open ground separated the deer from the birch tangles behind him, and I dropped him with a single shot from my .30/06.

When several other members of our party gathered to help drag the deer out, I performed a casual experiment. I asked one of my pals to climb into my tree stand, wearing my coat and hat. Then I stood where the deer had been. Because of the irregular swatches of cover around the stand, the various body features of the hunter in the tree blended so well they were almost indistinguishable. Yet two large chunks of safety orange (the coat and hat) could easily be seen, and their bright, glowing appearance did not fit in with the surroundings.

Two weeks later I was deer hunting on our combination farm and game preserve near Chesterhill, Ohio. The events were exactly the opposite.

I was in a tree stand, sitting motionless, making no noise, and

Illustration by Kip Lott

We are concerned with two basic things: being as nearly invisible to the deer as possible; being highly visible to other hunters in order to avoid hunting accidents. Both goals can be achieved.

wearing the same safety-orange coat and hat. A slight wisp of wind was in my face. I was keeping tabs on the intersection of two major runways. Only minutes after it was light enough to see, a doe and two fawns approached. Several times they looked toward me as the buck had done and apparently detected nothing amiss. Eventually, they came close, walked right beneath my tree, and slowly evaporated into the distance.

Moments later a forkhorn buck stepped into view, and I decided to try for him as soon as he came within range.

The slowpoke buck seemed intent upon savoring every morsel of food he chanced upon before advancing another step. Yet, like every whitetail I have ever been around, he was suspiciously alert. Between bites he repeatedly jerked his head up to pan the landscape. For long minutes he dawdled around, and looked straight in my direction no less than a dozen times. Finally the buck turned his head away, and that is when I slowly raised my 12 gauge and squeezed the trigger. The deer went down in a heap.

Every hunter can describe similar contradictory experiences. They add to the debate about how deer see the world around them, but startling breakthroughs have given scientists more insight. Research is still in progress, but after reviewing the latest studies I am convinced deer can see, or at least distinguish, various colors—with one major qualification. It seems that the context within which colors are seen and the time of day play important roles in determining whether a deer will register alarm or ignore colors that obviously clash with the natural surroundings.

Deer are shy and secretive and largely nocturnal. Though they may be up and around almost any time of day, they prefer to mate and travel under cover of darkness or in the dim light of dawn and dusk. Scientists have confirmed that deer are well adapted to nocturnal activity. A deer's eyes, in proportion to its head, are quite large, a characteristic shared by many night-oriented creatures—owls, bats, rabbits, flying squirrels, opossums, raccoons, and some fish such as walleyes.

Eyes are situated in an animal's skull so that it sees best what it needs to see most. Humans, like all mammalian predators, have eyes directly in the front of their skulls. This provides straight-ahead, binocular (two-eye) vision. Our lateral (side-to-side) vision is very poor. That's OK because we don't have great need for lateral vision. When we need to see far to one side, our flexible necks easily allow our heads to swivel.

Deer have relatively rigid necks. The ability to crane their necks would really be something of a disadvantage because frequent movement would reveal their presence to predators. It is better for deer to have good side vision. Frontal and wide lateral vision are provided by eyes well to the sides of the skull. This gives deer fairly good straight-ahead, binocular vision, but their eyes can also work independently of each other (monocular vision) to see to either side without head movement.

The comparatively rigid neck is the main reason a deer seldom looks up at a sharp angle. You've heard that deer never look up because they have no reason to expect danger from above. In fact, deer do look up from time to time, as any tree-stand hunter will tell you. But anatomy makes it uncomfortable, so they don't do it often. To demonstrate this, get onto your hands and knees and move around like a four-legged animal. Notice how difficult and uncomfortable it is to look up at the ceiling. And your neck is much more flexible than a deer's.

This is worthwhile information for hunters. It's obvious that the most effective tree stands are well above the ground, at least 12 and preferably 15 to 18 feet. Where laws affect tree stand placement (in Minnesota, for example, stands may be no more than 10 feet above the ground), it is imperative to achieve additional elevation by putting your stand in a tree on ground a good deal higher than surrounding terrain.

If you hunt from a ground-level blind, try to place it on high ground. Tree stands have never been popular among mule deer hunters in the Rocky Mountain states because the terrain is nearly vertical, and hunters can ambush deer without climbing trees. Yet where the terrain is flat, many mule deer hunters rely on tree stands.

Placement isn't the only thing about deer's eyes that adapts them to nocturnal activities. The eyes of deer—and of other nocturnal animals—contain millions of specialized nerve endings known as rods, which are very efficient at gathering light and detecting movement. This explains why deer can move about when most humans, who have fewer rods in their eyes, find it too dark to see their boots. It also explains why motionless tree stand hunters are more successful than stillhunters, trackers, or stalkers.

While rods are extremely efficient at gathering light, they aren't color sensitive. This is the function of the color-receptive cones. We know how these cones work in human eyes, but their function in the eyes of other animals has not been studied much. Until recently scientists believed deer had no cone cells in their eyes. Lately, though, there has been a small but important surge of interest in animals' color vision. Researchers have been able to respond to anglers' and tackle manufacturers' questions about feeding and striking responses in fish, for example, and this has produced some surprising information about deer.

This is not to say there has been an entire lack of information about color vision in grazing and browsing animals. As early as 1902 a Dr. Zurn described the color perception abilities of sheep and goats. His studies were confirmed in 1928 by a Dr. Menner. In 1952 a Dr. Hoffman reported upon the color vision of cows, camels, and giraffes, and a Dr. Grzimek revealed the color vision abilities of horses. Then in 1958 a Dr. Backhaus did a study of hooved mammals such as pigs, cows, and horses. Four years ago, Drs. Riese and Sambraus experimented again with the color vision of sheep. Evidence of color perception was found in many of these studies.

If members of certain animal families have some color vision, one would think close relatives should have a similar ability. If a domestic sheep or goat has the ability to perceive certain colors, then so should wild sheep, wild goats, and perhaps even pronghorn antelope (which actually are goats, not true antelope). And if European red deer can see certain colors, then why not also closely related species like whitetails and mule deer?

All the scientists I mentioned are German. Most of their studies were conducted in Europe, with European and Asian animals, and therefore do not apply to American deer. So most of what we believe about how deer see falls into the category of folk wisdom.

Last year I wrote a piece about whitetails and again, like my colleagues, parroted the same unsubstantiated information about deer being color-blind. I promptly received a response from the eminent scientist A.B. Bubenik, project leader of the Ontario Ministry of National Resources Wildlife Research Station near Maple.

"I have to say it is a pity that most editors and writers for hunting magazines in America do not have consultants among wildlife biologists," he wrote. "At least one highly respected study that was concluded just last year in your country will show you that deer are not color-blind. Perhaps you will find occasion to investigate this topic, and write about it . . ."

The study blew my mind. It was conducted by Drs. Witzel, Springer, and Mollenhauer at the U.S. Department of Agriculture's veterinary toxicology and entomology research laboratory in College Station, Texas. Many theories concerning whitetail vision were disproved.

The researchers trapped deer at the Aransas National Wildlife Refuge at Austwell, Texas. In the laboratory they studied the deer's eyes with high-powered electron-microscopes, using new chemical techniques. The first battery of tests confirmed that whitetails have rods in the retinas of their eyes. However, the second battery of tests provided proof positive that deer also possess an average of 10,000 color-sensitive cones per square millimeter of retinal tissue!

Having the visual equipment, shouldn't deer also have at least some degree of color perception?

"We decided to find out," Mollenhauer told me, "by conducting electroretinographic tests. Under highly controlled conditions, the rods and cones are separately stimulated to determine whether they respond to various cues. We began by capturing more live deer at the Aransas refuge, and then we mildly tranquilized them so they would be easy to handle." First, the deer were light-adapted to simulate their daytime responses to visual cues. Later they were dark-adapted to simulate their responses during the night hours. They were tested with individual flashes of white, blue, and red light. (Blue is a short-wavelength color, red is a long-wavelength color, and white is a neutral noncolor; therefore, these three colors represent the entire color spectrum, from one wavelength extreme to the other.)

Both rod and cone activity were detected in the eyes of the test whitetails. As in the human eye, the rods came into greatest use when the deer's eyes were dark-adapted and at presentation of the white light. When the deer were light-adapted, their cones responded to red and blue light flashes. The deer did not respond to color flashes in total darkness.

"As a result of our deer studies," Dr. Witzel told me, "we now know for sure that whitetails have cones in their eyes. Those cones function in a manner almost identical to ours, and they respond to color cues."

How sophisticated are deer's retinal cones? How clearly do deer see colors? Do their brains receive and interpret the color cues the same way ours do? Scientists are not yet sure about the answers to those questions.

"These questions about the efficiency of a deer's color vision will unravel a world of mysteries to us in coming years," said Tom Townsend, animal behavior scientist at Ohio State University. "We'll just have to wait and see."

"The fact that there are 10,000 cones per square millimeter of retinal tissue is strong evidence deer can see colors," Dr. Earl Smith, laboratory chief of the College of Optometry at the University of Houston, told me. "But keep in mind the human eye has a far larger number of cones in the retina. So even if deer have color vision, and I definitely believe they do, there is the likelihood it is not nearly as well developed as ours."

Larry Marchington, an animal biologist at the University of Georgia whose research regularly appears in scientific journals expressed a similar view.

"Whether you're talking about human beings or wildlife species, there are wide extremes in the abilities of individual animals to distinguish various colors," he says. "Some humans, for example, are quite adept at distinguishing between very subtle shades of just one color, other humans are mildly color-blind, and still others with congenital defects to their cones can't see any colors worth a hoot. The same is probably true with different wildlife species as well as specific individuals within each species.

"The Blaze Orange subject is really a controversy. Let me give you an illustration. I have a biologist friend who is also a hunter. He is color-blind and absolutely cannot distinguish between red and green, but he can easily see fluorescent orange. However, it's not the same orange you and I see. The way he describes it, the color is very bright and highly reflective in vivid contrast with its surroundings. If we apply a little logical deduction, deer should also be able to see Blaze Orange . . . as something bright and not belonging, much as my biologist friend sees it."

What scientists need to do next, Marchington suggested, are some of the same types of experiments that have been done with fish.

"You've probably read about them," he said. "Fish are given either food or mild shocks associated with certain colors." The fish soon learn to seek out the colors associated with food and avoid those associated with shocks. Scientists concluded that not only can fish see colors but distinguish between even the most subtle hues.

"We could easily do the same thing with deer in fenced enclosures," Marchington said, "but it would take a good deal of time, and someone would have to cough up a hefty grant."

Where does all this leave the average hunter? Well, we are still concerned with only two basic things: being as nearly invisible to deer as possible to avoid being detected, and at the opposite extreme, being highly visible to other hunters to avoid having lead mistakenly sent in our direction.

Both goals can be achieved.

First, wear an ample quantity of fluorescent orange. It saves lives. But you should also be aware that there are many different ways to use safety orange to make yourself a good deal less visible to deer.

Going back to 1979 and my Minnesota and Ohio deer hunting experiences, for example, I have a good idea why one buck readily detected my fluorescent orange clothing and spooked, and why the other deer paid me little mind. The key, I'm convinced, had to do with the time of day.

Remember that the Minnesota buck was encountered during midmorning when the terrain was brightly illuminated. That deer's eyes were light-adapted, meaning the color-sensitive cones were fully operational. Therefore he responded readily to safety orange.

The Ohio deer came by my stand just at the crack of dawn, when much of the landscape was still deep in shadows. These deer were almost surely still in a dark-adapted state. As a result, they were still relying heavily upon rod function, and their color-sensing cones were therefore unable to respond to the orange of my clothing.

It seems to follow, then, that hunters who wrap themselves in fluorescent orange from head to toe for stillhunting (stalking) or tracking should make a special effort to hunt in the early morning or at dusk. During these low-light times deer are dark-adapted and much less likely to see the hunter's fluorescent orange, especially if he moves slowly with long pauses between each step.

When deer are light-adapted, hunters wearing fluorescent-orange clothing would probably be well advised to stack the odds in their favor by waiting on stands. Since whitetails are often in their beds during the middle of the day, the hunter who takes to a stand would do best if drivers pushed deer to him. Fluorescent orange is not a disadvantage to a driver who is only trying to push a deer to a stander and does not intend to shoot the animal himself. The safety orange standing hunters wear may still be detected occasionally by deer, but at least the hunters are not adding to this disadvantage by combining high visibility with frequent movements.

Whether you hunt on the move or take a stand, it may be wise to seek another solution. One alternative is to wear fluorescent orange in small units—a vest, hat, and gloves—so long as the total area satisfies minimum legal safety requirements, if any, set by the state. This makes a hunter highly visible to other hunters, but because the garments are small and differently shaped, and because they are separated on the body by garments of other colors, your entire form will not stand out so starkly against the background.

Still another solution is attractive. This would be to wear safety orange clothing with a camouflage pattern of dull tans and greens printed on it. The glowing orange would be highly visible to hunters, but the floral camouflage would break up the orange and make it less startling to deer.

A few years ago, you could buy hunting jackets with a camouflage pattern printed on a bright background. Much of this clothing was made by Ideal Products of Sykesville, Pennsylvania. The bright background color, however, was red, not fluorescent orange. A spokesman for the company stated that this clothing is no longer made. Because the background is red, this clothing does *not* satisfy state laws that require hunters to wear fluorescent orange. Wearing that type of clothing in the mistaken belief that it enhances safety could endanger your life.

Sometimes it is difficult to tell the difference between bright red or bright orange and true fluorescent orange. This is particularly true when the fabric is dirty. After washing or dry cleaning it, look at the fabric in very dim light, so dim that you can hardly distinguish ordinary objects. Use natural light, not artificial lighting. True safety orange (Blaze Orange pigment as manufactured by Day-Glo Color Corporation) *glows* in dim light. Ordinary bright pigments do not. This occurs because the safety color has fluorescence, which is (Webster's): "The emission of or the property of emitting electromagnetic radiation usually as visible light resulting from and occurring only during the absorption of radiation from some other source. . . ." Quite simply, true Blaze Orange glows with unnatural brightness in dim natural light. If your garment does not do this, the bright color is ordinary red or orange. Another test is to examine the garment in dim light and compare it to a known sample of true fluorescent orange.

A manufacturer who could provide fluorescent orange with a camouflage overlay in dull colors would probably be able to sell a great deal of the clothing to hunters, but there are technical reasons why this is not being done. A representative of Day-Glo Color, manufacturer of the Blaze Orange pigment, states that it is impossible to make this kind of clothing and Ideal Products reports that the company has experimented with the idea but has found that manufacture is not currently possible. Day-Glo also reported that anything that breaks up the Blaze Orange pigmented area greatly reduces its usefulness as a safety color.

(If any clothing manufacturer has succeeded in producing fluorescent orange camouflage fabric, the editors of OUTDOOR LIFE would like to hear about it and receive a sample of the fabric. Please write to George H. Haas, Senior Editor, Outdoor Life, 380 Madison Avenue, New York, NY 10017.–*Ed.*)

Increasing knowledge of how deer and other animals perceive colors is sure to revolutionize big-game hunting. To date, we've only scratched the surface, but many pioneer scientists are on the brink of exciting new findings that will add more to our insight. Meanwhile, when the guys at the hunting club are once more talking about deer being color-blind, merely say, with a smug smile, "Don't bet on it."–***John Weiss.***

(For more on this subject, see the next chapter, "The Orange That Lets You Get Your Buck."–*Ed.*)

The Orange That Lets You Get Your Buck

Fluorescent orange, Blaze Orange (a trade name), safety orange, hunter orange, or whatever it is called is unnaturally bright. If anything would alarm deer, this color certainly would. Nevertheless, many states require deer hunters to wear safety orange-colored clothing to minimize "mistaken for game" accidents.

John Weiss has pointed out several steps that a hunter can take to lessen the alarming effect of safety orange on deer. For instance, he suggested that it's best to hunt early in the morning, when the animals' eyes are night-adapted and much less likely to see the hunter's fluorescent orange. Weiss also suggested that hunters wear camouflage clothing with a safety orange background and a camouflage pattern of other duller colors. This would break up the vivid orange and make it much less alarming to deer. Typically, state regulations require deer hunters to wear only 400 or 500 square inches of safety color. Seemingly, it would be easy to make a vest or jacket with the legally required minimum of safety orange (or even more) and print or overlay camouflage colors on it.

At the time that Weiss wrote, however, that type of clothing ap-

Since science has proved that deer do *see color, isn't wearing fluorescent orange, as required by many state laws, a sure way to ruin your chances to score? Some hunters feel that it is, but a compromise is available. Man on right wears solid fluorescent jacket; man on left has old-fashioned red-and-black plaid. In the middle is the compromise: safety orange with black camouflage blobs. Other fabrics that combine safety orange and some form of camouflage are now used to make hunting clothes.*

Photograph by Art Carter

parently was not available. Many hunters thought that it was and believed that they were complying with the law and assuring their own safety when they were not. Whole camouflage suits with bright orange or red backgrounds and neutral camouflage colors were on dealers' racks. Investigation revealed that the bright background colors were not fluorescent. They were merely red or orange and did not glow in dim light.

Readers have sent in many samples of this type of fabric. Many of them were archers. They stated that this type of camouflage works fairly well. It does not usually alarm deer, but it is bright enough to alert other bowhunters. Bowhunters who hunt during special archery-only deer seasons are not required to wear safety orange. Most sportsmen agree that they do not require true Blaze Orange for safety's sake because bowhunters shoot at very close range. "Mistaken for game" bowhunting accidents are almost nonexistent, despite the fact that most bowhunters wear complete camouflage suits without any hint of red or orange, much less fluorescent orange. In crowded bowhunting areas, however, nonfluorescent orange or red camouflage is a worthwhile precaution.

During the preparation of the Weiss piece, several industry spokesmen, including a Day-Glo Color Corporation representative, informed OUTDOOR LIFE that it was impossible to manufacture fluorescent orange camouflage clothing. Day-Glo should know, if anyone does, because that company makes most of the fluorescent dye used by makers of safety clothing. When the Weiss piece was published, we asked manufacturers and readers to tell us if this type of clothing had become available, and we're happy to report that there are several new developments. Apparently, the technical difficulties that prevented manufacture have been overcome.

Available now in many sporting-goods stores are safety-orange knitted camouflage jackets made by Winona Sportswear, Inc., Winona, Minnesota. The fabric consists of safety orange and black yarns knitted together. The knitting is done so that the black yarns show through in large irregular black blotches. The knitted fabric is quiet in the woods, and the manufacturer states that though individual yarns may pull out on thorns and twigs, a special knitting process prevents large-scale unraveling.

Uniroyal Corporation is making fluorescent plastic film bonded to an inner layer of cloth for added strength. Irregular blotches of gray and black are overlaid on the outside fluorescent film. The plastic is of a special kind that is not as noisy as the usual hard vinyl fluorescent-orange vest. This material is sold to clothing manufacturers, and several of them are now marketing safety clothing for deer hunters.

National Textile Industries, North Kansas City, Missouri, has developed a woven nylon cloth printed in fluorescent orange with light and dark-brown blotches. The outer, colored shell is lined with a light, feltlike Dacron material, and there is an inner lining of strong black taffeta. The three layers are quilted together by stitching in a diamond pattern. This material isn't waterproof. On the other hand, it permits perspiration to evaporate. Again, this material is sold to various garment companies that make safety clothing for hunters.

There may be other companies in this business. We can only report on those that responded to our request for information.

What if fluorescent-orange camouflage garments are not available in your area? Several readers told us about their solutions. All their methods are based on buying a genuine fluorescent-orange garment and then altering it to provide camouflage. One reader "sewed patches of brown and green cloth over 50 percent of the garment." Another purchased "indelible markers in brown and green and painted my own camouflage overlay." In doing this, the hunter must be careful not to reduce the fluorescent-orange background area below the legal minimum, if any, required by the state. Also, at least one state, Illinois, requires a *solid* safety-orange cap and outer garment. Check your state's regulations.

Still another reader merely remarked that there is no law in his state that requires a fluorescent-orange garment to be clean. Evidently, he flings his coat and hat into any handy source of dirt, perhaps a bog, to dull the safety color. That could be construed as illegal, and it could be dangerous too. Along these lines, a representative of the Day-Glo Color Corporation informed us that overlaying or coloring Blaze Orange with any other color greatly reduces the safety value. Without going into technical detail, the effectiveness of fluorescence is based partly on its covering a fairly large area. Perhaps this particular matter should be studied by state game departments to determine if any form of fluorescent-orange camouflage is really safe.

One problem is to determine if a garment on a dealer's rack or newly acquired elsewhere is really fluorescent. There are complex optical tests to determine the degree of fluorescence, but they can only be carried out by a technician. As we stated in the March article: "Sometimes it is difficult to tell the difference between bright red or bright orange and true fluorescent orange. This is particularly true when the fabric is dirty. After washing or dry cleaning it, look at the fabric in very dim light, so dim that you can hardly distinguish ordinary objects. Use natural light . . . True safety orange glows in dim light. Ordinary bright pigments do not. This occurs because the safety color has fluorescence . . . Quite simply, true fluorescent orange glows with unnatural brightness in dim natural light . . . Another rule-of-thumb test is to examine the garment in dim light and compare it to a known sample of true fluorescent orange."—*George H. Haas.*

Come Deer Hunting, Honey

My husband Ted begins getting ready for deer season in June. And usually I began getting ready too—not for hunting but for the chance to spend a whole week alone. I looked forward to hour-long baths, reading late in bed, no meals to serve, closet cleaning (what Ted doesn't miss won't hurt him), and all-day shopping sprees.

One summer day, while I sat in the kitchen making my list of things to do during that glorious week in November, Ted pulled out a chair and plopped down purposefully.

"I've been thinking," he said.

I looked up.

"I've been selfish all the time," he said. "You can go with me this year." He smiled.

"Go where?" I asked.

He paused and leaned across the table. "Deer hunting," he whispered.

I didn't know what to say, so I simply repeated, "Deer hunting!"

He could probably tell what I was thinking. Many men consider the days between January 1 and November 1 as numbered squares put on the calendar solely for the purpose of separating one deer season from the next. My husband is one of those men. He lives all year for the deer season. When I considered it at all, I viewed deer season as a time when I was most glad I wasn't a hunter. Ted and I managed to stay happily married for several years by respecting this difference in our otherwise compatible personalities.

"That should be interesting," I finally said, trying to be diplomatic.

I spent the next three months trying to back out tactfully. By the last week of October, I had given up all hopes of contracting strep throat, breaking a leg, or getting pregnant. I watched glumly out the front window as our Toyota pickup sank steadily under the weight of sleeping bags, a tent, ropes, food, a Coleman stove, lanterns, and various other gear, the usefulness of which I could only guess. For 11 months each year, Ted can't pack a shaving kit without help. Now he wrapped each article carefully in thick canvas bags and packed and repacked the gear until he achieved a perfect balance among equipment, truck, driver, and unfortunately, passenger.

Two days before The Big Day, we shopped for what Ted called grub. My husband sets foot in a grocery store once a year. This was it. I assumed a maternal attitude. I told myself that he would need my advice. But, no, the basket was full within minutes. It was piled high with canned chili, tuna, sardines, crackers, Oreo cookies, Bisquick, eggs, milk, soda cans, coffee, and bread. Also peanut butter, jelly, cheese, bacon, Kraft caramels, and butter. I couldn't have done better myself.

Ted usually sleeps through two rounds of the alarm clock, and various pleas and threats on my part. On the morning of our trip, however, the alarm never rang. He was dressed 45 minutes before 4 a.m. Still groggy, I was led to the four-inch space he'd left for me in the pickup's cab. There was no room in the back for the groceries; they were under my feet.

"Comfortable?" Ted asked, not waiting for a reply. "Babe, wait till you see the New Mexico mountains. You ain't seen nuthin' like 'em."

He had just lapsed into campfire talk, a language spoken by several million men only from November to January. Bank presidents and college professors who normally cringe at "ain't seen nuthin'," become fluent in bad grammar when deer season comes.

I managed to sleep the first hour of our drive. When I awoke, my feet and legs were numb.

Photograph by Bill McRae

"It ain't much farther," my husband said. "Seven or so more hours. Them mountains are beautiful. You're gonna love it."

I spent the next six hours trying to find a place where my legs and feet could rest without going to sleep. I was about to give up when we reached some foothills where Indians used to camp; you can still find arrowheads on the ground. The road began to curve and rise. The scruffy desert brush was replaced by equally scruffy trees. The road bent back on itself, and the scruffy trees gave way to small pines. About the time my ears popped, we turned onto a tarred county road.

"This is the last town you'll see for a while," Ted said happily.

I looked around for the town but saw only one building—an abandoned service station. *Goodbye, city lights,* I thought.

About two miles into the hills, the county road had been scalped of its blacktop. Our Toyota, its suspension already groaning, found one chuckhole after another. A few miles farther we turned onto what looked like two parallel cow trails, but the earth was sandy and the chuckholes were mere dips, so I started to enjoy the ride. That is, until we turned off even this token of civilization. What we began following now was *definitely* a cow trail, which led us finally into a valley. Hills loomed so high above us on all sides that dusk was already here at 3 o'clock in the afternoon. A small creek skipped along beside us. When we finally found our campsite it was dark.

I soon learned that erecting a tent in the dark is far more difficult than changing a baby's diaper under similar circumstances. While Ted ransacked a canvas bag for the stakes, I was delegated a more important task: clearing a 9-by-9 foot area of boulders and cow patties. The former were easy to find with the aid of a big toe; the latter tended to hide beneath unsuspecting feet.

After completing the job, I found out what veteran hunters already know—the directions for putting up a tent are written by borderline maniacs. "Pole A into Slot A" became a major feat, especially because subfreezing temperatures had numbed my fingers and the only light came from a two-cell flashlight. An hour and a half later, our five-minute-total-erection-time tent stood majestically.

The wilderness was so quiet I could hear our breathing. A strange, yelping sound came from a long way off. I guessed that it was a coyote's howl, and Ted confirmed it. As we crawled into our sleeping bags, I wondered how far we were from another human.

I awoke to the smell of frying bacon. It was still dark, and Ted was not in the tent. I poked my head through the flap. He was bending over the Coleman stove, deftly turning bacon and flipping flapjacks in the dim light of a white-gas lantern. I quickly snuggled back into my bag. The temperature must have dropped 100° since we'd gone to sleep.

"Come and get it!" Ted called.

I pulled the bag over my head and tried to ignore him. No good. He beat on the side of the tent with an oversize spoon. I grabbed my jeans and shirt from the floor beside me. Thrashing and struggling, I managed to dress inside the bag. Ted threw up the tent flap and handed me a plate piled high with crisp bacon and pancakes dripping with syrup. A cup of hot coffee thawed my insides enough so that I could appreciate the royal breakfast.

"Come on," Ted said after he'd finished gulping down his food. "The sun will be up pretty soon."

I quickly ate the last of my pancakes, threw on a coat, and followed my husband up the nearest hill. He was taking three strides to my one. Panting, I finally caught up with him on the crest of the hill. I'd hoped for a chance to rest, but we kept going. After what seemed like hours, Ted found "the spot" and we sat under a tree. At daybreak I could barely see the canyon below. I sat quietly and waited for a herd of deer to come thundering by us. None did. I sat motionless at least another five minutes. Still no deer. *Obviously, the deer are not awake yet,* I thought.

I looked at my watch: 6 a.m. I tried not to move much. Seemingly two days later, I looked at my watch again: 7. Ted suggested that we try another place. We spent the rest of the day trying new places. By 4 in the afternoon, I was tired and hungry. I'd lost any energy that I might have derived from the smashed peanut butter and jelly sandwich I'd fished from my pocket for lunch. By the time we'd trudged the two miles back to camp, our frozen Oreos looked good. We ate canned chili in the can. With Saltines and cheddar cheese, it wasn't bad.

The next two days were repeats of the first. I was about to change my belief that hunters have an unfair advantage over the deer. On our fourth and last day, from our hiding place under a tree, we watched the sunrise. We almost could have touched a blue-gray haze in the valley. Ted's happy mood had deteriorated over the past couple of days, and he'd become despondent. I was philosophical. *We didn't need the meat to survive,* I thought. *Considering the cost of the trip, beef would be cheaper anyway. The deer would still be there the next year.* I didn't express my thoughts aloud. Even I am too smart for that.

I continued to sit motionless, pretending that I could see frost forming on my fingernails. Thinking of beef prices reminded me of the budget we had been intending to organize for about six years. I decided it was a good time to talk about it.

"Honey," I began. "We really do need to take a look at . . ."

He shot me a look that zinged past my right ear and embedded itself in a tree trunk. I shut my mouth and tried to search through the half-light. Ted grabbed my wrist. Startled, I squinted into the shadows. Not moving his eyes, Ted picked up his rifle. I held my breath, still squinting but not seeing.

"About 175 yards that way," he whispered. "I saw something move."

I didn't breathe for fear that I'd move. My eyes began to water as I strained them to see the invisible. I was afraid that my thudding heart would give us away. Five minutes stretched into a year. Beads of perspiration broke out on my frostbitten cheeks. I began to breathe again, but slowly, and I kept watching the place that Ted was looking at. Then, inch by inch, bobbing slowly, a deer's antlers appeared above some cedars. Just as I realized what I was seeing, a deafening explosion scared my heart out of my throat and back into my chest where it belonged.

Ted ran toward the clump of trees and brush. When I reached him, I eagerly looked behind the tree where the buck had been. Nothing. I sank to the ground in disappointment. A week earlier I'd secretly wished that all the "poor little deer" would get away from all the hunters. Now I was ready to strangle the beast with my bare hands. Ted disappeared into the trees. I heard thrashing, then a jubilant shout.

When I found Ted, I also found out that I didn't have to strangle anything. A shot through the heart had given us meat to put in the freezer and a six-point rack for our wall. Ted's success made our long trip home bearable.

More than a year has passed since then. Though I still might not look forward to The Big Day with the same amount of enthusiasm and thrill of a seasoned hunter, at least I understand why Ted does.–***Debra J. Barber.***

PART 2 LOWDOWN ON GUNS AND ACCESSORIES

Will You Miss Your Shot of a Lifetime?

It's the last day of a two-week hunt in the high country, getting late, 15 minutes of shooting light left. You're on the dark side of a steep ridge, and there on the opposite slope, across a deep canyon, antlers pointing every which way, is the biggest muledeer buck or bull elk anyone ever saw.

There isn't enough time for a stalk, and your only hope is to blast him across unknown hundreds of yards. It will be the shot of a lifetime, literally, because you saved your nickels and dimes for 10 years to buy this hunt, and there'll never be another chance.

You fold your down jacket into a rifle rest and squiggle into a sort-of-prone position. Even with your variable-power scope turned to full power, your quarry looks tiny. The guide is breathless, and your hunting buddy looks as if he is about to choke. It's up to you, sport.

How many times have you pictured yourself in just such a scenario? Lot's of hunters do, I know, because I've received hundreds of letters from folk getting themselves outfitted for their first Western big game. Almost to a man they want to know what make of rifle, what caliber, and what kind of scope they should have for their personal shot of a lifetime. The inference, of course, is that if they flub they will not only forfeit a handsome set of antlers and freezer meat, but will forever be shunned by their friends, beautiful women will no longer make goo-goo eyes their way and their children will leave home in shame. Such disgrace, they imagine, can be avoided if they arm themselves with the shooting world's latest technological marvel, a big magnum that zips a sabre-tipped bullet out the muzzle as fast as forked lightning and as straight as a laser beam.

Quite a few of these letter writers say they have good deer rifles, .270s and .30/06s, but they've been persuaded that they'll need more horsepower west of the Mississippi. This troubles me because I'm rather old-fashioned and think there's a good sense in the old saying, "Beware the man with one gun because he knows how to use it."

Today's hunters have been fed such a heady diet of fancy hunting yarns, high-powered advertising and barnyard ballistics that we've come to liken the shooting of an elk or antelope to sending a rocket to the moon. The bitter truth is that the one great limitation of how far a hunter can bust a mule deer or elk is not so much a matter of ballistic technology but old-fashioned marksmanship. Let me say it again, MARKSMANSHIP—the ability to make a bullet go where you want it to go.

You can't buy good marksmanship, and no one has figured out how to load it into a cartridge. And believe me; you sure cannot make up for poor shooting with a pretty rifle or dazzling ballistics. A deer missed with a rock-splitting magnum is no more harmed than if he'd been missed with a slingshot. Every year many hunters rudely awake to the fact that hot-shot rifles are a poor substitute for marksmanship and are likely to make poor shooting even worse. High-performance rifles tend to be like high-spirited horses; they can be hard to master and often succeed in intimidating the rider. Old Dobin can be a lot surer. So for a while let's forget the velocity tables and talk about marksmanship.

Many hunters, I'd say most, actually do not have any idea whether or not they will connect on the shot of a lifetime. Some hunters are surprised when they miss, others are surprised when they hit.

Some hunters secretly suspect that they are good marksmen, others suspect they are not. The

Sitting position, above, is much steadier than offhand, and it puts rifle above low vegetation, unlike the prone position. Practice often at 100 yards, and when you know you can hit at that range, increase the range gradually until you find your maximum accurate range.

truth, however, is that few of us really know how we stack up as riflemen. Marksmanship seems to be a delicate topic that is not discussed in polite society. The absurdity of this situation is brought into dazzling focus by thousands of books and articles that describe in agonizing detail the performance of rifles and ammo but make absolutely no mention of the single most important element in getting a bullet on target—the shooter himself. Personal marksmanship apparently is such a touchy subject that most shooters prefer not to talk about it. Well, by golly, the tippy-toeing is over; let's talk about what we should have been talking about years ago.

HOW GOOD IS GOOD?

Hunter marksmanship is hard to put into perspective because we don't even have standards of performance with which to compare ourselves. So, for the sake of finding some place to rank ourselves, let's see how well target shooters do at the various ranges at which we might fire at big game. This will also give us a good idea of the upper limits of marksmanship. For example, firing from the prone position, with a super-accurate target rifle sighted to hit dead on point of aim, a top-notch long-range competitor will plunk most of his shots in the 12-inch 10-ring of the 600-yard target. This tells us two things: First, that a really good shot *can* hit a fairly small target at a long range, and second, that if hitting a 12-inch diameter target at 600 yards calls for the very best in skill and equipment, then most of us should forget about shooting game at that distance.

So let's back up a bit and see how target shooters fare at closer, more practical hunting ranges. A silhouette shooter who is good enough to hit five out of 10 chicken-size steel cutouts at 200 meters (220 yards), offhand, will win or place high in a silhouette tournament. This doesn't sound like very good shooting, does it? After all, the silhouette target is getting on to the size of the heart-lung area of a whitetail, and can't everyone hit a deer solidly, offhand, at 200 yards or a little over? No! The outside distance that the average hunter can effectively hit a *standing* deer from the offhand position *is less than 100 yards*. Remember, the shot is made all the more difficult by the excitement of the moment. It's like trying to thread a needle after holding your breath for two minutes.

Now, let's change the position from standing to sitting and see how well target shooters can hit the mark. The best example here is the 200 yard rapid-fire phase of the National Match course in which the competitor fires 10 shots in 60 seconds. During this time limit, the shooter gets into the sitting position and even reloads five rounds. Yet a crack rapid-fire specialist will crank 10 shots through his bolt-action rifle with time to spare and group his bullets inside a 7-inch circle! This gives us a good idea of how much more effective hunting marksmanship can be if the hunter shoots from a sitting position or takes advantage of natural rests such as limbs, stumps or whatever.

Sometimes hunters try to shoot from an improvised kneeling position with an elbow resting on a knee, but this is scarcely steadier than standing, and for most shooters not nearly as steady as sitting. In fact, the kneeling position is a mandatory phase of some U.S. and international riflery tournaments simply because it is so difficult.

The same target shooter who rapid-fires his shots into a seven-inch 10-ring at 200 yards, sitting, will, from the prone position, shoot about the same size group at 300 yards. But at this point the gulf between target shooting and hunting widens considerably. For while the target shooter, bringing all his skill and the excellence of his equipment to bear, can hit a pie-size target with relative ease, many hunters have neither the skill or the know-how to hit the vital zone of a pronghorn, a deer, or an elk at that distance.

GETTING THE RANGE RIGHT

"But," you say, "what about all those fantastic shots we hear and read about made at 600 and 800 yards?" Those stories are part of the problem. They've given too many beginning hunters the idea that such ranges are the norm on Western hunts for elk, antelope, sheep and goats. Every time I hear such a yarn I automatically cut the alleged distance in half, and even then I'm usually being generous. I don't think the bearers of such legends are deliberately exaggerating; they simply can't judge distance. I can't understand how the American male can spend so much time watching football and still be unable to judge 100 yards and multiples thereof.

Once when I was hunting pronghorn in Montana one of our party pulled off a neat shot on a trophy buck that sent him into spasms of ecstasy. "It's the longest shot I've ever made," he said, "500 yards if it's an inch." At his urging three of us paced off the distance to bear witness to his remarkable feat. The tally was 260 paces. Had we not paced it off the hunter would still be talking about his "500 yard" antelope, innocently misleading dozens of others into thinking that hitting game at such ranges is fairly common.

Another time a couple of my hunting pals and I came across a pretty fair elk poking along a hillside in northern New Mexico. The distance looked a bit longish, but the old boy gave me a broadside view that was too tempting to pass up. So, firing prone and using my hat for a rest under the rifle's forearm, I put in a shot that put him out of business. Both my buddies—and the guide—allowed it was the longest shot they'd ever seen and naturally had to pace off the distance. It was all of 320 steps, hardly the stuff hunting yarns are made of, but a revelation to my pals who, earlier would have dismissed a 300-yard shot as child's play.

I'm not being mean or critical; I'm only trying to make a constructive point. Since we very seldom shoot at game as far as we think we're shooting, it follows that our shots are easier than we think they are. Thus we don't really have to outfit ourselves for a 400-yard shot after all. If the average big-game hunter, firing from a reasonably solid rest or from the sitting position with a tight sling, can hit a gallon bucket at 200 yards he'll do OK on those "long" game shots. This will put him in contention to pull off the genuinely long shot at 300 yards (that looks like 500).

Nation of riflemen or not, the truth is that we are not born with genes that automatically make us crack shots. We have to learn to hold a rifle, how to align the sights on a target and how to press the trigger.

Back in the days of the great buffalo herds, hunters got to be good shots—and expert at judging range—simply because they shot dozens, perhaps hundreds, of buffalo day after day. The average big-game hunter won't shoot half that number of big-game animals in a lifetime, so we have to develop our skills elsewhere.

Traditionally, marksmanship instruction has been a family matter taught to youngsters by their fathers and grandfathers. This tradition seems to be fading away, and it troubles me somewhat because more young men and women than ever before are in need of sound instruction. Hunter safety courses offer good instruction in the fundamentals of shooting, but there are no follow-up programs to provide in-depth training. Thus, many beginning shooters have to go to it on their own or, if the opportunity exists, to join up with some target shooters. (Don't laugh at target shooters; they make the deadliest big-game shots of all.)

One of the big problems in preparing hunters to successfully pull off a "shot of a lifetime" is getting them to admit, even to themselves, that a bit of instruction might be helpful.

I don't know why it is, but men who unhesitatingly go to a golf pro to help smooth out a swing, and who have spent years dancing like puppets for football or basketball coaches, seldom seek help with their shooting. Since there is so little demand for professional coaching, there are few coaches. The next best course of action then is to visit or join a gun club and simply ask someone who is qualified for a little fine tuning. Target shooters who are proven winners themselves will probably spot your problem easily and put you on an effective training program. And I've never known one of these fellows who wouldn't fall all over himself to help a newcomer or fellow shooter in need of coaching and encouragement.

The best do-it-yourself training technique is simply dry firing,—aiming at a mark and snapping on an empty chamber. (Be *very* sure the gun is unloaded.) This form of practice is effective because it has the feel of firing a shot without the recoil, muzzle blast and cost of firing live ammo. Dry firing is a lot more than just snapping the firing pin. After a bit of practice you develop a smooth follow-through that actually let's you "see" where you would have hit the target. In fact, dry firing is often better than actual shooting because a recoiling rifle masks your tendencies to jerk the trigger or flinch at the shot. Shooters who have these bad habits usually aren't aware of them, and firing more live rounds only makes things worse. Dry firing quickly exposes such problems.

Don't worry about damaging a rifle by dry firing; it's unlikely to happen with most modern rifles. I'd say I dry fire some 50 to 100 shots for every live round I fire, and the really good shots I know dry fire a lot more. Karamojo Bell, the famous elephant hunter, who was reputed to be one of Africa's greatest marksmen, dry fired almost constantly. As he walked through the bush, he is said to have dry fired at every kind of target—birds, twigs, flowers and leaves.

When you practice with real ammo, work out a course of fire that lets you compare the results of each practice session with previous sessions. Many hunters feel that a sighting-in session at the bench is practice enough, but that is just the beginning. Fire 10 more shots standing and 10 sitting. If you can keep your shots inside 12 inches at, say, 100 yards, increase the range slowly until you reach your limit. You will not only improve your holding skills, but, equally important, you will gain a reliable knowledge of your abilities at different ranges. If you go through these practice exercises with your dad, your son or a hunting pal, they can be a lot of fun.

Years ago I read an article about long-range shooting at game in which the author speculated that a poor shot had a better chance than a good marksman at pulling off a super long shot. His argument was that the bum shot would scatter his bullets all around the target, thereby improving the likelihood that one lucky shot would finally find the mark. The good shot, on the other hand, would keep missing in the same place. I didn't know what to make of such a notion back then because I was young and innocent. But I sure know what to make of it now—balderdash! A good shot gets to be a good shot because he knows his rifle. Thus when he misses a long, deliberate shot, he will alter his point-of-hold somewhat and try again until he gets the range and hits.

I once asked an Alaskan sheep outfitter what kind of hunter he preferred to guide. "Pennsylvania woodchuck hunters," he answered at once, "because they can judge range and know how to shoot." And an African guide once told me that one of the best shots he ever took on safari was an Indiana farmer who came equipped with only a beat-up Model 70 rifle in .270 caliber and two boxes of ammo. He placed his shots perfectly, and everything went down in its tracks. It seems he had made a regular practice of carrying the rifle on his tractor, and was in the habit of sniping at groundhogs and crows. The practice, not a fancy rifle or dazzling ballistics, made him deadly.

So the next time Marvin Magmouth buttonholes you and starts unreeling the ballistic poop on his latest clod buster, just tell him that ballistic tables never killed anything but time. It's marksmanship that brings home the game.–***Jim Carmichel.***

The Eternal .30/06

If there's such a thing as the all American rifle round for deer hunting and other pursuits, it must be the ageless .30/06. Born and bred in the U.S.A., the .30/06 has been used in three wars (more than any other U.S. service cartridge). It's been chambered in more makes and models of rifles than any other cartridge in the world and earned for itself a reputation as an unequaled all-around hunting cartridge. It is the cartridge to which all others are compared. Whenever I start out to examine the performance or ballistics or accuracy of any new round, I always compare it to the .30/06.

The first head of big game I ever took with a .30/06 was a fair-size Southern highlands black bear which I shot on a Tuesday. I'm sure it was a Tuesday because I'd gotten married the previous Friday. My new wife and I had planned a 10-day honeymoon, but when the chance to go bear hunting suddenly came up, I naturally had no choice but to return my new bride to her parents, grab my rifle and boots, and head for the mountains.

I can't recall a time since I was 15 that I haven't owned at least one rifle chambered for the .30/06. At the time of my honeymoon bear hunt I had a matchgrade 1903 Springfield that had been fitted with target sights and honed until the bolt worked as slick as a snake's tongue. It was my first really serious big-bore tournament rifle and did me steady service for several years of intense competition.

The one I took bear hunting was one of those seldom-seen Remington Model 720 bolt guns made by Remington for only a few months of 1941 before the switchover to war production. The 720 was one of the most beautifully finished bolt-action rifles ever made, and I'd trade something really pretty to get that old rifle back.

Actually I killed two bears on that particular hunt, the first a fat one the dogs had chased up a slender poplar. One of the dog handlers had arrived on the scene sometime earlier and had passed the time pumping slugs into the animal's rump with a battered old .38/40 Model 92 Winchester lever gun. The bear was growling and squalling and acting so aggravated about the whole thing that the dog owner was afraid it would come down and wipe out his pack of hounds. So I angled around to where I could get a clear shot (and be out of the way when the bear fell) and finished him off.

Later that day I tried to head off some dogs on a hard chase and got so tangled up in a laurel thicket that the only way I could travel was on my hands and knees, dragging the rifle by the sling. Hearing a crashing ahead of me, I got my rifle around just in time to poke it in the chest of the onrushing bear and yank the trigger. The bear and I were so close that when the 220-grain slug hit its lungs droplets of blood sprayed out its nose and onto my shirt. The brush was so dense that the bear couldn't fall to my satisfaction, so I shot him again. So in the space of five days I got married, shot bears, and was toasted with Tennessee sour mash whiskey. Each for the first time.

The .30/06 gets its title from U.S. government nomenclature, which says that it is the .30 caliber service cartridge, model of 1906. This date is something of a puzzle to armchair arms historians; because the first service rifle which chambered a version of the round, the 1903 Springfield, was put into production three years earlier. What happened during those intervening years?

There existed for this brief span a service round known as, yep, you guessed it, the .30/03. The 1903 version of the case was almost identical to the current form except for a slightly longer neck.

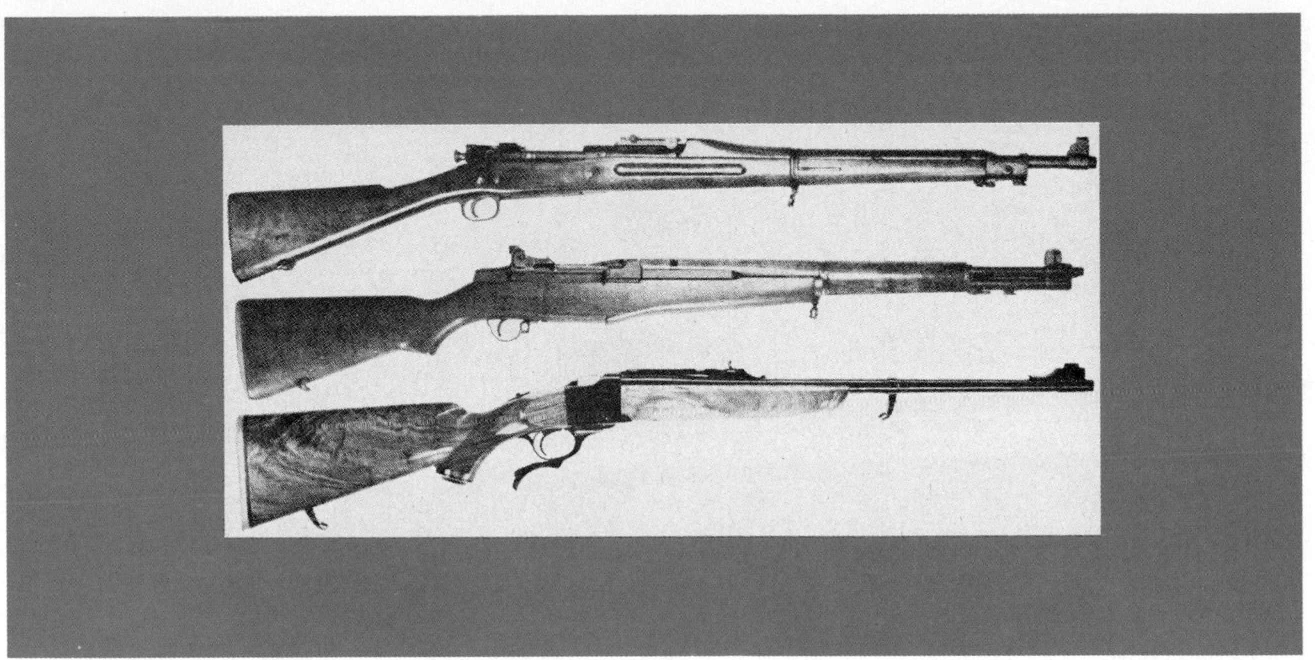

Three .30/06 rifles: the famed Springfield bolt-action used by the U.S. Army in World War I, a semiautomatic Garand, basic U.S. Infantry arm in World War II; a very modern Ruger single-shot, based on the old British Farquharson falling-block action. Because the .30/06 cartridge is a nice compromise between blockbuster loads and small-bore cartridges, almost any kind of rifle action can be adapted to handle it.

The change came when the Army brass, waking up to what was happening in the world, realized that velocity was more useful than bullet weight. The 220-grain bullet, carryover from the .30/40 Krag days, was dropped in favor of a 150-grain slug. This upped velocities from the .30/03's 2,300 feet per second to a new high of 2,700.

For several years, the .30/03—sometimes called the .30/45 because of its 45-grain charge of smokeless powder—was manufactured by sporting ammo makers alongside the virtually identical .30/06. As a matter of fact, the .30/06 can be safely and satisfactorily fired in .30/03 chambers, though the reverse is not true because of the .30/03's longer neck.

During the Spanish-American War, U.S. Ordnance officers had been much impressed with the Spaniards' high-velocity 7 mm Mauser rifles and ammo. (The 700 Spaniards defending San Juan Hill inflicted some 1,400 casualties on the American attackers.) They were so impressed, in fact, that their recommendations led to development of the 1903 Springfield rifle, based on the Mauser system, and the new cartridges. To give you an idea of how closely U.S. Ordnance was copying the Spaniards' ammo, consider that both the .30/06 case rim and base diameter are identical to the 7 x 57 Mauser.

It didn't take American sportsmen or sporting ammo makers long to discover the wonders of the .30/06. In 1908, for example, Winchester offered the heavy-framed Model 1895 lever-action rifle in the soon-to-be popular new caliber.

The legend of the .30/06 began to flower when Teddy Roosevelt used a sporter version of the Springfield in Africa and reported on its capabilities in rhapsodic terms.

It must be kept in mind that the .30/06 did not represent any sort of breakthrough in the ballistic world. Smokeless powder cartridges had been around for more than two decades, and some European military cartridges had been buzzing close to the 3,000 feet per second muzzle velocity barrier since before 1900. What the .30/06 did with such success was comfortably bridge modern ballistic thought with some traditional concepts. For example, it was of .30 caliber, the same as the .30/40 Krag round so familiar to thousands of Spanish-American War veterans. But at the same time it was of the sleek rimless case design which fed so smoothly through Mauser-type, stagger box magazines. But most of all it was the official U.S. government service cartridge, and that guaranteed its success as a hunting round, as had been the case with both the .45/70 and .30/40 Krag.

If there was any doubt as to the excellence of the .30/06, all such doubts were erased during the War to End All Wars. It was the superior infantry cartridge on Europe's battlefields. Even German arms makers admitted its superiority. As it turned out, they were more accurate than our own Army in pinpointing the advantages of the .30/06. For some reason the American soldier, in fact the whole American population, had fallen in love with the 1903 Springfield rifle. It was the world's most accurate rifle, they loved to tell each other, and went on to demonstrate its phenomenal accuracy by ringing up record target scores at all ranges out to 1,000 yards.

Actually the '03 Springfield, finely made as it was, was only a copy of the basic Mauser design with all the Mauser's faults plus a few extra faults of its own. What made the Springfield the most accurate repeating rifle of its day was the truly remarkable .30/06 ammunition made for it. Perhaps this calls for some explaining. Until the First World War, European small-arms design and manufacture were couched in the ancient tradition of massed musket fire. That's why the Europeans were so quick, by the middle of the 19th century, to convert to repeating-type infantry small arms. The idea of individual marksmanship apparently never occurred to them, or at least never had much appeal, as can be seen in their abominably inaccurate rifles and ammunition. It was common for rifle bores to be several thousandths of an inch out of size, and for bullet diameters to be nearly as bad. Accuracy was almost impossible except by accident.

American arms making, on the other hand, was philosophically predicated on the fine-honed marksmanship of the individual soldier. Accordingly, rifle barrels and especially ammunition, were held to exceptionally close tolerances. So when British, French and German armorers expressed amazement at the accuracy of the Springfield rifle carried by American troops, what they were really fascinated by was the beautifully uniform .30/06 cartridges.

This is one of the reasons European sporting rifle makers were so eager to adapt the .30/06. After the war, when continental rifle makers were again turning out hunting equipment, the .30/06 or 7.62 x 64, as they called it, was almost immediately a standard catalog item. The German firm of Mauser Werke offered a classy .30/06 sporter based on a fancied-up version of their Model 98 military action, and an Austrian outfit made a trim little 6-pound .30/06 Mannlicher-Schoenauer carbine way back in 1924.

In the United States, Remington got off to a head start simply by modifying its tooling a bit and offering a sporterized version, called the Model 30, of the 1917 Enfield produced during the war. In 1925, when Winchester introduced its Model 54, one of the original two calibers was .30/06. The other was a new round called the .270, made by simply necking the .30/06 case down to .277 caliber. In 1928 Savage offered another .30/06 bolt-action rifle, which was called the Model 40.

The apparent slowness of American gun makers to jump on the .30/06 bandwagon was due to a number of pretty important factors. One was that American sportsmen were still oriented toward lever-action rifles and other fast repeaters. Winchester's heavy Model 95 was the only .30/06 lever gun, and there were no .30/06 pumps or autoloaders until late in the 1930s. Another factor was the easy and low-cost availability of Springfield rifles. In addition to dirt-cheap service rifles, Springfield Armory produced a sporter rifle, very nicely finished and target accurate. This was the rifle used by Roosevelt in Africa, and thousands of American hunters were determined to follow his example. In 1930 a Springfield sporter, complete with star-gauged barrel and Lyman sights, could be had for about $60.

Also, during the 1920s a number of small gun making businesses specialized in making sleek sporters out of cheap '03 Springfields. Typical of these were Hoffman Arms, Griffin & Howe and Sedgeley. My 1939 Stoeger's Catalog shows a .30/06 autoloading rifle made by Krieghoff, a German firm specializing then, as now, in high-price shooting ware. I can't recall ever seeing one of these autoloaders and, with a price tag of 500 Depression-day dollars, I doubt if many were sold.

One autoloader that did succeed, though, was the Garand. Made by the millions during World War II and thereafter, this was the M-1 alternately loved and hated by American GIs. Since the ammo cartons said only "Cal .30 U.S." lots of soldiers never knew exactly what they were shooting. Many assumed, even to this day, that it was just a .30/30. I still get mail asking just what caliber the M-1 Garand rifle fired. The answer is none other than the .30/06. Likewise the .30/06 was the caliber of the beloved Browning Automatic Rifle and .30 caliber machine guns (but it was not the round fired in the little .30 Carbine). The .30/06 was the standard service cartridge throughout the Korean War and was not replaced until the late 1950s, thus becoming the longest-serving U.S. round.

Since its introduction the .30/06 has been a winning performer on the target range, and even today it is the second most widely used round in big-bore, long-range competition.

Over the years so many models and model variations of rifles in .30/06 caliber have been made, and so many different loadings offered, that it would take a thick encyclopedia to describe them all. I've used them for everything from Arizona jackrabbits to deer to 1,800-pound Australian buffalo, and thousands of other hunters have successfully used it for every species of game animal that walks the earth.

Among them America's three largest ammo makers—Federal, Remington and Winchester-Western—offer more choices of loads and bullet weights for the .30/06 than for any other *two* centerfire rifle cartridges combined. I counted no less than 22 load combinations in eight different bullet weights ranging from Remington's little 55-grain "Accelerator" hotshot up through 110, 125, 150, 165, 180, 200 and 220-grain slugs. The relative muzzle velocities of these bullets as factory loaded are:

55-grain Accelerator	4,080 fps
110	3,380 fps
125	3,140 fps
150	2,920 fps
165	2,800 fps
180	2,700 fps
200	2,550 fps
220	2,410 fps

The Accelerator is a varmint load, as is the 110-grain slug. The 125-grain bullet is fine for antelope as well as varmints, but until recently I preferred the 150-grain weight for all deer-size game. As a matter of fact, I used only 150 or 180-grain bullets for a number of years. The 150s were for mule deer and everything smaller, and I turned loose the 180-grain slugs on elk, moose and some big bears. The year Federal introduced its 165-grain boattail bullet load, I used it to take a nice elk and a couple of deer at long range and couldn't help being impressed. The 220-grain bullets have never done much for me because I don't care for their round noses. Federal's 200-grain boattail pointed bullet load, however, offers some interesting possibilities, especially for long-range shots at something bigger than deer. Its full ton of remaining energy at 300 yards is well above any other .30/06 bullet weight at that distance.

From the standpoint of internal ballistics the .30/06 is so well-balanced and untemperamental that it is ideal for hand loading. It is probably the most widely hand-loaded rifle cartridge of all. Without risk to his fingers or scalplock, the hand-loader can pretty well equal the performance of factory-loaded .300 H&H Magnum loads.

My longtime favorite hand load for both targets and hunting is 48 grains of IMR 4320 propellant with a 180-grain bullet of either hunting or match design. Depending on barrel length, this gives about 1,640 to 1,700 feet per second at the muzzle and unfailingly digests as smoothly as Aunt Grace's sweet potato dumplings. Sighted to hit 2 inches above point of aim at 100 yards, the pointed, boattail 180-grain bullet is almost dead on at 200 yards and 8 inches below aim at 300 yards. This is a fairly hot load, so use it only in well-made, well-kept modern rifles.

I used to have a notion that hunters with .30/06 rifles were more successful than hunters using other calibers. I suppose I felt this way because the abundance of low-cost, salvage GI ammo allowed them to practice more and thereby become better marksmen. There's not as much surplus ammo around as there was two decades ago, and it naturally costs more, but if you can find some cheap enough it's still great for practice. Tracer ammo, identified by a red-tip bullet, is no good because it is inaccurate and sets fires, but almost everything else, including the black-tip armor piercing bullets, is great for practice, provided your backstop will really stop the bullets. In case you use any of the old corrosive primer ammo, be sure to give the barrel three or four daily scrubbings and don't fire it in an autoloading rifle unless you're prepared to strip the rifle to clean the gas system.

The accuracy of the .30/06 is almost always described in a hunting context, meaning that it delivers satisfactory accuracy in a hunting rifle. But what is the true accuracy potential of the '06? Because it delivers more recoil than most benchrest shooters can tolerate, it has seldom been used in this ultra-precise accuracy game. However, a few years back I was lab testing a batch of carefully made .30 caliber bullets when, on a whim, I loaded a few in the .30/06 case and ran them through a heavy-barreled target rifle. Two five-shot groups fired at 100 yards measured .221 and .282, for an average of slightly over a quarter-inch between the centers of the widest shots. This, dear friend, is surpassingly good.

A while back I got caught in a conversation with a self-styled gun expert who grandly informed me that he had read all the ballistic tables and thereby concluded that the .30/06 was useless as a hunting round and should be scrapped. According to his logic the '06 is too big for varmints and even deer, but too light for the bigger stuff such as moose and bear and even elk. I was glad he told me all this because I hadn't had a good laugh all day and needed one.

Actually, I can't remember anyone saying that the '06 is supposed to be a varmint cartridge. At least not until a few years ago when Remington introduced the Accelerator load, which slings a 55-grain slug out the muzzle of a .30/06 at over 4,000 feet per second. With this load the .30/06 beats even such hot varmint cartridges as the .22/250 at their own game. This doesn't mean, however, that the .30/06 has suddenly become the No. 1 choice of serious varmint potters. Most stalkers of the wily woodchuck like to concoct their own special long-range medicine, and Accelerator components are not now available to hand-loaders.

If the Springfield rifle was adopted in 1903, and the .30/06 cartridge (left) was adopted in 1906, what round did the rifle fire originally? Answer is on right: the .30/03. It had a longer neck than the familiar '06, and it was loaded with a 220-grain bullet. Recoil was too much for many raw army recruits.

Long before the Accelerator load (which fires a jacketed .22 caliber bullet held in a sabot or sleeve) came along the ammo makers were (they still are) turning out a 110-grain bullet load with a 3,380 feet per second muzzle velocity and a 125-grain bullet which leaves at 3,140. When sighted in to hit dead on at 200 yards, either of these bullets will be about 3 inches low at 250 yards and close to 8 inches below aim at 300 yards. Nothing to rave about, of course, but plenty flat for some half-serious chuck bustin'! And too, there are all sorts of lightweight .30 caliber bullets available to '06 hand-loaders. Many hand-loaders, by the way, like to put together lower velocity "plinking" loads that are great for short-range practice because of their mild recoil and low noise level.

Some rifles do not shoot these lighter bullets as accurately as heavier slugs. This loss of accuracy is essentially—but not entirely—due to the '06's usual rate of twist, one turn in 10 inches, which theoretically is too fast for the short bullets. A rifling twist of one in 14 or even 16 inches would be more nearly ideal, but there are plenty of exceptions. Some rifles, for whatever reason, turn in remarkably good accuracy, even when the lightweight bullets are blown out at top velocity. But then the '06 was never intended to be a great dual-purpose cartridge. Varmint shooters who are serious about their sport shoot honest-to-goodness varmint cartridges such as the .222.

Just for the sake of shedding some much needed light, it's worth pointing out that the .30/06 is vastly more efficient—and useful—over a broader spectrum than are most of the dual-purpose or "compromise" cartridges. The popular image of compromise loads include cartridges such as the .243, 6mm Remington, .257 Roberts, .250 Savage, .25/06 and so on. You get the idea. Using these cartridges for varmints on the one hand and deer or antelope on the other is, when you think about it, a pretty skimpy compromise. It's also true that a good shot with the 25s can do the job on elk, but if you're thinking about trying them on moose, not to mention the mean bears, you'd better bring track shoes.

The good old .30/06, though, is plenty good for these bigger and tougher animals. In fact, I'd say that since 1920 American hunters have bagged more moose, caribou and northern bear with the .30/06 than any other cartridge. It has also been widely used in such places as Africa, Asia, South America and Australia for many big game species.

One of the reasons the .30/06 has been so overwhelmingly successful as a big game cartridge is because it is the "biggest" cartridge many shooters can shoot well. This, I know, takes some explaining, but the simple fact of the matter is that even in this unbridled age of magnum mania there exists on the cartridge scale a certain breaking-off point where hunter marksmanship begins to decline. Fear of recoil, both real and psychological, is one of the reasons for this phenomenon, and there are other reasons as well. Whatever the reasons, the .30/06 appears to hover just on the edge of the breaking point. This means that the average hunter is more likely to pull off a deadly shot with the '06 than with a round that is more powerful.

I have a secret desire to take an elephant with a .30/06 loaded with the Hornady 220-grain full-patch bullet, but I seldom use the '06 these days. I've already used it successfully on many head of game and simply want to try other calibers. But if I had to pick one cartridge and stay with it forever, I suppose I would go with the .30/06.–***Jim Carmichel.***

On Deer and Antelope Rifles

If you're thinking about buying a new big-game rifle, I recommend you do it during the balmy days of September, just before most open seasons. It's the best time of the year for getting acquainted with a new rifle, adjusting the sights to dead-on perfection, and tuning your trigger finger to razor-edge wickedness.

THE ALL-PURPOSE RIFLE

Inflation has done some ugly things to the cost of guns and ammo so more than ever, this year's gun buyer will be searching for the most gun for the dollar. I expect the big sellers will be rifles that fall into the "all-purpose" category, those that provide draft-horse service for whitetail, pronghorn, and mule deer hunting and, when called upon, are capable of delivering a knockout punch to elk, moose, caribou, sheep, goats, and bears as well as woodchucks and other varmints.

Gun writers are fond of fantasizing about the all-purpose rifle, and editors of the Shoot 'Em-Up journals learned long ago that they can sell a few extra copies by stirring the all-purpose kettle from time to time. A few months back one of the Blast and Stab periodicals featured a debate between two alleged experts on the all-purpose gun issue. One author allowed that if you picked just the right make and model rifle, in the correct caliber, using precisely his recommended bullets, you would achieve the Holy Grail of an all-purpose rifle for American game. His opponent declared that the all-purpose rifle is only a myth, and the battle waxed furious. Ballistic tables were wielded like battle axes, theories flew like thunderbolts, and the battlefield was strewn with the debris of common sense. Had the combatants slain anything much in the way of game, they would have blushed at the unveiling of their innocence.

The all-purpose rifle is not a myth, nor is it even elusive. You can walk into a well-stocked gun shop and select a rifle in any one of a dozen makes and models in about as many calibers, and go forth to slay any animal the law says you can hunt in North America. You see, all some rifles need to achieve all-purpose status are all-purpose *hunters*!

I like to poke a little fun at my fellow gun writers, but my real point is simply that the buying of a big-game rifle seems to have become an issue of unnecessary confusion and complexity. Rifle manufacturers contribute to this confusion by continually offering new models, upgrading existing models, and introducing new cartridges they claim kill longer, quicker, and deader. The purpose of most of this hype is to sell rifles to hunters who already own more hardware than most of them can use. The result is to confuse first-time buyers who only want a rifle that will get the job done reliably and perhaps offer some pride of ownership.

I have nothing but sympathy for anyone who goes forth to buy his first antelope or deer rifle. Everyone who has hunted these species has his own ideas of what the best rifle is, and he is more than willing to share his views with anyone who will listen. You can even get ironbound opinions from an army of theorists who have yet to center their crosshairs on anything more exotic than a paper bull's-eye. Shooters of bolt-action rifles, for example, tend to be elitist and love to scorn pumps, autoloaders, and lever guns. Eastern brush-busters say bolt rifles are too slow and that it takes firepower to bring home the game. And then there's the big-boom faction who insists that muscle conquers all, meaning that

Television and movie star Slim Pickens and I look mighty proud of our trophy-class pronghorns. Our rifles are Winchester Model 70 bolt guns in .270 Winchester caliber fitted with Weaver's new Auto-Comp scopes. The .270 does the job well.

a big-belted magnum will get the job done when lesser cartridges leave you in the lurch. So who are you going to believe?

Not that it makes much difference, but my favorite pronghorn rifle is a medium-light bolt rifle in .25/06 caliber. In my experience pronghorns are not hard to anchor. The trick is to hit them right, not blast them into the next county. The .25/06 has mild recoil, which makes it easy to shoot accurately, the trajectory is wonderfully flat, and wind effect is minimal. The .25/06 is also great for mule deer, especially in broken country where shots tend to be long. But this doesn't mean everyone should charge out and buy a .25/06. Actually, I have some reservations about the .25/06. If you are primarily an Eastern hunter and hunt out West only on rare occasions, you will be smart to tailor your rifle needs to the type of hunting you do most.

WHICH ACTION

Why not an autoloader? Or a pump? And no one needs to tell you lever-fed rifles are popular. But everyone says they're not accurate, right? Five or six years ago I got curious about what *everyone* (whoever that is) has been saying about the accuracy of quick loaders, so I assembled some two dozen assorted makes, models, and calibers of pumps, autoloaders, and lever rifles and spent a week testing them for accuracy. All testing was done from a benchrest at 100 yards, and the rifles were fitted with high magnification varmint-type scopes to make aiming as precise as possible. The results were remarkable.

On average the lever rifles were the poorest performers, the pumps were a bit better, and the autoloaders were significantly more accurate. Each rifle was fired 100 rounds in five-shot strings. The size of each five-shot group was tabulated into the average. The overall average for each classification was autoloaders 2.57 inches, pumps 3.20 inches, and lever 3.53 inches. The surprise performer was the least expensive rifle of the lot, a Savage Model 170 pump rifle in .30/30 caliber that had a habit of putting three or more of the Federal factory loads into a tight little cluster about the size of a nickel. Two of the groups measured under an inch, and the 20-group average was under two inches.

If you were to select at random a dozen bolt-action hunting rifles and test them from the benchrest, you'd find that the *average* 100-yard five-shot group measures a bit over two inches, about the same as my autoloaders tested. Don't misunderstand, the most accurate rifles in the world are bolt-action target and varmint models, but it is as unfair to compare these with the average off-the-shelf bolt-action hunting rifle as it is to compare them with pumps, lever guns, and autoloaders.

So don't let anyone look down his nose at your fast repeater. If you think an autoloader or lever gun best suits your needs, by all means go ahead and buy one. I'm inclined to recommend pump-action rifles only to hunters who use pump shotguns. It's hard to remember to pump the things unless you're in the habit. The three makes of autoloaders I tested—the Remington Model 740, Browning's BAR, and the H & R Model 360—did not malfunction once during several hundred rounds of shooting, so don't worry about reliability.

The only real problem with the quick shooters is that almost all of them have spongy, nonadjustable triggers. The stock dimensions aren't all that great if you use a scope, the problem being too much drop at the comb. The *ne plus ultra* of autoloaders is Browning's BAR, which comes in .243, .308, .270, .30/06, 7-mm. Remington Magnum, and .300 Winchester Magnum. The magnums are tempting, but the .30/06 has to be the best all-around choice in this rifle.

Remington's brand-new Model 4 autoloader and Model 6 pump, along with the lower-priced M 7400 and M 7600 rifles, offer some mechanical improvements over the well-proved M 740 and 760 repeaters. All models are available in .243, 6 mm., .270, .308, and .30/06. The Model 4 and Model 7400 also come in 7-mm. Express, which is probably the best caliber choice for all-purpose high performance shooting. The German firm of Heckler & Koch is sending some autoloading sporters in .243 and .308 to the United States but they've been hiding their light under a bushel, so I can't comment on quality or reliability.

The reason I've gone into such detail about my experiences with quick-fire repeaters is to point out that some of them, particularly the good autoloaders, put you to no particular disadvantage even when hunting the long-shot species such as antelope, elk, and mule deer. In fact, an autofeeder can be of considerable advantage when hosing down a fast-departing pronghorn. So go West young man, and take your autoloader.

The traditional .30/30 lever guns and their cousins don't really qualify as all-purpose rifles for American game. They have enough muscle for anything that roams east of the Mississippi but are too short on accuracy, too low on horsepower, and too crooked of trajectory for serious Western hunting. The exceptions are the Savage Model 99 in .308 or 7 mm./08 calliber and the Browning lever rifle in .308. Both of these rifles come in other calibers as well but they won't make you happy out West. The .243, for example, is great for whitetails and pronghorns but iffy for mule deer and out of its league on elk.

The Remington Model 788 bolt rifle had a 1981 suggested retail price of $239.95, about the most performance for your dollar, especially from the accuracy viewpoint. Among other calibers, the 788 comes in .308 and 7 mm./08 calibers, both of which are fine for Eastern or Western deer and antelope and will put a lot of hurt on elk.

The revamped 788's stock is better looking and more shootable than the earlier models, but the overall effect is still as plain as a stepchild and suffers the absence of an adjustable trigger. Accuracy can be remarkably good, though, and the 18½-inch barrel makes a 788 mighty handy in the woods.

The 7 mm./08, in case you haven't heard, is a new round Remington slipped in a couple of years ago. As the name says, the cartridge was formed simply by necking down a .308 case to hold a 7-mm. bullet. This configuration became a fairly popular wildcat among Arizona's silhouette shooters a few years ago, and it proved to be so adaptable that Remington gave it an honest home and name.

The beauty of the 7 mm./08 is that it adapts to short actions, such as the Remington 788 and the short form Remington 700 and Ruger 77. (Theoretically, a short action is more accurate than a longer one of equal cross section because of reduced flexing.) Short, high-intensity cartridges tend to be more efficient than longer cartridges of the same caliber. The 7 mm./08, for example, plays in the same ball park with the 7-mm. Remington Express and 7-mm. Remington Magnum and ranks head and shoulders above factory-loaded 7 x 57 Mauser ballistics.

The five-shot group, fired at 100 yards with a Browning Automatic Rifle, measured 1.038 inches between centers of widest shots. The cartridge was the .30/06 and the scope was a 3X-to-9X Leupold. Autos are about as accurate as most bolt guns.

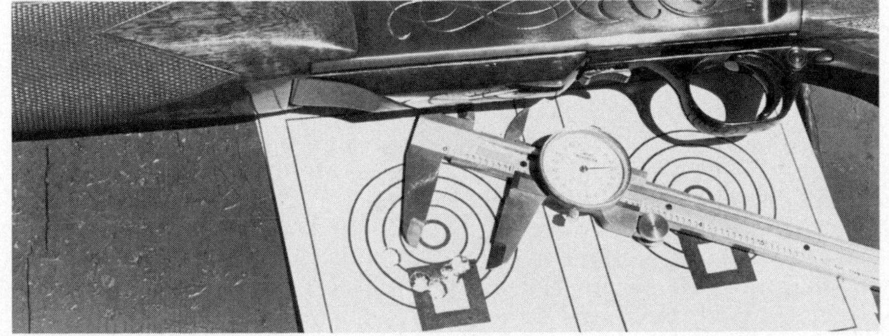

GETTING THE MOST VALUE

When I say more efficient, though, I don't necessarily mean better. Here's an example of the difference. Let's say that the above comments on the 7mm./08 convinced you that you can't live without one. But you don't like either the Remington 788 or Savage M99. Instead, you have always liked the Remington Model 700. So you figure that this rifle, teamed with the 7mm./08, will be the answer to your dreams. But wait. Is this the most gun for your dollar? Here's how to tell. You can get two versions of the Model 700 in 7 mm./08 chambering. One is the Varmit Special with a thick barrel built for accuracy. The 7 mm./08 caliber is a highly competitive silhouette rifle, but at a net weight of nine pounds the rifle is hardly a brush gun. The other choice in 7 mm./08 is the BDL hunting M 700, selling in '81 for $399.95. This seems like what you want, but is it? Look again. For the same money you can get the same rifle in 7-mm. Express, .270 Winchester, or .30/06, each of which may be theoretically less "efficient" than the 7 mm./08 but in the practical sense offer considerably wider hunting applications. Combined with the M 788 the 7 mm./08 is a terrific buy, but as a choice for the M 700 it may not offer all the punch and versatility you can get for your money. So how do you most wisely spend your hard-earned dough?

It seems to me that all too often we decide on a rifle we like and the cartridge we like without really considering if the two go together in such a way as to give the most gun for the money. A decade ago, hunters could afford the luxury of mismatched rigs, but shooters nowadays are looking for all the knockdown a dollar will buy.–***Jim Carmichel.***

Sighting-In Made Simple

During last year's deer season thousands of shots were missed because of improperly adjusted scope sights. There are no official statistics to cite, but every hunter knows it's true. Sadly, many disappointed hunters never discovered the cause of their bad luck and will miss again this season. How about you?

Some gun shops offer a scope mounting and sighting-in service and usually do a good job, but be sure to double-check the tightness of the scope-mounting screws. Keep in mind that most such sighting-in is done with an optical instrument that aligns the crosshairs with the *approximate* path of the bullet. *The rifle is still not sighted-in* and must be fired at a target for final zeroing.

Don't wait until the last minute to do your sighting-in. This is the single most important step in your hunt preparation so do it early, take your time, and do it right.

The ideal way to sight-in a rifle is from a solid shooting bench made of heavy timber or concrete, with your rifle resting over firm sandbags. Most rifle ranges have a benchrest or two just for this purpose, but if you don't have access to a range there are other techniques that work nearly as well. In any event, you will need sandbags. Make them yourself by using canvas shot bags (all shotshell loaders have plenty) or from the legs of old denim pants. Tie or sew up one end, fill with dry sand, sew up the other end, and you're in business. You'll need three or four bags depending on the bag size. Place two or three under the rifle's forearm and one between the butt of the stock and the top of the bench or other solid surface. This way you can shoot from a bench, the prone position on the ground, or even from the hood of a car.

The whole idea is to remove all human error when aiming and firing. With a few minutes of practice you'll find that you can hold the crosshairs dead on the target without so much as a tremor. With a scope, a good aiming point is a one-inch black square on white paper. It's a good idea to "dry-fire" a few shots (cocking the mechanism and snapping the trigger with the rifle unloaded won't hurt your rifle) to get an idea how the trigger feels, and thus find out how to pull the trigger so that it disturbs your aim as little as possible.

Wear shooting glasses and by all means wear hearing protection—the more the better. Unless you are already stone deaf, I absolutely, positively promise you that you cannot shoot a high-powered rifle well for very long without ear protection. Most cases of flinching are not caused by recoil but by muzzle blast. After a few shots from a magnum rifle, all your macho will turn to mush unless you protect your eardrums.

I usually sight-in my big-game rifles on a 100 or 200-yard range. Attempts to sight-in at 50 or 25 yards, and then interpolate a zeroed sight setting for a longer distance often run afoul of technical problems that make this setting invalid. Short-range shooting is handy to get the first shots "on the paper," but that's about all it's good for.

The usual method of sighting-in a scoped rifle goes like this: fire one to three shots at the target, measure the distance between where the bullet hit and the aiming point, make a series of adjustments to the scope's windage (left and right) and elevation controls to put bullet impact where you want it.

This is simple enough but I use an even easier method. My technique is to fire only one carefully aimed shot at the target and then locate the bullet hole. If the scope is 4X magnification or greater, it is usually possible to see a .30-caliber bullet hole at 100 yards through the scope. If not, make a mark around the bullet hole that can be seen through the scope.

With the rifle unloaded, carefully aim at the target again just as you did for the shot. With the rifle held motionless, and continuing to look through the scope, turn the adjusting knobs in the appropriate directions. There is no need to count the clicks or graduations on the adjustment's scales. We are bypassing all that. Instead, just keep your eye on the crosswire as it marches toward the bullet hole.

Obviously you can make only one adjustment at a time, and I like to make the windage adjustment first and then adjust the elevation.

When you coincide the crosswire with the bullet hole you simply bring the point of aim into mechanical alignment with the demonstrated point of impact. What could be simpler?

If you were careful and the rifle didn't move during the scope adjustment procedure (it is essential that the rifle be motionless), your rifle should now be perfectly sighted-in, that is, it is zeroed for the range at which you shot. In fact, you can sight-in for other ranges this way simply by altering the crosshair-bullet hole relationship. For example, let's say you want the bullet to hit two inches above aim at 100 yards so that you will be dead on at a longer range. Simply turn the elevation knob so that the elevation wire is positioned two inches below the bullet hole.

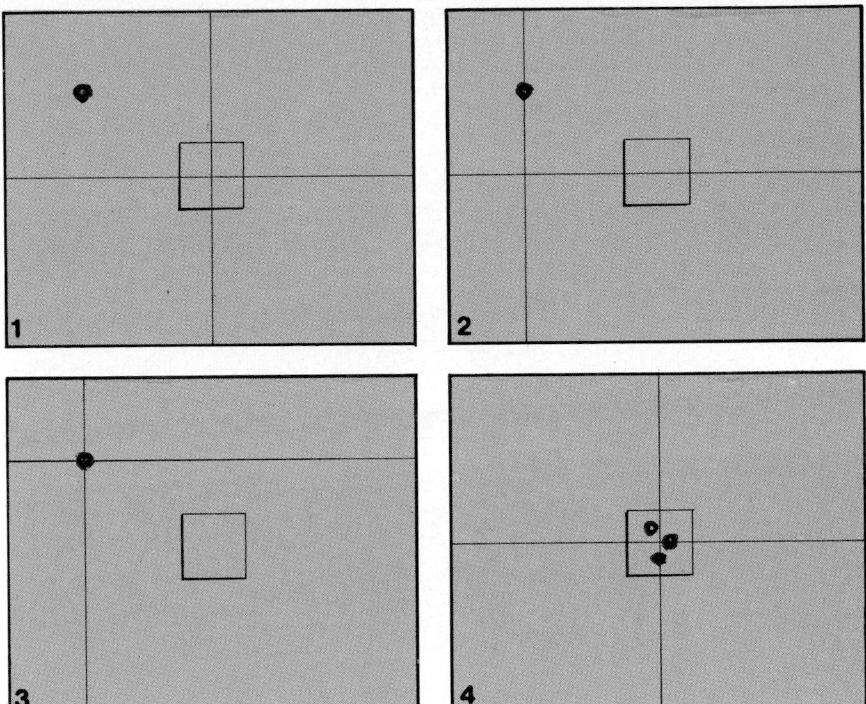

1. *With rifle solidly bedded on sandbags, quarter a square aiming point with crosshairs and fire. The bullet seldom hits target. It may be high, low, left, or right.* **2.** *Aim rifle at square again. With the rifle held motionless, walk crosswires across paper until vertical member intersects the bullet hole.* **3.** *Still holding steady, move crosswires so that horizontal wire intersects bullet hole. You have moved sights to the precise point where rifle shoots.* **4.** *Fire a few more shots to make absolutely sure.*

Some shooters find it difficult to look through the scope, hold the rifle motionless, and turn the adjustment knobs simultaneously. In this case have someone else turn the adjustments while you do the sighting and hold the rifle in place. Simply tell him to stop when you are where you want to be.

This method is so easy that one shot usually gets your rifle perfectly sighted-in. Don't take a chance on it, though. Be sure to fire several more shots to make sure your bullet hole is really where you want it.

If possible, you should fire your rifle at longer ranges to make sure of the point of impact at ranges longer than the one for which the rifle is zeroed. For instance, if the rifle is dead on at 200 yards, how much lower will the point of impact be if you fire a 300-yard shot? If it is too low, you will, of course, hold high when you shoot. See the accompanying diagram.

That's all there is to that.–***Jim Carmichel.***

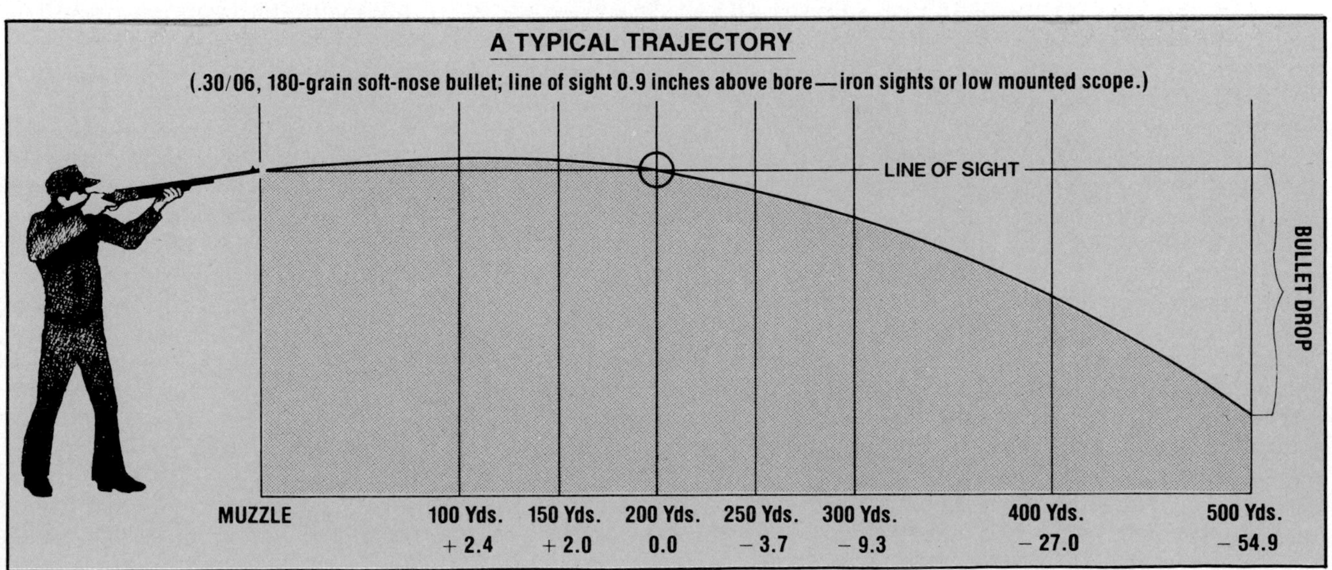

Ready— Aim— Ignition!

What could be simpler, or faster, than firing a gun? For instance, you squeeze the trigger on your deer rifle and an imperceptible instant later the bullet thunders out the muzzle. Yet, in that almost measureless instant of time an astoundingly intricate series of events takes place. Mechanics, physics, and chemistry join forces and interact so swiftly that their individual roles are played out in time spans measured to the *millionth* part of a second. In fact, once you press the trigger, releasing the sear and setting the hammer or striker in motion, the time periods needed for each action actually get shorter and shorter.

The first element in this chain-lightning process is *you*. You are the first energy source, the first drop of water that turns the wheel. You do this when you load and cock the gun. When you pull back the slide on an autoloader, break down the barrels on a double, cycle a bolt gun or thumb the hammer of a revolver, you are also *cocking* the mechanism. Your physical action withdraws a hammer or striker to the ready-to-fire position, where it is held in place by the sear, and transfers energy from you to the striker or hammer spring where it is stored until you pull the trigger. This energy can be stored there for seconds, days, or years, though it is very unsafe to leave a loaded, cocked gun lying around.

When you pull the trigger of your shotgun, rifle, or handgun you create a mechanical action by releasing the sear and thereby remove the restraint that has been keeping energy stored in the hammer or striker spring.

If you could see an ultra-slow-motion movie of a falling revolver hammer you would note that for the first few microseconds (one microsecond = 1/1,000,000*th* of a second) after the sear releases, the hammer scarcely moves at all. This is because it has been a static object, a body at rest and, according to the laws of motion, it wants to remain at rest. So there is a momentary tug-of-war between the hammer and the energy that you stored in the mainspring.

Gradually, as microseconds skip by, the energy wins and the hammer or striker begins moving, picking up speed as it accepts more and more energy from the mainspring. Naturally, the rate at which the striker accelerates is dependent on its weight in addition to the energy, or force, provided by the spring. If the striker is relatively light it accelerates very quickly, like a lightweight dragster, but if the striker is heavy it will accelerate like a heavily loaded tractor-trailer rig. These differences in striker speed pose something of a dilemma for gun manufacturers. Let me explain why.

The interval between the sear release and the impact of the firing pin on the primer in the cartridge is called *lock time*. All other factors being equal, a short lock time is desirable because it is a definite aid to accuracy. Let's say that you are aiming a revolver at a difficult target. Since it is physically impossible to hold any firearm with either one or both hands so that it is motionless, the revolver tremors and bounces about a bit as you align the sights on the target. Finally, when the sight alignment looks perfect, you press the trigger, releasing the sear and setting the hammer in motion. While the hammer is falling, the revolver continues to tremble and jerk in your hand, and by the time the hammer completes its fall the revolver may have wandered some distance from where it was when you pressed the trigger. This occurs to some extent with all hand-held guns, and we easily see that we will hit closer to where we aim if the gun has a short lock time. This is why makers of target-type rifles, shotguns, and handguns try to achieve the briefest possible lock time in their guns. But, alas, it's not easy to do—hence the dilemma faced by gun makers.

At first thought it would seem that all we need do to speed up lock time is to use stronger mainsprings. But there are mechanical limits to this because most trigger mechanisms can withstand only a limited amount of mainspring pressure. If the design limits are overburdened, sears may crack and crumble and become unsafe.

Another way we could shorten lock time is to lighten the hammer or firing pin. This is why the firing pins of sophisticated target rifles are often little more than slender pieces of wire. Some custom gunsmiths, in an effort to improve lock time, drill holes in revolver hammers or turn excess metal from strikers and firing pins. But here again, what seems like a simple solution can lead to other problems. You see, the heavier a firing pin or hammer the better it does its job. When it reaches the end of its travels and strikes the cartridge's primer, the firing pin must have *momentum*, and the two components of momentum are velocity and *weight*. One without the other won't do the job because the firing pin must hit the primer at high velocity and have enough weight to back up its punch. Otherwise the primer won't be indented quickly enough or deeply enough. Gun designers are torn between demands for fast lock time and the need for reliability. The usual result is a compromise, but there are extreme examples in both directions.

If you disassemble the bolt of a Model 98 Mauser rifle or a 1903 Springfield you will note that the 98's firing pin and the Springfield's firing-pin assembly are truly massive. When you pull the trigger on either of these famous rifles you hear and feel the pin or striker fall with a distinct *thump*, after a perceptible lock-time delay.

"Why do these rifles have such sluggish lock time?" you may ask. The reason is simply that their respective designers wanted utter reliability of cartridge ignition. These rifles were designed for the battlefield, not the target range, and a heavy firing pin with its added reliability was more desirable than fast lock time and possible loss of reliability.

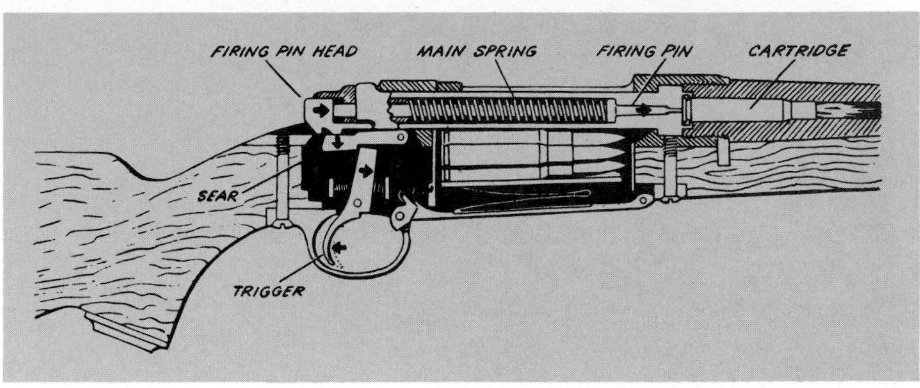

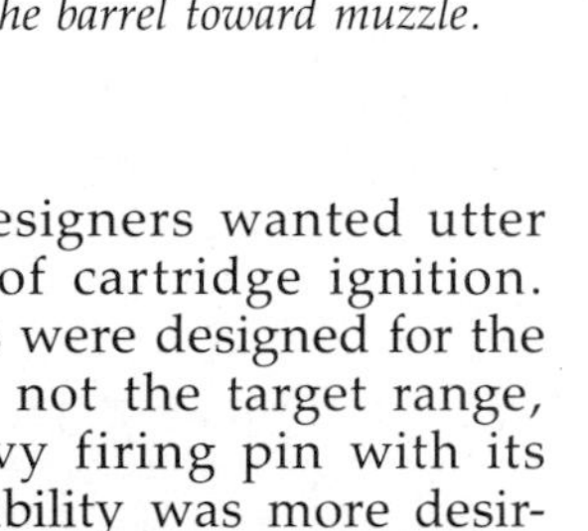

Modern rifle or handgun primer, right, is result of many years of development and is direct descendant of the early external percussion cap. After rifle is cocked, pulling trigger causes sear to release firing pin, and the pin impacts primer. The chemical primer mix explodes and ignites powder charge. Gas pressure in barrel reaches about 50,000 psi but falls rapidly as bullet moves down the barrel toward muzzle.

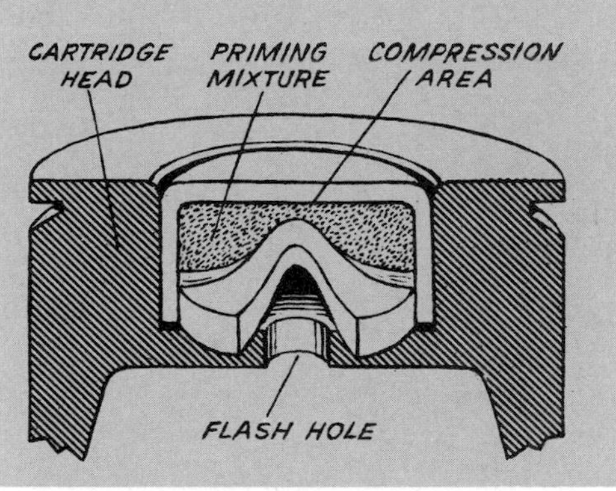

To give you a realistic comparison of actual lock times, the 1903 Springfield striker falls in about 5.7 microseconds. A Remington M700 striker takes about half as much time, and the much touted lock time of the Remington M788 bolt gun is a 2.25 to 2.5 microseconds.

Until this point, events have been moving at a rather leisurely pace, but as soon as the firing pin hits the primer face the tempo quickens considerably.

IMPACT

When the tip of the firing pin hits the primer or cartridge rim (in the case of rimfire ignition) it immediately begins to indent the encasing metal, but it may also have to move the entire cartridge forward in the chamber, which is not at all good.

Though cartridges are manufactured to exceedingly close dimensional tolerances and firearms are similarly chambered, there is, by necessity, a certain amount of play between the ammunition and the gun in which it is chambered. If tolerances were held too close the inevitable result would be failure of some ammunition to feed and fire in some rifles chambered for that caliber ammunition. As it is, even ammunition of maximum allowable dimensions almost always functions perfectly in rifles that have minimum chamber dimensions. This is as it should be, and the fact that sporting firearms by a dozen makers can function and fire ammunition by as many different manufacturers is no less than a miracle of modern manufacturing technology.

Yet sometimes even these tiny variations can be seen, and they may even have some effect on performance. If, for example, you were to compare the fired cases from five different rifles of the same caliber you would quickly note some differences in the way the cases expanded in the different chambers.

When the firing pin strikes the face of the primer it not only begins indenting the metal cup but also shoves the cartridge forward in the chamber. If, as sometimes happens, we have loaded a minimum dimension cartridge case in a maximum length chamber, the free space (known as headspace) might amount to a few thousandths of an inch. Not much free room, to be sure, but a centerfire rifle cartridge can weigh several hundred grains and a 12-gauge shotgun shell several times that. Therefore, a considerable portion of the firing pin's momentum has been exhausted in moving the cartridge to the deep end of the chamber. Once the cartridge is "fixed" in the chamber, the remaining energy in the firing pin is utilized to indent the primer cup and explode the chemical priming mixture. How then, you may wonder, can there be any problem so long as the cartridge fires? Actually there isn't much of a problem, certainly nothing that would be noticed in most hunting situations unless, of course, the round misfires, but accuracy buffs *can* detect some differences.

Let's say that the first round happens to be deeply seated in the chamber when the striker falls. Since the cartridge does not move, the firing pin hits the primer cup full strength with a quick, sharp blow. The primer explodes efficiently, and the powder charge ignites instantly. On the next shot, the cartridge is lying well back in the chamber with several thousandths of an inch of free play ahead of the shoulder. Again the firing pin hits the primer squarely, but instead of instantly exploding the primer mixture, much of the striker spring energy is spent shoving the cartridge forward. Finally, when the case is jammed to a stop against the chamber's shoulder, the primer is indented sufficiently to explode the priming mixture. But the explosion is less crisp, and there is a resulting erratic powder ignition and subsequent variation in chamber pressure and muzzle velocity. This is probably nothing you would ever notice unless you were shooting a high-performance target rifle, in which case you would notice some loss of accuracy. That's why centerfire target rifles, especially those used in benchrest competition, have specially cut minimum-dimension chambers. Some .22 Rimfire target rifles are so tightly headspaced that they won't even accept field-grade ammo.

The primer of a centerfire rifle or pistol cartridge of U.S. make is made up of three elements: the cup, the anvil, and the priming mixture. The cup holds everything together. The anvil is a metal structure inside the cup that performs the service its name suggests. The priming mixture is a dry chemical compound of rather unstable properties, making it a *percussive* explosive. It explodes when struck a sharp blow. The chemical mix commonly used in today's primers is lead styphnate, but many different kinds of mixes have been tried.

A familiar example of a percussive explosive is the cap used in a cap pistol. The mix used in cartridges, of course, is considerably more sophisticated. If you were to remove the bullet and powder from a centerfire cartridge and pop the primer in a gun you'd discover that the resulting crack is quite loud, much louder than a cap pistol and almost as loud as the report of a .22 Rimfire cartridge. This gives you some idea of the power of today's primers.

When the firing pin strikes the primer cup, the inward indentation smacks against the upturned point of the anvil. This percussive effect literally explodes the priming mix, sending a hot tongue of flame through the flashhole and into the powder chamber of the cartridge case. The explosion of the primer mix, by the way, is the only explosion in the whole firing sequence. Modern smokeless gunpowder, as we shall see, does not explode. The explosive force of the priming mix is so powerful that it may cause the primer to back out of the primer pocket somewhat, especially when there is clearance between the case and the bolt face. But we rarely are aware of this, because later events hide the evidence.

BURNING POWDER

When the hot jet of primer flame flashes through the loosely packed main powder charge about 50 to 75 percent of the powder granules are ignited instantly (depending on case size, powder type, and primer intensity) and the rest quickly follows suit.

So-called "smokeless" powder is peculiar stuff. Around the turn of the century thousands of guns were blown to smithereens before reloaders caught on to how it was to be used. If you ignite an unconfined charge of smokeless powder you'll be disappointed at its performance. Unlike old-fashioned black powder, which burns with a quick flash and produces lots of smoke, unconfined smokeless powder burns rather slowly with an orange flame. This is scarcely more sensational than burning a scrap of paper. Black powder burns at a constant rate whether confined or unconfined; smokeless powder burns a lot faster when you confine it. That's why smokeless is called *progressive burning* powder. The burning rate becomes progressively faster as the pressure of expanding gases increases. When confined in a tight cartridge case, the burning rate of smokeless powder becomes astounding and gases are generated in such terrific volume that the pressure inside a modern high-intensity rifle cartridge may jump to 50,000 pounds per square inch before the bullet has traveled more than two inches.

When this happens the brass cartridge case expands so tightly against the chamber walls that the two metals are temporarily held very firmly together. This is good because the expanded case forms a seal that prevents the maelstrom of gases from blowing back around the case and into the mechanism, and perhaps your eyes. While the forward four-fifths of the case is plastered tightly to the firing-chamber walls, the rear portion is expanded rearward so that it fills the few thousandths inch of space between the case and the bolt face. When this happens the primer pocket settles around the recently protruded primer so that they are again flush.

Part of the art of manufacturing ammunition is determining how far a cartridge case will stretch before it becomes thin and weak enough to pull apart. Brass, though expensive, is obviously the preferred material for cartridge cases because of its combination of strength and elasticity. However, there is a definite limit on how much a brass case can stretch and yet retain needed strength. That's why rifles with excessive headspace are dangerous. The unsupported brass may stretch too far and rupture, allowing gas under thousands of pounds of pressure to blow rearward like a rocket exhaust.

The critical time occurs only during the first few inches of bullet travel. Once the bullet's inertia is overcome it accelerates at a tremendous rate even though the gas pressure is dropping off rapidly. The bullet takes less than one thousandth of a second to travel the length of the average barrel. As soon as it exits the muzzle the internal pressure drops to the normal atmospheric level and the brass case, springing inward somewhat, releases its grip on the chamber walls and is easily extracted. The entire sequence ends.

The temperatures inside a centerfire rifle may be as high as 4,000°F, but the time period so short that relatively little heat is transferred to the gun itself. If the firing sequence lasted for a few seconds, rather than a thousandth of a second, the gun would literally melt in your hands.

That's what happens when you pull the trigger. It's all over in no time, but it's something to think about.–*Jim Carmichel.*

What Benchrest Shooting Has Done for Hunters

When I finish writing today, I'm going hunting. The duffle is packed and my rifle, sighted in during the dead calm of late yesterday afternoon, is zeroed to put its 150-grain 7mm bullets on the mark at 200 yards. After a couple of scope adjustments the bullets were hitting where I wanted them to, so as is my habit, I pulled three more rounds from the ammo box to fire a final "proof group." I like to do this to satisfy myself that the zero is stable and to see if the barrel "walks" (changes point of impact) as it heats up.

These three shots, fired from a stout benchrest at 100 yards, went into a tight little overlapping cluster that, through the spotting scope, looked to measure no more than a quarter-inch between the centers. This is not too unusual with a good rifle and ammo, but as often as not, good three-shot groups are a matter of luck. When I get tight groups like that, curiosity forces me to fire at least two more shots. This weeds out some of the luck factor and also gives me a fair idea of how the rifle stacks up against other rifles of a known accuracy level.

The fourth shot skipped a bit to the right, barely touching the main group, and the fifth printed a bit low. If the last two shots had gone into the hole made by the first three, I would have taken the target home and measured the group with calipers. As it was, the five shots probably measured some $^{6}/_{10}$ to $^{3}/_{4}$ of an inch between the centers of the two widest holes—very satisfying, especially from a big game rifle, but hardly a bragging group by today's standards. The target went into the trash.

Let's shift the scene back to 1955 and see what shooters were talking about then. The big news was a new breed of "super rifles" that had riflemen and shooting editors as giddy as a covey of teenyboppers at a rock festival. The rifles were monstrous affairs weighing up to 40 and 50 pounds (some had to be wheeled around on golf carts) and the name of the game was benchrest shooting. The idea was to see how close together all the holes in a 10-shot group could be. It wasn't necessary to hit a bull's-eye to win; all that counted was group size, the smaller the better.

To that end, firing was done from rigid tables with the rifles resting on sandbags or any other support the shooter figured would result in the tightest groups. Rules were simple. The shooter had to pull the trigger. Machine rests weren't allowed, so there was some semblance of aiming and squeezing. Otherwise the only limitation was one's own ingenuity. And to be sure, the early

Here's a typical modern benchrest rifle. It weighs $13^{1}/_{2}$ pounds (heavy varmint class) and features include: fiberglass stock, vibrationless trigger, special benchrest action, stainless steel custom barrel, and scope mounted entirely on the receiver.

benchrest shooters were an ingenious group.

Though the benchrest game got a good bit of publicity during the early '50s, it was mostly of the "gee-whiz" type which described the funny looking rifles without really explaining how they were built and used. The ponderous rifles, and the game itself, came to be regarded as some sort of two-headed calf. Sport hunters and target shooters saw benchrest as a game apart with few if any elements linking it to other rifle sports. If they had only known.

Benchrest shooting was—and is—a game of pessimistic optimism. It's optimistic because the ultimate goal is a perfect one-hole group no larger than the diameter of a single bullet. It's pessimistic because the rifleman deals only with negative factors. In the strictest sense nothing can cause perfect accuracy. Inaccuracy is caused, and the shooter tries to discover the causes and eliminate them one by one.

I illustrated just how far benchrest shooters have traveled along that road of discovery when I sighted my hunting rifle in yesterday and casually fired a group that would have been astonishing just a generation ago. In fact,there are at least a half-dozen makes and models of rifles you can buy off your dealer's shelves that are at least as accurate as those 40-pound benchrest "super rifles" of the 50s.

WEIGHT NOT A FACTOR

One of the most interesting things hunters have learned from the benchresters is that rifles do not have to be heavy in order to be accurate. Not too long ago weight and accuracy were thought to be synonymous. The heavier the rifle, the more accurate it was judged to be. Now we know that this is not at all true. Other than causing it to lie steadier on the rests, a rifle's total mass contributes very little to its accuracy. This was discovered soon after some farsighted leaders in the benchrest game realized that the very heavy, unrestricted rifles were leading them down a developmental blind alley, and created the varmint, sporter and hunter rifle classifications of benchrest competition. The light varmint and sporter bench rifles can weigh no more than 10½ pounds with scope. That's not much heavier than many scoped hunting rifles.

The hunter class bench rifles must have a magazine, carry a scope of not more than 6X and be of 6mm or larger bore size. They must be chambered for a cartridge case with at least as much powder capacity as the .30/30 and weigh no more than 10 pounds. In other words, they must be what their name suggests—rifles you can use for big game hunting. Yet, with just such a rifle, a top bench competitor will hit a dime every shot at 100 yards and will bet better than even money he can nick the period at the end of this sentence.

Until the 1950s many riflemen believed that a finely accurate rifle performed well simply because it had a well-made, accurate barrel. Until that time it was common for long-range target shooters to have two rifles—a "pet" rifle for use in tournaments and a less accurate "practice" rifle. The reason was to save the presumably irreplaceable "pet" barrel, from which all accuracy sprang, for serious competition. By the 1950s, however, custom barrel making techniques were so good that a really fine barrel was not a one-in-a-thousand oddity but an easily available commodity. Barrels by the top makers of that time became so reliable that when a rifle did not group well, it was probably for other reasons. This got shooters to thinking about other factors that affect accuracy: actions, stocks, triggers, sights and ammunition—especially ammunition—and the accuracy revolution was on.

THE ACCURACY REVOLUTION

Until then, if you complained to an ammunition manufacturer, or a maker of bullets for reloading, that his product didn't shoot accurately he would often take refuge in the countercharge that your barrel wasn't any good. With the advent of really good barrels made by, say, Douglas or Hart, a shooter could weed out the makers of bad bullets. And a lot of them were bad. In fact, very few were really accurate. The shortage of truly accurate mass-produced bullets was so acute that benchrest shooters had to make their own ultraprecise bullets in custom swaging dies. These efforts reduced group sizes so much that other variables could be isolated.

The first benchrest rifles were usually built on any available action, mostly military Mausers because they were plentiful and cheap. Sometimes Springfields, Winchesters and other bolt action designs were used. It didn't take long, however, for serious shooters to discover that most of these actions made their own contributions to poor accuracy. The Mausers and Springfields, for example, were found to flex under the stresses of firing and thereby create peculiar barrel vibrations. The fit of the action in the stock was found to severely affect accuracy, and proper "bedding" was subjected to much experimentation. The "free floating" barrel, now universal on target rifles, was just one result.

Another innovation was the currently widespread use of "fiberglass" or resin bedding compounds which rigidly lock the barreled action in the stock. As these and other bedding improvements were put into use by benchrest shooters, manufacturers of hunting rifles, who always watch closer than you think, began to pay more attention to the bedding of their production rifles. New bolt action rifles, in particular, were designed to take advantage of the bedding secrets discovered by bench shooters. The Model 77 Ruger bolt rifle, for example, features large expanses of flat surfaces on the bottom side of the receiver that make for a highly stable metal-to-wood contact, plus a front action screw set at an angle so that the recoil lug is pulled tightly against the lug mortice when the screw is tightened. The Colt-Sauer rifle features a bedding "foot" under the recoil lug which is obviously intended to take advantage of the bedding technology developed on the benchrest range. The actions on some modern hunting rifles are quite obviously copied from custom actions originally built for bench rifles.

When light, ultrastable fiberglass stocks were first used on bench rifles in the later 1960s, they were only curiosities and rather ugly ones at that. But it didn't take long for hunters to find out that the new glass stocks were strong and light and went a long way toward eliminating the "zero shift" caused by the warping of wooden stocks. Fiberglass stocks do not absorb moisture. Now a number of hunting style fiberglass stocks are available for most models of bolt guns. This autumn a new production-made hunting rifle will be introduced which features—you guessed it—a superaccurate fiberglass stock as original equipment.

Drawing on the new standards of accuracy established by bullets handformed in custom-made swaging dies, big-name bullet makers such as Hornady, Sierra, Nosler and Speer began producing ultraprecise "BR" bullets. It took several years for these manufacturers to catch up with the excellence of the handmade products, but what they learned about making ultraprecise bullets on a mass-production basis naturally spilled over into the production of hunting bullets. The bottom line is that *all* bullets, especially hunting bullets, are much more accurate than anything you could have bought two decades ago.

HANDLOADS STILL THE BEST

Handloaded ammo continues to be a cornerstone of benchrest shooting. I've never seen or heard of anyone using factory loads in a bench match, though I'm sure it happens occasionally. This sounds like a fearsome condemnation of factory loaded ammo, but that is not as true as it once was. Actually, certain calibers now loaded by the major ammo makers are so accurate that the ammunition could have been used to win bench tournaments in the 1950s and '60s. Back then, however, the accuracy of factory stuff was quite poor.

With the growing popularity of benchrest shooting in the 1950s and the publicity given to "1-inch" or "half-inch" rifles, hunters finally had a reliable standard against which to judge their own shooting equipment. Hunting rifles and ammunition fared very poorly when that standard was applied. Handloaded ammo, for example, was vastly more accurate than factory loads, especially when the shooter used precision reloading techniques pioneered by benchrest shooters. Stung by these comparisons, the big makers of factory cartridges improved their loading techniques and components to the point where their products are more accurate, and certainly more reliable, than most reloaded ammo. This statement would have been ridiculous 20 years ago.

All this doesn't mean that reloading has stood still. Really well-developed handloads are still the most accurate ammunition you can put in a good rifle, mainly because of improvements in components. Primers and cases, as well as bullets, are considerably more uniform today than they were a few years ago, and they continue to improve. This is because today's benchrest shooter is so demanding that even lot-to-lot variables in primers are recognized and decried. As a result, component manufacturers constantly try to improve their products and thus win favor with bench shooters. Naturally, when a new component, say a primer, offers a recognizable improvement in accuracy, it's not long before it is used in factory loads.

TRIGGERS AND SCOPES

To give you a better idea of the wide-ranging discoveries made by benchrest shooters, consider what has happened to triggers. Back when the benchrest game first got rolling, it was common to fit bench rifles with double-set triggers. This seemed like a good idea because once the rear set trigger was cocked, a slight touch on the front trigger would fire the rifle without disturbing it. The need for careful squeezing was eliminated. But then some astute bench shooters got to wondering why some of the set-trigger-equipped rifles didn't shoot as well as they should. They soon discovered that the "kick" of the spring-activated set trigger unleashed a cycle of vibrations that conflicted with normal barrel vibrations. So double set triggers were abandoned, and the custom trigger makers were given the task of devising new nonvibrating triggers. The upshot of this was a whole new family of trigger designs, more adjustable and more uniform over a broad range of weight-of-pull settings than anything that had been offered before.

Consider scopes. Since shooting for tiny groups calls for high magnification, the early benchrest rifles were equipped with long, target type scopes, partially or wholly mounted on the barrel. This arrangement was acceptable for a few years, but by the late 1960s, the whole system came under critical scrutiny. The long, hefty scopes attached directly to the barrels created stress and vibration problems that hurt accuracy. At first the problem was dealt with by mounting the long scopes on ungainly looking bridges and trusses that were attached only to the receiver. This worked well enough to demonstrate that the shooters were on the right track. Then the scope makers themselves lent a hand by designing and manufacturing high magnification (20X and over) scopes short enough to mount entirely on a rifle's receiver just like traditional hunting scopes. The technology that grew out of the development of these highly refined telescopic sights was naturally carried over into the production of hunting scopes. Many of today's hunting scopes have vastly greater precision than those made only a decade ago!

When I took up target shooting back in the early 50s, my single burning desire was to own one of the great European "free" rifles used in 300-meter international competition. At that time they ruled the ranges, and nothing else was considered equal to the test. Fortunately I never raised enough money to buy one of those things because they are now obsolete. They were outmoded by rifle building techniques first tried and developed on bench rifles. When an American Olympic shooter goes to the firing line he carries a rifle that is little more than a benchrest barrel and action bedded (by benchrest methods) in a target stock. He shoots benchrest-developed components loaded to standards refined in benchrest competition.

When the varmint shooter or big game hunter levels his sights on a distant target, the odds are better now that the bullet will go where he aims—thanks to benchrest shooting.–*Jim Carmichel.*

Scopes and Mounts

I don't mean to sound unkind, but someone has got to talk tough about scopes and it may as well be me. Frankly, I'm more than a little worried about the direction—or lack of direction—of today's scope buying habits.

Just a generation ago articles on telescopic sights for rifles usually amounted to a hard sell. To be sure, in that era of leaky lenses, questionable reliability and uncertain mounts, scopes *needed* selling. Depending on who you talked to, scopes tended to be a rather touchy subject, either sworn by or sworn against. I can recall very few neutral opinions.

Many of the early criticisms were justified. Scopes did fog, their adjustments did tend to come apart and they did occasionally drop off after a few shots. But these problems have long since been solved and are so far behind us that any criticism in this context is as out of date as four-bit haircuts and Sunday drives. Today's rifle scopes, with few exceptions, are marvelous pieces of equipment. They are tough, reliable, backed by solid guarantees and about the best dollar value in the shooting world. They have become so much a fact of shooting life that many, perhaps most, hunters do not even consider an unscoped rifle as usable hunting equipment. This *could* be a very good thing. But is it? Could it be that our passionate affair with the telescopic sight is causing some—too many—shooters to abandon common sense and even loose touch with the purposes and advantages of scopes? Consider:

MISTAKEN CHOICES

Recently I got a letter from a young reader who wanted to tell me how he had run a trap line all winter so he could buy his "dream" hunting outfit. He had bought a handy autoloader in a sensible caliber which, for snap-shooting whitetails in his northeastern state, I'd call a practical rig. Then he went on to tell me that he had topped it off with a lovely 6-to-18X scope! His reasoning, as he explained it, was that since this was the most expensive scope on his dealer's shelf, it had to be the best. But for what? Whitetail? If this were a single instance I'd pay it no mind. But it is not isolated; there's a pattern.

Another reader, experienced he says, and presumably wiser, wants to know if a 3-to-9X or 4-to-12X will be best for his .444 Marlin lever gun, and what kind of see-through mounts I recommend. And a chap with a pretty little Sako .222 writes me that he's going to equip it with a 2½-to-7X scope for potting woodchucks. Would, he asks, one of the scopes with a television-screen eyepiece be any advantage?

All three people bought or wanted to buy the wrong scope! Now, I'm not going to say that these hunters, and hundreds of others with similar ideas, are not going to enjoy their grossly miscoped rifles. After all, it's hard not to enjoy shooting a rifle, no matter how it is sighted. But I am saying that their rifles would be more efficient, more effective, easier to shoot and easier to carry if they had the right scopes.

Let's be honest, guns are status symbols. Why else do we proudly show off our best ones in racks and cabinets? Scopes too have become status symbols, and at their symbolic best when they are big and expensive-looking and festooned with the latest gimmickry.

This is by no means a slam at scope makers. My personal knowledge of them as businessmen, engineers and shooters convinces me that they would much prefer that their customers buy the

Though all the equipment in these pictures is of good quality, it is mismatched, causing big trouble for the shooters. The rifleman above has a scope that is mounted very high on a rifle with a low comb that was designed for use with iron sights. Result is that his face is too high on the comb when his eye is aligned with the scope. It's very unsteady.

From the other side, we see that his mouth is open. This results from an unconscious effort to keep as much of the head in contact with stock as possible. With this rifle/scope combination, the only way is to open the mouth, but it really doesn't help.

Here the same shooter ignores the scope and snuggles up to the stock as he should. With the high tunneled or see-through scope mounts, his eye is well below line of sight. He actually can't see through the scope at all! High, tunneled mounts require high comb.

model that is best suited to their needs and therefore gives best satisfaction in the field. After all, a satisfied customer is a good customer. But the scope business is highly competitive, and one of the ways scope makers compete is by offering an ever-wider array of models, styles, variations and combinations. Have you looked at a major scope maker's catalog lately? The offerings can be absolutely bewildering. In one catalog I count no less than 71 different models or model variations.

With such an assortment to choose from, the buyer can easily be led astray, especially if he has been conditioned to believe, as most American consumers have been, that the most elaborate and expensive model is the best.

THE RIGHT SCOPE

So how does a hunter select the *right* scope for his dream rig? First of all, a scope should not be considered as a fancy telescope that sits on top of the rifle. Once it is mounted it becomes *part of the rifle,* a vital component which contributes to the performance of the rifle just as do the stock, barrel and action. If in any way the scope prevents the rifle from performing at the full potential and efficiency of which it and the shooter are capable, then it is obviously not the right scope. This is why it's so important to plan your rifle and scope outfit as a single working unit and not as two separate mechanisms screwed together. It is equally important when planning the perfect outfit to consider which scopes work best with what rifles. The importance of matching the two is far more important than is generally realized. Here's an example of how a shooter can go wrong.

Let's say our old friend Marvin Miscue has saved up the cash to buy a lever-action rifle and scope for hunting whitetails in Pennsylvania. He looks around and decides he wants a Savage Model 99 in .308 caliber. So far, so good. This is a great deer round, and the 99 is one of the all-time great woods rifles. The Savage 99 comes in three or four variations, and after looking them over Marvin decides he likes the 99-A because of its trim lines and traditional styling. It's a great rifle, but remember, Marvin wants to use a scope. So right here he's made a wrong choice. The traditional styling he likes so well dates back to 1899, when scopes on hunting rifles were virtually nonexistent. The stock dimensions are for iron sight shooting and ill suited for scope use.

Knowing that he was going to equip the rifle with a scope, he should have chosen the Savage Model 99 CD, which has a higher comb designed especially for scope use. The high comb supports the cheek in a higher position so the shooter's eye is naturally aligned with the scope. This can save long moments when you're trying to get the cross hairs on a highballing buck.

Marvin is savvy on scopes and buys a good 4X glass that should serve him well for his kind of hunting, but then he goes wrong again. His buddies tell him he ought to get a set of see-through mounts which give him an instant choice between using the scope or looking through the holes in the mounts to use the rifle's open sights. This sounds like a smart idea to Marvin, and that's what he buys. So now he's got a great rifle, a good scope and a useful set of mounts, but when he puts them all together they're not worth a thing. The scope, propped up on the high see-through mounts, is so high above his natural eye alignment that he can't see through it without craning his neck and lifting his face off the stock. When this happens he loses about 50 percent of his rifle control. In short, it won't work. His dream outfit is a shooter's nightmare. The pity here is that poor Marvin thought he was getting the perfect rig, the best of everything. The problem is that the best of everything often doesn't go together.

Now let's go back to our young reader who mounted a 6-to-18X variable power scope on his deer rifle. It's a beautiful scope and costs a lot of hard-earned dough. It's probably the most elegant piece of sighting equipment he's ever looked through, and he has every reason to be proud to own it. But in the region where he hunts whitetails, the average shot is fired at about 50 yards or less. So he needs a variable scope like he needs a rock in his boot. If he needs a scope at all, he needs low magnification, 4X at most, and a wide field of view. Since he will be shooting fast, the weight of his outfit is a vital factor. His big variable weighs a full half-pound more than most 4X scopes. But worst of all, he simply can't get a fast sight picture with his fancy scope. Even at the lowest power setting the field of view is too restricted and the eye relief too critical. Tax and all, the scope cost him about three bills, nearly $200 more than a top quality 4X scope. It's an expensive mistake, but think how much more it could cost if he booked an expensive guided hunt and flubbed the shot of a lifetime because he had the wrong scope for the job.

Of course he might argue that he wants a variable power scope because he intends to clobber a few woodchucks in the orchard this summer and will need some additional magnification. That's fine, but again, match the scope to the rifle and to the purpose. With his autoloader he's not going to pull off very many long-range shots at groundhogs. Hitting one at 200 yards with that kind of rifle would be a good effort. For his sort of dual purpose shooting one of the little 2½-to-7X scopes would be just the ticket.

This takes us to the groundhog hunter who wants to use a 2½-to-7X on his .222. A straight 7X scope would be OK, though for most varmint shooting he could use more magnification. For woodchucks, though, the lower end of the 2½-to-7X scale is all but useless. Perhaps our friend has succumbed to the spreading belief that variable power scopes are somehow inherently superior, even when only one power setting is ever used. Such notions are off target.

I used to do quite a bit of complaining about variable power scopes but during the last few years the chief cause of my vexation, zero shift with magnification change (as much as three or four inches), has been pretty well eliminated. Now I often use variables on my hunting rifles. One must still keep in mind that there are certain prices to be paid for the variable power feature. In addition to the initial higher cost of the scope, you'll have to carry more bulk and weight. The optical clari-

This shooter suffers from a scope that is mounted too far back, which causes him to hold head in a very awkward position, strained to the rear. No one can shoot well or fast this way. Nevertheless, the scope is mounted as far forward as is possible with these rings. This is an obvious case of mismatching rifle, scope and mounts.

ty will be slightly inferior to that of a fixed power scope of similar quality. This occurs simply because you're looking through more glass. The field of view at any power setting will be less than that of a fixed power scope of the same power—as much as a third less. Even so, when matched to the right rifle the variables offer some wonderful advantages. They are best in a situation where a hunter wants to use his outfit both for big game and some really serious varmint shooting. In this case it is as important to match the rifle to the scope as the other way around. You can't, say, mount a 3-to-9X variable on your .300 Magnum and say, "Look at me, I've got a varmint rifle too." The really good dual-purpose combination outfits are in the .243, 6mm Remington, .25/06 bolt-action class. These rifles offer the range, accuracy and *shootability* that make the high magnification end of the variable scope worthwhile. In fact, I wonder if some shooters wouldn't do well to carefully consider the hunting they will be doing, select the scope which best suits this need, and then buy the rifle that best suits the scope. Interesting viewpoint to ponder, isn't it?

THE MOUNTS

And what are we to do about the scope mounting situation? Select five scoped rifles at random, and I'll bet two of them will have either the wrong mounts or the scope incorrectly positioned. There are all sorts of great mounting systems available, but all too often the buyer doesn't get what he really needs. This can happen in a number of ways. One of the most common problems is caused by rings that position the scope too high above the bore. Ideally, the hunting scope should be mounted as low on the rifle as possible without the front lens bell actually touching the barrel or otherwise interfering with the gun's operation. A low mounted scope is easier to see through, gets the line of sight closer to the path of the bullet, and is less likely to be snagged on limbs and brush. To this end most scope mount makers offer rings in varying heights so you can select the height that gives ample clearance but still positions the scope as low as is practical. Even so, too many outfits are fitted with rings that are too high to be practical. I suspect this is largely the fault of dealers, especially less-than-knowledgeable discount store clerks, who figure the "safe" thing is to sell you the highest rings in the store.

It's not all that much bother to attach the bases to your rifle in the store and try different ring sets. Always start with the lowest and keep trying until you find the one that gives you the lowest workable scope position. If the dealer doesn't want to do this, go to someone who will. I promise you that it is an important factor in how you aim and handle your rifle. Don't settle for the easy way out if that means mounting your scope too high.

Another common problem is mounting the scope too far to the rear. It's an easy mistake to make because many shooters do not hold a rifle the same way when they are just looking through the scope as when they are actually firing. When we position the scope so that the eye relief seems right, we tend to stand upright with our heads well back on the stock. Thus the scope tends to be clamped in the rings farther back than it ought to be for a natural shooting position. When we shoot a rifle we tend to angle the body away from the direction of fire, pull the stock tighter into the shoulder and lean the head forward. This is when a scope mounted too far back gets awkward and even dangerous. Shooters who get whacked on the nose or eyebrow when the rifle recoils nearly always have the scope mounted too far back. It also causes awkward aiming and handling, and the semiconscious fear of being hit by the scope causes flinching.

When I mount a scope on a rifle I position it as far forward as possible while still getting a full field of view in the eyepiece. Sometimes this feels extreme, but when I'm actually shooting it always works out just right. Some variable power scopes have large power setting rings which, when standard mounts are used, prevent the scope from being positioned as far forward as it should be. To solve this problem most mount makes offer special bases which set the rear, or both, rings forward and thus permit proper positioning. I expect many dealers don't stock these special bases because it complicates inventory, but don't settle for anything less than perfection.–***Jim Carmichel.***

Buying a Used Rifle

So you're thinking about buying a used gun? You won't get any argument from me. I think it's such a good idea that about two out of every three guns I own were bought off a dealer's used-gun rack or from a private owner.

I buy guns second hand because that is sometimes the only way I can get specimens of certain discontinued models or calibers. I often buy them because the bargain is too good to pass up and, like many gun collectors, I like the treasure-hunting excitement of prowling through a rack of "experienced" guns, hoping to discover a jewel. Used-gun racks are filled with firearms that didn't work out for their previous owners but, who knows, one of them may be a match made in heaven for the next guy who snaps the gun to his shoulder and snuggles cheek to cheekpiece.

Unlike buying a used car, you aren't taking much of a blind risk when you buy a used gun. Potential trouble spots can be spotted easily, and any necessary repairs can often be tended to in the home workshop. Best of all, if you buy a used gun at a fair price, and take reasonably good care of it, that gun will never be worth less than you paid. Almost all guns increase in value so that you can get, say, five or 10 years steady use then sell or trade at a profit.

Certain "collector" guns such as Parkers, old Colts, and Winchesters command a price that is much greater than their utilitarian function would dictate. Guns of this type bring whatever the market will bear, and you'd better know what you're doing before you hock the farm. So let's discuss only the rifles we might buy *to use.* I will discuss used handguns and shotguns in a future column.

BE SUSPICIOUS

My first rule for buying a used gun, especially if I do not know the previous owner, is to be suspicious. In fact, if the gun looks new, or nearly so, I'm even more suspicious. Why did anyone want to dispose of a new gun? Was it unreliable? Inaccurate? Poor fit? That's why I always ask the dealer why a nearly new gun was traded in or sold. If I'm dealing with the original owner, I always ask why he doesn't like the gun. Usually the answer is simple and straightforward: the gun was a gift but the owner prefers golf; it was bought for a special hunt never to be repeated; need to raise cash for kid's braces. Some shooters, especially trap and skeet buffs, are chronic gun traders and are continually buying and trading in their search for the perfect gun. These are safe bets too. But if the reason for selling is a bit mysterious, I'm inclined to be cautious. I get even more cautious when a shadowy figure offers me a gun at a price that is too good to be real.

WHAT TO LOOK FOR

A certain amount of visible wear is unavoidable if a gun is used. Do not confuse wear with abuse. What I call honest wear is a certain amount of blue rubbed away on a gun's sharp edges and corners, bolt handle, trigger guard, and at the muzzle. The stock will have a few dents and scratches and the finish may be chipped, cracked, or worn away in some spots. The stock may also have dark spots where sweat and oil have seeped into the wood. Action parts will show bright spots where moving parts have rubbed together.

Abuse is something else. It is apparent in splotches of rust, bent and dented metal parts, mangled screw heads, and unnecessarily deteriorated wood and metal surfaces. If a gun looks really bad on the outside you can almost always figure that it is pretty bad on the inside as well and was probably traded in simply because it stopped working. Abused guns are seldom a bargain at any price.

I will always choose a gun with visible signs of use and wear over one that has been reblued. Very few reblueing and stock refinishing shops are capable of restoring a gun so that it is indistinguishable from the original factory product. So take a close look at older models that somehow look too new to be true.

Refinishing and reblueing a gun is a fairly expensive and time-consuming operation and is not usually worthwhile unless the gun was a real dog to start with. If the reblued gun shows signs of heavy preblue polishing such as "saucered" screw holes, splayed lettering, and rounded edges it's a safe bet that it had been pretty rough. Sometimes even heavy buffing will not erase all the scars and you can still see rust pits, dents, and dings. Steer clear.

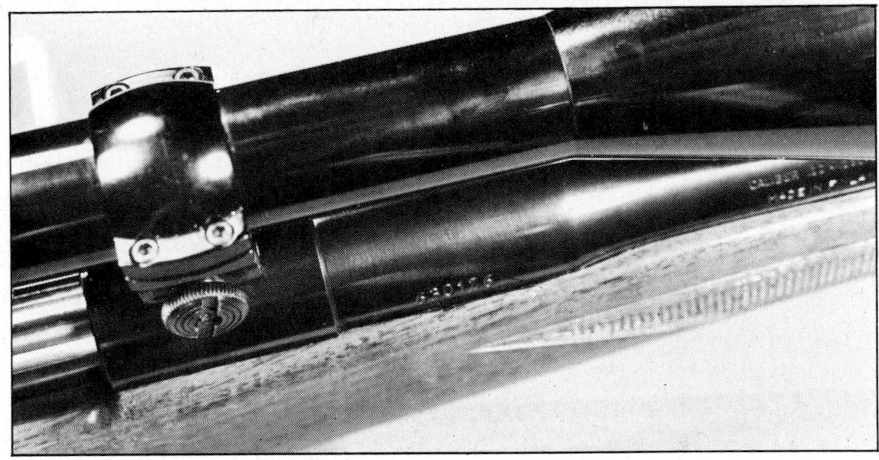

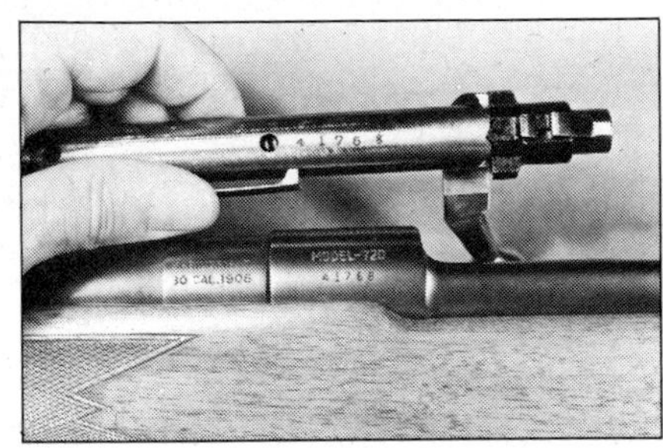

If the edge of the inletting is chipped or broken, top, it may be the result of a previous owner's attempt to free-float the barrel, which is often done to cure poor accuracy. Could be that he didn't solve the problem. Be sure to check for matching serial numbers on bolt and receiver of bolt-action rifles, right. If the numbers do not match, the bolt was not made to fit the rifle and there may be dangerous headspace trouble.

RULES FOR BUYING RIFLES

Except for target and varmint rifles, which we'll talk about later, there is almost no chance that any hunting rifle will be worn out by use alone. Modern rifles chambered high intensity cartridges such as the .270, .280, and 7 mm. Remington Magnum are good for at least 4,000 rounds before any accuracy loss can be detected, and the useful life of the rifle is much longer. Medium pressure rounds such as the .30/30 and .35 Remington create even less barrel wear, so you can figure a life of upwards of 10,000 rounds. That means a deer rifle made today should still be going strong in the year 2200! Rimfire barrels last even longer. Target shooters note that rimfire accuracy begins to decay after some 20,000 to 30,000 rounds. This translates to firing a box of .22s (50 rounds) every week for 10 years.

Clearly then, how many times a hunting rifle has been fired is of little concern. What we really want to know is has the barrel and the rest of the rifle been *cared* for. Even though today's smokeless powders and priming mixtures are noncorrosive, that doesn't mean a barrel won't rust if it isn't cleaned after use. If there is any question about a barrel's condition give it a good cleaning and study it carefully. Be particularly alert for dark-looking areas that may be patches of shallow pitting caused by rust. Also look closely at the condition of the rifling at the muzzle. Any uneven wearing or disfiguring of the lands here is a sign of overzealous use of a rough cleaning rod, and its effect on accuracy is often disastrous. (This is why barrels should be cleaned from the breech end whenever possible.)

Swollen spots in the barrel caused by firing with the bore obstructed (with mud, snow, or a cleaning patch) are also ruinous to accuracy but can be easily detected by feel. Just run a thumb and finger over the length of the barrel. Even the slightest "goose egg" will be obvious.

By all means, compare serial numbers. Nonmatching numbers on the receiver and bolt could mean that the bolt was taken from another rifle and that a dangerous headspace condition exists. This situation is seldom encountered with commercial sporting guns, but is not uncommon with surplus military bolt rifles. If the numbers don't match have the headspace checked before firing. Most gunsmiths have the necessary gauges.

Snap the trigger a few times. Be wary if the weight of pull seems excessively light, especially if the trigger mechanism is of the nonadjustable variety found on pumps, autoloaders, and lever-action models. A trigger mechanism of this type usually has a five pound or heavier pull. If the pull feels lighter it may mean the mechanism's sear engagement has been altered and could be unsafe.

Whenever possible, check the condition of the firing pin. Those on centerfire rifles should be smooth and evenly rounded. Rimfire pins should be square and reasonably sharp at the edges with no signs of battering. Firing pins that have obviously been repaired by welding or brazing should be regarded with deep suspicion.

If the rifle is clip-fed pay particular attention to the "lips" or upper edges of the clip. Signs of bending or alteration are a signal that feeding problems may exist. Also look for signs of tinkering in the clip mechanism. Deformed followers and springs are bad news because they too indicate that feeding wasn't smooth.

Extractors with rounded or battered edges are a forewarning of ejector problems, but small problems of this type are easily corrected. If the rifle is a takedown model be sure that the barrel threads are not badly worn and that the barrel locks rigidly in the receiver. Any slop will cause accuracy problems. Also, if the rifle has a two-piece stock, be wary of any looseness in the butt section. This is usually correctable by simply tightening a through-bolt. If, however, the rifle was fired very much with the bolt loose, the threads in the receiver could be stripped. In extreme cases this can lead to a ruined receiver.

A cracked stock is nearly always a problem, and no repairs should be considered permanent. Check for hidden cracks by twisting the stock somewhat, paying particular note to the grip area.

If an excessive number of scope mount holes have been drilled in the receiver and/or barrel, you can safely guess that an amateur tinkerer has had his hands on the rifle and may have performed other mischief.

Don't be particularly impressed if the rifle has a fancy scope sight; make your judgment on the overall condition of the gun only. And don't be gulled into paying a bonus for a scope. Used hunting scopes, even very good ones, have relatively low resale value. So don't add much more than 25 percent of the scope's retail price to the price of the rifle alone. As often as not it will not be the right scope for the rifle anyway. Some dealers try to sell used rifles by "packaging" them with scopes. Ask what the price of the rifle is *without* the scope.

VARMINT RIFLES

Varmint rifles tell a story all their own. Since tack-driving varmint rifles are things of beauty and lasting joy, their owners are usually not inclined to trade them in until the barrel is beyond the pale. A varmint rifle may have more shots run through it in one weekend than the average deer rifle in a lifetime. This high use factor, combined with the errosive character of high-velocity varmint cartridges, means that the barrel may very well be shot out. Lower velocity varmint rifles such as those in .22 Hornet or .222 Remington are less likely to be burned out than rifles in faster calibers such as .22/250 and .220 Swift. Some varmint rifles can look nearly new externally and still have a badly worn barrel. One external clue though is a bolt knob with the blue worn off—evidence of much use.

Give the barrel a good cleaning, then inspect the bore carefully from both ends. Pay particular attention to the area just ahead of the chamber. Flattening of the lands or an overall frosty appearance are signs of wear. If black streaks can be seen you can figure accuracy is gone.

This does not necessarily mean that you should avoid the rifle. Some of the best bargains available are shot-out varmint rifles. Barrels are easily replaced, either by the factory or custom gunsmiths. By fitting a custom barrel to a good action you might well have a rifle that is more accurate the second time around.

I'm suspicious of a varmint rifle that looks nearly new inside and out. Why did the original owner dispose of it? The first guess is that it wasn't accurate enough. So ask questions and ask for a three-day trial. Also be suspicious of any rifle, especially varmint models, that have been glass-bedded. Why was bedding necessary? One has to assume the glassing was done because of accuracy problems, so beware. A glassing job improves accuracy no more than half the time, and in any event such modifications reduce the gun's resale value.

If you are buying a used gun for actual use and not necessarily as an investment, it doesn't make all that much difference if it has been altered somewhat so long as it is still safe and completely usable. But when you consider a used gun put yourself in the place of the guy who may eventually be buying it from you. What are the minus points? A barrel that has been shortened two inches, for example, may be of no consequence to you but it might be of considerable importance when you try to sell it. Such minor points translate into dollars, sometimes lots of dollars.–***Jim Carmichel.***

PART 3 GOING FOR WHITETAILS

Get Your Buck On Opening Day

If you want to kill a whitetail buck this year, be sure you hunt on the first day of the season. If you don't you may be passing up your best chance to bring in the venison.

Most big-game hunters know that opening day offers rich potential for killing a buck, but many would be surprised to find out just how fruitful this first day is—and how bleak prospects are for scoring during the rest of the season in comparison.

Figures compiled by state fish and wildlife agencies show that the first-day kill of bucks often adds up to from 33 percent to 80 percent of the harvest for the entire season. In Pennsylvania, for example, one of the nation's premier whitetail states, two-thirds of all bucks taken during the 12-day season are dropped on the opener. That means twice as many deer are killed in Pennsylvania on the first day of hunting as during the entire remaining 11 days of the season.

While opening day is not as important in states that have longer seasons, it is for the vast majority of hunters the high-odds time to take a deer.

I always had considered opening day to be important, but its full significance really began to strike home on the first day of West Virginia's deer season several years ago. Dawn came slowly to the wooded hollow where I sat perched on a rough-hewn lumber tree stand. Almost immediately after dawn, I saw a doe and two fawns come ambling down from a nearby field. They paused near my stand, and the doe looked back.

That was the giveaway. Far in the distance a buck appeared, then disappeared quickly. When he showed himself again he was sneaking through thick brush on an adjacent knoll. I raised my rifle and shot when he paused in a patch of open woods. The hunt was finished, the first day barely an hour old.

The woods echoed with the sounds of rifle fire that day. In the county I hunted, nearly 1,000 hunters took home venison. Many also took back handsome racks. Not only does opening day offer the greatest number of deer, but it also yields some of the heaviest-beamed antlers that will come out of the woods and fields all year.

My buck wouldn't make any record books, but at 138 pounds

One way to tag a buck on opening day is to wait on stand near a trail likely to be used by fleeing deer.

dressed out, the six-pointer was large for that area and yielded many delicious meals. That buck also did something else. He started a tradition with me of devoting the bulk of my preparation and most intense hunting efforts toward opening day.

I've learned that by hunting hard and exploiting the unique conditions found on opening day, you can greatly improve your chances of killing a buck. By developing a strategy that takes advantage of the potential of this important first day, I've managed to take a buck on every opener I've hunted since that six-point West Virginia deer fell, except when I chose to pass up a small buck in hopes of getting a larger deer later.

The year after taking that six-pointer, I hunted in Virginia and killed a three-pointer that was ambling down Massanutten Mountain. Next I went to West Virginia, and a tall-racked buck tried to ghost past my stand while light was still so dim on opening day that I was afraid I'd have to pass up the shot. But with the aid of a 2.5X scope, I was able to put a 200-grain bullet behind his shoulder. The deer trotted 40 feet before dropping dead. The following year a seven-pointer fell to my .35-caliber Marlin on the first day.

Last season I hunted Virginia on opening day. Well before light I perched on a comfortable oak branch on a Blue Ridge mountaintop. After passing up a small spike at first light and watching several does slink through the winter woods, I settled the crosshairs of my scoped Remington .30/06 on a thick-beamed, three-point buck. The 150-grain Federal bullet dropped the deer instantly.

A week later West Virginia opened its season. Shortly after dawn a forkhorn tempted me, pussyfooting about within 30 yards of my stand for 10 minutes. I held off, waiting for a larger buck, but for the sixth time in a row the effectiveness of my opening day strategy had proved itself. The techniques allowed me to get within easy range of a standing buck.

On several of the seasons described above, I hunted for a second deer *after* the opener and failed to get a single shot at another buck. Some years I didn't even see another buck.

Nor was I alone. Those hunters using the later phases of the season face much more dismal prospects for killing a whitetail, particularly in the most heavily hunted states.

But if you have a proved opening-day strategy, you won't have to worry about seeing your odds drop drastically. You'll have your buck in the freezer by the time those low-output days roll around.

Opening day is a rewarding time for several reasons. For starters, except for minimal bowhunting pressure, deer have not been hunted. They've become a bit placid since they last had to contend with hunters, and they've let down their guards a trifle. Not much, mind you. But deer generally become just careless enough to give you a slight advantage when you pursue them on the first day of the season.

On the opener bucks often move in open, easily reached places such as fields and hardwood stands. After the barrage of first-day shots alerts them, most bucks hole up in thick cover where it's all but impossible to find and get clean shots at them. Big bucks travel and feed almost entirely at night after the season opens, bedding for the bulk of the day in overgrown tangles and conifer thickets where hunting quietly is difficult.

Another reason that hunting on opening day is so productive is that many other hunters keep deer moving. For the savvy hunter, that can be an advantage rather than a disadvantage. Few of those other hunters have the patience or willpower to sit still on their stands for more than a few hours. When the itchy hunters move around, they also move deer. Many smiles on opening-day hunters are results of the large number of other hunters milling through the woods, acting unintentionally as part of a huge, unorganized, but very effective drive.

Still, success demands more than simply wandering into the woods and hunkering down on the first stump you see. If things were that simple, more hunters would take deer. In most whitetail states, less than 10 percent of hunters score on the opener.

Among those who take a buck, many are plain lucky. But many opening-day-success stories are those of repeat performers. Some hunters score on the first day for eight or 10 seasons in a row.

What do they do that's different from what the typical hunter does? Quite a few things, in most cases. The important differences, though, boil down to two factors: effort and strategy. A strong hunting effort is born of determination, willpower, and desire. These are vital for repeated success in the deer woods. But without a strategy, effort will net you only sore muscles and frustration.

Those who succeed on half or more of the openers they hunt have developed a strategy based on the unique circumstances that exist when the season opens. I have two effective approaches. One is to hunt on private land or remote public areas. I can learn the deer's movement patterns before the season and intercept them on opening day without fearing that another hunter will scare them out of their routine.

I like this kind of hunting because it involves pitting my skills as a woodsman and hunter in a one-on-one challenge with a buck. If you hunt this way, you'll take deer that haven't sensed they're being hunted.

The second approach, which most hunters will find most useful, applies to hunting on crowded grounds. This strategy doesn't involve getting away from the hordes that flock to national forests and wildlife-management areas on the opener, but rather depends on using them to your advantage.

I'll describe this technique in detail later, but let's take a look at the first method. Countless deer that live out their lives more than a mile from the nearest road are never subjected to serious hunting pressure. The sad fact is that few

hunters ever venture farther than a quarter-mile from their car. If you're willing to hike in just a mile or two, you can find hunting areas where it's possible to waylay a buck while he's going about his daily routines in a natural way, unpushed by other hunters. You can hunt this way on private and public lands.

To find remote areas, study recent topographic maps. Pinpoint tracts of land that do not have roads within a mile, preferably two or three miles. Get back this far and you're not likely to see another hunter.

It's important, though, to find spots that are not only remote but also choice deer habitat that provides ample food and cover. Look for old homesites, logging trails, clear-cuts, fields, oak ridges edging conifer stands, and new-growth timber.

Scout the area well, as close to opening day as you can. This will give you current information which you need because deer movements alter as foods change and the rut comes on. Tracks, trails, bedding sites, droppings, and scrapes and rubs will help you determine a pattern the deer seem to be using.

Opening-day hunting is productive partly because many hunters keep deer moving.

For example, deer often feed in fields before and right at daybreak, and then they munch their way through open hardwoods before bedding in thick cover at 8 or 9 a.m. If deer follow this pattern, a logical stand site is in the open hardwoods, preferably where several trails meet and lead into thick cover. You have open shooting in such an area, and you will not likely disturb the deer when you get into your stand before daybreak because they will still be feeding in the fields.

During the rut, hunting over an active scrape or series of them is a good approach. Most bucks visit these sites at least once a day during light hours.

For those who hunt in crowded areas, opening-day prospects can still be bright. But decidedly different tactics are called for than those used by hunters in remote areas. If you hunt where lots of other gunners roam the woods, you want to use them to push a deer to you.

To do this, you should understand how sensitive whitetails are to the presence of humans in the woods. A buck knows his home range the way you know your living room. He hears the commotion early, as the first eager beavers arrive. Car doors click shut, not-so-soft conversation fills the night air, and soon the hunters make their moves, tripping over branches and crunching twigs beneath their boots. The buck scents a heavy mixture of cologne, alcohol, gun oil, and perspiration. If he sticks around, he also sees his pursuers as soon as daylight arrives. Some are late and come wandering in after first light. Others are not dressed warmly enough to stay still on their stands. By 9 or 10 a.m. these hunters start milling around to keep warm.

The deer's three major defense mechanisms—hearing, smell, and sight—have thus been triggered virtually as soon as legal shooting time arrives. A few bucks, mostly young, naive ones, are taken by hunters within a few hundred yards of roads. But most bucks flee these areas of human activity, seeking places where they can hide.

They don't always travel far—just far enough to get away from the commotion and find a thick or difficult-to-reach area where they can feel safe. Dense pine thickets, overgrown swamps, brushy cutover areas, and hard-to-climb craggy ridges all can be used, depending on local terrain.

By studying the layout of public-hunting areas on maps and hiking through them before the season, you can pretty well determine where the deer will go once hunting season starts. *Be there waiting!*

Parking areas indicate where other hunters will be as first light arrives. You can then pinpoint trails that escaping deer will likely use and the heavy cover in which the animals will hide. In some areas it's common to see dozens of whitetails moving toward such hiding spots. By planning ahead, you can dramatically increase your odds of getting a buck over those who enter the woods randomly, relying on luck to send a deer past them.

To get to the best places, sometimes you must walk into the woods hours before daylight. But when you fill your tag, the effort seems worthwhile. Be at your ambush site well before dawn because many bucks, particularly big ones, head for cover early. If you don't see a buck at first light, be patient. More deer will be disturbed and they'll move during midmorning on the opener when hunters start getting cold or bored on their stands and begin moving.

Since a rigorous hike is often required to get into these prime ambush sites near thick hiding cover, it's best to dress lightly at the start and carry extra clothes in a pack

SOME FIGURES TO PONDER

I asked game biologists in nine states what percentages of their buck harvest came on opening day or in the early part of the season. These are their responses on recent seasons:

West Virginia. Whitetail deer specialist Thomas Allen put the first-day tally for bucks at 15,730. That was 40 percent of the total buck kill for the 12-day season. The first three days accounted for 69 percent of the bucks.

Michigan. Joel Vogt, a biologist with the Department of Natural Resources, said Michigan hunters account for 33 percent of the total deer harvest on the opener. Translated to the proportion of *bucks* taken for the season, the opening-day figure rockets to roughly 43 percent of the 96,700 antlered deer taken during the season.

Ohio. Division of Wildlife Biologist Dave Urban said 38 percent of the bucks taken in a season are killed on the first day.

Georgia. Gib Johnston, chief of information for the state's wildlife agency, told me 33 percent of the deer taken during a recent season were killed on opening day. About 71 percent were killed during the first week of a seven to 10-week-long hunting period.

New York. The opening-day tally of bucks varies according to region, said Nat Dickenson, big game unit leader. In the Catskills, 51 percent of the harvest takes place during the first two days of the season. In the heavily hunted central and western parts of the state the figure is 58 percent. In the remote Adirondacks only 9 percent of the harvest occurs during the first two days of the hunting season.

New Jersey. George Howard, chief of the Bureau of Wildlife Management, estimated the first-day take at 30 to 40 percent in south Jersey, where thick scrub oak and pine predominate, and at 60 to 80 percent in the north where dairy farms are common. Statewide, Howard said 50 to 60 percent of the season's whitetail bucks are downed on the opener.

Pennsylvania. Pennsylvania's opening-day buck harvest is usually about 65 percent of the season kill, according to Dale Sheffer, chief of the Division of Game Management.

Alabama. Deer season lasts several months in Alabama, and the limit is one buck a day. The opening-day harvest there is less significant than it is in many other states. Keith Guyse, a biologist with the Department of Conservation and Natural Resources, told me the first-day kill is only 6 or 7 percent of the total 150,000 deer harvest.

Texas. Biologist Fielding Harwell said the deer kill varies from region to region. On the Edwards Plateau, which has one of the highest densities of deer in the United States, 50 percent of the bucks are taken in the first two weeks of a six-week season. In the eastern third of the state, 71 percent of the harvest takes place in the first two weeks. In contrast, hunting in the famous south Texas Brush Country, which yields many trophy bucks, is best during the last two weeks of the season, when 50 percent of the harvest occurs.

on your back. This way you avoid getting overheated and sweating heavily on the trek in, which can create deer-spooking perspiration odors and also leave you shivering in short order once you have to sit still.

I learned this lesson the hard way the first time I hiked up a 2,000-foot peak in the Blue Ridge Mountains of Virginia. The temperature hovered at freezing and a howling wind whipped across the mountainside as I left the pickup in the black of night. The chill factor was down close to zero, so I bundled up to ward off the cold.

A third of the way up I was already warm, and by the time I reached the peak sweat was pouring off me. I loosened my collar and unzipped my coat, but before I could dry out the wind and cold began cutting through me. Wet and chilled, I was forced to give up my stand by midmorning without a buck.

The next time I hiked up that mountain I started earlier so that I could take the hike slowly and avoid breaking into a sweat. Equally important, I wore only a light layer of clothing though the mercury read 25°. I carried the warm clothes I'd need on stand in a backpack.

When I reached the crest of the mountain, I cooled down easily from the climb, broke out the extra clothes, and settled in for a warm, dry watch for deer. Less than two hours later I had my buck.

Though some hunters like driving or still-hunting on opening day, these methods are usually far less productive than hunting from stands. In crowded areas stillhunting, which involves easing slowly through the woods at the same halting pace as a buck, can be dangerous. And if you're moving, you'll seldom be able to see a buck before it sees you since the deer are so fidgety and wary from the sudden influx of humans.

Organized drives usually aren't as effective as stand hunting on the first day either. It's hard to tell where other hunters are and how they might interfere with your plans.

By scouting before the season and finding either remote areas where you can hunt undisturbed by the crowds, or by pinpointing the deer's escape havens and allowing other hunters to unwittingly drive the deer to you, chances for scoring on a first-day buck are excellent.

I've outlined the tactics that have put venison in the freezer for me in every recent season I've hunted. If you hunt hard, the same strategies could produce for you.—***Gerald Almy.***

A Lifetime of Whitetail Hunting: How to Hunt and Where

My whitetail deer hunting began in the forests of the Great Lakes region. I recall the first three years with some amusement. I collected a buck each season and began to believe I had whitetail hunting down to a surety.

By the end of 10 years my views had changed. Although I honed my craft diligently, many frustrations and uncertainties intruded. Now 40 seasons are behind me, not one missed. I've been privileged with varied opportunities—in Maine, Michigan, Wyoming, the Virginias, the Deep South, Texas, and several states in between, Northern forests, Southwestern deserts, Midwest cornfields, Plains creek bottoms, Western mountains, and Southern swamps. The single most important conclusion I've drawn from these four decades is: No matter how much you learn about the whitetail it remains to some extent unpredictable and enigmatic. That's why it long has been America's most admired and intriguing game animal.

The fact that the whitetail—exceedingly shy, physically fragile-appearing compared with the mule deer—was able to colonize an immense and varied expanse on this continent, and to adapt to man's massive settlement, should tell hunters something important about it. It is a tough, resilient animal. Wariness and a facility for keeping its private life private are facets of its personality that have nurtured its success. I concluded long ago that a thorough understanding of the whitetail personality is the first requisite for the serious hunter.

Here is a creature of cover, chiefly *edges* of cover. Either when undisturbed or fleeing, whitetails seldom cross open areas. A single bush will focus movement, the deer using it as a screen. Many times in Texas I've rattled up whitetail bucks in rut, taking a stand by a small opening with scattered trees or bushes. Unfailingly, a buck coming in would dodge behind and around a succession of shrubs. Large openings are a waste of time for whitetail stand hunters. Even when whitetails feed in fields, it's invariably only the edges near escape that draw them.

Whitetails are nervous, intense, excitable, never placid. Hundreds of times I've watched a whitetail feed on my own property. Down goes the head—two nips—up it comes with a jerk, twisting, turning, ears flicking this way and that, stares intently, puts the head down again, instantly jerks it up. No whitetail at its fattest is as fat as a mule deer. It's too much a bundle of nerves. That's why it is a superb survivalist.

For more than 20 years, on our ranch in the Texas hill country and also on our 27-acre home place, I have observed whitetails almost daily. If a bird flits from a bush, a deer feeding nearby lifts its tail in panic and bounds away. A flying buzzard draws its shadow across the ground, and the deer flees. An expert deer-hunter friend says, "A mule deer runs up a ridge, then stops to look back at what scared it. A whitetail runs over three ridges without curiosity about what it is fleeing."

Understanding whitetail personality is important because every hunter tactic relates to it. For example, anything strange in a whitetail's home bailiwick, which is of only moderate size, is quickly noted by the deer. A deer knows every bush, rock, tree, natural sound, and scent in its domain. The human voice or face are horrors to a whitetail. So is the sound, sight, and scent of a prowling hunter.

Hunters ask me, "How can I travel to Texas (or some other place) and hunt successfully when I've always hunted in Pennsylva-

During the rut, whitetail bucks lose some of their usual caution. This one was called to the gun by rattling antlers to ape the sound of two bucks fighting.

nia (or elsewhere)? Aren't the deer different?" The personality of the quarry doesn't change at all, from north woods to southern swamp to desert. Only the forage, cover, and terrain change. The deer simply have adapted to differing surroundings. A hunter who can spot lie-up havens for deer in Vermont can quickly pinpoint their counterparts in the thornbrush of southern Texas. The hunter who understands whitetail behavior in one part of their range exchanges physical attributes of terrain in a different locality, and sizes up where food, safety, and comfort are available.

Years ago when I was trying to nail down basic hunting rules that would help to make me more consistently successful, it occurred to me that once I knew what kind of animal the whitetail is the rest would be quite simple. How does the whitetail spend its day? What deer are doing at a given time will determine what the hunter should be doing.

On a normal day, whitetails are actively feeding and moving during the first couple of hours after dawn and the last couple before dusk. What only a few hunters realize, however, is that they don't bed down and stay there throughout the six or seven hours in between. There's a distinct midday activity period when deer are on their feet, relieving themselves, moving into shade as the sun moves, into a warmer or cooler spot if wind switches. They may not leave cover but move about in it, eating as activity brings on hunger. Sometimes they move to edges, potter about, wander briefly, then seek a new bed. Few whitetails are killed at this time because hunters are in camp.

Obviously, numerous influences change how whitetails spend certain days. Bright nights may diminish dawn activity in some areas. Severe weather may force deer into dense cover. Abundance of food may make for short feeding periods, and the scarcity of it for longer ones, especially late in the year, when the food supply is very thin.

I learned through exasperation on several occasions a fact that few whitetail hunters are aware of in relation to the deer's day. Dawn hunting, when whitetails have been on their feet feeding and moving in an area during predawn, finds them bolder and more confident than they are late in the afternoon. They're more vulnerable then. Predusk hours are when the deer, previously safely bedded in cover, are first coming out to the edges. What dangers may have moved into the feeding areas while the animals rested? They may stand long in shadows, peering, listening. The slightest inkling of danger late in the day will send them back. Hunters must be extra quiet and crafty during these hours.

Which is best, to prowl quietly or to take a stand? As a young hunter I argued about that, but it slowly dawned on me that the whole argument was ridiculous. An old-timer in a northern Michigan deer camp pointed the way. He'd taken a buck every season for more than 25 years, and he said his success hinged on doing just the opposite of what the deer were doing. When deer were moving, he'd stay put. When they were resting, he'd move.

When I was teaching my two boys to hunt deer, I remember drawing a simple map in the dirt. Point A was where deer rested, B was where they fed. Water didn't get a letter, because except in arid terrain deer are seldom tied to a specific location. They drink anywhere. In the North they even eat snow. I explained that going to and from A, and while at B, whitetails were moving and exposing themselves. Therefore, instead of taking a chance of disturbing them during that time, the hunter should be on stand, either at B or along a route between A and B. When the deer were at A was the time for the hunter to do his moving. The illustration may be oversimplified, but the bulk of whitetail hunting basics is wrapped up in it.

Because the most important hours of a whitetail's days are spent foraging, a successful hunter must be familiar with what deer eat where he hunts. Filling the paunch is the main reason for moving from A to B and moving around at destination—movements allowing hunters opportunities. It takes about six pounds of food to fill a whitetail. Some foods, such as acorns, are distributed over much of the vast range. Scores of others are localized.

On our ranch we have five kinds of oaks. In good acorn-crop years, deer gorge on them. This isn't necessarily a help to hunters. The more abundant any prime forage is the less the deer must move to fill up, the quicker they do so, and the less their exposure to hunters. However, we can judge by the abundance or scarcity of acorns what the deer are eating and where they're likely to be. About 100 miles south of us oaks are scarce. Varied browse—huajillo brush for example—is a diet mainstay. Far west in the Chisos Mountains, mountain mahogany is a favorite.

Whitetail forage changes in kind and quantity not only from locality to locality but from hunting season to hunting season. So every year hunters should check what is available to make sure just where point B and travel routes between it and point A will be. Pay little attention to the whitetails' summer and early fall habits. At home I can watch deer out of a window almost any day all summer and fall. Come fall, however, food changes and movement routes with it. Scouting done too early may get you excited about trails and sign that are worthless when hunting season arrives.

If I were to pick the one area of lore I feel is most important in the world of whitetail hunting, it would be the differences between bucks and does. Most hunters think in terms of looking for deer, lumping the sexes together. To be sure, enlightened management requires that we do our part in harvesting does. One must understand, however, that the sexes are like two different species, especially during fall, and that whitetail *buck* hunting is a highly specialized endeavor.

Whitetail bucks are only mildly gregarious. They are 10 times more secretive than does and fawns. On four consecutive days during the 1980 season I counted more than 100 antlerless deer along the edges of a huge winter-oat field near the Mexican border. There wasn't a buck among them. Most whitetail hunters see far more does than bucks. Yet at birth the sex ratio is almost even, tilted slightly in favor of males. Hunting changes the ratio. The fact remains that whitetail bucks are numerous, and they are masters at keeping out of sight. The buck hunter who is seeing numerous does and fawns is hunting in the wrong places. The most secluded feeding and bedding areas are where the bucks will be.

How many tales have you heard about that monster buck suddenly spotted, just once, on a certain range? Hunters love to claim he wandered in from some other territory. Don't believe it. He became a monster because of his secretive ways and his hideouts. These might have included small pockets such as unknown headers of draws in hill country, a high-and-dry motte of trees or brush in the middle of a Southern swamp, the willow-fringed creek bottom in farm country where no one looks because there "isn't enough cover for a deer" and from which he forages forth only at night.

A classic example of this secrecy

Photograph by Erwin A. Bauer

This nice whitetail is "frozen" and trying to decide if it's wise to bolt or wait till danger passes. Make just the slightest quick movement, and he'll vanish.

Photograph by Erwin A. Bauer

Photograph by Bill McRae

Photograph by Jerry Smith

Photograph by Roy Morsch

If you can get a clear shot at a bedded buck (top and above), you're doing something right. It's very difficult to do because of the noisy cover and the hair-trigger senses of the deer. A good buck in the open during the hunting season (middle left) is a rare sight, and when they must cross open ground you can bet they are alert. The buck at left was feeding along the edge of forest cover. Raised "flag" shows he's aware of the human intruder, but he's moving slowly and there's time enough for a hunter to get off a shot.

This buck came down a well-used deer runway, but he stopped short when he came to photographer's high stand. Sometimes, whitetails do look up!

has occurred recently on our home place. For two years we've seen a whitetail far larger than average deer in this area each summer in velvet and each fall during the season, but only once each summer and fall. We are certain from tracks around our ponds that he lives right here, and we are around the place day after day. How does he avoid us?

Once he has filled in the broad brush strokes of the whitetail picture, the accomplished hunter refines it with details. Wrapped up in hunters' schemes for success are perhaps the most intriguing facets of the *advanced* art of whitetail hunting. For years I've listened to other hunters whose prowess I respect divulge odd bits of lore that had filled tags for them. I've also hatched a few schemes of my own.

For example, blowing a coyote call where it is legal to use it as a deer call will often move hidden whitetails from cover. John Finegan, who runs a large whitetail-hunt operation in Texas, uses a leather sling to hurl stones far into canyons to spook out hidden deer. Several hunters I know have learned to mimic the snort of a deer. Bedded deer often move out or peer out to see what's going on.

Good hunters meticulously case every square foot of a small hunting territory, rather than range widely, looking for something that ties whitetails to a specific place. During rut, a buck scrape can be a tag-filler. In farm country, sign at a sagged spot in a fence between forage edge and woodlot indicates a jump habitually used—or it may be a dip in the ground forming a crawl-under. That old apple orchard or a green succulent crop such as winter oats sprouting during deer season—these are daily magnets.

Some concepts are so obvious it's surprising everyone isn't practicing them. For example, it has long amazed me that one of the positive methods of success is ignored by probably 90 percent of whitetail hunters. This is just adding hunting time—not adding days to a trip but becoming an *all-day* hunter. Perhaps because I am not a midday napper, for years I've barely taken time to eat between dawn and dark of each deer-hunting day. Keep in mind that whitetails, just like hunters, make mistakes. The more hours you are in the woods, the better your chances of catching one at it. The early-and-late syndrome so mesmerizes most whitetail hunters that they waste the bulk of each hunting day.

Another simple approach involves heavily pressured deer. On many whitetail ranges, swarms of hunters flounder aimlessly, especially on opening day and on weekends. It should be obvious that all any expert hunter has learned about his quarry and how to outwit it is shot to bits by such intrusion. Hunting spooked deer is quite another matter from hunting undisturbed animals. Feeding animals are frightened and scattered. Bedded deer are bumbled into and sent fleeing. Under normal circumstances, you can almost bet that a whitetail moving in a certain direction will, when startled, whirl and go back the way it came. This habit has been used by hunters working together to collect many a buck. It, and the A and B business I outlined, can be discarded when hunters swarm. Remember, many of them are inept and too eager. They change all the equations for the deer and the astute hunters.

I dislike hunting under such conditions. But I learned the hard way years back what to do. I pick a spot near dense cover that has a natural flight route leading into it and then sit. In the woods is a swarm of unorganized drivers. Harassed deer will try to get away from them. I let the bumblers send one to me.

When things quiet down and your time comes to hunt, appraise the area for the least likely places a deer might find refuge. I once killed a big buck in a Southern river bottom after a mass of hunters had combed the timber, by watching at dusk a tiny copse of trees out in the middle of a soybean field. The buck had taken refuge there, where surely no one would look. Another time a companion and I both took good bucks by floating a stream deep into a big swamp where hunters couldn't walk because of fringe bog holes. The deer had fled all the disturbance and never expected us.

In 40 years a lot of whitetails have gone into our freezer. I've never tried to count how many. Years of experience and diligence make success come easier. Of course, I've never tried to count how many *didn't* go into the freezer because the craft I prided myself on wasn't crafty enough. If I could count 'em, I'd not divulge the figure here—but I will admit it certainly would be by far more than the meatpole count. That's why I'm still a dedicated whitetail hunter.–***Byron W. Dalrymple.***

Mad About Whitetails

I'm 33 years old and I work as a carpenter in my home area near Bay City, Michigan. When October 1 arrives—the opening day of Michigan's archery deer season—I quit working and go deer hunting. I hunt with a bow until our two-week firearms season opens in November. In December I go with a muzzleloader until that season closes, then I finish out the month with archery gear. I hunt all types of whitetail terrain from southern Michigan farm country to the dense wilderness forests in the state's Upper Peninsula.

The only years I don't hunt the full three months is when I fill my two Michigan deer tags with truly outstanding trophy bucks before the respective seasons close. I have head-and-shoulder mounts of 11 of my huge whitetails, and a lot of them were taken with arrows. I wrote a story about how I got some of those big deer. "Swamped by Trophy Bucks" was published in the December 1980 issue of OUTDOOR LIFE.

I get so much satisfaction out of trying to outwit big bucks that my loss of income doesn't bother me. When you hold out for trophies you let a lot of average-size bucks go by. These bucks teach me a lot of things that some hunters never get a chance to learn.

The sketch (page 64) explains two of the most important principles I've learned in more than 1,000 days of hunting whitetails.

The situation shown represents an area I hunted 12 years ago near Rose City, Michigan. At that time I fully understood the runway principle that's illustrated. It's simply that deer leaving a big feeding area will utilize many runways leading toward bedding grounds. These are feeder runways. They always merge into major runways much like tributary streams merge into a river.

Deer use whatever cover is available when leaving feeding areas, but as they get closer to bedding grounds they use the thickest and best cover. As the sketch shows, eight or more runways leaving large feeding areas will merge into two or three leading into bedding areas. This is one reason why a hunter on stand will see more deer near a bedding area than near feeding grounds. I selected a stand site that was close to a major runway.

The first day I hunted the area I parked my Jeep near the cabin and followed route B to my stand. It was an hour before dawn when I started walking, and I got my feet soaked in the marsh. Between dawn and 9:30 I had 23 deer walk by me. Four were small bucks. I didn't try for any of them. I was holding out for a trophy deer.

The next morning I took route A to my stand. I saw only two deer in the distance, and neither came down the runway. I used the same route the following morning, and didn't see any deer. I reasoned that the animals were feeding somewhere else, so I hunted other areas for the next few days.

About a week later I again parked my vehicle near the cabin long before dawn. This time I was wearing rubber boots, so I took route B and tried going through the marsh without getting wet. I didn't succeed, but my soaking feet didn't bother me a bit during the next couple of hours when 19 deer used the runway.

After that hunt I assumed that the deer were using the area again, so I decided to keep hunting it. The next morning I used route A because it was the shortest and easiest route to my stand. I didn't see a single deer. It occurred to me that the only times I saw deer from that stand were the times I got to it via route B. The next day I went through the

The drawing of a real hunting situation encountered by the author illustrates two important principles. The deer were feeding in cropfields and bedding in thick security cover. Almost always deer spread out a bit to feed, so there are many small runways at the feeding area that join to form one or two runways at the edge of daytime bedding cover. Therefore, it's usually best to locate a stand near the bedding area. The whole herd funnels onto the heavily used major trails. When the author first hunted this area, he often crossed all the minor runways near the feeding area in order to reach his stand. On those days he saw no deer because they got his scent on the trails and abandoned the bedding area, never reaching his stand. When he used the roundabout route through the swamp, he saw many deer because he crossed the major runways beyond the place where his stand was located, and the deer could not scent him until they were beyond his stand.

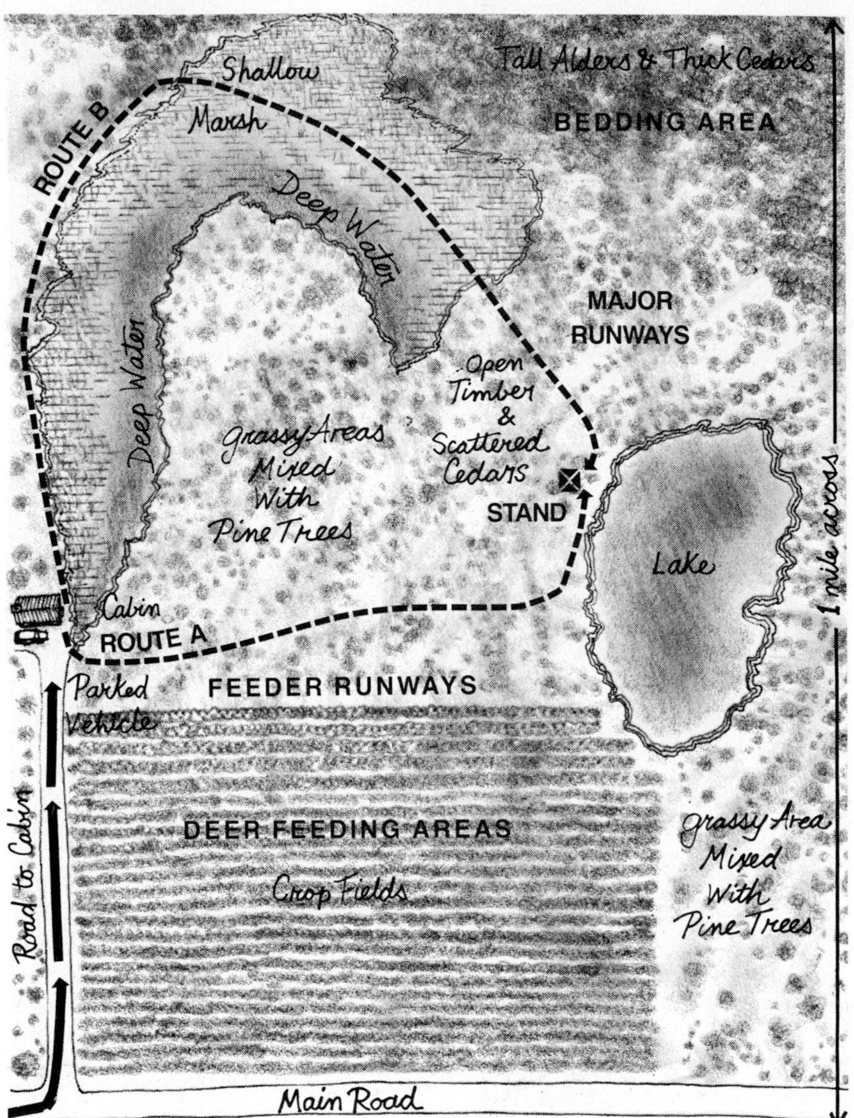

Illustrations by Bob Ritter

marsh. Again I saw many deer, and the significance of what had been happening dawned on me.

Note on the sketch that when I used route A I walked directly across the feeder runways. When I used route B I didn't cross any feeders, and I crossed the major runways only at points far downtrail from my stand. The deer were long past my stand before they could be alerted by my scent.

The importance of this principle can't be overstated. If a hunter crosses a deer runway shortly before the animals begin using it, the runway will be abandoned for that day. No matter how much you know about other phases of deer hunting, you WILL NOT see deer on a runway beyond a place that has recently been crossed by a human.

Another very important lesson I learned years ago is that rainy days are by all odds the best times to hunt whitetails. It took me a long time to figure out the reasons, a good share of the 1,000 or so days I've hunted these animals.

One morning years ago I headed for my stand in a light drizzle. Normally dawn would have come on about 6:45, but it was still dark after 7:15 because of very heavy cloud cover. By 8 o'clock it was pouring rain. I was so cold I was shaking, and I had yet to see a deer. I was ready to call it quits at 8:30, then I saw a small buck coming down the runway.

During the next hour about 30 deer walked by me, including four bucks with average antlers. I was really surprised because I'd hunted from that stand numerous times. In normal weather I'd been used to seeing about 10 deer each morning, of which only one or two would be bucks.

All of those rain-soaked animals walked by me at a fast pace. None exhibited the caution that whitetails normally show when moving from one area to another. Through the years since I have watched the same strange behavior many times, but only on rainy days.

Two years ago hunting in the rain paid off with astonishing success. Thirteen of us were in our camp in Michigan's Upper Peninsula. During five full days of hunting we'd hung only four bucks on our buck pole. On the sixth morning it rained, and we brought in four big bucks and a black bear.

Rain dramatically reduces use of the two senses that deer rely on most heavily for safety—hearing and scent. Rain drives a hunter's scent into the ground. It also dampens sound. But it does something else that is even more significant; it disturbs a whitetail's timetable to such a degree that it abandons normal caution.

Here's what happens. When a night is clear, it takes at least 45 minutes to an hour for darkness to turn into dawn. First there is a dim lemon-yellow glow near the horizon. The sky gradually lightens and visibility slowly improves. A deer has lots of time to leave its feeding area and cautiously use runways leading into its bedding cover before full daylight comes on.

But that timetable is drastically upset on a rainy morning when the period from full darkness to dawn is much shorter, sometimes as short as 15 minutes.

On such days deer tend to stay in feeding areas much later. Since they have no idea of time, they depart on the basis of how light the sky has become. On really dark and rainy mornings deer are caught in feeding areas long beyond the time when they would normally depart for bedding grounds.

This makes even wary bucks much less cautious than usual because they know they have to hurry to reach daytime security cover. A buck that would normally stop every 20 yards to test for danger with his ears and nose now may go 100 yards or more between stops. And when he does stop, his two most useful senses are drastically dulled by the rain.

There's still another factor that makes a rainy day the best time to hunt. A deer that's been bedded all day in nasty weather—especially freezing rain—is very uncomfortable. He'll get up and start moving toward a feeding area much earlier in the afternoon than normal. This is the reverse of what happens in the morning. When dawn comes quickly, and deer are late getting into bedding areas, the hunter has a longer period of good shooting light before the animals settle down in beds. Conversely, because deer are on the move earlier during rainy afternoons, the hunter again has a longer period of shooting light. All of these factors emphasize why a hunter on stand will see more deer near bedding areas than near feeding areas.

As far as nice days are concerned, the average hunter doesn't appreciate the importance of thermal currents. Even the casual hunter knows that his stand should be downwind from runways, but he'll seldom see deer if he doesn't understand how thermal currents can alert the animals to his presence.

A thermal current is a wind drift that moves vertically up or down. It contrasts with winds that move horizontally. Temperature changes on calm windless days create thermal currents. As daylight comes on and air temperature warms, a rising thermal current develops because warm air rises. In the evening, when air temperature begins dropping, a downslope thermal current develops because cold air is heavier than warm air.

I'll never forget the first time deer proved to me how important the thermal current principle is. I had a stand on the side of a ridge. About 20 yards away a well-traveled runway ran along the side of the ridge above me. Near the bottom of the ridge, about 35 yards from my stand, there was another runway that ran through a stand of cedars (see sketch page 46). My stand was located where I had a good view of both runways.

I first started hunting the spot in the evening, and it wasn't long before I discovered deer behavior that seemed very strange. On quiet days when there was no wind to eliminate thermal currents, the whitetails that used the runway above me passed by without a hint that they knew of my presence. The deer that used the runway below me always spooked even though they were almost twice as far from my position. I couldn't figure out why this happened.

Some time later I began using the stand at various times, often in the morning. I discovered that deer using the high runway early in the day when there was no wind always became alert to my presence while the deer on the low runway never scented me. Even though I didn't know what a thermal current was in those days, my many experiences taught me that a stand hunter in hilly country should always locate above a runway or other likely spot in the morning and on low ground below the hotspot in the evening.

All the things I've mentioned won't help a hunter if he doesn't hunt deer-concentration areas. An old-timer once said to me, "Don't look for deer where they've been, look where they are!"

Your first step should be to check potential feeding areas because it's far easier to find deer sign on feeding grounds than in the much denser cover used for bedding. Whitetails have food preferences based on the time of year, and they're smart enough to know when various foods will be available.

In my opinion, whitetails love winter wheat and farm crops more than anything else. They also know that when the crops are harvested they have to rely on winter wheat or natural food like acorns.

Let's say that one large area of several square miles includes well-separated cornfields, winter wheat fields, and hardwoods showing good amounts of acorns. During October the odds are high that the area's deer will feed mostly in standing corn or other crop fields. When the crops are harvested by late October, the herds will shift to the growing winter wheat or to grassy areas. Deer in farm country seldom go for acorns and other natural food until the choice man-produced food is gone. During wet years, when muddy ground prevents farmers from harvesting their crops, deer continue to feed on crops late in the year. Find a field of standing corn in late November or during December, and you'll find a prime whitetail feeding area.

Farm-country deer use the same runways every day (unless spooked or the food availability pattern changes) because good runway cover is limited. Feeder runways always begin along edges of feeding areas, usually along those edges closest to or bordering

On calm days air rises or falls as the temperature changes. In the morning thermal currents rise toward ridgetops and other high points as the sun heats the air; in the evening the thermal currents move downhill as air cools. Therefore, it's best to take a high stand in the morning and a low stand in the evening. In the drawings, the hunter on his morning stand can observe four major runways, and the thermal currents rise above him so that traveling deer are not alerted by his scent. His evening stand is below two major runways where the descending currents waft his scent downhill. Of course, if the wind is blowing, the hunter has to choose his stand accordingly, no matter what time of day it is. One of the author's bucks, at right, scored 238 2/8 in the nontypical whitetail category—certain proof that his theories are on the ball.

brushy or woodland cover. When I'm scouting, I always walk these edges looking for runways showing fresh tracks. When I find lots of fresh tracks I know I've located a feeding area that's being used.

My next step is to find bedding areas by following feeder runways to major runways and then looking for nearby thick bedding cover. I don't look for actual beds for several reasons. Often it's difficult to see beds on hard ground. Even when bedding deer make depressions by crushing grass or leaves when they lie down, it's easy to miss seeing them. A well-defined bed in fallen leaves may disappear in a hurry when a strong wind begins blowing. Rain can also destroy visual signs of beds. I know from many hard lessons that a lot of whitetails can bed in a small area and leave few signs of their presence.

There's only one sure way of determining if a potential bedding area actually harbors deer, and that's by jumping the animals. The best time to jump them is on a warm, sunny, and windless afternoon. On such a day the animals can hear you coming at a distance, and they're far more likely to jump and run than stay hidden. Once you actually see deer, you know a bedding area is being used and you can hunt it with confidence a few days later.

Everything I've said so far applies to the choicest whitetail terrain, which is a mixture of agricultural lands and woodlots. Whitetails in forests where there is little or no agriculture are different animals from a behavioral standpoint.

The first thing to consider is that forest deer have little or no need for runways because they're not going to and from crop fields.

Though the best places to hunt are areas showing new low growth, these deer are browsing animals and browse is almost everywhere. Unlike farm-country deer that use runways every day, forest deer tend to wander. They do have a movement pattern, but they may not return to the same spot for three or four days. This means that hunting near any runways that you do find can be a losing game.

Buck scrapes are small areas scraped bare of leaves and vegetation by buck deer. The bucks urinate in them to attract does. A buck in farming areas may find 20 or more does in a single field at night. He may make scrapes, but he doesn't have to advertise his presence, and so he may never return to them. Conversely, a doe in heat doesn't have to look for a buck scrape to find a mate because there are plenty of bucks to go around in good farmed deer country. But in forests, where the deer density per square mile is far lower, waiting downwind from a scrape can be deadly.

A lot of so-called deer-hunting experts have written that hunting near scrapes is the best way of getting shooting anywhere in whitetail country, but *only* during rutting periods. I disagree on both counts. Bucks are ready to breed and are continuously looking for does in heat during most hunting seasons. Because the forest has far fewer deer than farm country, the bucks are well aware that does in heat are definitely attracted to scrapes. My experiences have shown that forest bucks will make scrapes and check them for doe activity long before and after the peak of the rut.

This knowledge enabled me to get one of my trophy bucks last fall. He had a huge eight-point rack, and he was also the heaviest buck I ever killed. He had made two scrapes only a few yards apart in a big cedar swamp, and both were about six feet in diameter. I found them in late October when I was bowhunting. I saw that buck twice while on stand, but couldn't get a shot.

The first time I heard him coming over a knoll to my right. He walked behind some cedars, stopped, and stared at his scrapes. He didn't move a muscle for over five minutes, then he disappeared. His rut-swollen neck was so huge it looked like it belonged to an elk. I saw him again several days later from the same stand under the same conditions. I decided to leave that buck alone and then try for him again during firearms season.

Three weeks later, when my group got to camp the day before rifle season opened, I could hardly control myself. I desperately wanted to check those scrapes for fresh signs of the huge buck. It took all my willpower not to do it, and I'll tell you why in a moment.

Opening day dawned dead still and freezing cold under a cloudy sky. It was about 11 a.m. when I heard leaves crunching 90 yards to my left. I knew a deer was coming, and my heart was banging my ribs when I got my first view of the animal. It was the same huge buck, and he was heading toward a big windfall poplar.

I figured on taking him when he stopped to jump the deadfall. But he lowered his head, squatted, and bellied under the trunk. His head was stretched out, and his neck—which had appeared so huge to me weeks earlier—now seemed even bigger. It made an ideal target, and I broke it with a .30/06 slug. That buck hung on our northern Michigan buck pole for 10 days before we broke camp and headed home. Even after all that time his field-dressed carcass weighed 214 pounds.

The reason I refused to check those scrapes after I first arrived in camp ties in the biggest mistake deer hunters make in northern forests. Unlike whitetails in agricultural areas that are used to human activity, forest deer panic at the sight or scent of humans. Many forest-deer hunters wait all year and use their vacations to hunt in the woods. Then they blow their chances for success by scouting hunting areas only a day or two before the season opens.

Remember that forest deer follow a travel pattern over a very large area, and they may not return to any given spot for several days. Wherever a scouting hunter leaves his scent the deer will leave, especially wary bucks. The worst thing a forest hunter can do is check out his hunting area just before he actually uses it. And when he does use it, he should sneak into and out of it with minimum commotion.

Forest bucks make several scrapes along their extended travel routes. These scrapes are usually a few hundred yards apart. When you find two or more, an imaginary line drawn between them will come close to representing segments of a travel pattern.

Finding buck rubs is a big help. Rubs in farm country don't mean much because there are many bucks using the same limited cover areas. But in a big forest, rubs are usually made near or on travel routes. The combination discovery of rubs and scrapes can give a knowing hunter a fine indication of a buck's travel route. After that it's a matter of selecting a stand site in a good ambush area.

Once on stand, don't give up nearly as soon as you would in farm country where most deer are usually bedded shortly after daylight.

Food supplies for forest deer are far more limited. These animals are likely to feed much longer in the morning, especially following moonless or very dark nights. On such nights it's difficult for browsing deer to find food, so they'll feed from dawn until they're no longer hungry. I've killed a lot of my forest bucks between 10 a.m. and noon, and one of them was that big buck I shot in the neck last November.–***Paul Mickey.***

Watching for Whitetails

I must have been daydreaming because a deer suddenly appeared and had walked almost 60 yards from cover before I saw it. It wasn't much farther away than that and was staring right at me. Small antlers were visible. I froze.

The buck took a step and lowered its head. Quickly I shouldered my Remington model 700 in .270 caliber, centered the crosshairs of the Weaver K4 scope on the deer's chest, and fired. The buck whirled and headed for the woods. I had time for a second shot but hesitated. Suddenly the buck was down.

I could hardly believe my luck. I'd been deep in the boondocks of north-central Minnesota all day and now I'd flattened a buck only yards from a road and my truck. It was getting to be a familiar story.

For 25 of the 31 years I have hunted deer in Minnesota, I've resisted the notion that there are more whitetails around the roadside farm fields than in the backcountry. Like many hunters, particularly young hunters, I wanted to believe that I was improving my chances by hunting deep in the woods. More recently I have conceded that whitetails have adapted well to civilization because they like the food found in farm fields, pastures, clear-cuts, and other openings near the roadside.

Now my serious hunting efforts are directed toward posting along the edges of such openings. I limit my posting to the last two hours of daylight. Early evening usually is the best time to see a buck in large openings.

My preference for the early evening is reinforced by Wisconsin-based Al Hofacker of "Stump Sitters" fame. Stump Sitters is a Wisconsin-based organization that studies the habits and movements of whitetails. Hofacker suggests that deer could be just as active in the morning, but hunters are moving to their stands at the same time deer are active. Deer may detect them and move out of the area.

Radio-tracking studies have shown that when bucks return to check their scrapes, they do so five times more frequently during the early evening than at any other time of day. This same study revealed that scrapes and rubs are often found along the edges of woods that suddenly yield to open meadows, fields, and clear-cuts.

Three years ago my son Dave killed his first deer, a six-point buck, when, just before sundown, it burst from cover and into the center of a mowed hayfield. When my son fired the buck ran to the edge of the field and collapsed. Only then did Dave find a string of scrapes and rubs just within the trees and bushes edging the field.

In Minnesota we usually have a heavy leaf fall by mid-October. At that time deer can be seen almost any evening feeding along the edges of farm fields and other openings. The reason for this exodus from the woods lies in the deer's desire for green vegetation, still to be found in openings. Although deer will eat the newly fallen leaves from shrubs and trees, a leaf that has lain upon the ground for several days is of little interest to them.

Because this same area is poor farming country, most field-watching will be over hayfields, either wild or seeded, or pastures that are normally unoccupied during fall.

A hayfield that has recently been plowed and reseeded probably holds the greatest attraction for whitetails in the northern forested region of the Great Lakes states. In 1978 I killed a small buck in a wild hayfield full of weeds and coarse grasses. In 1976 I had a stand by that same field. Five minutes before sundown a broad-racked eight-pointer burst from the woods 150 yards away. At my fourth shot the buck appeared to melt from view into the woods. I

Solitary hunter keeps watch over a hayfield during the last hours of daylight.

ran across that field, hoping that I would find blood or some sign of a hit. I found the buck instead. My last shot had killed it cleanly.

My bowhunting friends know that deer feed actively in open fields in early evening. Yet these same hunters rarely watch fields when they switch from longbows to rifles. Most believe that deer shy away from such fields during the heavy hunting pressure of the rifle season, feeding there only at night.

Yet confirmed field-watchers see a surprising number of deer in early evening. One group of observers reports that deer have such short memories they often cannot recall something that may have alerted them only three minutes before. This probably goes double for bucks in rut since their minds are more in tune with romance than feeding.

When you hunt deer by conventional methods in thick woods your vision is severely restricted. When you watch fields, pastures, and clear-cuts you extend your field of vision, in some cases by many hundreds of yards. In openings that are bordered by woods on two or more sides, one may see deer traveling across the field from one wooded area to another. If there is a light line of trees or bushes or a brushy fence line, the deer will follow it for the tree cover. Because the deer may be a great distance away, scent is not a problem. Biologists say deer must be within 50 to 100 yards of a scent source before they react.

Though fields offer a greatly extended field of vision, it doesn't necessarily follow that if a deer is in a field you're going to see him. Many hunters don't spot deer in fields because most persons take in a wide-angle view of open areas. Look for details. It's easy to miss seeing deer, especially those that are partly hidden by high weeds, brush, or other terrain.

Remember that a big buck seldom stands taller than 40 inches at his shoulder. If such a buck is standing in weeds 200 yards away, it's likely that the hunter will miss seeing him in poor light. Veteran field hunters have trained themselves to spend half their time with the wide-angle view; the other half is spent studying details. Good binoculars can be just about as important as a rifle. The best shot in the world isn't going to eat venison steak unless he can see a deer to shoot at.

One of my favorite hunting sites is an area of woodland with numerous connecting wild hayfields. But the competition has become keen because a number of good bucks have been taken by hunters watching these fields during midday. While I'm the first to admit you can see deer at any time, the chances are more remote of seeing one in open fields during the day. Fortunately, most of my competition head out to their trucks and cars just about the time the hunting gets good.

Although I live in a heavily forested area, I have many fields and openings to choose from. I often spend a few hours during midday scouting new fields. If I find buck scrapes or rubs I know that a buck is nearby. If I am patient I'll get him.

I've watched the edges while does and fawns have fed in a field, but the times I have killed a buck, the animal has been the only one around. My brother has filled his buck tag every year for the past nine with lone bucks that have entered fields or clearcuts. Perhaps they are exhausted from chasing does and want a quiet meal. Whatever the reason, lone bucks are the rule.

Watching fields in the early evening requires tenacity and patience. When an evening's stand proves futile, the nagging question of whether to continue watching the same field again or try another finally surfaces. Being in the right spot at the right time still holds true.

Because I rarely watch for more than a two-hour period and generally have a long-range view, I rarely use a tree stand. Sometimes, however, I will nail a board or two to nearby tree limbs to use as a rifle rest. If you are not handy at estimating ranges, you can step off yardage during midday scouting trips. Once you know the approximate distances, binoculars are handy.

Legal shooting hours and other regulations differ from state to state. Be sure you know what they are where you hunt. This is especially favorable for early evening posting because you can be out until dark. Every minute you stick to your stand during this early evening time period swings the odds in your favor.

Almost any potentially good spot for deer is better as sundown approaches. If you are on a deep-woods stand, but not far from a logging trail or other easy route out of the woods, I urge you to stick to your stand until the legal closing time. I like to carry a small flashlight with me. It can be handy for following a blood trail in poor light, and is a precaution that I will not be mistaken for a deer.

Have I given up on conventional deer hunting? No way. I still enjoy poking through the woods, rifle in hand, in pursuit of whitetails. Most days I combine early morning woods posting with midday stillhunting. But I no longer have qualms that I should have stayed on some deep-woods stand longer, or moved more quietly while stillhunting, because the most productive time of day is still ahead.

I'm constantly amazed that hunters will get up long before daylight and stumble off into the woods in total darkness, yet give little attention to early evening hunting. If I could hunt only 30 minutes each day, I would still be confident of killing a buck because I would choose the last 30 minutes of the day and spend it watching a large opening. When I kill my buck I have only a short drag to the nearest roadside. It's really the easiest way to hunt Great Lakes' whitetails.–***Bob Gilsvik.***

Author's brother Ken admires a fine whitetail shot where woods met a hayfield. Patient watching made the kill possible.

The Easiest Ways to Strike Out on Whitetails

About 20 years ago I missed the best trophy whitetail buck I've ever seen. The place was 20 miles southeast of Superior, Wisconsin, and there were 10 hunters, all specialists in deer driving. I was a guest, and it was the first time I'd hunted the area. Dick Johnson was outlining plans for the final drive of the day.

After Dick finished giving directions to the drivers, he and I took off in one of the pickup trucks. We drove around a section of woodland and then headed down a two-track cutting through a big clearing that separated the timber stand from a creek bottom edged with swamp. Dick stopped the truck near a roadside clump of willows.

"Stand right here," he instructed me. "If the drivers put out any deer they'll run across the clearing in front of you and head for the swamp. I'm going down the road half a mile, and then cut in south to my stand."

Back then I had little experience with driving deer, but I knew a lot about stillhunting and working from stands in the swamps and thickets in Michigan, my home state.

"No buck in his right mind is going to run across that open clearing when he could just as easily cut through these willow clumps behind me," I said to myself.

With that conviction in mind I faced west instead of east, and began looking for cover that would provide a good stand. I was still looking when I heard distant yells announcing the beginning of the drive. I was beginning to feel the cold when something told me to

Heavy antlers of my Saskatchewan buck prove that I was ready when it really counted. But there have been other times.

turn around and check the clearing Johnson had told me to watch.

The buck was already halfway across it. He was broadside to me, running like a racehorse. His head was held low, and the massive antlers looked like an ivory-colored crown. The range was about 200 yards, and there wasn't a twig between us.

The buck's speed was increasing rapidly. It would be only seconds before he'd reach the heavy cover of the creek bottom. I picked him up in my Redfield 3X-to-9X scope and sent the first 100-grain, .243 slug on its way. I expected him to crumple, but he never missed a step. Somehow I missed the buck with four more rounds before he was swallowed by the bottomland thickets.

I was dumbfounded. I numbly realized that I'd goofed the greatest chance I'd probably ever have at a truly outstanding trophy whitetail. When we regrouped I told everybody what had happened.

Lyle Laurvick, a gunsmith in Superior and the friend who had invited me on the hunt, asked, "How come you didn't start shooting as soon as the buck entered the clearing?"

"I didn't see him until he was halfway across," I answered.

Lyle gave me a strange look. Somebody said, "Well, a lot of the best ones get away. Let's get on with the hunt."

I had the definite impression that nobody wanted to embarrass me by asking more questions. It wasn't until years later, when I'd had a lot more experience with drives, that I realized I'd made three really dumb mistakes.

Right at the start I ignored good advice. When Johnson told me to watch the clearing, he was speaking from years of experience with hunting that area. He knew which way the deer would run. Moral: Don't try to second-guess local experts when you're hunting new country.

My second mistake was that I hadn't expected a deer to appear so soon after the drive began. Since then I've learned that it's all-important for posters to be on stand and ready to shoot before the drivers start. When whitetails sense the drivers they almost always do one of two things immediately. They either bolt or they hide. That big buck ran for safety as soon as he heard the first sounds the drivers made. If I had known what was likely to happen, and if I'd been looking where I was supposed to look, I would have had that big brute in my scope when he was running toward me rather than away from me.

Even so, I had time to fire five shots at the buck. My biggest error was lack of shooting skill. On that cold day in Wisconsin I vowed to greatly improve my marksmanship, and I did it too.

Some years later I had a chance at an enormous whitetail buck under similar conditions. He was running across a stubblefield in Saskatchewan. I put two bullets in his chest at 150 yards. The 11-point head-and-shoulder mount now hangs over my fireplace. The reason I scored on that buck was I had practiced shooting my deer rifle until I could use it with confidence.

Most deer hunters never touch their rifles from the time one deer season closes to shortly before the next one opens. They simply don't have the shooting skills they need to cash in on many hunting opportunities.

My hunting buddy Bob Wolff is a fanatic about shooting. He loads him own ammunition and shoots all year informally and in competition. It's a very unusual year when he doesn't get a buck with his rifle and another with his bow.

"Think about how often deer hunters miss easy shots," he said while we were discussing this article. "I spend a lot of time on shooting ranges, I sight-in rifles for many friends, and I see and hear about some very strange misses. I believe that nine out of ten deer hunters can't hit a pie plate from a firm rest at one hundred yards, and the same nine guys can't hit a washtub at that range when they're shooting offhand.

"One day last fall a fellow showed up at the range to sight-in his rifle. He had an old five-gallon bucket that he placed at the one-hundred-yard marker. He shot ten cartridges before he finally creased the bucket, and then he said, 'Well, that's plenty good enough.'

"I watched another guy shooting offhand, monkeying with his scope adjustments after every shot. He couldn't get a bullet to hit anywhere on a paper target. I finally suggested that he use my bench rest to sight-in. He shook his head and said, 'You can't carry a bench rest around in the woods.'

"I didn't say anything. If he hadn't been so bullheaded I would have told him that it's almost impossible to make killing shots unless your rifle is shooting precisely at point of aim. A lot of deer hunters can't properly sight-in their rifles because they don't know how. (See chapter entitled "Sighting-in Made Simple," by Jim Carmichel.) No matter how much you know about other phases of deer hunting, the odds are high that you can't get a buck unless you can put a bullet where you want it to go."

Bob works night shifts in our local school system. Before that he worked a night shift as a Class A machinist in a factory. Bob won't work days because it would interfere with his hunting, fishing, and golfing. He hunts every day during each fall open season, and he gets more hunting experience in a single year than most of us get in a lifetime. When a man like Bob tells you how to hunt deer, you're getting expert advice. Here are more of his tips.

Many hunters hunt the wrong places. During preseason scouting trips they see lots of deer and deer sign in relatively open places such as hardwood ridges, edge cover along clearings, and in cropfields. Any whitetail that has survived at least one hunting season is well aware of what the opening day invasion of hunters and the first rifle shots mean each fall. The big bucks immediately move into the thickest swamps, pine plantations, or similar cover.

"Every fall I see scores of hunters sitting on their stands, and often I spot them over one hundred yards away," Wolff told me. "Any time you're in whitetail country, and you can see a hunter one hundred yards away, you can be sure he's in the wrong place. He's not going to see many bucks unless a few happen to get spooked by him. No worthwhile whitetail will travel in thin cover by choice after the shooting begins. Statistics prove it. Many studies show that the majority of harvested whitetails are downed at ranges of less than fifty yards. It's common sense to hunt the thickest stuff you can find."

Two of the best time periods to be on stand are late morning and early afternoon. Late in the morning many hunters leave the woods and walk to camps or vehicles for lunch. In early afternoon they return to hunting areas. These hunters jump bedded deer that may travel past hunters who are still on stand.

"Also," says Wolff, "many of today's hunters are far too impatient. A lot of guys say to themselves, 'I didn't see a single deer from that stand this morning. After lunch I'm going to do some still-hunting and look for a new spot.' These fellows are unknowingly driving deer for the man who stays on stand."

Don't build new blinds a few days before the season opens. Blinds should be built at least a month in advance of being used.

"Look at it this way," Bob told me. "Suppose you come home from work tonight and notice that your TV set has been moved from one side of the room to the other. The change in the completely familiar scene catches your eye immediately. The same thing happens to deer when something new shows up in their home area. It takes at least several weeks for the animals to decide that any change in familiar terrain is harmless.

"There's another thought that ties in here. Every veteran whitetail hunter has heard about fellows who down their bucks from the same stand every fall. These men hunt from stands that are in place year-round. Once you find a spot that deer travel past every year, don't give up on it. Sooner or later you'll get a shot. I have several of these blinds that my friends and family use. At some time during the season these blinds offer shooting opportunities."

One of Wolff's pet subjects is the art of seeing deer. He isn't talking about the overworked theory of looking for parts of a deer's body, checking out-of-place colors, or other such clues. He's talking about what to do when you actually see one or more deer.

"Almost all of the forty-some bucks I've killed were by themselves," Bob emphasizes. "Seeing a single deer is far more promising than seeing several. A small herd usually consists of does and fawns. Most hunters like to watch the animals, so they try to keep them in sight as long as possible. While they're doing this they're not going to see a buck that may be passing nearby.

"I look for a single deer and determine as soon as possible if the animal is a doe. If it is, I discount her presence immediately and begin looking for another animal. Most hunters are not attentive enough. I keep telling myself, 'Hey, there's no sense watching does. Somewhere in there there's a buck, and I'm going to see him.' The hunter who always maintains the optimistic approach is the one who's going to see bucks."

If you feel that Bob Wolff is a deer-hunting fanatic, then consider the case of Paul Mickey. He's a Michigan carpenter, except that he doesn't touch a saw from October 1 through December 31. Unlike Wolff, who will work only night shifts, Mickey won't work at all

Illustrated by Ken Laager

The buck was already halfway across the clearing, running like a racehorse. I whirled around, fired five shots, and missed every time.

during deer-hunting seasons. I've worked with him on two whitetail deer hunting stories for OUTDOOR LIFE. Mickey is very emphatic about a very important point.

"Many hunters scout an area and see lots of deer before hunting seasons open, then they hunt there and see few, if any," Mickey told me. "They assume hunting pressure has driven the animals to another area. This is seldom the case because whitetails hate to leave a home area. They stay in home territory, but they move to heavy cover, and they hide so well that most hunters never see them.

"One time I left my stand and headed for a cedar swamp to do some stillhunting. I was walking on a logging road through a stand of pines. Way ahead of me I saw a deer lying on the ground about twenty yards off the road. It was by pure accident that I saw the animal through an opening in the pines. I kept on walking and staring at the spot. By the time I closed the distance to forty yards I picked out three does, two fawns, and a four-point buck.

"I wasn't interested in that little buck, and I wanted to see what would happen if I kept on walking without giving any indication that I was aware of the animals. When I first saw the deer they were all lying with their heads up, but as I got closer, they slowly laid their heads flat on the ground. They didn't move a twitch as I walked by within twenty yards. Farther down the road I turned and looked back. Every deer had disappeared, and I never heard them move. I'd bet anything that the same sort of thing happens all the time, but most hunters aren't aware of it.

"My most dramatic example of a whitetail's hiding ability came when I was bowhunting with two buddies. We were driving my jeep into a new area in farming country when two bucks ran across the road in front of us, raced out into a plowed field, and disappeared into a ditch. They didn't reappear, and we figured we had at least one of those bucks for sure.

"The ditch was narrow, about thirty feet wide at its widest point, and brush grew along both banks. We put Rick Havercamp on stand near one end of the ditch. Then Terry Horner and I circled around to its other end half a mile away and pushed back toward Rick. We thought we covered that ditch well, but when we reached Havercamp, he said that we failed to move either buck.

"The three of us then went back down the ditch, working through every piece of the thickest cover. The two bucks finally jumped within twenty yards of Terry, but he couldn't get a shot. The biggest, at least a twelve-pointer, ran out into the field and into a little swale not much bigger than a farmyard. He didn't come out, and though we crisscrossed that swale four times we couldn't jump him. There was no way that buck could have moved out without us seeing him. We must have almost stepped on him several times, but he wouldn't run."

How do you hunt such bucks? Mickey claims that the best way is a two-man drive. Both men must know the bedding areas and escape routes used by deer in a given area. One man takes a stand on an escape route, the other stillhunts at an extremely slow pace in the bedding thickets.

"A wary buck will get up and try sneaking away when he figures he's faced with only one hunter," Mickey explains. "But the hunter has to really pussyfoot around, actually stillhunting instead of merely driving. He has to take a couple of steps, stop, look in all directions for several moments, then take a couple more steps in a new direction. This ultra-slow progress spooks most bucks. They get more nervous by

One way to get at the big bucks that retire to hummocks in cedar swamps during the open season is to don waders and go in after them.

the moment. They figure that sooner or later the stillhunter will see them, and that it won't be difficult to sneak away from one man. That's good figuring, except that it doesn't take the other hunter into account. He is waiting in hiding along the known escape route.

"We get a lot of bucks with this system, but the average hunter won't. He doesn't scout enough to discover the exact bedding areas and escape routes, and he doesn't really understand that whitetails would much rather hide than run, except when they can run with little apparent danger."

One of my friends and his two sons almost always have bucks hanging in their garage early each season. They often base their hunts on the fact that clever bucks will move to specific areas within their home range where there is little or no hunting pressure. One favored hotspot is a 20-acre island in a river that's too deep to wade.

"The only way to get to the island is by boat," Jack Thiel told me. "There are lots of hunters on the mainland on both sides of the island, but when they get to the river they can't cross it. I doubt if a lot of those hunters even know the island exists. When you look at it from the mainland, it looks just like any other part of the opposite shore. Before the season we carry a little pram through some thickets and swamp, hide it, and then use it to get to the island when we hunt. We have never seen another hunter there. That's why the island is loaded with deer during the season."

I think most hunters make the mistake of not realizing that such bonanzas exist in many whitetail areas. Cedar swamps where there is standing water are good. In many of them, there are patches of solid ground. The man who takes the time to put on hip boots or waders and get past the mucky or flooded edges may find prime deer areas that most hunters never see.

Cattail marshes may also contain islands of solid ground. Make no mistake about a whitetail's swimming ability, or his ability to get through marsh and swamp. A buck can easily get to places that most deer hunters would consider inaccessible. The hunter who discovers one of these places has his own private shooting preserve.

A whitetail knows its home area so well that it can conceal itself in areas that hunters seldom bother with. These are very small patches of thick cover surrounded by open fields or clearings. The average hunter makes the mistake of thinking these places are too tiny for deer, so he doesn't hunt them.

Some years ago while grouse hunting I flushed a bird along the edge of a big woodland. I missed the shot, and was amazed when the grouse flew out over the adjoining cropfield and sailed into a tiny swale no bigger than an average living room. The swale was just a low spot in the field. It had never been plowed, and it supported a tangle of brush.

I figured I had that grouse for sure. There was no way it could flush out of that little piece of cover without offering me a shot. I walked into the swale and jumped a big eight-point buck. He crashed out of there across the open field, and it took me several moments to get over my astonishment.

Almost the same thing has happened on other occasions.

Last fall I missed a woodcock that flew out over a hayfield and alighted in a tiny stand of poplars. I walked out there to reflush the bird, and I almost stepped on a six-pointer. Most of these hotspots are only 50 to 150 yards away from a much bigger woodland. A buck wants to be in a spot he figures is safe from hunters, but he also wants to be relatively close to a large area of cover to escape into if he's accidentally discovered. I'm convinced that a great many bucks lie in their tiny sanctuaries and watch unsuspecting hunters in the nearby woodlands.

Check them out, and sooner or later you're going to jump a buck and get a wide-open shot as he races across the open ground.—*John O. Cartier.*

The Otis Wyman Story

It's 6:15 a.m., only 15 minutes into deer season. A whitetail buck, nine points, Eastern count, whiffs Otis Wyman's trail. It lowers its head. Sniffs. Doglike, it follows.

Otis peers through the leaves and limbs of the blowdown that blurs his outline. The business end of his slug-loaded 12-gauge Marlin bolt action rises an inch. Nothing else moves to indicate he has seen the deer. Two squirrels have been scolding him. More of their chatter could draw the buck's attention to the blowdown.

The deer is 175 steps away. Otis is sure of that. He counted them two weeks previously when he located the buck's stomping grounds and his improvised blind in the blowdown. At 5:30 opening day he closed the door of his pickup with a key instead of slamming it. And then silently, by moonlight, no flashlight to alert a deer, he entered the LaRue Scatters, a group of islands in a marsh. Just as Otis followed a narrow neck of land to the "island" where he planned to hunt, the moonlight faded into darkness. But that was timed and expected too. In the dark, Otis counted off the 175 steps and found himself at the blowdown.

Now with daylight, the buck reaches the narrow neck of land, 175 steps away. The deer is walking in Otis' tracks, head low, following a scent. The odor gets hotter, easier to follow. The deer's head comes up. The deer breaks into a lope and comes straight at the blowdown!

A fast-moving deer isn't part of the Otis plan. He whistles sharply to halt the buck, but it doesn't work. Twice more he whistles. The buck is passing the blowdown at 35 feet. Too close! Otis can't find the speeding deer in his 4X Weaver scope. Trees flash between them. But then Otis gets a glimpse of the buck's chest, and fires.

It's a bad shot. The buck runs 100 feet and stops, facing straightaway from the hunter. Possibly the deer is unwilling to leave the scent trail it has been following. Possibly it can't pinpoint where the noise of the shot came from and is afraid to move until certain it won't be running into danger.

"Can't shoot a deer in the rump," Otis thinks as he bolts another load into the chamber. The clicking sound brings the buck's head up. Ears flick. The deer moves slightly and the head bends around to the right to look back. Otis can see a little of the shoulder now. The big slug will range into the neck.

He fires, and the deer falls. It weighs about 200 pounds. At 2½ years, the buck had survived two other hunting seasons in a hard-hunted public area. The animal couldn't have been entirely stupid, yet it followed Otis like a curious dog, and it ended up being the first deer of the 1980 season to arrive at the Union County, Illinois, checking station.

The deer was Otis Wyman's 51st. At 62, and after 51 successful deer hunts, Wyman has learned a great deal about deer hunting. Most of his experience was gained in Illinois where the firearms deer season lasts only six days and is split into two three-day units. Both bucks and does are legal game. Illinois restricts deer hunters to shotguns loaded with slugs, muzzleloaders, or archery tackle. Long-range shooting is impossible, and Otis and other successful Illinois hunters really have to know deer well to take their venison. Some of them say that the average Illinois hunter knows more about deer hunting than hunters in some other states that have seasons that last for months and where the limits are very liberal. In Alabama, for example, it has been perfectly legal to kill one buck a day during a season that lasts for months!

The buck that Otis killed in the Scatters was a good example of the kind of hunting problem he has learned to solve. In preseason scouting, he learned that the buck regularly followed the long, narrow neck of land to the wide place (called an island) at its end. The deer followed an established game trail on the narrow neck. Because the surrounding marshes are impassable, Otis had to come in along the narrow neck too, and he had to walk on the trail or close beside it to reach the blowdown where he wanted to conceal himself. On opening day, he had to get to the stand early before the buck's arrival, but his human scent would have spooked the deer.

His solution was typical—very simple and very effective. He tied sheepskin pads to the bottoms of his boots at the instep after soaking them in red-fox urine bought from a trapper's supply house. As it turned out, the buck came right along to the hunter's stand, and Otis believes that the deer was actually following the nonexistent fox by scenting the trail. Why?

There are conflicting theories, but Otis believes that there are two reasons. First, he told me, deer feel confident when they scent foxes because they sense that foxes are very alert to danger. His theory is that deer like places where they smell foxes because they "know" that a fox readily smells human beings and avoids them. Also, Otis believes that deer are very curious and interested in foxes in a way that human beings find hard to understand. He believes that a deer sometimes follows a red fox simply to find out what the animal is doing. Thus, using a very strong fox scent to mask his own odor enabled him to reach his stand without spooking the buck and may have attracted the animal. He freely admits that fox scent doesn't always work, but

Wyman's basic hunting method is to move very slowly from one natural hide to another. Almost any cover will do, even a tree with low branches to break up the hunter's outline (top). He often whistles to stop a moving deer for an easy shot (above). To mask human odor, he attaches sheepskin pads soaked in fox urine to his boots.

Photograph by the author

in this case and in many others, it worked well. But Otis often points out that other things are more important.

"Awareness is the main secret of successful deer hunting," Wyman told me and cited a negative example.

"I was making a terrible racket dragging a deer out of the woods. I pulled it a ways and then went back for my shotgun. I did that several times. Then I saw another hunter and got within 200 feet of him before he saw me. He should have heard me or seen me first since he was well hidden. You won't kill a deer if you're not paying attention."

Otis pays attention to every detail, and he remembers every hunt in detail. He took his first deer on November 17, 1938. He can tell you that it happened at 3 p.m. He and a buddy were trapping in northern Minnesota. It was his first time in the big woods. To this day he remembers the swamp, picking his way through tag alders and cattails, the small island covered with quaking aspens, and the 15-point deer that was unable to locate Otis because the crosswind blew his scent away.

Wyman also recalls how green he was. Everybody told him that if you castrate a buck right after you kill it, the meat never tastes strong, but he had forgotten his knife. He pulled, he twisted. Then he realized that he was trying to tear a buckskin bag, and he gave up. The deer was gutted later, and the meat was fine. Two lessons were etched in his mind: Pay attention to wind direction and don't believe everything old-time deer hunters tell you.

Another trait that helps Otis to do his own thinking is his natural enthusiasm. Whether it's business, or the business of deer hunting, it's a fascinating game to him. He competes. He thinks. He schemes. He's downright gleeful when he finds a better way, and he knows just as much about hunters as he knows about deer.

"If you tell most hunters about using fox scent, they think it's the only thing they need to know," he says. "They will walk into the woods, any old place, and expect a buck to come along. When one doesn't, they'll say using fox scent is all bull."

Wyman usually does some preseason scouting because he enjoys it, but he doesn't regard it as essential, especially if he knows the area where he intends to hunt. Deer use the same kind of habitat year after year. Even in strange territory, a good hunter should be able to recognize good deer cover. Otis killed his biggest deer, a 13-point buck, the first time he hunted a new area in Missouri.

One important thing he does is to get farther away from the road than he thinks the average hunter is willing to drag a deer. Then he crosses one more ridge or stream.

From that moment, he constantly asks himself, "Where would I be if I were a deer and I knew hunters were in the woods?"

The answer to that is based mainly on two variables—weather and terrain. In reasonably good weather, deer often sneak off to hills and ridges where they can watch for danger coming from all directions. Sometimes three or four deer will bed down at a vantage point with each watching a portion of the countryside. Wyman studies the high places for locations that provide three or four escape routes. When he also finds heavy cover in that type of location, he has found deer. If food is nearby, the location is perfect.

During inclement weather deer move off exposed locations. Although their coats are so well insulated that they can bed down in snow without melting it, deer usually drop down between ridges during bad weather or last out storms in very thick cover of valleys. They don't like to be pelted by rain or sleet. They may bed or stand behind a screen of honeysuckle, in a brushy thicket, or sometimes they merely stand beside a tree when the weather is bad.

"Rainy days are ideal for hunting," says Otis. "There's so much noise you can forget about the little sounds you make, and your scent isn't likely to reach the deer. All you have to do is be all eyes. If deer are disturbed in a rain, they don't move far before they settle down again."

Late in a recent season, the 20° temperatures and a mild sleet storm forced most hunters to give up, but Otis had seen tracks going up a hollow and he felt the deer would be weathering out the storm between the two ridges. The wind was from the northwest, so that Otis could sneak along the top of the southeast ridge. He couldn't stay on its wooded top because the high humidity and strong wind intensified the bitter cold of the sleet, but at least the sleet masked the sounds he made as he moved along below the crest on the sheltered southeast side. Every 15 yards or so he eased up to look over the top.

Almost at the head of the hollow, after three quarters of a mile of agonizing caution and just as all chances of finding the deer were about to run out, there they were, four of them, low on the opposite ridge. They were at least 125 yards away. He took careful aim. The bead of the automatic he was using at the time almost covered the deer. He made a judgment, raised the muzzle, and slowly pulled the trigger. The shotgun didn't fire. Perhaps the cold had stiffened the lubrication. Maybe moisture had frozen in the mechanism. Otis aimed and pulled again. The shotgun boomed, but he had jerked too hard and missed. The semiautomatic didn't eject the empty. Trying to eject it manually with numb fingers, his glove caught in front of the sliding bolt and had to be pulled out. During the confusion three deer scattered, leaving one uncertain doe looking around for the danger.

It was the last chance of the season. Otis fired, and the doe slowly bounded off, but she didn't go far. When Wyman field-dressed her, he cut a numb finger on a broken rib. The German Brenneke slug had gone all the way through the deer at 125 yards! That was when Otis decided to buy a bolt-action shotgun with a barrel especially made for slugs and have a 4X scope mounted on it for accurate sighting at 100 yards. His slugs group in three to four-inch circles at that range. Nowadays he seldom fires at a longer range, and he advises hunters who use ordinary shotguns without special slug barrels and scopes to keep their shots under 80 yards or so.

By hunting, Otis doesn't mean finding a deer trail and perching in a tree stand all day to watch it. He will spend time in a natural hide, but if deer don't show up in reasonable time he goes looking for them.

Few hunters kill deer by still-hunting, but Wyman is quite successful. Otis doesn't stalk in the sense of knowing where an animal is and trying to approach it stealthily. He actually hunts from hundreds of different natural blinds such as blowdowns by moving quietly from one hide to another.

Before moving he plans where the next hide will be—behind a bush, blowdown, boulder, vines, a tree—anything that will break up his outline and isn't more than three to five *steps* away. Then he plans the steps one by one—around sticks that would pop, over moss because it is quiet, up the moist bed of a dry wash. If the forest floor is noisy, he moves when other noises begin. A crow cawing, a jet plane passing, a blue jay screaming make his own low rustling less noticeable.

At each new hide, Wyman waits at least 10 times as long as he spent getting there from the last hide. "If you're standing still and the deer is moving," he says, "you see the deer. If the deer is still and you are moving, the deer almost always sees you."

The direction of Wyman's slow, tedious travel is east in the morning and west in the afternoon, except when the wind would carry his scent ahead. He pulls his cap down low to keep the bright light out of his eyes and moves into the sun because he believes deer prefer the sun at their backs.

Where to hunt also depends upon time of day and weather. Otis points out that the weather influences where the deer will be (high or low) and time of day makes a difference in air currents, especially on sunny, calm days. Warming air (in the morning) rises, so it's necessary to be on high ground to prevent human scent from wafting up to the deer. Cooling air (later in the day) descends, so keep to low ground.

Taking a stand or moving with nothing to break up one's outline is a sure way for a hunter to reveal himself to deer, and Wyman feels this is especially critical when topping a ridge. When Otis looks over a ridge, he stops with his eyes just above the crest and scans the top of the next ridge. Then he moves up just a little so he can see farther down the opposite slope. He works upward very gradually until he can see the entire ridge, the hollow, and the other side of the hogback he's standing on.

Rubs reveal the presence of deer, but bucks don't return to them. Scrapes are different. Bucks make several and check them at regular intervals for does. However, Otis has never seen big old bucks checking scrapes, so he believes they do it at night. Anyhow, Wyman isn't inclined to wait very long in any one place.

When in the woods, Otis avoids talking to anyone. A deer's big ears can hear humans talking a mile away.

"If a deer zeros in on you with two of his senses," Otis says, "he has you located. With just one of his senses he may be uncertain. So if you spook a deer and it's moving away, take a chance and whistle sharply. More often than not, the deer will stop and try to pinpoint the source of the sound."

Otis has found that he often sees deer where there are a lot of gray squirrels. Both animals eat nuts, so Otis pays a lot of attention to stands of nut-bearing trees. Not as obvious is the fact that gray squirrels are active early in the morning and late in the evening and prefer calm, warm days for foraging. Deer do too, so when you see a lot of squirrels look for deer.

"One more rule I used to observe all the time is never to cross a deer trail or walk along one," Otis told me.

"Used to observe?" I asked.

"Yes," Otis answered. "When deer smell you they turn around and go back, or they leave the trail. But now that my friends and I have been using fox scent, we've found it often helps to cross their trails. In fact, it has become a new way of hunting. We now watch our backtrails almost as carefully as we look ahead."

To illustrate the importance of using scent, Otis told me about Harold Delashmit who encountered a problem while bowhunting. One excellent stand was inaccessible without crossing a deer trail. Available commercial scents didn't mask human smell well enough, and neither did crushed acorns. The deer would smell Delashmit and turn back.

Finally, Delashmit doused fox urine on patches of coon skin (hair side down), tied them to his boots, and walked through known good deer territory, crossing the trail, to the stand. Before long a doe was following along the ridge, sniffing Delashmit's tracks. Presently, a second doe came along smelling the trail. The bigger of the two approached within 100 feet, and Delashmit made the shot.

Otis made sheepskin pads, doused them with fox scent, and tied them to the insteps of his boots. He walked along the top of a ridge late one afternoon. The downdrafts would carry the scent to any deer below him. One deer picked up the trail and followed the ridge, walking in Wyman's footsteps. It, too, came within 100 feet.

Adding more scent to the pads on the bottoms of his insteps about every mile seems to be enough to mask human smell and lay an attractive trail, Otis told me. He wound up his discussion of deer hunting by emphasizing again the fact that using red-fox scent won't transform an inept hunter into a great deerslayer. "You have to do everything else right too," he told me. That's no cinch.–*Larry Mueller.*

The Deer of December

December 8, during a recent Michigan deer season. There wasn't a cloud in the sky, the mercury barely registered above zero, and the wind intensified the cold. The day wasn't what many deer hunters would consider ideal, but we knew better.

Dave Raikko and my brother Bruce were hunting with muzzleloading rifles. I had my bow and a quiver full of arrows. We live in Marquette, Michigan, and were hunting about 70 miles south of there. Our plan that morning was to regroup about noon—if we could withstand the cold that long. As it turned out, it wasn't necessary to post until the prearranged time.

About 10:20 I heard Dave shoot. Minutes later a doe came bounding past my stand from Dave's direction. She was alone, so I assumed that Dave got the buck that was probably with her. When the doe passed my tree stand at about 20 yards, I released an arrow that just missed her. I climbed down to retrieve my arrow, then went to check on Dave, expecting to find him standing over a buck.

Unfortunately that was not the case. The round ball from Dave's .50-caliber Hawken had simply grazed the eight-point buck's belly. We found white hair on the snow, but no blood. After tracking the animal several hundred yards we decided he was unhurt. The buck separated from the doe after the shot, which is why I didn't see him.

Dave explained that he hurried the 50-yard shot at the walking buck because the doe was almost in his lap. He was concerned about the doe detecting him and spooking the buck, but he was mentally kicking himself afterward for not waiting. The buck trotted past Dave in the open at about 20 yards after he emptied his rifle.

While we were checking the tracks of the buck Dave shot at, a shot sounded from Bruce's direction. I thought it had to be him because we didn't see any signs of other hunters. My watch read 10:40.

Bruce met us when we drove up a half hour later.

"How big?" I asked when he walked up.

A smile flashed across his face as he answered, "Six points."

Bruce said he dumped the buck at about 40 yards. The ball from his rifle, also a .50-caliber Hawken, hit both heart and lungs. That buck was the tenth whitetail my brother saw that morning. Dave saw four other deer besides the buck and doe.

Deer hunting in Michigan is legal during the last three months of the year, with seasons for bow and arrow, firearms, and muzzleloaders. If I could hunt during only one of those months, I would choose December. Days like the one described are part of the reason why.

Bruce and I hunted hard during the regular gun season that fall, and neither of us filled a tag. My brother saw only one buck during the season, and he missed it. I thought I saw what might have been antlers on one animal, but it vanished before I could be sure of it. By the end of November it would have been easy to believe that few bucks were left in the area we hunt, but we knew better.

The eighth was our first day of hunting for December, and two of us had good chances within 20 minutes of each other. What a difference. I'll take that kind of action any day. This kind of action in December is not unusual.

Two major factors increase the vulnerability of bucks in December. The rut is usually over and winter is rapidly approaching. Dominant bucks often use up much of their fat reserves during the breeding season, and in an effort to regain weight before winter sets in they spend a lot of time feeding. Bucks seem to know instinctively that quality food may be in short supply during the months ahead, so they eat all they can while they can.

Whitetails also move from summer to winter range during this time. Winter quarters are referred to as yards in the northern portion of the deer range. Yards vary in size but usually encompass expansive swamps. Studies have shown that deer travel as much as 20 miles, and sometimes more, between some summer and winter ranges on the Upper Peninsula. These deer use the same routes every year. Whitetails aren't normally thought of as migratory, but they are to some extent in parts of the Midwest.

Even in the southern half of the Midwest, where whitetails don't actually yard, they will concentrate in thick cover, such as river bottoms and swamps. In these areas the shift from summer to winter quarters may involve only one to several miles.

Between heavy feeding and the change in habitat, bucks as well as does are very active during December. This activity often results in bucks leaving the hiding places they occupied during earlier seasons. And they seem to move more freely during daylight hours than they do earlier in the fall, perhaps because there are fewer hunters afield. All of these factors boost the odds of December deer hunters seeing plenty of game.

The scarcity of hunters is another reason why I like to hunt deer in December. By then some hunters have filled their tags, others who failed to score have had their fill of hunting, and there are some who have tags to fill and would like to hunt but are scared off by December weather. The cold is bearable for those who dress for it though.

I have found stand hunting to be most productive late in the season because the deer are generally active. I usually spend mornings and early afternoons posted along migration routes. My evening stands are in or near feeding areas. Occasionally I post along a runway between feeding and bedding areas before dawn in an effort to intercept animals that leave feeding grounds.

Photograph by the author

With the rut over and winter rapidly approaching, bucks become much more vulnerable.

The three of us were watching migration trails the morning Bruce nailed the six-pointer with his muzzleloader. Every year deer in that area use the same trails when traveling from summer to winter range. It took time and effort for us to pinpoint the routes, but any hunter can do the same in his or her area.

Simply find an area where deer winter, then go around the perimeter of it looking for well-used runways heading into it. Hunters who aren't familiar with places used by deer during the winter usually can get reliable information from local wildlife biologists or conservation officers.

In early December much of the movement on migration trails in upper Michigan occurs during darkness, immediately following gun season. Deer are still jumpy as a result of heavy hunting pressure. Early morning is the best time to see a buck then.

However, after about a week with little or no hunting pressure, coupled with winter-like weather, whitetails start developing typical December movement patterns. Then migration trails are used most heavily between 9 a.m. and 2 or 3 p.m. The pattern probably is similar in other Midwestern states.

You'll need a lot of clothes to make sitting comfortable during December. Temperatures often dip below zero. The best thing to do is dress in layers. I generally wear two pair of long underwear on both top and bottom, unless temperatures will be at least 10 above all day. A pair of jeans and heavy wool pants go on over long johns.

On top I usually wear a flannel shirt over the underwear. I slip two or three sweat shirts or sweaters over the shirt and I top off the outfit with a pair of white coveralls for camouflage. There is almost always snow on the ground in upper Michigan by December. If I'm hunting with a muzzleloader, I wear an orange-colored hat as required by Michigan law. A camouflage cap goes on my head when bowhunting. I avoid using ear flaps or hoods while deer hunting because they reduce my hearing.

Each garment should be large enough to accommodate underlying layers without restricting movement. For this reason, sweat shirts, wool pants, and coveralls should be purchased in large sizes. The same goes for boots. I use the sorel-type with felt liners. The boots I wear in December are one or two sizes larger than my feet. This enables me to wear three to five pairs of heavy socks. Even then, feet tend to chill faster than the body. Gloved hands are kept in pockets whenever possible until an opportunity for a shot presents itself.

Some bucks lose their antlers during the early part of the month. Most trophy bucks hang onto their headgear until late December, but not always.

A few bucks drop their antlers during late November and early December in upper Michigan. Some probably lose their racks about that time every year, which reduces the number of potential targets for hunters limited to bucks only. Antler loss is probably delayed farther south in the Midwest.

Some of the highest concentrations of bucks I have seen while hunting in December have been in the vicinity of fresh cuttings. Tops of felled trees, especially those of white cedar, contain plenty of nutritious browse that antlered whitetails really go for. Trails leading into cuttings, as well as to other feeding areas such as apple orchards are the places to watch during afternoons and evenings.–***Richard P. Smith.***

Swamped by Trophy Bucks

I'd bet 10 to 1 there are at least 20 whitetail bucks within a 50-mile radius of my home that have racks good enough to be listed in the Pope and Young or Boone and Crockett record books. I live near Bay City, Michigan, not far from the other big cities of Flint and Saginaw and less than 100 miles from Detroit.

There are millions of people in this area, but there are also farmlands and swamps that produce some of the nation's finest trophy whitetails. They are so smart, and so used to coping with the activities of humans, that most hunters never see them.

In 1976 I shot a nontypical whitetail that scored 238 2/8 points. It won the first award at the Seventeenth North American Big Game Awards program in 1980. It was the best nontypical whitetail taken in North America during the previous three years, and it's the best ever taken in Michigan.

I shot that buck about 9 miles from my home. There's another buck as good or better than him even closer. He has an 18-point rack. He has outsmarted me for two years, but I think I'll get him. There's a 16-pointer in the same area. I'm confident I could take that buck with my rifle, but I'm determined to get him with a bow.

I'm 32, but I decided 10 years ago not to shoot any bucks with a rifle unless I got chances at really outstanding trophies. I have head-and-shoulder mounts of 11 of my bucks now, and a lot of them were taken with arrows.

The main reason I get big bucks is that I hunt deer full time for two to three months every fall. All that time without earning a paycheck produces some financial problems because I work as a carpenter, but my wife Kay doesn't say anything. We lived together for 1 1/2 years before marrying, so she knew what she was getting into.

I used to hunt everything in season years ago, but now I concentrate exclusively on Michigan deer. I'd love to be able to hunt other big game in Western states or Alaska, but I can't afford to. Anyway, I'm obsessed with trophy whitetail bucks. And when you hunt them as much as I do, you're bound to learn some strange things about deer behavior. Here's an example.

In 1972, Rick Havercamp and I were bowhunting along a bank of the Saginaw River on a cold but sunny afternoon in late December. The 300-yard-wide river had recently frozen over. Rick was close to the shore, I was a few yards up the bank in some brush. Suddenly my partner said, "Get down, there's a whole herd of deer running out there on the ice. They might come across. Get ready, here they come!"

I looked out there and saw about 40 deer. There were at least 10 bucks, and the whole herd was coming dead on. I nocked an arrow on the string of my 70-pound Jennings compound bow, then squatted down.

As the deer got close to our side of the river they began breaking through the shoreline ice. I don't know if they saw us, but for some reason they veered to our left and crashed into a cattail marsh about 500 yards long. The going was tough for those deer. I figured if I ran along the bank at full speed I could get to the end of the marsh before the deer did, and that I could intercept them as they came out.

I was puffing hard by the time I got there, but I knew right away that I was ahead of the herd. I could hear the deer breaking ice and banging through dead cattail stalks. Then the commotion suddenly stopped. About half an hour passed without my hearing a sound. I couldn't figure out what was going on, so I walked back to confer with Rick.

I met him half way around the marsh. He was as confused as I was.

"I'll climb a tree and see what's going on," he said.

When he got up the tree and looked, he said, "Hard to believe. They're all out there, standing still as statues. Some of 'em are through the ice, up to their chests in water. There's a couple of really huge bucks. What're we going to do?"

"I'll give you 10 minutes to get back to where they ran into the cattails," I answered. "Then I'm going back to the other end and drive those deer back your way. If that ice is thick enough to support the deer it's thick enough to hold me."

When I returned to the far end of the marsh I cautiously tested the ice near shore. It seemed OK, so I took off. I covered about 50 feet, then I dropped through that ice as suddenly as if I'd walked off a plank. My boots hit the mucky bottom about 3 feet down, but I was already making my move to get out of there.

I rolled up onto the ice at the edge of the hole I'd made, and the whole edge broke off. I was soaked by the time I made my next roll, and again the edge gave way. I broke through once more, and then I found ice that supported me. By the time I reached the shoreline I was covered with black muck and marsh weeds.

I had lost all concern for deer, then I suddenly heard loud noises. It dawned on me that all those deer were crashing through the marsh again, and they were coming straight toward me. I nocked an arrow and squatted low in a kneeling position on the edge of the wall of cattails, and shook my head when I realized that, almost unbelievably, I was seconds away from having a whole herd of whitetails in my lap.

Photograph by John O. Cartier

Smart old bucks in heavily-hunted farm country soon learn to go where most hunters won't or can't go. That's where I hunt, and that's where I shot a record-book whitetail—right in the middle of one of the most heavily populated parts of North America.

The first deer out was a doe. She broke through the cattails about 10 feet to my left, stared wild-eyed at me, then bolted up the bank. Another doe came out just to my right and did the same thing. Now the crashing diminished. Somehow the rest of the deer had been alerted that those two does had run into something that wasn't right.

Then I spotted movement above the cattails a few yards in front of me. A rack of antlers was moving slowly toward me. I couldn't see any part of the buck except his 10-point rack, but it was obvious what was going on. That buck wasn't about to run out of the marsh as the does had done. He was going to peer over the edge of the cattails to see what the problem was.

It seemed like that deer's neck was stretched out 5 feet when it popped into view at a range of about 3 yards. I was already at full draw, and I drove my arrow dead center into the white spot on his throat. When I had that head mounted I told the taxidermist to mount it with the neck straight out, exactly as I'd first seen it.

That hunt taught me one of the most important buck-hunting lessons I've learned. When I broke through the ice and began floundering about, I was producing exactly the same sounds as the deer were making when they broke through. They assumed that I was a deer making my escape through that end of the marsh. So on they came, intending to use the same escape route.

Since a deer's range of vision in thick cattails is only a few yards, you can actually walk or wade right up to a buck because the sounds you make won't seem unnatural to the animal. An important part of the equation is that smart bucks in heavily hunted farm country soon learn to go where most hunters won't go. Those places are swamps, the rougher the better. If you hunt whitetails, and you have thick cattail swamps in your area, you can bet that they hold a lot of deer.

One of the best bucks I've taken out of a cattail marsh was an 11-pointer I arrowed in 1979. Though it was a great rack, it wasn't nearly as impressive as one belonging to another buck in the same herd. The inside spread of the 11-pointer's antlers measures 19½ inches. I saw both bucks only moments apart, and I'd bet everything I own that the bigger buck's antlers have a 23-inch inside spread.

It was windy and clear that day, but the 20° temperature made for colder than usual December hunting. Though there were traces of snow on the ground, there was none on trees or cattails. That called for brown camouflage outer wear, including a brown face mask. I usually wear camouflage face grease, but when it gets so cold that makeup would freeze, I wear masks.

When I go with a bow I'm camouflaged completely according to weather conditions. Early in the season, when the foliage and ground is green, I use green camo. Later I switch to brown. If there's lots of snow I'm dressed in white, and so is my archery tackle.

I began that hunt by walking up to a big marsh and climbing a sloping deadfall in the oak bottomlands that edged the cattails. I immediately spotted two big racks. They seemed to be floating above the stalks only 60 yards away. I've seen similar sights several times. Deer will stand in water for hours without moving. You won't see most of them because the cattails completely hide their bodies. But when you get a buck that's not alerted—when he's not trying to conceal his antlers—his rack will be above the marsh terrain when he's standing.

I slithered down the deadfall, then stalked along the edge of the cattails to a spot that was about even with those bucks. There I eased up another deadfall, just far enough to see one of the bucks. He was walking slowly down the marsh, but he was only about 30 yards out in the cattails. Again I began sneaking along the edge of the marsh. I wanted to get ahead of him before I began wading into the swamp.

Right then that enormous buck—the biggest one I've ever seen—stood up in the cattails 20 yards from me.

He was looking dead away, but he quickly turned his head and looked right at me. Though I was perfectly camouflaged, and still as a stone, he knew something wasn't right. Our little game lasted at least 30 seconds. I don't think he ever figured out what I was, but he whirled and bounded out of range before I could shoot.

I stalked on for 25 yards and stepped up on another of the maze of sloping deadfalls that littered the edge of this marsh. I spotted the huge buck I'd spooked. He was more than 100 yards away, standing near the other side of the cattails and looking back. The two bucks I'd originally spotted were 40 yards straight out in front of me. They didn't seem nervous.

When I hunt these marshes I always wear hip boots or waders, depending on the water's depth. I stepped into the cattails and began wading without making any attempt to conceal the sounds of my approach. When I figured I was about 20 yards from the closest and largest buck, I pulled my arrow to full draw in the compound bow and kept right on wading. At a range of about 17 yards I saw his shoulder through the maze of cattails. I picked out his heart area and drove my Bear Razorhead right into it. He bolted, but died on his feet.

I sincerely feel that a bow in the hands of an expert is almost as deadly as a rifle. If I can get within 40 yards of a buck I can kill him because I can hit a grapefruit-size target every shot at that range. I can do that only because of dedicated practice. It's extremely unusual if I don't practice shooting arrows at least an hour every day.

I learned how to hunt on my own. My folks were divorced, but I lived with my mother on 15 acres of land near Kawkawlin where I live now. Even when I was a little kid I was out in the woods most of my free time, studying birds and animals and shooting arrows or my BB gun.

I shot my first buck, a spikehorn, when I was 14. I didn't know much of anything about deer hunting then. I just blundered into the little buck in a pine plantation and knocked him flat with my grandfather's .300 Savage.

Though I bowhunted deer for several years I didn't get one until I was 18. He was a five-pointer. I've taken bigger bucks with arrows every year since. A few years ago, when it became legal for Michigan hunters to take a deer with a bow and another with a gun, I've always scored on another big buck with my .30/06 sporterized Enfield.

I used that rifle to shoot an 11-pointer in his bed in 1975. Rick Havercamp was with me that day too. He's 36, and a carpenter. We were in an area 3 miles across, that borders the Au Sable River near Cook Dam. It's laced with beaver ponds, tag alders, and muck.

You have to wear hip boots or waders to get in there, and even then you usually get wet because the mucky bottoms are so treacherous. Every year I have to chop out trails with a machete because there's no way I could find my way in or out of that place in darkness. I throw the chopped off alder branches in muddy places that would be impassable without their support.

The middle of that place is so rough I've never seen another hunter in it. That's why it draws deer like a magnet.

There had been a blizzard the

day before that had left a foot of snow on the ground, but there were a million stars in a clear sky when Rick dropped me off near one edge of the swamp. His plan was to drive around to the opposite side and hunt in from there.

I took a stand on an island, and I sat there until a forkhorn and six does browsed to within 25 feet of me. The little buck finally saw me and panicked. He charged into brush and through some skim ice, and he took the does with him. They made such a racket I decided to go still-hunting.

Because of the recent blizzard, every deer track I found was fresh. When I came upon a set of enormous tracks I began following them. I stayed on that track for five hours, taking a few steps at a time and then stopping to inspect the area ahead. I'd squat and bend to look under branches, around clumps, and behind deadfalls.

Because the snow was deep and soft my extremely slow progress was almost soundless. Once I almost walked up to a doe. When about 20 feet separated us she jumped out of her bed and crashed into a thick stand of snowladen cedars. She produced a miniature blizzard of sun-sparkling snow when she blitzed through those trees. As time passed I jumped several deer, including an eight-pointer. It was impossible not to surprise at least some deer; there were deer tracks all over. It was a job to keep the tracks I was following separate from the rest.

Finally, during one of my staring-ahead sessions, I saw a brown spot 40 yards to my right. I figured it was a dead cedar stump, but I turned up my 3X-to-9X Redfield scope to full power for a closer look. I still couldn't tell if the spot was a deer or a stump, so I inched forward a couple of yards. Another look through the scope proved nothing. I just couldn't identify any part of a deer. Then the stump suddenly became a deer and shook snow off its body like a dog shakes off water.

I had to crawl a couple of yards to my left before a massive rack suddenly popped into focus. I broke the buck's back with a 180-grain handloaded slug. When my rifle went off that place erupted deer. They seemed to be rushing off in all directions. Rick, who was a few hundred yards away at the time, said later, "After you shot I had deer running by me for five minutes."

A different kind of stalk produced my award-winning buck. John Miller, another hunting buddy (he's 29 and works in construction) saw the buck just after the 1976 archery deer season opened. The buck was on a ridge eating acorns when John saw him, and he figured the buck was working toward a runway leading down into a stand of tag alders. John guessed correctly, but it was almost dark when the buck went by his stand. He missed his shot, but he sure got excited. He was waiting at my home when I returned from hunting.

"Paul, that buck is unreal," he said. "I couldn't get a good look at him, but he's got a rack that's so wide it looks preposterous. He's got at least 12 points, maybe twice that many. The antlers are so massive I just couldn't believe what I was looking at. I overshot him because he was closer than I thought. When my arrow hit a rock I could see sparks fly, that's how dark it was."

John and I were back in the area before dawn the next morning. He wanted to be on stand near the oak ridge, but I had a different idea. I figured that if the buck went into a stand of alders at night there was no way he wanted to stay in them. I assumed he would go through the alders, then cross a road and go down into a winter wheatfield that edged another stand of alders. So I went down in there and picked a stand near a runway.

I hunted that area for five straight days and never saw a deer, the worst run of bad luck I've ever had. Miller saw several deer every day, but no big bucks. We finally got disgusted and went to Michigan's Upper Peninsula (U.P.) for two weeks of bowhunting.

When we got back, an ironworker friend told me that his two boys jumped the giant buck in a field of weeds while they were pheasant hunting. He said the animal's rack was so big it wouldn't fit through a doorway. But what really shook me was that the kids had jumped the buck in the same area where I'd been hunting him. John and I were back on our stands the next morning.

I hunted three days without seeing a deer, but I found a clump of tag alders and willows that were ripped and shredded from near the ground to eye level. It was by far the biggest buck rub I've ever seen. I wondered aloud how many points the buck must have to do that kind of damage.

The next morning I saw three does. They went into a jungle of alders, so I decided to leave my stand and follow them. About an hour later I jumped that buck 40 yards ahead of me.

When the buck leaped up his antlers slammed into a maze of branches thick enough to stop his up and forward motion. He was in a half-standing position, and he was actually trying to pull those trees out of the ground. The muscles in his hindquarters were standing out like whipcords, but my attention was riveted on his massive and almost pure white antlers. I was so startled that the whole show was over before I could nock an arrow. The buck dropped low, then bolted away.

I saw him once more before I got him, and that time he almost ran over me. We came as close to a full-speed collision as you can get. If he had hit me he probably would have put me in the hospital, or worse.

It was Halloween, cloudy and very foggy. I was on a stand in some weeds edging a drainage ditch about 6 feet deep. John got bored with the miserable, wet morning before I did, so he decided to drive a cornfield toward me. A stubblefield about 100 yards wide separated my position from the standing corn. I knew John was in the corn, but I didn't think anything unusual was happening until he suddenly yelled, "Here he comes!"

I heard the buck before I saw him. He was crashing through cornstalks and flattening them as he ran. He burst out into the stubblefield and bolted for a corner in the drainage ditch 150 yards to my left. Spray flew as he hit shallow water. Then he disappeared and everything became still. I knew there was a runway down there, and I was positive he used it to get into a thick stand of alders.

So I stood up, put my quiver on my bow, put the arrow I had nocked in the quiver, and jumped across the water in the ditch. One more step would put me on top of the ditch and on level ground. To understand what happened next you must know that the buck did not go down the runway as I assumed he would. Instead, he jumped back up on the ditch's bank and ran straight toward me at full speed. He was not aware of my presence, and I was sure he was gone. When I took that last step out of the ditch, I popped up into his vision and route of travel at point-blank range.

The first thing I saw was the buck hunching up as he slammed on the brakes. All his legs were stiff, and he was jamming his hooves into the soft ground like spears. I could have hit him with the tip of my bow, but I was so startled, I couldn't move. He reacted like a giant coiled spring. He seemed to bounce backward and hit the ground, bounce again as he whirled toward the ditch, then bounce across it into some willows. He was gone before I could even think about reaching for an arrow.

John had watched the whole episode from 100 yards away. He was still dumfounded when he ran up to me.

"I couldn't believe what I was watching," he said. "I saw him change course at the corner of the ditch, and I knew he was going to run right past you. I figured that buck was as good as dead. Then I saw you stand up and put your arrow back in your quiver. I just groaned when I realized what was happening."

I kept hunting the buck for almost two weeks without seeing him again. By now it was time to head for the U.P. for the rifle season. Every fall, 13 of us hunt from a cabin there. It's the highlight of the year for all of us. I couldn't get that big white-racked buck out of my mind, but I figured I'd get him in December with my bow.

I usually stay at the cabin through November, but this time I went home for Thanksgiving, mostly because it would give me three days to try for that buck with my rifle.

John Miller and I hunted the next morning in pouring rain. We went home about noon, got out of our sopping clothes, then headed out again about 4 p.m. I was about 700 yards from my stand near the winter wheatfield when I spotted something out of place in the wheat. Visibility was poor because of the rain. My first thought was that somebody had put an old junk car out there because the thing I'd spotted resembled a car bumper. I checked it out with my scope. The car bumper immediately turned into the enormous white antlers of my giant buck. I had missed seeing his body because it was dark with the rain and blended in almost perfectly with a background of wet and dark alders.

I was in a field of weeds about 4 feet high. I immediately dropped down out of the buck's sight. I could close the distance by 200 yards just by hunching over and running through the tall weeds to the edge of a stubblefield. The buck hadn't moved much during the few moments it took me to reach the foot-high stubble. He appeared to be grazing without any hint of fear, so I rested a minute to control my gasping breath.

Then I flattened out in the mud and began crawling. I knew if I could make it through the 300 yards of stubble I'd be within a shooting range of about 200 yards. If he detected me sooner, I'd have to shoot when he began running.

I hadn't crawled far when I found that the buck was going through a precise routine. He'd graze for a few seconds, then jerk his head up fast. He'd look straight ahead, then inspect things to his right for another few seconds, turn his head left and do the same thing, then conclude his check for danger by craning his neck around to the side and looking straight to his rear. After that he'd take two steps forward, lower his head and resume grazing. He did the same thing every time.

I had a definite advantage now. I timed my crawling periods to start when he lowered his head, and to end just as he jerked it upright. When I got to the end of the stubble I wiped my scope clean of water and pieces of weeds and seeds. Then I waited to make one last move that would give me a wide-open shot.

When his head went down again I made a complete roll from the stubble into the very short wheat and then spread out into the typical prone shooting position. My 180-grain bullet broke his back and put him down instantly.

The excitement of such a stalk exhausts you as much as the exertion. By the time I ran full speed to the deer I could hardly breathe. I was gulping for air. I finally managed to tape the outside spread of the rack at 26½ inches, and then I tried counting antler points. I kept losing count, but I finally counted 31. By that time, John was running onto the scene. From over 100 yards away he yelled, "Did you get him?"

"Yeah, I got him. I finally got him!"

"Does he have more than 12 points?"

"John, he's got more than that on one side."

When John got to me he was so happy he was laughing. I was still in a state of shock. I couldn't think of anything appropriate to say, so I started grinning and laughing too. We stood there in the rain, staring at those fantastic antlers and laughing our tensions away.–***Paul Mickey.***

A Compact Deer Hound for Dixie

Deer and hounds are as much a part of the Southern outdoor tradition as dove perleau and Jack Daniel's. Hounds not only make hunting the thick brier hills and swamps far more productive, they add tremendously to the spirit of the chase. The explosion of a pack in a creek bottom on a still, foggy morning sets any hunter's blood boiling.

Hound music sings to something older than the tradition of hunting in the South, harking back to a time when the dogs and the men were still half wild, and when the hunt meant life or death to both hunters and hunted. Large, powerful, long-winded and strong-throated dogs made the difference between eating and going hungry. The season was always open, there were no bag limits, and the woods were endless; good hounds could feed both themselves and their masters yearround. The Walkers, Triggs, Plotts and Redbones became the favorites of generations of woodsmen, praised from Florida to the Carolinas as the finest hunting machines alive.

For many hunters they still are. But the days of the big woods and the endless seasons are gone forever. The big hounds are ever more expensive to feed and kennel, and suitable training areas shrink each year. Like the big luxury automobile, the large hound is becoming less economical and practical.

Fortunately, a "fuel-efficient" compact is available. A growing number of Southern deer hunters have found this new champion easier to feed, keep, train, hunt with and perhaps (keep this to a whisper around confirmed Walker men) even more productive than today's large dogs. It's no new, exotic or imported breed. It's the most familiar hunting dog in America—the stubby-legged, friendly little critter better known as *Peanuts*'s Snoopy than as a serious big-game hound—the ubiquitous beagle.

But the beagle that is gaining the American Kennel Club's attention is a far cry from the sometimes pudgy and lethargic backyard beagle most of us know. Florida breeder Frank Pemble and other hunting-dog enthusiasts in the South have been working hard to earn the recognition given by AKC field trials for a strain of beagles they classify simply as gundog beagles. These tough, rangy little animals have gigantic voices, finetuned noses and a hunting instinct so strong that they can switch from deer to rabbits to foxes to bobcats and back again without missing a track. Recognition for this strain is starting to come. AKC recently acknowledged the Deep South Beagle Gundog Federation.

Pemble, a foliage farmer who hunted with Walkers for 30 years before switching to beagles, notes that the little hounds cost only about one-fourth as much to keep as traditional deerhounds.

"Of course," Pemble wryly points out, "it didn't cost me much to feed my Walkers during the hunting season, because most of the time they were lost." The larger dogs' speed and range often took them so far into the woods that they were days getting back out.

Pemble hunts both the "big Scrub" area of Ocala National Forest in central Florida and the vast lowlands just north of the Georgia-Florida border. In both regions the short legs of his 13-inch beagles are the perfect length for scooting under the palmetto bushes and briar tangles that make the going tough for larger hounds.

"When a deer takes off for a swim, say across the St. Mary's River," Pemble says, "the big hounds go right with him, and that's the last you see of them, maybe for a week. The beagles stop at the shore, backtrack out to where you put them on track, and can be picked up for another chase that same day. We often run four or five races in a single day, while a Walker pack is likely to go off on one long run that takes them clear into the next county."

Beagles are also a lot more compliant than many hardheaded hounds. They can be called off a trail or caught by standers if the deer turns out to be a doe or fawn. Then the beagles can be put on another trail more likely to have horns at the end. This is usually a tough proposition with fast, headstrong dogs. But using beagles, Pemble and his companions regularly outhunt other dog men in their hunting areas, sometimes by a margin of four deer to one.

Beagles come in a wide variety of bloodlines, resulting in various sizes, strengths and weaknesses. The so-called "hare-hound" beagle of the Northeast is characteristically fast-trailing, slender, long-legged and long-winded, capable of trailing a snowshoe hare's giant leaps for hours without tiring. "Cottontail beagles" tend to be smaller, stockier and usually slower and more precise at chasing the cottontail rabbits of the Midwest and South. "Brace trial" beagles, of the cottontail class, are bred to work slowly each track put down by a bunny. These dogs bark the whole way, and have earned the nickname "walkie talkies."

The gundog beagle being developed by Pemble and others of the federation, is more closely related to the hare hound than to the brace trial beagle. The gundog beagle is long-winded, has good speed, excellent cold trailing ability and a powerful voice. And though he's a natural cottontail specialist, he has a particular love for the scent of deer.

Training small deer hounds is easy, as their boosters have discovered. If you have rabbits near your home, you can teach your dog the basics of trailing, strengthen his voice, nose and endurance, and let him learn to handle himself afield, all without ever showing him his first deer track. Nearly all beagles from good hunting stock take to rabbit scent immediately. And with the slightest bit of encouragement, most of these dogs become fervent deer trailers, readily applying what they learned while chasing cottontails.

The big, long-winded deer hounds of the South have become expensive to feed and kennel, and hunting land seems to shrink each year. Fortunately, there's a fuel-efficient hound available that's easy to train and is proving to be even more productive than the big dogs. It's the beagle.

By training close to home in cottontail country, you can see your dog at work and avoid the possibility of getting lost. The pup makes short, circular chases and doesn't go as far as he would on a deer track. Training at home offers other obvious advantages as well.

Pemble suggests starting a pup young, even actually carrying him into the field when he's too small to make a long chase. Set him down where you've seen a rabbit, encourage him a bit, and his instincts will soon take over. After a few weeks, when he's thoroughly engrossed in the new sport, you can follow him and make gentle corrections if he leaves the track, begins to backtrack or is distracted by other scents or sights. Beagles tend to be "soft" dogs, and a yell or at worst a brief cuff on the shoulder is enough discipline for most.

Pemble likes to run his pups alone for a time, so that they can build confidence and he can correct them without having other dogs to worry about. But they should be introduced to pack work as soon as they have learned the basics. Running with other hounds quickly increases field sense, and competition encourages a pup to give tongue more readily and to trail harder.

Another advantage in states such as Florida where the rabbit season never closes, is that training can go on year-round. Training deer hounds on deer, though, is restricted to a few weeks before the fall season. Beaglers can keep their dogs in excellent shape running cottontails all summer, then fine-

After 30 years of hunting deer with Walker hounds, Frank Pemble has changed to hunting with the swift and long-winded gundog beagles.

tune them during the short legal training season on deer.

Dogs trained on rabbits do not have a tough time switching to deer. Southern beagle fans have learned that the little hounds actually prefer deer to rabbits. In fact, deer-hunting beagles from Northern states such as Michigan can often be had dirt cheap because they persistently run deer against their owners' wishes. Since deer are not legal game for dog hunters in Northern states, deer-hunting beagles are not in demand. They're not even worth feeding, say most confirmed rabbit men. That's music to the ears of Dixie deer hunters like Frank Pemble. A dog that readily brings $200 in Florida can often be had for the cost of shipping it south. (Beagles have not undergone the price inflation that runs rampant among larger hounds; a well-trained, hard-hunting beagle costs $150 to $200, while a good, big hound can sell for two to three times that. A few outstanding field champions may go for up to $2,500, but untrained pups with field champion blood often cost less than $100, making the beagle one of the best bargains a person can get for a hunting dog.)

In the woods, even a fast beagle acts as a slow-trail dog compared with the speed of full-size hounds. Beagles move deer steadily, but don't panic the animal into headlong flight. A buck is more likely to stop and check his backtrail, and consequently offers more chances for a clean kill by a stander placed along his route.

When game is wounded instead of stopped cold, the little dogs are as efficient on a blood trail as any of the hounds. Dog hunters rarely leave wounded deer in the woods—a statement many other hunters sadly cannot make. Because of their small size, however, beagles usually don't bring any but severely wounded deer to bay, and neither their temperament nor physique suits them to pulling a wounded buck down. This might seem a handicap to hound men who own fiercer dogs such as Plotts, but it benefits does and fawns caught in a race with the hounds. Like it or not, most deer-hunting beagles are doomed to spend their entire lives chasing something they will never see alive.

The smaller dogs, whose short legs are an obvious handicap, must give way to the traditional hound in deep swamplands or extremely mountainous country. Beagles are also no match for dangerous game such as wild hogs, or bears, encountered in many deer-hunting areas. Even wildcats may be a problem if your pack is small. And if you enjoy the endless chase, either on horseback or by four-wheel-drive, the bigger hounds can provide dawn-to-dusk action through hell and high water.

But Pemble and other breeders may be on the trail of a strain ideally suited for deer hunting in the 80s. With the developments that AKC-sanctioned trials are sure to bring in the future, the little beagles might become the preferred breed among Southern deer hunters who love hound music but find larger hounds difficult to buy and maintain.

These compact deer dogs, because they're easy to train, also make a good choice for the hunter just starting out in dog hunting. They provide an inexpensive entry into a great Southern tradition, double the chances of taking a deer any time you're in the woods, and allow the opportunity to dish up a platter of fried rabbit anytime the mood strikes. How much more could a hound man ask for?–***Frank Sargeant.***

PART 4 GOING FOR MULE DEER

Deer of the Wide-Open West

Regardless of how many more years I hunt mule deer, there will never be a hunt quite like my first one. It was a boyhood dream come true. I'd been hunting whitetails for some years in the dense forests of the Great Lakes country and elsewhere, and I thought I knew quite a lot about deer hunting. On the long drive to Wyoming for that first mule-deer hunt, anticipation rode with me every mile, along with visions of forested mountains.

My interest in wildlife, and deer in particular, had started when I was a small boy, sparked partly by some superb paintings in a book. To this day I have that ragged volume, inscribed on the fly leaf: "Christmas, 1921, from Dad." It is *Wild Animals of North America.* It was published by the National Geographic Society and has paintings in it by that all-time great among wildlife artists, Louis Agassiz Fuertes.

One painting especially gripped my interest—that of the mule deer. There was something about those dark, blocky animals of the Western mountains that excited me, and I wondered if I'd ever look at one down a rifle barrel.

My arrival at the hunting ground in Wyoming was a shock. Nothing was as I'd visualized it. I stood in a ranch yard, and there was not a mountain in sight, no forest, not even a tree. I was in a vast expanse of treeless range country slashed by deep coulees and stippled by bare, reddish shale hills. In the draws were threads of low brush. The area was the then all but roadless region south from the confluence of the Powder River and Crazy Woman Creek far west of what was at the time the small plains village of Gillette. Posed against what I'd pictured as deer country, this was a godforsaken wasteland.

Cow-country style, the rancher pointed with his chin where I should hunt. What a letdown! I descended a long, steep incline to the bottom of a draw, then started up it. He'd told me deer rested in side pockets of these gullies and some bedded on the shale upthrusts. Things brightened considerably when I moved up the coulee. Deer tracks!

This first hunt couldn't have been better chosen. It launched a long course in learning that the mule deer is a totally different personality from the whitetail. Although sometimes found in heavy forest cover, the mule deer doesn't need that; in fact, it dislikes heavy cover. It is fundamentally a crea-

Photograph by Erwin A. Bauer

ture of such open places as mountain meadows and sparsely timbered foothills.

That first day I jumped several does and forkhorns. The terrain still puzzled me, but at least I felt better. By the third day I knew that I was in prime mule-deer country. Curiously, over many years since, I've watched hundreds of hunters pass up open terrain and head for mountain forests. Sure, they kill deer in the meadows and sparse timber and along the rims. But, over the past 35 years, I have made at least one mule-deer hunt a year, and in some years several in different locations. I've hunted mule deer in seven states, from the Canadian to the Mexican border. Without fail, all the places where I've found the most deer have been decidedly open, with only thin to scattered timber and brush.

On the third day the rancher sent me on a seven-mile hike to work my way up an especially deep and narrow erosion. He'd pick me up near its beginning.

During the long prowl I saw tracks galore but no deer. When at last I climbed out where the rancher leaned against his pickup, I was discouraged and exhausted. He got in and cranked up. I started to unload my gun. Behind us a doe came bounding up over the opposite lip of the 40-foot-deep coulee. I vividly remember thinking in astonishment that the deer had been bedded down below all that time, and that had it been a whitetail it would have sneaked away along the bottom, never showing itself. Nor would it have waited this long.

Then a tremendous buck vaulted up over the lip. It stretched out in a dead run across the flat plain that separated the coulee from a pair of red shale upthrusts several hundred yards away. As the years were to teach me, mule deer commonly react in these seemingly improbable ways. They almost always want to move *up* to get away from danger, and they seldom pay much attention to cover en route as whitetails do. I dislike running shots. But this buck was just too big. When I shot, the deer crumpled. It was a 10-pointer (full count), one of the largest mule deer I've ever killed. Field dressed it weighed 235 pounds.

A spotting scope is valuable for locating mule deer in the vast, open territory of the arid West.

As I learned more about mule deer, I began making it a point to hunt in steeply sloped, broken country with lots of rimrock, rugged canyons, abrupt coulees, and deep, brushy draws. I've never seen big bucks using flats between mountains except to cross from slope to slope. Even does and small bucks usually cling along the foothill bases. If a deep wash runs across a flat between slopes, big bucks will follow it. I've cut off a couple that did. But one basic fact that years of observing this fascinating creature has taught me is to stay with the rolling areas, the slopes, and the stand-on-end country for consistent results. Mule deer as a species are tied irrevocably to the slopes.

This is one fundamental facet of mule deer personality. Knowing that personality in detail, in my view, is perhaps the most important part of successful hunting. For example, mule deer are extremely gregarious. Even the old does get along quite well. I have counted as many as 40 does, fawns, and young bucks in a group. Adult bucks are not nearly as aggressive as whitetails. Many times I have watched bucks during the rut, when groups of both sexes were together. Last season, for example, I sat watching for half an hour the antics of a group of 12 mule deer. Three were adult bucks, two of them very acceptable specimens. One doe got attention from both bucks, which sparred half-heartedly. There was no real battle.

I have written often about rattling antlers for bucks during the rut. Under optimum conditions whitetail bucks are easy to bring in. A couple of times I've wondered if an especially wild-eyed one wasn't going to get right into a thicket with me. I have tried repeatedly to rattle up mule deer, most times when I could watch their reactions at modest range. I have yet to have one pay more than routine attention. Never has one come rushing in or sneaking in close.

Adult bucks hang out in buddy groups all summer and fall. One of my most unnerving experiences happened when I guided a companion to a group of seven bucks I'd seen on the same rocky knoll several times. The bucks didn't seem irritable or excitable. They were social creatures. My friend picked out one he liked and from about 200 yards dropped it. The others darted away, then all came back and nosed around the fallen buck as we walked toward them in plain sight. They seemed to be wondering what had happened.

One fall the day before the season I glassed a group of 14 10-pointers feeding scattered out along a slope. Toward dusk they formed a group and trooped over the ridge. They were all back the next morning. Two or three whitetail bucks together are not rare, but I've seldom observed much congeniality among them. Big whitetail bucks invariably are loners.

Such observations tell a lot about the mule-deer personality. An experienced hunter once said

Mule deer are gregarious and often feed on open slopes, as the above photograph illustrates. A telephoto lens made the hunter look closer to the deer than he really was. Below: This muley was caught where no hunter would look for a whitetail in midday.

to me—and it fits my own observations perfectly—that he'd never killed a mule deer that was not larded with fat. I could have added that I've taken many a whitetail buck that wasn't. Just watching mule deer, especially when they know you are around, tells why.

A couple of seasons back I walked up a slope and sat down, while six mule deer on another ridge watched me. I was far enough away so that they didn't seem worried. Whitetails would have turned wrong side out at first sight of my movement and would have been still running when they crossed the third ridge. The mule deer looked a few minutes, went back to feeding and fiddling around, and paid no further heed.

From a photo blind on my Texas ranch recently I watched a feeding whitetail. Down went its head for a nip of forage. Seconds later up it came with a jerk. The deer stared, flopped its ears, and switched its tail every few seconds. Not 10 seconds passed without nervous, visual sweeps. No wonder these deer seldom are as fat as mule deer. They're nervous wrecks from watching, listening, and scenting, while mule deer are placid, trusting creatures.

Are mule deer therefore plain dumb? I believe they're simply naive—true wilderness animals that never really learn to cope with man's incursions as whitetails have done. Big-game managers have often explained to me that mule deer are far less adaptable than whitetails. They cannot take severe hunting pressure either—simply because they are far easier to kill. It seems curious that these blocky, rough and rugged-appearing deer are far more fragile in relation to environment than the almost dainty whitetails.

My hunting experiences in two areas illustrate the vulnerability of mule deer. One is northeastern Wyoming, where whitetails are spreading their range and mule deer are giving way. During one hunt there a few years ago I was determined to take a whitetail. In a week I could have tagged a dozen fine mule deer bucks. All I saw of whitetails were their distant flags waving. In a sector of the Big Bend country in western Texas where I hunt, Texas whitetails are common and desert mule deer are abundant. In nearly 20 seasons of hunts there, I have never failed to take a mule deer. But on the Texas multiple-deer license I have shot only one Texas whitetail.

Mule deer are inordinately curious. I recall a Colorado incident that today is comical to me, but at the time was exasperating. Using binoculars, I'd found a small group of mule deer, including one excellent buck, at the foot of a steep slope. I made a stalk. As I came into easy shooting range I jumped a doe I'd not seen previously.

She flew up the ridge. The other deer joined. I had a wide-open shot at the buck, which looked enormous. My rifle held five cartridges. I slammed away, trying to ground him before he reached the top. At the fifth shot I'd still not cut a hair.

Wildly and four-thumbed, I grabbed for more shells in a box in my hip pocket. All the deer stopped. Broadside, nicely below the crest, the buck stared down at me, presenting an easy shot. As I fought frantically to reload, he strolled casually over the top. I should have had better sense. I've seen mule deer go through this pause-and-look-back routine many times.

As one friend experienced with both muleys and whitetails put it: "A whitetail runs first and never pauses to wonder what scared it; a mule deer wonders first if there's any use running, then wonders midway if there's any use running far."

That brings up another experience illustrating one more common mule deer trait. During an east-slope foothills hunt in Montana I jumped a good buck, and it ran up and over a ridge, going at what I call spooked gait.

The buck was such an old buster I decided to make a long circle to see if by any chance I could find him again. The way he was going, I guessed he'd be at least half a mile away, possibly over a couple of higher ridges. I made my huge circle. No buck. He'd eluded me. Annoyed at the time and effort I'd wasted, I headed straight back toward where I'd jumped him. As I climbed the ridge over which he'd run, there he was, *lying beside a single juniper bush.* I anchored him right there.

Countless times mule-deer operate with an out-of-sight-out-of-mind attitude toward danger. I've killed several spooked bucks by simply walking up a slope over which they'd disappeared running. All they'd done was to crawl behind a few bushes where they unconcernedly went about their business.

Perhaps because so much fine mule-deer range has only moderate cover on the ridgesides, and the fact that it is sloped, causes the animals to select bedding and hiding places that by whitetail standards sometimes seem ridiculous. When I was learning this trait, a guide in Utah drove me one early afternoon along a valley between two high, steep ridges. There were only widely scattered single bushes or clumps on either slope. I kept wondering why he went so slowly and paused so often to glass such barren terrain. Then he said, "There's one."

In a patch of shade barely big enough to cover it lay a buck, its antlers thrusting up out of the shade. I was eager to go after him. The guide said, "We'll drive along and see if there's a better one. He'll stay right there."

Within a couple of miles we spotted four acceptable bucks in similar bed situations, then went back and settled for the first one. The guide explained that even in cool weather, fat mule-deer seek shade and breeze. Usually the breeze is a rising thermal, which means as a rule the deer move *up* to bed down. Also, quite opposite from whitetails, which bed where they can't be seen and can see little, mule deer usually want to be able to see out of their beds. He also noted that dozens of hunters never look for mule deer in such "unlikely" places as we had, and thus pass by scads of them.

A Wyoming rancher added to all this a unique bit of lore. Where we hunted, the terrain, with pale rocks and grass, was dotted by clumps of juniper and other low bushes. He pointed out the deep, black shade each clump made. The day was bright and warm, the air, as always in that region, was dry.

"See that shiny round spot over yonder in the shade?" he asked, pointing across a draw to a juniper clump. "It's a deer's nose. I always look for noses. In this dry altitude, they lick their noses constantly, and that makes them shine. Once you see a nose, glass closely and as your eye adjusts you can see what sort of deer you've found."

Along with curiosity and naiveté, mule deer often exhibit an ostrichlike head-in-the-sand mentality when trying to hide from danger. In western Texas one fall I jumped a 10-pointer that ran full-out up a slope on which grew nothing but a scattering of low yucca, a few Spanish bayonets, and some sotol bunches. All he had to do to elude me was sail over the ridgetop. Instead, at perhaps 300 yards he whirled behind a bayonet, lay down, and put his head flat out on the ground. He wasn't remotely covered.

Another time I shot at a buck feeding on a slope and missed. At the shot and sight of me, the deer bounded away, straight toward the ridgetop, then swung behind a dense clump of shin oak not much larger in diameter than the deer was long. All it had to do was keep going another 30 yards, and it would have been over the top. I got down, rested off one knee, and filled my tag. I stepped off the distance—71 paces.

Granted, it's not always that easy. Nor are they always that unaware. There are times that don't make very dramatic anecdotes. You comb the country days on end, wondering if the deer are extinct. However, 35 years of hunting mule deer over such a vast amount of border-to-border range puts together a lot of pieces. You form a type of hunting style that you know works. In all those years there's not been a single season when I failed to fill a tag, or at least could have filled one.

My two sons, both adult and experienced deer hunters now, chuckle about my special love for mule deer. Needling me, they call them *venado por viejo*—old men's deer because they're easier to hunt than whitetails. Maybe they have a point. Regardless, occasionally I pull that ragged book off my library shelf and look at the Fuertes painting, remembering the dreams of boyhood and that first hunt in Wyoming. Happily, the thrill hasn't diminished one bit.–***Byron W. Dalrymple.***

Work Hard for Big Muleys

It was late afternoon when our packstring finally arrived at our camp high in the Colorado Rockies. Well-known outfitter Cap Atwood had ridden in several days before, put up a spike camp, and stocked it with provisions for four. An early snow had flattened our tents, but we soon had them up again and a campfire crackling.

The sun was sinking behind the mountains to the west when Cap climbed into his saddle. "I'll be back in three days to bring in more grub and to haul out meat and horns," he drawled. "Hunt hard, guys. Some monster bucks are up here."

As I watched Cap ride down the winding trail I could see the silver thread of the Colorado River far below, and the splashes of gold in each bend of the river where the cottonwoods grew. Finally, the sun faded, and the moon illuminated the peaks around us. The excitement of another opening day at dawn made sleeping difficult, so we lay in our down bags and talked about big mule deer until after midnight.

Dawn was only a gray line in the east when we shouldered our rifles and left camp. We agreed to spread out half a mile apart and hunt toward the rim of a dark mountain that rose to the south.

The sun was just beginning to slip down the hillsides when I topped out on a brushy saddle. Pausing to catch my breath, I checked the sunlit ridges ahead. In bitterly cold weather mule deer often bed where they can bathe in the first rays of the sun.

A dark spot in a snowbank on the next ridge caught my attention, and I focused my binoculars

One way to find big mule deer is to get far from roads, as these horseback hunters, below, are doing. At right, a long stalk results in a close-range shot.

Photograph by Erwin A. Bauer

The author, shown here with a four-point buck, says mule-deer hunting is much more difficult than many writers have implied.

on it. A huge buck was in his bed, his eyes fixed in my direction.

My heart raced as I studied his huge rack. The beams were massive and dark with long, heavy tines and deep forks. From tip to tip the distance between a mule deer's ears is about 20 inches, and the inside spread of this buck's antlers extended well past both ears. He had all the characteristics of an exceptional trophy.

I estimated the range at about 450 yards. I needed to work much closer for a sure kill, so I slipped forward and worked through the brush for 100 yards or so.

The old monarch had chosen his bed with care. If I moved closer the branches of trees below him concealed his position. An almost vertical ridge fell away to his right, while the terrain to his left was too open for me to try a stalk.

I carried an old Winchester Model 70 chambered for .270 and equipped with a Redfield 2X-to-7X variable scope. I'd carried the rig for years on Western hunts, both as a hunter and as a professional big-game-hunting guide. My cartridges were handloads with 130-grain Sierra boattail bullets, which had proved accurate and flat shooting. This old buster was too big to pass up because of the range, so I found a solid rest on a flat rock. I padded the forend of the rifle with my down jacket, turned the power ring up to 7X, and put the horizontal crosswire on the edge of his back above the shoulder.

At the crack of the rifle he jumped up and lunged through the snowbank. I had missed. Then, as mule deer often do, he paused. I repeated the same sight picture and squeezed off again. This time he collapsed. I have no idea where the first bullet landed. The buck had five points on each side, and his antlers were even better than I had hoped.

By the time we broke camp, my three pals had also taken large bucks. Though the hunt was short, it yielded one of the finest bucks I have ever taken. That all happened many years ago, but his handsome head still graces my den wall.

Over the years I've been able to hunt mule deer in several Western states and in a variety of ways, but I prefer to hunt from a spike camp with two or three close friends. Since such hunts don't involve guides, cooks, wranglers, and horses, they aren't as costly as fully outfitted expeditions.

My first mule-deer hunt was a guided hunt, and despite the added expense, I strongly recommend that any novice should sign on with a reputable guide whose references have been checked. Regardless of a hunter's experience with other game, and no matter how much he has read about hunting mule deer, it is difficult to apply this experience and book learning on an actual mule-deer hunt. During a single trip with an experienced guide, a beginner can learn more about how, when, and where to kill a mule deer than he could by making three hunts on his own.

A number of years ago, while working as a guide for a ranch near New Castle, Colorado, I learned that virtually all first-time mule-deer hunters shared two problems.

First, almost to the man they overestimated their physical abilities. The hardships of a mountain hunt would usually whip them within three days. Once they were tired and sore, and once they discovered that there wasn't a buck behind every rock as they had imagined, their will to take a buck would wane.

The solution to this problem is, of course, to arrive on the mountain in top physical condition for your age. Then take it easy the first day or so to allow your heart, lungs, and legs to adjust to thin air and rough country. Don't be timid about asking your guide to slow down his pace, for he intends to carry you along as fast as you'll allow. It usually takes several days to locate prime hunting areas. Being able to scramble uphill quickly on the last day of a hunt is often the difference between bagging a buck and getting skunked.

The second problem that most beginning mule-deer hunters share is unfamiliarity with their rifles. Many of the hunters have taken a number of whitetails, so they think they know their rifles as well as they know their wives. In almost every case their whitetail bucks were shot at ranges from 30 to 200 yards. As skillful as he is in his own bailiwick, the typical whitetail hunter has no idea how his rifle performs at 250 to 350 yards. In the mountains, sometimes your only shot is a long one.

I am always amazed by the guy who borrows his buddy's big magnum for a Western hunt. Instead of using the old .30/06 he has been shooting for years, the hunter totes a cannon he is unfamiliar with and more than just a little afraid of.

One Southerner I guided was a crack whitetail hunter in his home state. He was physically tough and the 10,000-foot mountains we hunted weren't a problem. But hitting a mule deer with a borrowed Weatherby .300 Magnum was another matter. On his five-day hunt he fired 28 rounds at six bucks and did not draw blood. After each miss I checked his rifle to be sure it was zeroed, and it always was. The hunt would have been a cinch if the guy had carried the .280 Remington he'd used at home.

Over the years outdoor writers have created the false impression that mule deer bounce around the hills like so many cattle in a pasture, and that the hunter simply selects a buck that suits his fancy. In truth, finding a big buck is usually tough. I agree that the species isn't as wily as the whitetail, but weather, hunting pressure, and the vastness of the country can all have an effect on the number of deer seen.

One year a friend and I hunted an area in the Book Cliff Mountains on the Colorado-Utah border, where we counted 10 to 20 bucks a day. When we returned the next fall, bucks were scarce. We combed the rims where we had taken two good bucks the previous year but came up empty.

We finally moved into oak brush, rocky draws, and deep ravines. It was tough, dirty hunting, but the effort paid off for me at sundown on our last afternoon when I kicked a fat four-pointer from the bottom of a brushy ravine and punched him through the ribs with my .270. He was a young buck, but because I'd done so much work to collect him, I was proud of him.

Barring really bad weather, bucks usually start up a mountain just before daylight. They might feed as they go, but they move steadily upward before lying down for the day. If the mountain has a band of rimrock just under its crest, the largest bucks usually bed just under the rims. Thermal updrafts during the day warn them of danger approaching from below, and the rimrock offers protection from critters above.

Consequently, it pays to reach high elevations as early as possible. I try to be in position by the time there's enough light to shoot by. This is when chances are best to spot an old mossyback slipping into the rims to bed. To get there on time might require a long, cold ride or a two-hour hike in the dark.

In the day two hunters can team up to take these rimrock bucks. One hunter takes a stand on a ridge with a good overview, while the other hunter skirts the rims on the opposite ridge, kicking rocks into the brush below. When a buck slips out, the watchful hunter on the ridge gets his shot. Occasionally the driver comes out with the venison.

One fall I was walking the rims for a buddy on the next ridge. I kicked a big rock and watched until it crashed into the ravine below. Seeing no deer, I continued my hike. I had taken only a few steps when I heard the click of a rock below. Quietly I peeked over the ledge. There, 100 yards below at the base of the rimrock, stood a big buck looking at me. As he turned, I drilled him between the shoulder blades.

Many hunters concentrate their efforts in stands of aspen and in the open woods of the high country. These picturesque areas are easy to hunt, but they don't hold as many deer as does brush at lower elevations. Whether called oak brush or buckbrush, it is often avoided because it is tough to hunt, especially for the lone hunter.

But two men can often make brush pay rich dividends. One hunter moves slowly along a ridge while his buddy weaves through the brush in the hollow and on the facing hillside. The stander should keep pace with the driver, and he must be alert to spot deer on the move. Alerted bucks usually try to slip uphill.

As a guide, I made just such a drive one afternoon for a visiting hunter. The outfitter stayed on a ridge to spot deer for the hunter. During the course of plowing through a quarter-mile of oak brush I did not hear or see a single deer. My partners later told me I had put up 16 deer, including one big buck they glimpsed from the ridge. They said the buck simply moved uphill 30 yards or so as I approached, waited for me to pass, then dropped back down to the same bed. The hunter didn't get a clear shot and they weren't able to spot the deer again. As it turned out, another hunter bagged the buck two days later by using the same tactic.

Hunting on horseback has a number of advantages. You can find concentrations of deer by sweeping across the country in only a fraction of the time it takes on foot. There's less wear and tear on the hunter, and a saddle horse can pack your buck off the mountain. Also, a horse makes it easier to reach high country early in the day and to hunt late in the evening. But even if horses are used, once a hunter reaches prime areas he is wise to tie his horse and hunt on foot.

Horses are also useful for making drives through brushy hills. Last fall, my 17-year-old son Bruce and I hunted Nevada mule deer with an old friend, outfitter Jerry Hughes of Las Vegas. Most of the deer were along the brushy sides of the mountain we hunted, so Jerry determined we should drive it on horseback. We spread out 100 yards or so apart and moved across the brushy ridges and shallow coulees. I had just ridden to the top of a narrow ridge when my horse cupped his ears forward, and a buck jumped up and tore down the ridge toward my son.

As it turned out, the deer all but collided with Bruce and his horse. But the boy jerked his little Ruger 7X57 from the scabbard, bailed off, and nailed the buck as the animal streaked across the next ridge. It was his first mule deer, and he was justly proud of a nice buck and a superb shot.

Most of the mounts I've seen outfitters use are gentle, vacant-eyed, lazy plodders for the most part, but even so, interesting things happen. One October a friend and I rented some horses and rode into the high country. We rode the rims for a couple of days, and both animals proved themselves to be strong, dependable mountain steeds. And then one noon a jet caused a sonic boom overhead. My horse, named Bud, possessed a Dr. Jekyll and Mr. Hyde personality, and that sonic explosion released the merciless beast in his soul.

Believe me when I say that Larry Mahan at the pinnacle of his career as a bronc rider never had such a horse between his legs. My tail was clearing the saddle by four feet with every leap. What's more, the camera that hung from my neck was in effect a medieval mace battering me about the head with all but deadly result.

After he pitched me off in a 20-foot somersault that featured a nearly perfect headfirst dismount, he continued to run and buck for another quarter-mile. Other than appearing as though I had faced Roberto Duran for 15 rounds of boxing, I was OK, and Bud and I finished out the hunt with no further acts of depravity on the horse's part. After that I was far more interested in spotting jets than I was in seeing mule deer.

I learned two important lessons: Beware the gun-shy horse, and put cameras in saddlebags.

However it is done, hunting mule deer is a rewarding experience. Fall is a wonderful season to be in the mountains after these animals that offer fine venison and impressive heads. And trophy bucks can still be taken, though they appear to be getting more like whitetails every year. This improved wariness should keep them around for a long time.–*Bruce Brady.*

Mule Deer Tips for Eastern Hunters

As our Cessna 180 started final letdown, the heat-hazed, stark landscape below became clearer. The vast land from several thousand feet looked like a wrinkled, tawny tarpaulin.

Pat McFall, my flying partner, adjusted the elevator trim and looked moodily out the window.

"Where the heck is this great deer country you've been telling me about all these years?" he asked. "There's nothing down there but a million miles of jackrabbit pasture."

We were flying over northeastern Wyoming in our trip from homes in Minnesota. His skepticism was understandable. For many Easterners to whom "deer" and "forest" are as related as "fish" and "water," the sunbaked, treeless terrain below looked hopeless. I'd learned otherwise years ago and kept heading back to Wyoming every fall since.

Yet next morning Pat was dressing out a mule deer buck. I teased him for taking only a three-pointer.

"Self-defense," he said unabashedly. "This buck and about 50 other muleys were about to run right over me when you came over the hill at the far end of that alfalfa meadow."

Pat had just learned a great truth of Western mule deer hunting. Don't be fooled by the apparently coverless, open nature of much of the West. Those seemingly empty spaces can hold lots of deer. Don't underestimate how well big mule deer can use their often-open country to evade hunters.

The major hunting difference between mule deer and whitetails is this: Most of the time, the muley prefers to use distance as its defense against hunters. The whitetail uses cover as its safeguard.

Last fall my son and I hunted deer in eastern Washington's mountainous Okanogan country, which has both muleys and whitetails. The two were cleanly separated, however. The whitetails stuck to the brushy, densely timbered valley forests. The muleys were 1,000 feet or more higher in the thinner timber with plenty of naturally open parklands.

These habitat differences are basically due to different lifestyles. A muley is more of a wanderer than the homebody whitetail. A muley may travel two to three miles or more from nighttime feeding to daytime bedding. An Eastern whitetail often beds only a few hundred yards (or feet) from where he fed. A whitetail likes to be close to water. Mule deer in rocky uplands may travel long distances for a drink. The desert mule deer even gets much of his moisture from water-containing plants.

Eastern whitetail range may be a square mile or less, and even when starving a whitetail won't leave that area. Mule deer are often semimigratory, summering above timberline in mountain country and wintering miles away in sheltered valleys. Obviously some of the best mule deer hunting takes place when animals are strung out on their migration routes when winter strikes. The so-called Interstate Herd of mule deer near the Oregon-California line move up to 70 to 80 miles in seasonal migrations.

Mule deer often are rated as easier quarry than whitetails. That statement invites a lot of rebuttal. A muley hunter often must cover far more mileage on foot than the whitetail hunter. Some mule deer terrain is a gutbusting challenge in itself. In Washington's special high-country season, I've found myself in Cascade crags looking at mountain goats well *below* me when I gathered enough nerve to even look down those dizzying cliffs.

Rancher friend Dean Hall has spent his life in country that has both muleys and some whitetails.

He says, "In today's stepped-up hunting pressure, any muley that lives long enough to be a four or five point buck gets very smart in the process. You'll find he's no pushover and has all kinds of tricks."

Whitetails in their usual timber and brush environment are not noted for keen eyesight. Ears and noses are their main detectors. By contrast, mule deer have excellent long-range vision, at least for moving objects. More on this later, since it's tactically important in hunting them.

Some hunters underrate the mule deer's sense of smell. Don't kid yourself; they have keen noses. I've seen muleys react with alarm after picking up my scent from a good quarter-mile away under conditions where it was impossible for them to see or hear me.

A mule deer's hearing is very good too. The big, mule-size ears were not provided by nature just for decoration. My favorite example is a heavy-bodied four-pointer that Jim McFall, Pat's brother, was after. The buck bedded on calm days on a great rimrock steeple sticking up from a ridgetop. He could see anyone approaching from half the compass points. Loose-rock slopes behind him on his blind side were noisy for a hunter to climb, as Jim found out on two tries. The buck heard him coming up the talus slope and vamoosed sight unseen in the other direction.

On day three Jim got smart. He put on tennis shoes. He had some painful encounters with prickly pear as he approached the back side of the buck-steeple ridge, but the tennies let him move with surefooted silence up the talus slope. Jim finally topped out just a few feet from his soughtafter buck that was still bemusedly watching the other face of the ridge and the valley beyond. And that was that.

Not all of the West is open hills and rangelands. A great deal is timbered. Forests range from doghair-thick stands of pine and other evergreens to open, cathedral-like forests of big ponderosa and white fir. Where timber is available, muleys use it skillfully for cover. Like whitetails, they'll bed where they can hear, scent, and see the approach of danger. The usual tactics of the forest whitetail hunter sometimes can be used against timber-dwelling muleys. There are some problems.

Western forests are dry in the fall and noisy to walk through except in more open stands. On a calm day when even little twig-cracks can be heard by sharp-eared muleys at a distance, the stillhunter must move slowly and with great care. Some forests are simply impossible to stillhunt. A dense stand of lodgepole pine has so much drybranch debris underfoot that quiet walking is out of the question unless there's a stiff wind to drown out noise. But during a strong wind, muley bucks are shrewd enough to stay out of the timber and bed elsewhere.

Another problem of hunting mule deer in timber is their lack of reliance on specific trails. Because the usual Western forest is not as clogged with brush and windfalls as typical Eastern whitetail cover, deer can more easily move where they please. You're not likely to find the well-established trails to watch that an Eastern whitetail stump-sitter capitalizes on. Stand-and-drive hunts work on muleys if there's enough manpower to handle the area involved. But Western forests are not Eastern woodlots, and all too often driving isn't practical because the area is too big.

The mule deer has one ingrained habit that a hunter can often play upon. When spooked, a muley's automatic reaction is to head uphill. It may bail off one ridge but it does that only to get to another, better one. Its weird, pogo-stick leaping gait is not very fast on flat ground. But it takes the deer uphill like a low-flying bird. Ernest Thompson Seton in his classic *Lives of Game Animals* describes how his wolf-hunting dog pack flushed a muley doe with twin fawns. The hunters couldn't stop the pack that steadily gained on the fleeing deer. Tragedy seemed so imminent that Seton was almost ready to start shooting the dogs. Suddenly the muley led her flagging offspring to a steep hillside. Up and away the deer soared, leaving even the pack's greyhounds behind. No four-footed predator can catch a muley under those conditions.

With that in mind, the mule deer hunter's best bet is to hit the high country at or even before daybreak. Dawn can be spent with good binoculars from a top-level vantage point, particularly if it overlooks a sidehill canyon that offers a natural pathway into the hills. There's a chance of intercepting deer returning to the hills from night's lowland feeding.

If nothing worthwhile is seen, the hunter should begin stillhunting ridgelines and hilltops, working into the wind, watching well ahead for the telltale white rump that's often the first sign of a distant muley. Use any cover for all it's worth, because the deer is capable of spotting you almost as far as your unaided eyes can see it.

My son puts this basic tactic well. Paraphrasing Gen. Nathan Bedford Forrest's famous remark, "I git thar fustest with the mostest men," Peter told me as he gulped a hasty breakfast in Montana's predawn darkness, "Hunting muleys, I like to git highest at the earliest."

Except during the rut, the biggest and best bucks won't be with does, fawns, and lesser bucks. The old codgers tend to be loners, although often two or more live together in a buddy arrangement. These busters leave their hilltop fastness after dark and return well before dawn. You may think there's not a big buck in the country. Try driving a valley road about midnight, and your headlights will often disclose mule deer big enough to plow a forty with. But you won't ambush them on the move in daylight (except in remote, lightly hunted country), because all their commuting is done on the owl-hoot shift.

However, careful daytime stalking of the highest, roughest country nearby will locate these big bucks. Find the highest rimrocks or timber copses on the skyline, then plan a quiet, upwind approach keeping out of sight until you're in good range of likely bedding spots. Don't be fooled if you don't see deer at first. A bedded muley can curl up into a gray ball that's almost invisible under a clump of sage or a rock overhang (they love shade on a hot day, wind shelter when it's cold). Often a mule deer will let a hunter mooch past within a few yards before the buck quietly sneaks off behind the hunter. It pays to look behind often when working good mule-deer range.

Once Ed Ollila and I worked our way along parallel ridges several hundred yards apart. This is a good pincers play, since deer chased off one ridge may cross right over to the partner's ridge. Suddenly I saw Ed doing an arm-waving war dance. Spinning around, I saw a huge muley disappearing over another fold of ground behind me. That buck lay doggo in a little clump of incense cedar while I passed 20 paces away. When I was about 200 yards beyond, he ghosted out, head down, like a big, gray cat, which is when Ed happened to spot him.

An Eastern whitetail jumped in thick cover often goes a short distance, then stops to detect any sign of pursuit. Unchased, he may circle right back to his old bed or close by. Not the big muley. Once disturbed, he usually lines right out of the country for the rest of the day. In open hills you can often track a spooked, big muley a couple miles with binoculars and he'll still be traveling when last seen.

Mule deer are famous for that last-look pause before topping over a ridge. Don't forget this habit. If your jumped buck is beelining for a hillcrest within decent rifle range, it may be smarter to sit down and get ready for a stable, well-aimed shot when he pauses to check on your pursuit rather than burn ammo trying to hit him on a run. The high-bounding gait of a scared muley makes for a tougher target than the flatter run of a whitetail. But, for safety's

Big muleys often bed near thick brush where they can hide while watching for danger.

Photograph by Erwin A. Bauer

sake, never take a skyline shot unless it is safely backstopped by higher ground beyond the deer.

Because of the longer ranges usually involved, more marksmanship and more rifle and cartridge capability are needed than are required for the usual 30 to 50-yard shots at Eastern forest whitetails. Years ago mule deer beyond number were killed with .30/30s as well as lowball loads such as the .44/40. Even today good hunters get big muleys with blackpowder rifles and bows. Usually this takes lots of hunting time, great stalking ability, and plenty of luck.

The typical mule deer hunter uses a modern big-game cartridge and rifle. Almost any of them from 6 mm. on up will do very well. Among resident Westerners, the .270, 7 mm. Rem. Magnum, and .30/06 with 150-grain bullets are favorites because they're also good elk loads. But smaller cartridges such as the .243, .250-3000, .257, and .25/06 will handle most muley opportunities.

However, the Eastern hunter who is not a bona fide rifle nut had better do some preseason practice. He'll find himself up against much longer shots than most Eastern whitetail hunting offers. Also essential is properly sighting in the rifle. With the typical, flat-shooting loads cited above, sighting in for dead-on hits at about 250 paces will put you two to three inches high at midrange and still not require any significant holdover out to 300. And that, in spite of how easy it appears in print, is a long shot on deer-size targets anytime, anyplace.

The reputation of the 4X scope was made in mule deer hunting. It's the ideal magnification for this. A 6X riflescope is tempting for open country use but doesn't have enough field of view when you get into timber.

Most Eastern whitetail hunters initially have trouble sizing up good mule-deer heads. Used to the compact, low racks of my native Lakes States whitetails, I shot a rather scrawny forkhorn as my first muley 30 years ago. At 200 yards his rack looked good. If you want an impressive mule deer rack, hold fire until you're scoping a buck with an antler span substantially wider than his big ears and at least 18 inches or so higher than his head. At first look, a really good muley head will make you think a junior bull elk wandered into view.

Advance planning is essential to a good mule deer hunt. To find an outfitter or guide, check outdoor magazine advertising sections; the National Rifle Association's "Denali" listing of guides and outfitters, which is now incorporated in the "NRA Hunting Annual"; and the game department of the state you'll hunt. Once in contact with a guide or outfitter, take pains to ask him for references and check them by mail or phone.

Beware of off-duty gas-station attendants masquerading as guides in some Western towns. Typically, those good ol' boys are much more interested in the fast, green buck than the big, gray buck you're after. Their mode of hunting is to pile the maximum payload of hunters into the back of a pickup truck for a quick ride into the country. The pilgrims, for their money, get a very bumpy, dusty trip, some sagebrush and barbed-wire scenery, and (with luck) a shot or two at a 130-pound forkhorn. If that's all the time or ambition you've got, fine. But a serious, well-planned hunt on a big private ranch or on your own in a national forest or other public area is much more satisfying with far greater chance of a rewarding kill.

Since most Western deer seasons open when weather is still mild to hot, don't come overdressed with snow-hunting togs only. Most of my muley hunting in three decades has been done in jeans and a cotton shirt. But check your host state's fluorescent orange regulations. Don't forget to carry a large canteen and wear a comfortable pair of hiking boots. But particularly in high country, the West's weather can be treacherously changeable in autumn. A spare set of cold-weather clothes is advisable, including boots suitable for snow and mud.

Although it's pretty hard to spoil venison during cold-weather hunts, certain precautions must be followed in the West's early and midfall seasons. After field dressing, get your game into a shady location to cool. Don't haul it around all day in a pickup truck under a hot sun. In dry weather, I prefer quick skinning for better cooling. If rain or snow threaten, I'll leave the hide on to help keep meat from getting wet (which can really touch off spoilage) unless roofed shelter is available for the carcass.

If your hunt includes several days, an early kill may have to go to the nearest town's commercial walk-in cooler. But over the years, hunting partners and I have had no problem keeping unrefrigerated game in the West's arid, cold-nights climate for several days. For the trip home, plan to leave in early morning. The night-chilled game will stay cool all day if kept out of the sun (no rooftop transporting except at night) and covered with a sleeping bag for insulation.

The mule deer is great quarry in a great country. It homesteads from spruce forests in northern British Columbia down to saguaro and octillo thickets in central Mexico. At its western limits, it overlooks Puget Sound from the Cascade crest. The Missouri River is supposed to be its eastern boundary, but don't bet on that. A few years back, a mule deer buck was a traffic casualty in a Minneapolis suburb a good 375 miles east of the Big Muddy. If we don't convert all its winter range to miserable "ranchette" subdivisions or sheep-off its uplands with overgrazing, our children's children will hunt these big-antlered mountaineer deer as the conquistadores and Lewis and Clark did.

–Norm Nelson.

Mistakes Muleys Make

Something has happened to America's mule deer hunter. He isn't the same as he used to be back in the 1950s and 1960s. He hasn't been ever since most Western states went to some form of buck-only hunting several years ago. Average hunting success has plummeted. Hunters have grown pessimistic.

The negative attitude has been due, at least in part, to the fact there are fewer legal targets than there used to be when does could be hunted. Also, there are more hunters in today's hills, and that has made the deer warier. Hunters have changed too.

In my own native Utah—one of the best mule-deer-hunting states—83.5 percent of hunters tagged a deer in 1951 and 58.2 percent did so in 1964. Then, with buck-only regulations, only 34 percent of hunters got venison in 1980. The 1980 success rate was about the average of the previous several seasons and typical of hunter success in other Western states. That's a decline of some 50 percent in the success rate in less than 30 years. Only one hunter in three is now bringing home the venison. A shocking two-thirds are "failures!"

Much of the lack of success is due not only to the switch from either-sex hunting but to greater competition as well. Utah had 112,911 hunters afield in 1951, 169,178 in 1964, and more than 200,000 in 1980. Such fierce competition can cause a hunter—if he seems to see a rifle-toter in every clearing and on every ridge—to doubt his own chances. Are there any other reasons for such a high rate of failure? Deer populations haven't dwindled much, and in most states are actually up slightly. Are the reasons really physical—more guns and fewer targets because does are no longer legal in most states?

I'm convinced that at least part of the reason is psychological. As more hunters meet with less success they expect even less. They hunt less alertly and for shorter periods of time. *Since I probably won't score anyway,* a hunter thinks, *why venture far from camp or road?* Some talk wistfully about the glory days of their fathers or uncles who just waited by a meadow or a saddle until a deer showed up. I've watched many hunters making cursory checks of the woods. After seeing nothing during the first half hour, many of them stop hunting. Then they simply hike around with a gun. Recently I was returning for help to get out a high three-pointer I'd just taken when I came to a camp and met an orange-vester who was lying on a cot.

"Quitting, too, huh?" he asked. "I've been out looking around too, but I didn't see anything. I guess it's all shot out."

Though the time was 11:45 a.m. on opening day, his companion poked his head through the tent door and added, "But the weather's nice. We'll probably stick around for a while. We have to be back to work Monday."

What they were doing, communing with nature, was certainly better than sitting in an apartment all weekend, but it can't be called hunting and it isn't conducive to bringing home venison or antlers.

As an outdoor writer for several Utah newspapers over the past 25 years, I've witnessed the self-defeating trend for some time. But it's worse now than ever before. As more and more people move from farm to city, beginning hunters become less familiar with wild creatures. They seem to get the idea that even a little buck is a rare phantom, a wizard that never makes mistakes and can't be beaten. Many city-bred sportsmen doubt that deer exist out there at all. Many hunters are defeated before they load their rifles. They feel they won't see a buck, and by golly they find that they are right.

Many make no effort to scout before the season to make sure they are in deer country to start with. Thus, they announce that "there are no deer left," unwittingly playing into the hands of antihunters who don't know any better either.

If you doubt that there are mule deer about, visit almost any Western foothills area in December. On winter range, the deer are concentrated in large numbers and they are easy to see. If they're there, and you know it, you can hunt with more confidence next season.

One new license-buyer told me, "I'd be happy with just a young, tender spike, but what chance do I have? Any buck can run faster than I can, has better ears and nose, good camouflage, and knows his home range better than I could ever know it."

I've lived most of my life in mule deer country, hunting or studying them from New Mexico to Canada. I'm also amazed at how quickly they often outwit the careless. The mule deer is one savvy hombre. But if I envision in my mind only the ways in which a buck can outfox me, I will become discouraged. Why hunt with only his strength in mind? Does a boxer work to his opponent's strongest points or does he play on the weakest ones? Does a salesman go out with the idea that he will be rejected at every door? Does a basketball coach tell his own players that the other team's players are better than they are?

Let me illustrate. I know a football player who went to a hypnotist. The hypnotist told him, "The guy across the line may be 6 foot 5 inches and 265 pounds, and have blinding speed. But I want you to think of him as a 'pile of jelly' and a 'wet hunk of clay.' " The player did so and did well thereafter.

We can't all rush to a hypnotist for treatment of our troubles, but we can apply optimistic thinking to deer hunting. We can look for exploitable weaknesses. We don't need a whole basketful of Achilles' heels. It takes only one!

What are a mule deer's liabilities?

Yes, mule deer make mistakes, and with the right attitude you can

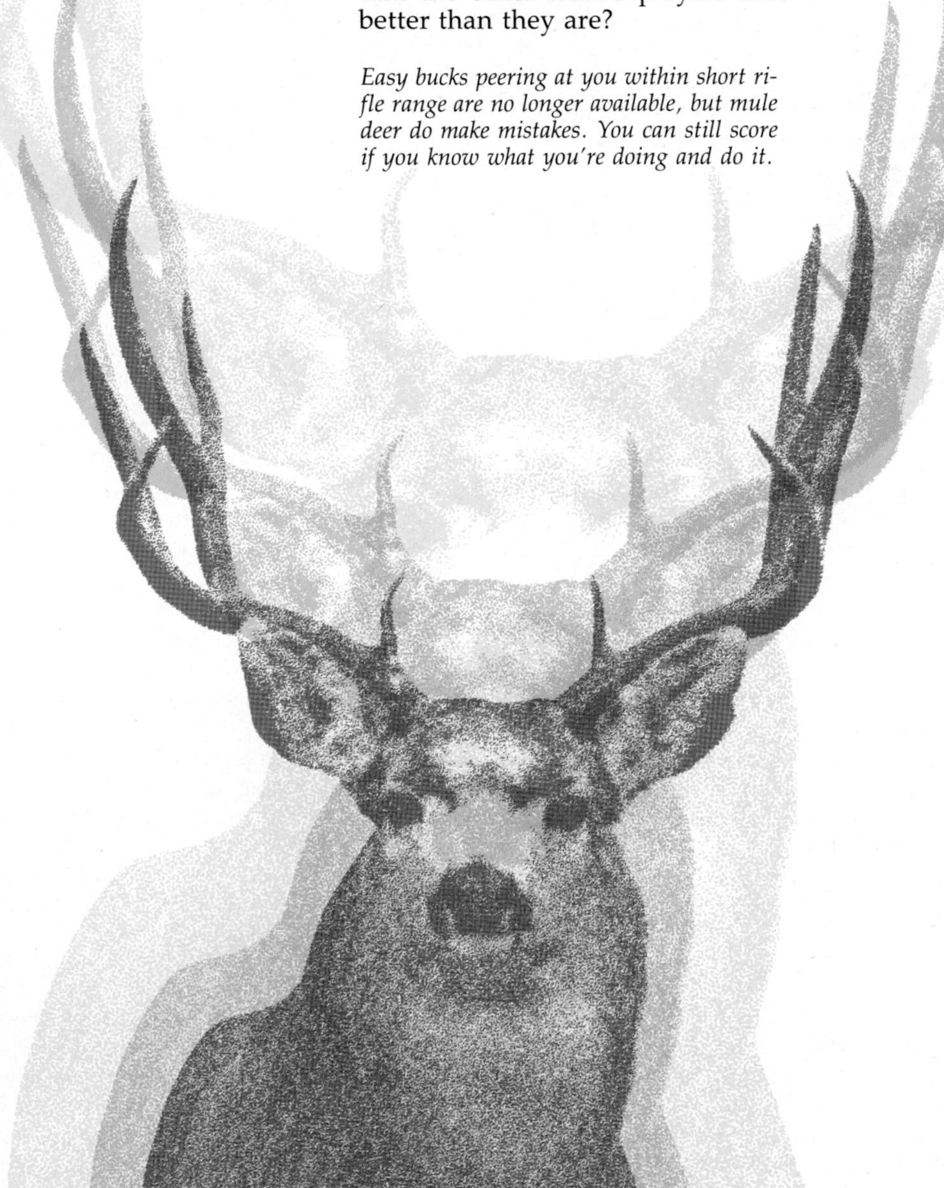

Easy bucks peering at you within short rifle range are no longer available, but mule deer do make mistakes. You can still score if you know what you're doing and do it.

Photograph by Michael S. Quinton

take advantage of them. Take camouflage for example. Many discouraged hunters amble along carelessly. What they get is a tough shot—a buck in high gear going away, often in thick cover. If you do more meticulous searching than walking (I'd venture some two-thirds do more of the latter), you won't have to try running shots at 300 yards. The deer are likely statue-still, waiting for you to pass by. Since this mule-deer stratagem usually works, it's an asset most of the time. But if you take advantage of it and spot the motionless buck, it's obviously a mule deer's mistake. It all begins with the frame of mind with which you hunt.

Of course, it makes a difference where you look. A friend of mine insists on hunting in juniper forests. You can find muley tracks in most juniper forests, but I don't hunt deer there for a good reason—the deer have all the advantages. Jump a deer and he will keep a tree between you and him if not a clump of them. The same is true with other evergreen vegetation that grows in thick profusion such as mountain mahogany and conifers, and it is especially true of north slope conifers that grow in greater density due to higher retention of moisture on the dark slopes. In such places deer have few exploitable weaknesses.

One of my favorite covers consists of quaking aspens. Mule deer frequent them. Even after leaves have been stripped by October's chill winds, the deer often trust in them for cover. This false sense of security exists even though aspen branches sprout from quakie trunks well above the antlers of even a Boone and Crockett buck. If you are searching for a motionless deer, it isn't all that difficult to locate a horizontal form among all those thin, vertical tree trunks. And if there is snow on the ground, the deer really stand out, as they do in open sage. While a buck would be skitterish in the low sage, he often gives you a longer look in the aspens.

Visibility is reduced somewhat in the aspens, of course, when you're hunting on level ground. To gain still another advantage, avoid hunting on the flats. All any animal has to do there to get out of your sight is to step behind a bush or a big boulder. Go high and look downhill. Mule deer least expect danger from above, and you have "window vision" to the slopes below. Remember that you are glassing for a deer with a russet-hued coat during bow season, tawny in October, and slate-gray during November.

I read in someone's hunting primer that mule deer seldom go into the aspens, but I haven't paid it much heed. Seventeen of my last 20 bucks have been taken in or around them. Mule deer often feed on wet aspen leaves, and many other favorite deer foods grow along quakie edges. The ground under or on the edges of thick conifers is likely to be a desert so far as deer browse is concerned because there is no sunlight. That is only one reason I often spend hours on one fairly large aspen patch. I scout for such cover before open season because once I've found it I've usually found mule deer.

A muley's reliance on camouflage is not limited to trees, brush, and other vegetation. I once walked within nine paces of a giant four-pointer that didn't budge until I stopped to stare at him eyeball-to-eyeball. He had flattened himself against the bare earth after being cut off from the timber by the four-wheel-drive vehicle I was riding in. Another time I noticed two hunters who were walking along a ridge but never looked down at one big patch of brush. I tied my tag to the three-pointer that was standing behind it. Fortunately, I took him on the first bounce. One more bound, and he would have gone into a thick wall of pines. Why wasn't he bedded there to begin with?

The answer, I believe, involves another weakness, and any hunter can exploit it. I believe that mule deer—particularly big bucks—often suffer from claustrophobia. It seems unlikely that a big buck would flush readily from very thick cover, but such is frequently the case. Whitetails I've observed in Nebraska and Wisconsin usually respond to heavy hunting pressure by sneaking into the thickest swamp or cover they can find and staying there. Perhaps mule deer in thick cover fear attack by cougars or other predators. They seem to stay near an open exit where they can bust out when tension mounts. I've capitalized on this by heading into blowdowns or heavy timber and then quickly exiting to the side where I can watch at least one exit. Quite often I've got a shot.

Mule deer are really creatures of the semiopen spaces and seem to dislike heavy cover. Yet they often move reluctantly when danger approaches, having learned their legs can get them into just as much trouble as staying put. Watch for a big buck to mince away furtively, attempting to melt into the landscape instead of merely bolting. If you look for a racing animal, you may not see one that sneaks.

Another muley asset that can be turned into a liability is his knowledge of home territory. Studies by the U.S. Fish and Wildlife Service in Nevada indicate that does seldom venture more than 1½ miles from their birthplace, and that bucks seldom wander 2½ miles. Even when forced out of a given haunt by horseback drivers, the deer in the study returned home again within a short time. Thus, you have some "wet clay" to work with. Mule deer are totally unlike elk or antelope, which often change counties when mildly skittered. For this reason, pass up difficult shots and hunt the same place again later on.

Even a buck's ears can be used against him. I once helped a nonresident friend locate a high-antlered buck. But my buddy could not get off a shot before the buck stepped behind a spruce ridge. We were about to leave when we noticed some does heading toward us. They sensed our presence and ran wildly into the spruce. We sat down to see what effect the running does would have on the buck. Those does must have sounded like a thundering horde to him. He could not have seen them, but the noise they made panicked the buck back into the sagebrush where we had last seen him. My friend was ready, and the beautifully high and symmetrical rack now hangs on his wall in Reno, Nevada.

A mule deer's nose can get him into trouble too. Sniffing your approach, he may leave his bed and move out. To take advantage of this you should keep checking ahead from knobs and other high points rather than merely plugging along. Hunt into the wind. If he does not scent you, he can be lulled into unjustified complacency.

Habit is another downfall. On one Wyoming hunt, a nice buck eluded our drives several times by heading out the far side of the cover before the horses of the drivers started. On the third morning, I persuaded the guide to let me move into a likely position before the mounts stirred a hoof. I walked to the stand I had chosen. Sure enough, at the first movement of the mounts that buck trotted right to me. I could not have had an easier shot.

Naturally, there are times when hunts don't go as planned. On one Colorado foray, southwest of Montrose, we went where the antlers had always been, but not one of the 17 hunters in that canyon had sighted a deer by 4 p.m. of opening day! Fourteen of the hunters departed, but three of us sat down to think things out. We believed that if the deer had always been here they couldn't be far away. By asking local ranchers, we discovered that the elk hunt had been held just the week before. Besides, the local ponds had frozen over because of unusually cold temperatures. There was no snow so there were few tracks to follow, but the logical thing was to believe that the deer had moved out downhill. We couldn't head directly down, because most of the land below us was posted. A Bureau of Land Management map showed us what we were looking for—springs and cover away from roads at a lower elevation—and we circled around to get there. We killed three bucks before dusk. There were no signs of any other human activity in the area. As a result, we found the deer concentrated and reluctant to leave quiet terrain that offered abundant food and unfrozen water. It was a matter of locating an exploitable weakness.

Some bucks seem to come by sheer luck, but closer examination often contradicts that conclusion. I once put in 36 consecutive hunting hours without seeing a single shootable buck. Then I noticed a horseman nearly half a mile away. Figuring any buck in flight would cross to the opposite side of the ridge from him, I crossed over myself and waited. Soon a pebble trickled down from above, and I assumed a shooting position. A buck with a 30-inch spread almost skidded into me. A dozen other times this tactic didn't pay off, but it sure does pay to try it now and then.

If you keep trying, some strange things can come your way. I've spotted bucks on the fourth day of the season miles from the nearest tree. Apparently they were bent on switching ranges. I've also seen bucks feeding openly in Colorado alfalfa fields below town while hunters searched in vain in the traditional high hunting ground above it. One giant buck broke through my packtrain on a mountain trail only to bust right back through it again because he had been blocked by a yawning chasm. Either he had a short memory or he was on unfamiliar ground. I've also found bucks in river bottoms during the summer heat when they were supposed to be as high on the mountain as they could get.

Some of the mistakes I've mentioned weren't fatal for the deer, and I'm sure those animals learned from their miscues, which is more than I can say for the many hunters who keep making the same mistakes again and again. But the worst mistake any hunter can make is to stop looking for deer. Easy bucks peering at you within short rifle range are no longer available, but you can still score if you know what you're doing and *do it!*–***Hartt Wixom.***

The Trouble with Muleys

Crumpling the pop can, I stuffed it along with the empty sandwich bag into the corner of my day pack and got up to leave. After five hours of tough hunting in the rough, precipitous terrain along the east slope of the central Montana Rockies, the half-hour lunch break had been a welcome respite.

I had climbed the high ridge because from a distance I could see deer tracks in the snow, and it looked like an ideal place to find a big mule deer buck. The buck hadn't materialized, but since the view was spectacular I had decided to relax a bit and chow up.

I was shouldering the pack when I saw something strange. A gray, gently rounded rock at the base of a small spruce about 50 feet away was exactly the same color as a mule deer. *It can't be a deer,* I told myself, *not so close and* . . . Then the thing began to take the shape of a buck lying flattened out, neck stretched, with his chin almost on the ground. Massive antlers were all but lost in the snaggy lower limbs of the spruce. I should have looked away as I reached for my gun, but my gaze caught his and he knew he'd been seen. He literally scooted from under a thin layer of new snow on his back and in two bounds was over a ridge and out of sight.

I enjoy any kind of hunting, but if I had to pick a favorite it would be playing the game of "who's the smartest" with big old mule deer bucks. The score card has the deer considerably ahead, but with teachers like the buck I just mentioned I'm at last beginning to learn a few things that are increasing my score too.

With a deer, lying down and hiding are synonymous. When a deer hides, it wants to keep a low profile. So it lies down. When it beds down to rest or chew its cud it is most vulnerable to predators, so it seeks a safe place in which to do so.

Here is what a mule deer, and especially a wise old buck, looks for when seeking a place to bed.

First, the place must provide a good view in as many directions as possible, and it must also keep the deer from being seen. In the thousands of times I've seen big bucks bedded down, I can't think of once when these criteria were not met. I'll go into more details later, but keep in mind that such a place usually is at a higher elevation than most of the surrounding area.

Second, since even big bucks don't have eyes in the back of their heads, the bedding spot must offer protection from behind. This can take several forms, such as trees and cliffs. In the case of a tree, a buck is more likely to lie down in front of one than behind it. Why? There are several possible reasons. In order to jump on the deer's back a predator such as a cat in its final rush would have to come around the tree, and that's not easy for a leaping creature to do. Also, because of his natural camouflage, the buck is hard to see, especially since the tree breaks his outline, and, being in front of the tree, the deer's field of view is unobstructed.

Third, a hiding place must provide quick access to two or more escape routes. The best places, used again and again, allow the deer to get out of sight in a jump or two.

A factor that's hard to appreciate because our own senses are so dull is that deer rely as much on their sense of smell as on their vision to warn them of danger. They invariably use both senses when choosing a bed.

How does all this theory translate into reality? Where in the mule deer's extensive domain do you look for him?

Aspen groves are choice spots. Strangely, I can't remember having killed a buck in an aspen grove. But I've photographed more deer in or near such groves than anywhere else, and I've pho-

tographed many more than I've killed. The several varieties of aspens tend to grow in small patches or clumps, and they dot the mountains and hillsides over much of the mule deer's range. The reasons deer like them are that they offer an abundant food supply, are often small enough so deer can see out of them in any direction, and they are noisy places to walk in.

Another topographical feature often found in most mule deer country are cliffs, the higher the better. Bucks seem to like to bed down below them, especially if there are steep slopes running down from the bases of the cliffs, which is usually the case. The deer then has solid rock to his back and a good view of the country below.

The trouble with hunting mule deer is finding them. Masters of deception and camouflage, heavy-racked bucks know exactly how and where to hide. What makes them choose the places they do? I've spent a lot of time trying to find out, and what I've learned is making me a better hunter.

He can elude danger by going in either direction below the cliff. And, more often than not, there will be some place nearby through which he can pick his way up and over the top of the cliff.

Small benches or flat areas on hills or mountainsides are favorite bedding places. They provide level places to lie on, and are also excellent vantage points. All that is visible from below, where most threats originate, is the top of the buck's head and his antlers, and neither is easy to see.

The shoulders or points of big ridges are also favored hideaways. I found one such place while hunting mountain goats. Yes, big bucks go right up there with the goats and get around just about as well. While climbing the mountain, I had seen four respectable-size bucks. They were moving out high above me across the upper end of a large cirque just below the top of the ridge that extended down from a stark snow-capped peak. They were at least 600 yards away. Later in the day I found their beds. The place was a small bench from which the ridge fell away steeply in three directions. The bucks had close to a 300° field of view, and they could see anything coming up the mountain at least a mile away. No doubt they had watched me for a long time.

Patches of sage or other short brush in open country are good places to look for bucks. Much of their effectiveness as hideouts lies in the fact that they don't seem to be big enough to hide anything. Believe me, it's a revelation to see a buck and maybe several does and fawns disappear into a patch of sagebrush 30 feet across and no more than two feet tall.

My favorite hunting area is a place in the Rockies where the earth's surface is folded into a series of great high ridges that, viewed from the air, roughly resemble a washboard. On the west side, the mountains are steep but slope consistently from their crests. On the east side there are cliffs, some 1,000 feet high, and below them steep slopes descend to timbered valleys. Timberline is not consistent, but it extends in long fingers up underneath the cliffs. Single bucks, and at times whole herds of deer, bed near the tops of these narrow strips of timber. I have taken several good trophies from such places.

When I hunt I like to wait until there is snow on the ground and then glass the fingers of timber with binoculars. Occasionally I see deer, but most times I see tracks where the deer have been feeding on brush that grows along the edges of timber. If I see tracks and think the deer are still there, I plan a stalk. Here's a situation where it pays to have a buddy. One hunter can spook the deer while the other cuts off the most likely escape route.

When hunting a new area, the first thing I do is find a place where I can see a lot of country. I sit down and study the terrain, looking over all the spots that meet the criteria for buck hideaways. If it is good deer country, I often find a buck.

By far the easiest way to find a buck's bed is to watch him go to bed. This means being up in deer country with good binoculars at the crack of dawn. Though the first cursory look at the area may often reveal nothing, keep looking, searching, visually taking the landscape apart bush by bush and rock by rock. Sooner or later you'll see a deer that will likely be feeding his way up to higher elevations where he'll bed down for the day.

Another technique that works well is to hunt deer from above. This is a hard and sometimes dangerous business, but it pays off in trophy racks. The main advantage in doing it is that deer usually look for danger from below and lie facing downhill. I don't mean to imply that they never look up. They do. So you still have to be quiet and keep a low profile. A hunter who strolls along the top of a ridge, silhouetted against the sky, is probably wasting his time. When I work both ridges and cliffs, and expect to find bedded bucks below, I move along quietly back out of sight and intermittently peek over the edge to thoroughly—and I mean thoroughly—scan the area below.

Another big advantage in hunting high up is that you can invariably see more by looking downhill than you can when looking up. A good case in point is the buck that may be bedded behind a windfall or on a bench. While he's almost invisible from below, he sticks out plainly from above.

One thing that becomes more apparent to me each season is that most hunters, including myself, move too fast. No one gets trophy bucks by galloping over the terrain. In fact, we usually pass by more deer than we see.

Frequently a deer's greatest allies are the hunter's own impulses, specifically the one that says, *Because there isn't a deer here, I'll rush over the next hill and find one.* There are two factors involved here. First, to see game consistently you must look a long time, not just glancing around but hard, serious looking. A mule deer buck in his natural habitat is incredibly hard to see. So much so that if you take persons with 20/20 vision and point to a deer standing in typical country, 90 percent of them will say, "Where? I don't see any deer." Sometimes you have to draw a picture before they see it.

A hiding place must provide quick access to two or more escape routes. The best places, used again and again, allow deer to get out of sight in a jump or two.

Another reason for taking it slow and easy is that a wise old buck chooses his hiding place with care, and he has great confidence in it. He feels safe where he is and is reluctant to leave. So, if you move along at a fairly steady pace, he'll just stay put and let you walk by. If you dillydally and look around, though, he's likely to get nervous and show himself.

Before I leave the subject of spotting deer, I want to tell you what I consider to be the most important single item of gear the trophy mule deer hunter should have. A flat-shooting, scope-sighted rifle? No. A pair of high-quality, precision binoculars. It's nice to have a fancy rifle, but if you're going to stretch the family budget do it on binoculars. Get the very best you can afford.

Higher-power glasses, at least 8X and preferably 9 and 10X models, are best. If your budget forces you to buy something less than the finest, you're wise to stick with 7X. The often heard advice that 7X is the most magnification that can be handheld is bunk. Anyone who can hold a rifle still enough to shoot at deer will have no problem holding a 10X glass.

Of all my experiences, the one that best illustrates what I've been trying to say here took place about 15 years ago. I was hunting in Montana's Bob Marshall Wilderness. After glassing the area, I made a long, circuitous climb that brought me out on top a 100-foot cliff overlooking the upper end of a large alpine basin.

At first I saw nothing. Figuring that I had the situation well covered, I stepped out into plain view. In less than a minute two bucks bounded out from below me and took off across the basin. One was a three-point, but the other had a respectable four-point rack. I sat down, chambered a round, and waited for that buck to stop and look back, as I had come to believe a stupid mule deer would do. He did, and the crack of my .30/06 was followed instantly by a reassuring thud. The buck made one gigantic leap and cartwheeled down the mountain.

I got up, mentally patted myself on the back, and was looking for a way down off the cliff when I heard a stone roll below me. I looked straight down, and what I saw haunts me now. There, not running but sneaking away, was one of the biggest bucks I have ever seen.–***Bill McRae.***

Blacktail King

George Shurtleff may know more about hunting trophy blacktail deer than any other hunter. Consider his record.

On Oct. 2, 1969, Shurtleff shot an enormous blacktail that scored 172²/₈ points, a Pope and Young record for bow-killed blacktails. Firearms hunters should notice that the score was higher than the Boone and Crockett No. 1. In other words, this bowhunter outscored the riflemen.

In 1977 Shurtleff bow-killed another record blacktail. This one scored 163⁷/₈ points for second place in the Pope and Young book. Only a handful of Boone and Crockett bucks score higher.

In 1978 he killed a third huge buck. Had he been concerned about records at the time, this animal might have been No. 3 in Pope and Young records with a score of 162⁴/₈. But the hunter split the skull to lay the antlers neatly on his pack, which disqualified the buck from official competition.

In 20 years of bowhunting deer, the 62-year-old Shurtleff has killed 18. Several of these, besides those listed above, are large enough to place in the record books. The Pope and Young Club honored him at its 11th annual awards banquet in 1979 with the Ishi Award, the highest honor given to bowhunters. Shurtleff's overall hunting record is just as impressive as his world record buck. Anybody can get lucky once. But over and over? This hunter has not been lucky.

Shurtleff has no secret or special advantage He's a refreshingly average man, slight of build, bald headed. He hunts land open to the public, primarily in his home state of Oregon. As a life-long working man, he hunted only during vaca-

George Shurtleff killed the greatest blacktail buck ever recorded — the hard way, with a bow during rifle season. Among his many trophies is a blacktail that would have ranked No. 3 had Shurtleff not chopped its rack in half with a hatchet. For more on record bucks, see page 179.

tions and regular off hours, as most other hunters do, until he retired last November "because work was interfering with my hunting and fishing." He's had no special advantage over rifle hunters by taking his bucks during low-competition bow seasons—his two largest bucks were killed during the rifle season. Shurtleff simply has discovered the perfect combination of location and hunting method for taking huge blacktails.

First in this combination comes locale. Some regions grow larger animals than others. Record books show that Oregon produces the largest blacktails. Many of these come from the lower third of the Cascade and Coast ranges bordering the rich farmland of the Willamette Valley in northwestern Oregon. This is the country Shurtleff hunts.

He doesn't keep any secrets about the best spots, either. One time a man asked where he'd killed the world record blacktail. George gave precise directions. An onlooker gasped.

"He's telling right where he got it!"

"Well, why not?" Shurtleff replied. "Somebody's going to hunt there. It might just as well be one of my friends."

He killed his two largest bucks within a mile of each other in the Cascade foothills near Silverton. His third largest buck came from across the valley in the Coast Range. In 1979 he killed another large buck in the Coast Range.

Many Western hunters think they must go high for big bucks. For mule deer, that rule may hold, but for blacktails the opposite is true.

"You find the biggest bucks low," Shurtleff says. "I think the fertilizers and farm crops may grow bigger animals. I've taken my largest bucks within a mile of fields."

Oregon Department of Fish and Wildlife harvest records verify that this is productive country, although big game biologist Paul Ebert gives different reasons. He says the mild winters, long growing seasons and frequent sunshine, a quality lacking in the cloudy high country, produce better forage for deer than that found at higher elevations. Blacktails in the foothills live much of their lives in small localities.

Picking the right spot is not the whole answer to killing trophy deer, of course. Oregon hunters kill about 35,000 blacktail bucks every year. A good number of those come from the Willamette Valley region, yet no other hunter has a record of taking trophy animals equal to Shurtleff's.

How has one man, a bowhunter at that, so surpassed all others at collecting trophy blacktails?

For most big game, the long ranges and quick-handling qualities of firearms give rifle hunters an edge over bowhunters. But in western Oregon, junglelike vegetation and the elusive nature of the deer diminish this advantage. The challenge in hunting trophy blacktails is not so much in making the long or difficult shot as in seeing a deer.

"Blacktails are sneaky. They hide and rarely bolt into the open as mule deer do," Shurtleff points out. "Blacktails may be numerous, but you can walk all day and not see a deer. You walk right by most of them."

Shurtleff has adapted to conditions, forsaking still-hunting, his approach in years past, for stand hunting. As he stays motionless, letting the bucks come to him, he sees them before they see him. That's the greatest advantage a blacktail hunter, whether using bow or rifle, can have.

In addition, a hunter on stand can always be prepared.

"One time I was still-hunting and sneaked up on a big buck, a perfect shot," Shurtleff recalls. "But before I could shoot, I slipped on a wet log and crashed to the ground. When you're moving, you invariably have limbs in the way, or you're caught off guard. Something is always going wrong. On a stand, you can get set up so you're always ready."

Similarly, a bowhunter on stand can shoot at known distances, a rare possibility while still-hunting. Shurtleff often measures the distance from his stand to surrounding points.

"I'm only a fair archer," he says. "So I set up to get the kind of shot I'm sure I can make. Stand hunting eliminates a lot of guesswork."

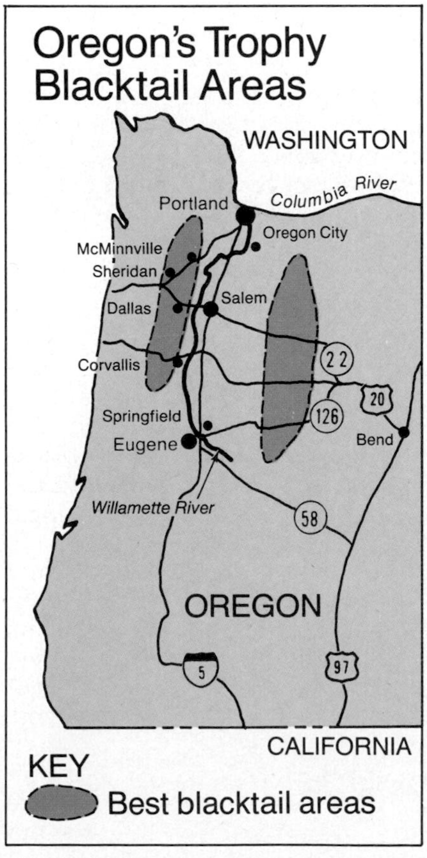

Oregon's Trophy Blacktail Areas

KEY
Best blacktail areas

Shurtleff uses two important tactics when hunting from stands. One is calling. He may call from a tree stand, but often he walks about, selecting temporary stand sites to call from.

He got the idea for calling deer in 1960 while hunting fox. He blew his predator call, and an animal came running—not a fox, but a deer.

"That set the pattern for a type of hunting I'd never done before," he says. "Since then I've killed about half my deer by calling."

Shurtleff uses a predator call that imitates a screaming jackrabbit. Sometimes he blows lightly to make a low bleat, which brings deer in slowly and will draw back one that has been spooked. Other times he blasts hard on the call to produce a shriek. Or to make a similar sound, he holds a piece of plastic between his thumbs and blows across it, as a person would whistle through a blade of grass.

"Whether deer come to these noises out of curiosity or to protect one of their own that's hurt, I don't know," he says. "But they usually come on the run. And with their hackles up.

"One time I'd forgotten my call and didn't even have a piece of plastic. So I plucked a blade of grass and held it between my thumbs," Shurtleff says. "I gave a couple of blasts on that and heard thumping in a nearby thicket. *Here comes an old doe,* I thought, and didn't reach for my bow. A nice three-point buck charged into the open, 15 yards away. By the time I got to my bow, he was long gone. Experiences like that have taught me to always expect a buck."

Calling success is varied. Shurtleff has called for many days in a row without a response. At other times, deer seem to come from everywhere.

Calling gives a hunter the advantage of remaining motionless as game comes to him. But calling has a drawback—deer usually have their eyes fixed on the caller. For the rifle hunter that presents little problem. But the bowhunter may have a hard time getting off an unhurried shot.

"I've called in a number of large bucks, but I've never taken a real trophy by calling," Shurtleff says. "Seeing a deer and getting a shot are different things. For that reason I use calling as an alternative method of hunting."

His primary approach is trail watching from a stand. This is how he's taken his largest animals.

Surprisingly, Shurtleff puts little emphasis on scouting. Because he hunts many different areas, he scouts as he goes, looking for a particular type of country. He especially likes old logging skid trails grown up with grass and brush. Deer frequently travel these. He also likes to hunt draws that top out at saddles. Trails may traverse each side of a draw and meet as they pass through the saddle.

"I'm looking for places where two or more trails cross. A confluence of trails is always a good place for a stand. It may be no more than a few feet long, but if trails come together there, that's the place to hunt."

Ideally these crossings are in thick cover, dense alders or blackberry brambles, that confine animals to well-defined trails. In old-growth timber and clear-cuts where underbrush is sparse, animals can wander randomly and may not come near a blind.

Whitetail hunters commonly evaluate country according to rubs, scrapes and other signs of the rut. Blacktails leave little such sign, so Shurtleff sizes up a trail system in terms of tracks. Obviously, a big track means a big deer. And sign must be plentiful.

"I won't spend much time putting up a stand where there are few deer tracks," Shurtleff says.

Shurtleff uses whatever workable blinding method is simplest. To take his world record blacktail, he perched on a rock bluff. He'd discovered the trail while fishing a nearby creek. He arrived early and made his way to the bluff by the first light of morning. About 7 a.m. he saw antlers coming through the brush.

"I got so excited I wondered if I could draw the bow," he recalls. "The buck walked right below me, maybe 15 to 20 feet away. When he was just past I let fly with an arrow. It was a good shot, and I watched him go down."

Frequently Shurtleff hunts from a portable tree stand. He killed his No. 2 buck from a tree overlooking a trail intersection.

Although he took his third largest buck from a ground blind, he prefers to be above the trails he's watching.

"It gets your scent off the ground. And I've always had the idea that predators hunt from above, say from a ledge or tree," he says. "I think hunters should learn from that. It obviously works.

"But getting high isn't always the answer. One time I was in a tree, watching downhill. To my surprise, a little buck came from above. On that steep ground, he was at my eye level. He spotted me right away and tore up the ground getting out of there. That made me think a little more about selecting a stand site."

The success of stand hunting, of course, depends on the movement of animals. As all hunters know, deer are most active early and late in the day. Shurtleff especially likes the morning because he's consistently seen the largest bucks then. His normal pattern is to trail watch early and late, then to call throughout the day, when deer are least active.

Under some conditions he may spend all day on stand. For example, blacktails may feed all day following a heavy storm at night. The hunter on stand could score at any time of day.

The same applies when a lot of hunters are in the woods. When the practice was legal (a hunter in Oregon must now choose to hunt either the rifle or the bow season), Shurtleff often bowhunted during the general firearms season in addition to the bow season. Numerous hunters walking about pushed deer to him, and he killed his two largest bucks under these circumstances.

To kill his third largest buck during an August bow season, Shurtleff planned his hunt around a concentration of bowhunters.

"I knew where a large party was camped, so I found a confluence of trails above their camp. The ferns were high there, so I just sat down in them, 20 yards from the trails. At the time, my wife Kay was in the hospital, so I'd told her I'd be back by noon. And I was. With a good buck. It was simply a matter of letting those hunters push the deer to me.

"Incidentally, that's the buck I split the skull on. Boy, did Kay chew me out for that."

Shurtleff killed his first deer, with a rifle, at age 16.

"For many years, deer hunting was a driving force. I had to be in the woods by daylight of opening day, and I'd continue there until I got a deer.

"When I started bowhunting in 1960, I decided it would be different. I'd take a fishing pole along with my bow and just enjoy the trip. But hunting is as much of an obsession now as before. Maybe I just like the challenge of the bow."

Shurtleff bought his first bow—a cheap solid-glass model—for carp shooting. Amost as an afterthought he went after deer and killed a yearling doe that first year. But he didn't dream of killing record-book bucks.

"I've always tried for bigger animals," he says. "But as I told the boys at the Pope and Young banquet, I'm a trophy hunter early in the season. As time grows short, my requirements get smaller and smaller. I like to eat venison."

George Shurtleff eats at least his share of the venison. But he collects far more than his share of trophy racks. His hunting record makes it seem easy. Unquestionably, his method is one of the best, if not the best, for this type of hunting. But it's not a matter of just climbing a tree and shooting a deer.

"Many times I've spent all day on stand without seeing one deer. Watching the birds and chipmunks is the only thing that keeps me going. I'm not particularly patient," he says.

"It boils down to one thing—to kill a trophy animal, you have to spend a lot of time at it. I average hunting about 20 days a year.

"And you have to hold out for the big one. If you kill the first deer that comes by, you'll probably never kill a trophy animal."–*Dwight R. Schuh.*

Nine Bucks for the Records

Kirt Darner rested his rifle on an aspen branch and watched the two mule deer bucks. They both had respectable racks and were in full view only 50 yards away. Darner wasn't interested in either one. He believed there was a truly great trophy buck somewhere in the dense cover behind the other two.

It was a gamble because the daylight was fading. Darner had only two or three more minutes of shooting light in which to spot the incredible buck he had seen the day before. He couldn't be sure, but the two feeding bucks looked like a pair that had accompanied the great buck the previous afternoon. If so, the trophy deer might be just out of sight.

Darner used his big Navy-surplus binoculars to take the oak brush and aspens apart, one branch at a time. His eyes watered with the strain.

Then a slight movement caught Darner's attention. An oak branch stirred at the edge of the thick aspen grove as though something had brushed against it. Was it his imagination, or was a third deer moving from the thick timber into the scrub oaks? Darner stared even more intently, but he saw nothing.

A moment later a horizontal form took shape in the brush. It was the body of a deer. Darner spotted huge antlers when the buck lifted his head to feed on the frosted leaves of an elderberry bush. The deer was shielded by a heavy brush, and a shot would have been risky. Darner had to wait for a clear target.

It was 1962. Darner, 23 years old at the time, was hunting New Mexico's Carson National Forest near Chama with several friends. Kirt had killed several deer in the past, but he had high hopes of getting a really big buck on this trip. The men in his family often discussed their trophy bucks with pride, and Kirt wanted to take a big buck too.

Most of all, he wanted to better the 31-inch outside spread of a buck his brother had killed.

Kirt had plenty of reason to be optimistic. Big mule deer were common in much of the West then, and New Mexico had a two-deer season that year. Many Western states offered two deer tags per hunter in those banner mule-deer days.

Kirt's dream came true early in the hunt. He was crossing an oak thicket when five bucks flushed from the cover. He took a running shot at the biggest and hit it in a leg. Kirt jerked the bolt back, but the rifle was new, and the stiff magazine spring somehow tossed the remaining cartridges out. He grabbed one off the ground and loaded it directly into the chamber, but the buck was gone. Disgusted with his bad luck, Darner trailed the wounded buck. If the gun had functioned correctly, he might have been able to fill his tags.

Five hours later, Kirt caught up to the wounded buck and downed it. The deer was a magnificent animal with heavy antlers that measured 31½ inches, outside spread. Each main beam measured an astonishing 8¼ inches around at the base.

After field-dressing the buck, he backpacked the cape and antlers to camp. Shortly afterward he saw the three bucks, including the great trophy deer, but he couldn't get a shot at him. Kirt was determined to try for him the next day. While he packed the meat from his first buck back to camp early the following day, his mind constantly strayed to the huge buck. With the chore over, he hurried back to the place where he had seen the trophy deer. There, he finally spotted the enormous buck feeding in the fading light.

Kirt's break came a moment later. The buck moved and raised his head to feed on a high branch and he exposed his shoulder. The hunter fired once, and the buck slumped to the ground dead. The huge antlers had an outside spread of 35 inches, and there were five long, massive tines on each side.

As soon as Kirt got back to Chama with his deer, he went to Ozzie

Kirt Darner shows the magnificent nontypical mule-deer trophy he took in 1977 in Colorado. The Boone and Crockett score is 273 6/8.

Washburn's house. Ozzie—a guide, trapper, and experienced woodsman—was impressed when he saw the big buck. "That's the biggest mule deer rack I've ever seen," he said in amazement. "You ought to have it measured for the records."

Kirt did, and the buck placed comfortably in the Boone and Crockett records with a score of 197 3/8. Currently the trophy ranks 189th in the typical mule deer category.

Taking that buck obsessed Kirt Darner with a giant mule deer, and he devoted a lot of time each year to scouting mule deer country and planning hunting trips so that he would have as many chances as possible to hunt trophy bucks. Today, 19 years after he took his first record deer, he has taken eight more record-book bucks. Four are listed in the current (7th) edition of North American Big Game Awards Program (Boone and Crockett) record book; three are scheduled to be listed in the next edition; and two qualified for earlier editions were dropped from the listings when the minimum-score requirements were raised. A tabulation of all nine record deer appears later in this article.

How does he do it? Why has Kirt Darner been able to take so many record-class bucks?

"There are several answers to that question," Kirt said when I asked him, and he settled down comfortably to tell me all about it.

"I've lived and hunted in country that produces record-class mule deer," he told me. "Out of the 293 typical mule deer in the current record book, 123 were shot in Colorado, the No. 1 state, and 37 more were taken in New Mexico, the No. 2 state. I was raised in New Mexico, and I killed my first buck when I was in the seventh grade. Most of my deer hunting has been done in New Mexico and Colorado, but I do hunt in other states if I know of a place that produces big bucks. Recently, I killed a record-book buck in Wyoming's Greys River country."

Darner and I were sitting at his kitchen table, and he pointed out of the window to the jagged snow-capped peaks of the San Juan Mountains.

"There's the best big-buck country in the West," he said. "Doug Burris killed the No. 1 world-record typical buck there in 1972, and those mountains have produced many other great heads. There are record-class bucks in those mountains right now."

Darner's home is on the outskirts of Montrose, Colorado, and that fact made it difficult to interview him. It's great game country, and we were constantly distracted by assorted wildlife in his backyard. Pheasants appeared now and then to feed on corn kernels, and a muskrat lazily swam across the pond he keeps stocked with rainbow trout and channel catfish.

At 41, Darner is lean and trim, and well groomed. He bears a slight resemblance to Neil Diamond, the popular singer. His work as a forester for a lumber company keeps him in excellent physical condition. His daughter and three sons, and his attractive wife, Paula, share his outdoor interests. Mrs. Darner killed a big six-point bull elk during the 1980 season.

There were distractions inside the house as well. Mounts of a desert big-horn ram, a Rocky Mountain ram, Coues deer, elk, several mule deer, and a grizzly bear rug were displayed on the aspen-lumber walls of the living room and kitchen.

Again Kirt pointed out of his window, this time in another direction. "That's the Uncompahgre Plateau," he told me. "It's hunted hard every year. During the deer season, it's like Grand Central Station, but there are still some fine bucks up there. I hunted a huge buck there last year, but he gave me the slip. What I'm saying is that I live right in the middle of great deer country. Five years ago, my company told me I could live anywhere in southwestern Colorado. I chose Montrose, and you know why."

I still had no real answer to my most important question. Other skilled hunters hunt where Darner hunts, but he has set himself apart by taking nine record-book bucks. I asked him about it again.

"My work as a forester really helps," he told me. "I worked for the United States Forest Service in New Mexico, and my current job as a forester for a private company helps, too. While I'm working on timber sales, I constantly look for deer as well as good timber. And on my own time during weekends and vacations, I ride horseback through new country, to look for big deer.

"I talk to a lot of people too—game wardens, ranchers, road surveyors, and other foresters. Sheepherders are especially helpful. They live in the high country all summer, and they see a lot of deer."

I know sheepherders, too, and I asked Kirt how he communicates with them. Many sheepherders are Basques or Mexicans and speak little or no English.

Kirt chuckled at the question. "I know enough to get by," he responded. "And many sheepherders do speak a little English. A few years ago, for example, I got wind of a huge buck in the San Juans. During the summer before deer season, I looked up a Spanish-speaking herder who was with his herd right where the big buck was supposed to be. I asked him my standard question. I raised my hands over my head like antlers and said: 'Muy grande venado?' The sheepherder smiled and told me: 'Si, Señor. I see beeg wan week ago. That way—two mile.'

"I checked out the area and found a set of huge tracks. I didn't see the buck, but I did find out where he was watering, and I waited for him when the season opened. I almost wore a hole in the ground waiting, but he finally showed up one afternoon, and I was ready. His rack was the widest I've ever taken—41½ inches—but there were so many penalty points that he didn't make the book."

Though it's a great help to know about a big buck beforehand so he can be hunted in his home range, there is no guarantee he can be *seen* and *shot*. Darner does several things that give him an advantage.

"I hate to sit on a stump or rock and wait for a deer to show up," he said. "I do it only when I must. My favorite way is to ride my horse into the back-country where I know there are big bucks and then still-hunt on foot. Record-class bucks are smart. They're at least five or six years old, and they know all the tricks, and they remember them on opening day. I like to look for big deer at about 8,500 feet where the oak and quaking aspen cover meets. Foresters call it transition forest, and I think it produces the biggest deer because of the dense escape cover and excellent feed.

"If I'm hunting where I think there are some big bucks, I may not walk a half a mile all day. I really want to cover the area in detail. On the other hand, when I'm scouting, I may walk eight or ten miles to locate the buck I want.

"Hunting slowly—and I do mean slowly—is very important. I look for something a bit different in the brush—movement that might be the flick of an ear, the gleam of an antler, a horizontal shape, a patch of white.

"I often hunt in what I call the fishhook pattern. All it means is that I like to circle off to the right or left and come around parallel to my original route but a short distance away from it. When a hunter disturbs a wise old buck in his bed, the deer often waits until the hunter goes past him and then

Seven of Kirt Darner's trophies. They are regularly displayed inside the store in Montrose, Colorado. Outside spread ranges from 35 to 45 inches.

slips away quietly, but he'll often circle back to the place where he started. Most of the time, the hunter doesn't see or hear the buck, but if he circles back fairly often, he has a chance of meeting a buck."

Many skilled hunters believe the biggest mule deer live in the alpine forest near the timberline. Darner has his own opinion.

"Sure, there are big bucks up in the rimrock and in the high evergreen country," he told me, "but there are so many summer backpackers and hikers in many places that the big bucks just pull out and head for thick brush where they won't be disturbed. A big old buck doesn't like to be around people. He'll always head for country where he can be alone. In Colorado and New Mexico, that often means scrub oak and dense aspen forests, fairly low."

I looked out of the window and watched storm clouds forming over the rugged San Juan peaks. Kirt must have been reading my mind.

"Now is the time I like to hunt," he said. "Some people say the deer lie up during a storm and stay put until it clears. I don't believe it. I've killed some of my biggest bucks during storms when deer were actively feeding. Most of them never knew I was there because they were so intent on filling their bellies before the snow covered up their grub. Besides, their vision is hampered during a snowstorm, and I'm convinced the snowflakes hitting their ears interfere with their hearing. And you can move around quietly on the soft fresh snow."

Kirt Darner's Record Mule Deer

Year killed	Area killed	Score	Rank	Category
1962	Chama, NM	197 3/8	189	Typical
1964	Chama, NM	193 2/8	*	Typical
1965	Chama, NM	223 6/8	*	Non-typ.
1965	Chama, NM	196 7/8	205	Typical
1968	Chama, NM	209	17	Typical
1969	Pagosa Springs, CO	203 3/8	56	Typical
1973	San Juan River, CO	199 6/8	**	Typical
1977	San Miguel River, CO	273 6/8	**	Non-typ.
1979	Greys River, WY	209	**	Typical

*Not listed in current edition; minimum scores were raised.
**To be listed in next edition.

Before I left, Kirt showed me his old reliable Remington 700 ADL 7 mm. Magnum, the rifle he's used to shoot most of the deer he has taken. "This gun is like a part of me," he said. "I own others, but I never hunt deer without this rifle."

As I turned to leave, I pointed into the distance and asked one final question: "Is there a new world-record buck somewhere out there?"

Kirt frowned and took time to think. "I really can't say," he finally said. "Doug Burris's fantastic No. 1 buck is tough to beat, but the right bloodlines are still out there in those mountains. There's a good chance that a better buck is wandering those ridges, but if he is, I'll bet he's killed by some guy sitting on a stump eating a sandwich. When it comes down to it, you really have to know your trees."

"How's that?" I asked.

"You have to be sitting under the right one when muy grande venado comes along," he answered with a grin.–***Jim Zumbo.***

PART 5 OUTDOOR LORE CAN MAKE THE DIFFERENCE

Lost!

There's a new scientific approach to search and rescue. Teams are now trained to analyze the behavior of a person lost in the woods and predict his movements with surprising accuracy.

Harry knew he was in trouble, but it was beginning not to matter to him. The snow people would not help him. They were in their little snow houses, sitting by fires warming themselves. But they wouldn't let him in. Had he been lost two nights or one? He couldn't even remember when he had lost his rifle.

Harry really was in trouble. He had gotten lost the day before and was now spending his second night in the snows of New Mexico's Pecos Wilderness. He was entering that dangerous stage of hypothermia (cold exposure) in which his brain was affected. He could no longer make safe judgments and was experiencing delusions: the "snow people" and that "lodge" that suddenly disappeared. He was barely standing; if he was not found soon, he would die in the snows of the Sangre de Cristo Mountains.

He had started out for a weekend of deer hunting with two friends in the Santa Fe National Forest on Saturday morning. At about 8 a.m., when the snow became too deep to drive through, they left their vehicle and separated, each to do his own hunting. They agreed to rendezvous at an old cabin a few miles away between noon and 2 p.m. But in the heavily forested steep canyon of the Cow Creek and Elk Creek drainages, Harry became lost. He had fired two shots, the previously arranged signal. His partners searched for him Saturday afternoon and Sunday morning and then went to report the incident to the New Mexico State Police.

Like most people who get lost, Harry was unprepared. He was wearing cotton clothing, which may have been sufficient for the time he had planned to be outside. But now the snow was 15 to 18 inches deep. The temperature during the day was in the 30s, posing a danger of hypothermia because cold wetness soaks cotton clothing and wicks heat away from the body.

By Sunday afternoon, search teams were in the area. Officials called the Rescue Coordination Center at Scott Air Force Base, Illinois, and received a mission number so they could use military and Civil Air Patrol aircraft. But the weather—heavy cloud cover close to the ground—was keeping them out of the air.

Near the vehicle, searchers found Harry's footprints, but blowing snow obscured them a short distance away. Since the man had been gone for so many hours, and was in such bad weather, the search coordinator decided to saturate the most likely area for finding him with seven field teams. Snowshoes wouldn't be practical on steep terrain, on top of blowdowns and thickets. The team members, each with full pack for self-reliance in the wilderness, would have to slog through the snow. It was going to be hard, slow going. A tough search.

The science of lost-person search has developed tremendously over the past several years. New techniques and equipment help, but the big gains have been in improved search team training and a systematic, well-coordinated approach to managing the search. This has come about in part as a response to the increasing number

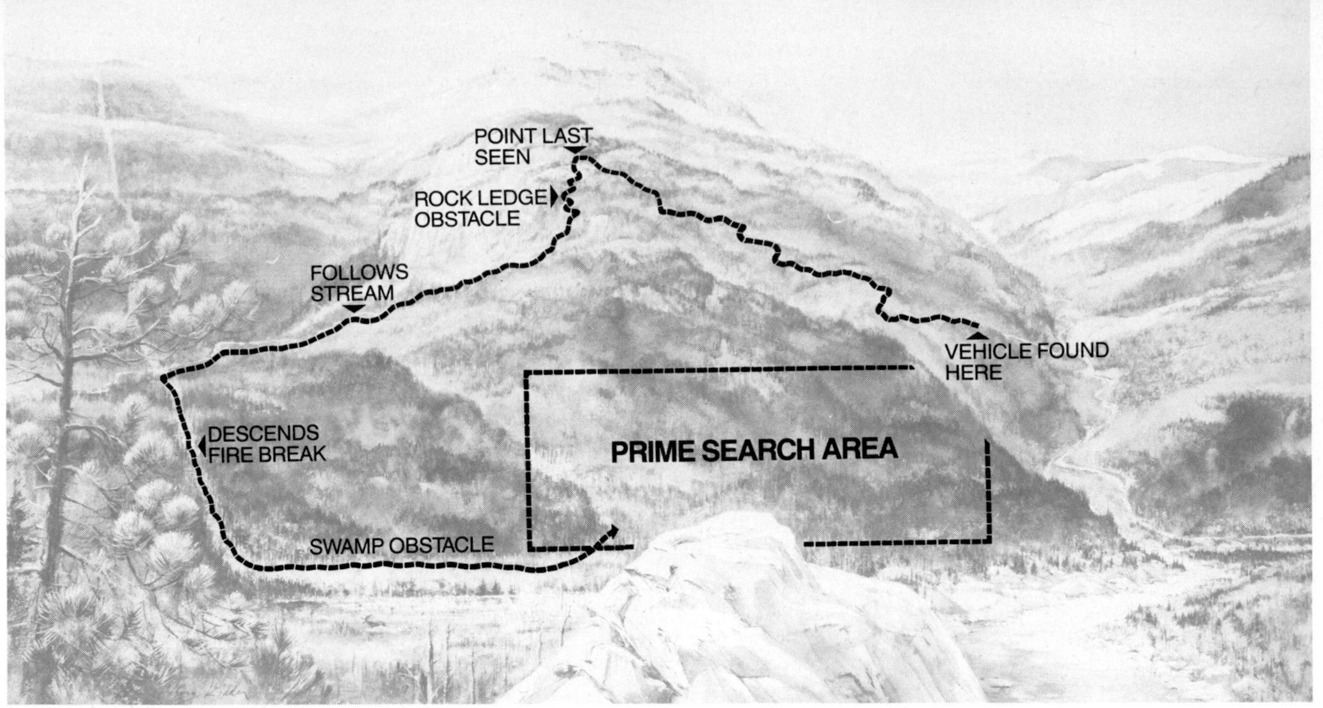

This drawing shows the path of a lost hunter. Note how he heads downhill when he realizes he is lost. He avoids natural obstacles, such as rock ledges and swamps. He follows travel aids, such as firebreaks and streams. All these factors will lead him into the prime search area or area of probability, a location which has already been predicted by search and rescue teams.

of outdoor recreationists, but also because of some well-publicized searches which, despite enormous expenditure of man-hours and money, ended in failure.

One of the most publicized of these was the Dennis Martin search in the Great Smoky Mountains in 1969. Dennis, 7 years old, was last seen at about 4:30 p.m. on June 14. When his father looked for him a few minutes later, he could not locate the boy. Rangers were notified, and they began a search. The effort escalated until 1,400 men including Green Beret units, the Air Force, FBI and 58 rescue squads were searching. The cost was said to be more than $287,000. No trace of Dennis was ever found.

A search for a teenager missing in Colorado several years ago probably cost well over a million dollars. In addition to civilian teams, it involved 500 army troops along with helicopters and support equipment. They did not find the youth. Fifteen days after the search began, he walked up to a search team and said, "Can someone help me? I'm lost."

Searches like these made it apparent that sending many people with vast amounts of material into the woods was simply not the best way to go about the job. Wilderness, even just a few square miles of it, is much too vast and complex for even thousands of men to cover completely. And hundreds of people, even if military, are too many to supervise and coordinate adequately.

The old method of conducting a search (and in some areas it's still used) was to empty the pool halls and the junior high school, line everybody up and run them up and down the mountain. There may have been a few coronaries and a few more lost adolescents among the searchers, but generally, if they were working a large area, they never found anything. This was not surprising, since the untrained and unskilled volunteers usually were working under poor coordination.

Many search teams still are made up of volunteers, but today organizations like the Mountain Rescue Association and the National Association for Search and Rescue seek out searchers who are well trained and in good physical shape. Often, the crews are fast-moving mobile units, well coordinated by a search boss who may be a professional, such as an officer of the law or a park ranger. Search bosses get training in a search management course devised by the National Park Service and NASAR.

Teams are now trained to look for clues. Few people can go through the woods without leaving a multitude of clues: footprints, broken branches, gum wrappers, spent shells, and so forth. The search boss keeps track of the progress by radio, compiling the results on his status map, trying to solve the riddle of where the person is.

One of the most important things is to know where to look, and recent research has turned up methods for predicting a lost person's behavior. Depending on whether the subject is a hunter, fisherman, backpacker, berry picker, or whatever, the search boss can estimate where he is likely to be. This is known as establishing the *area of probability.*

A search often follows the classic mystery pattern. Some of the clues are physical, like footprints; others are found in the subject's personality, and still more come from an analysis of the area in which he is lost. Would this person go uphill or down? Follow a stream or cross it? Seek shelter or keep moving?

Popular lore says that following a stream is the way to find civilization, but in certain areas of the West, streams lead deeper into wilderness. A West Virginia stream might suddenly disappear into a sinkhole.

Clues as to what a lost person will do are often found in interviews with friends and relatives. If the lost person is someone who generally needs to see in order to get oriented, chances are he will travel uphill to a vantage point. A person with an assertive personality might travel a greater distance and place himself in more danger than a less assertive person would. A logical thinker might be likely to stop, build a good shelter, and wait to be found.

Compiling a profile of a lost person enables a search boss to deploy his resources efficiently. Scientific methods for doing this were developed by Bill Syrotuck, a researcher from the state of Washington, and after his death, updated by a New York researcher, Al Kreutzer.

Syrotuck and Kreutzer found that the large majority of lost hunters would go downhill when lost. Most would also use travel aids such as foot and game trails, forest roads and firebreaks. A good proportion (34 percent) were found within the first mile, with diminishing numbers beyond that. This contrasts with the behavior of hikers, who are more often than not found beyond the one-mile area.

The actions of hunters are most often related to the game they are hunting; often they get lost because they are more interested in the chase than in navigation. When they get into trouble, it generally is because the excitement of pursuing game leads them into deep snow, underbrush or rocks. Hunters also tend to push themselves beyond their physical limits and into darkness when they are unprepared for it.

Experienced searchers know to expect a search call at the worst possible time in the worst possible weather. Many people, particularly hikers, get into trouble because of changing weather, and with lost hunters, the correlation is direct.

Foul weather, particularly heavy storms, often stimulates animal movement and improves hunting. Deer hunters know that deer often start moving before a storm comes through. In mountainous areas especially, storms can appear with little warning. So the hunter on the trail of game may be a prime candidate not only for getting lost but for having weather problems.

Searchers have also compiled some profiles of lost fishermen, but they tend to be somewhat less useful. Fishermen tend to be well oriented for navigation because they are particularly aware of the direction of water flow or the lay of a lake. A missing fisherman often has had an accident—slipping off a bank into water, falling over a cliff, or being swept off his feet in a fast-moving stream. A high percentage of these are boating accidents. Often the search for a fisherman is a "recovery mission" which is rescue terminology for going in to bring out a body.

A New York state incident a few years ago combined the two kinds of profiles. After a hunter had been reported missing on the Fort Drum military reservation, searchers concentrated on what they considered the area of probability, but found nothing. They were puzzled, since the region had very thick underbrush and swamps, and they did not see how the man could have wandered very far. But the spring thaw and rains brought the answer. He had attempted to cross a creek on a beaver dam—in the primary search area—and he had fallen off and drowned.

On the second night, one of the search teams found Harry's tracks in the snow leading into a canyon. The searchers were nearing exhaustion, and in the deep canyon radio communications were spotty. But they pushed on. They were on their own now, four men hunting to save a life.

Typical of the changes in search techniques is the use of dogs. The traditional image of a search dog is that of a bloodhound, nose to the ground, straining at the leash as it follows the tracks left by the lost person. Tracking dogs are still used, particularly where there is a fresh trail, but in some circumstances other dogs may be needed.

Search bosses have recently increased the use of "scenting" dogs such as German shepherds, particularly where it is not practical to employ tracking or trailing dogs. Every human body, alive or dead, gives off a constant stream of scent, sort of like an invisible smoke grenade. Experienced hunters understand this principle, knowing that game approached from upwind will be alerted to a hunter's presence.

Under good conditions, search or scenting dogs can detect a subject at 1,000 feet or more, even if he is hidden in vegetation, rocks or fog. Since the mechanisms of detection vary, the techniques for using scenting dogs are different. They do not need a scent article and generally do not follow the trail left by the person. Working off lead, but near their handler, they crisscross an area, noses in the air, searching for a scent. Once they find it, they head generally in a path to the subject. There are disadvantages to using scenting dogs. They have to work downwind from the subject. Searchers also have to clear out of the area, since the dogs may "find" them instead of the subject.

Image also plays a role in the selection of a search dog. Because law enforcement personnel are familiar with shepherds' "K-9" work, they may be more likely to use this breed, even though there are other good scenters—for example, the poodle. But, as Alice Stanley of the Virginia Search and Rescue Dog Association is fond of pointing out, "Imagine the reaction of a group of deputy sheriffs on a search if you were to drive up with a car full of poodles."

They were calling his name, but Harry was sure it was the snow people tormenting him, so he ignored them.

The team had found his tracks and followed them into the canyon. Harry was leaning against a tree; in a short while he would have been on the ground. Quickly, the rescue team removed Harry's wet and frozen clothes, put him in a sleeping bag and fired up their stove to heat hot drinks. As his body core temperature began to approach normal, Harry became rational once again.

Now the problem was how to evacuate. The prospect of carrying a stretcher 1,000 feet through the snow was too much for the fatigued rescuers, who requested a helicopter. The weather had cleared, so at 10:20 a.m. a helicopter from Kirkland Air Force Base hoisted Harry aboard and flew to an Albuquerque hospital. Although Harry is not his real name, the man today lives in Albuquerque.

One of the biggest headaches faced by the search boss is the possibility that the lost person may not stay in the primary search area. Every mile that the person travels multiplies the search area, extends the time needed to find him, and perhaps takes him beyond help.

A search in Baja California is an example of the frustration that searchers may experience in trying to narrow their search area.

The Baja has always had a certain mystique that attracts adventurers, some of whom never return. For those who are unprepared, the Baja is one of the most unforgiving of lands.

Fred Mundy went there on his motorcycle in November 1970. After his tour, Mundy was to rendezvous with friends back at the border. On the appointed night, he did not show. Fred Mundy was to be another victim of the Baja's Pole Line Road.

SEARCH AREA

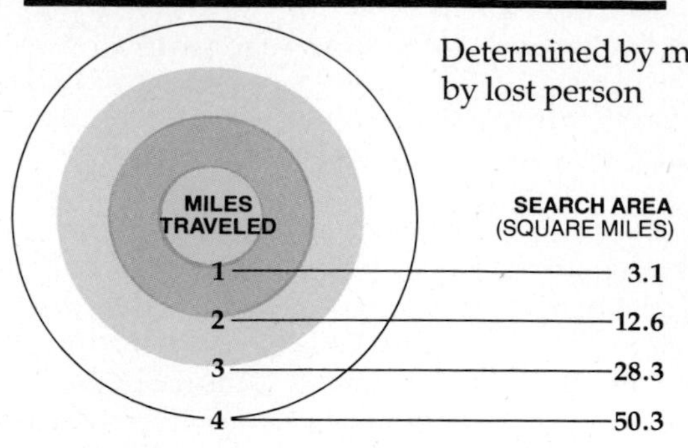

Diagram, left, shows that search area multiplies tremendously when a lost person does not stay in one place and wait for rescuers. Chart, below, indicates that in cases of lost hunters and hikers, the majority will travel downhill rather than up

WHERE THEY GO

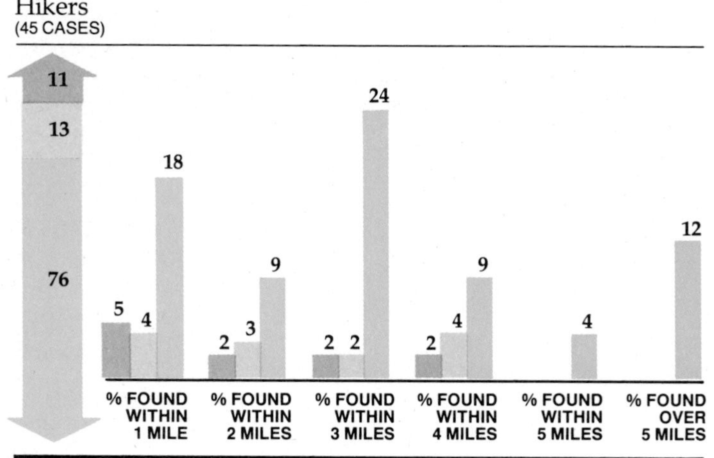

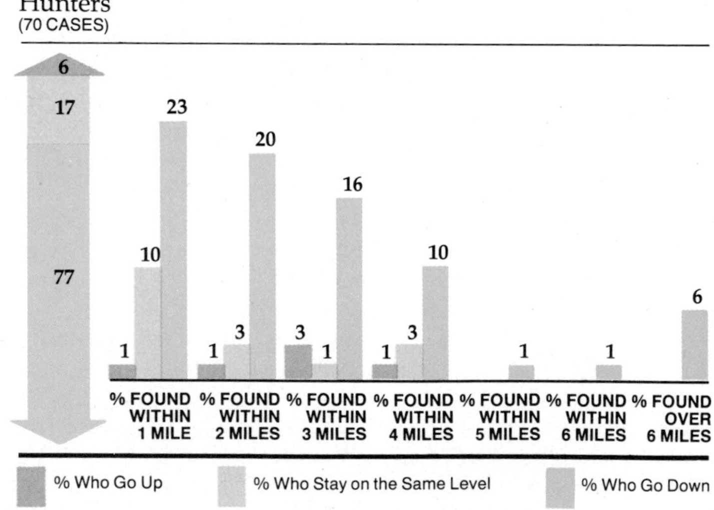

The road runs through the Tinaja Desert and connects with the road which runs to San Felipe on the Gulf of California. At the junction, the road drops into a wash where the correct road is invisible. If a man misses it, he blunders into a maze of roads used by the *leneros,* or woodgatherers. These roads branch and rebranch into the desert, leading nowhere. It was into this area that Fred Mundy disappeared; soon he ran out of gas searching for the way out.

Mundy's friends reported him missing; U.S. military planes and California search teams mobilized. Later that day a pilot spotted his motorcycle. A helicopter brought in a search team, but Mundy was not there. His tracks led into the desert. Tracking teams would have a difficult time finding him before he surrendered to the desert and its heat.

In popular mythology, trackers are a sort of mystical fraternity of mountain men and Indian scouts. Actually, mantracking has developed into a science with modern techniques. Its best practitioners are a group of men whose job is tracking people who do not want to be found and take every opportunity to cover their trails. These trackers are, of course, members of the Border Patrol who follow illegal aliens.

Most trackers who work in searches have been trained by the Border Patrol, or use its techniques. An expert tracker can follow a person through rocks, across streams, into vegetation—almost anywhere a man can walk. The trackers who followed Fred Mundy into the Baja would need every bit of their considerable skill. To know where to look for these clues, these men use a tracking stick. When they begin the track, they find two definite prints made by the lost person and use these to mark the person's stride on the tracking stick.

Mundy was known to his friends as a desert survival enthusiast, and although he had shown questionable judgment in leaving his vehicle, he was showing good sense by holing up during the day and traveling at night. Trackers found the places where he had found shelter during the heat of the day. The presence of animal tracks over Mundy's footprints told them he was moving during the cooler nighttime hours.

Jon Wartes got his first search experience as an Explorer Scout in Washington state and went on to write text books on search techniques. His first search was for a hunter missing in the Cascades. After days of search, with no sign of the missing man, the effort was abandoned. Several years later, the hunter's bones were found. Had he gone north, west or south of the search area, he would have come to a road. But the man had gone east.

Confinement—making sure the subject does not leave the primary search area—is one of the most important techniques in search, Wartes found. It can shorten search time and save the person's life. Typical confinement techniques include using vehicles on perimeter roads, running personnel along area trails and posting observers at trail junctions and high observation points.

Wartes and his Explorer Scouts have developed sophisticated confinement techniques. His personnel pay out miles of string in a grid pattern around the area of probability, attaching cards with arrows indicating which direction to go to find help.

After he has made his field assignments and tried to confine the subject, a good search boss assigns someone to do the "bastard search." This is so named because in some instances the searchers, after a night of tromping through thick underbrush in freezing rain, find the "victim" at the Tune Inn Bar & Grill with a bucket of suds, or in the arms of a local floozie. That's when they say, "You bastard!"

In fact, though not all of these are "bastard" searches, about one search in four is for a person who is not really lost. Sometimes this happens because of bad communications when a group of people separate and make plans for a rendezvous. A hysterical relative might be confused about the time a person was supposed to return.

TIPS FOR BEING FOUND

1) Plan for being lost. Carry a compass and a simple survival kit. Have wool clothing which prevents heat loss when wet.
2) Think. If lost, sit down and have a smoke or a chew—whatever puts you in a contemplative mood. Your best weapon is rational thought. In good weather, move to a high place to find landmarks.
3) Survive until found. In foul weather, hole up and build shelter and fire. Keep warm and dry. Don't travel during storms. In the desert, travel at night.
4) Make yourself seen. If you must travel, leave signs. Scratch your initials in the ground with direction-of-travel arrow. Build a fire. For aircraft sightings, spread out your belongings in the open; make a very large X or SOS in the ground, vegetation or snow.

And then again, there are desperate persons who elaborately stage "disappearances" in order to escape problems and start a new life. It seldom works, and it puts friends, relatives and the search team through many hours of distress.

The character of Fred Mundy's trail changed. Instead of the tracks of a healthy, resolute man, trackers began to find evidence that he was dragging his feet and, every so often, impressions where he had fallen to his knees. Why, with his knowledge of desert survival, was he traveling during the heat of the day? That mistake was beginning to take its toll.

The containment teams did not intercept him; Mundy had veered east of his motorcycle. He had no compass. The tracking team was desperately trying to catch up with him, but they were still about a day behind. They now found the words scratched in the sand: "Help" and "No Water."

On the fifth day the searchers found Mundy's body five miles northeast of his motorcycle.

There are limits to the technology of lost-person search. Airplanes, for example, rarely find an individual on the ground. Survival beacons, such as the so-called ELTs used to locate crashed airplanes, have an extremely high rate of false signals. Infrared photography picks up not only the lost person but every deer and bear in the forest.

Perhaps the hardest question of all is when to terminate an unsuccessful search. Search bosses generally do this by estimating how long the lost person could be expected to survive, taking into account the weather, terrain, subject's clothing, and so forth. Then they search three times that long. In the Adirondacks, for example, a typical deer hunter lost in winter weather might be expected to survive for three days if he was dressed warmly and had some outdoor experience. So the team would search for nine or 10 days before deciding that the wilderness had claimed another victim.–*Tom Vines.*

Your Feet Can Cripple You

Healthy feet are an outdoorsman's most important asset. A hunter or hiker won't go much farther on sore feet than a car will go on a flat tire. Principles of foot care are vital knowledge for all outdoorsmen.

Let's start with footgear. A friend of mine wears canvas deck shoes for hunting. He's an exceptionally fine hunter, and his lightweight shoes undoubtedly contribute to his stealth. But after a two week elk hunt, his feet look like tenderized steaks. The fact that he can still walk on them is a tribute to his fortitude, but it doesn't say much for his good sense. Deck shoes, moccasins and tennis shoes are fine for day hikes and slow-paced still-hunting, but for carrying heavy loads and for prolonged hiking in rough terrain, they're inadequate. I think a person should sacrifice some stealth and light weight for the comfort, durability and protection of good boots.

For general hiking and hunting, plain leather boots are fine. However, most companies now make insulated leather boots. I prefer these. My ankles bend out, causing leather boots with single wall construction to wear down easily. The two thicknesses of leather in insulated boots give better ankle support and are less inclined to break over to the side. Insulated boots also have a soft lining that makes them as comfortable as bedroom slippers.

Insulated leather boots come in waterproof and nonwaterproof styles. The waterproof models with 8-inch tops are now my choice for all-around hunting and hiking.

Insulated leather boots are not much hotter than standard leather boots in warm weather. I also don't find them much warmer in cold weather. Some companies claim their leather boots are good to zero or below, which they may be if you're hiking hard, but they perform no magic in bitter cold. Heavy socks are needed for warmth.

When really cold weather sets in, I recommend insulated shoepacs with rubber lowers and leather uppers. These have thick felt liners that keep feet warm in most conditions. I've worn these boots for several consecutive days on snow and ice and have never suffered cold feet. Also, contrary to some people's opinions, I've found them adequate for long-distance hiking. They work well with snowshoes.

One precaution to take with these boots is to dry the felt liners regularly. The boots do breathe, but the liners still soak up a lot of foot moisture. After a few days of hard hiking, they'll get soggy and your feet will get cold. A good idea is to alternate two pairs of liners so one always can be drying.

All-rubber, insulated boots are good for stand hunting or slow going in wet or cold weather, but they're less than ideal for prolonged activity. The rubber doesn't breathe, so moisture in the boot can't escape. Your socks soak it up, and when you stop moving your feet get cold.

The right socks, of course, are important for comfortable hiking. Two pairs of socks will prevent blisters. Next to your feet, wear lightweight, snugly fitting socks that won't slide. Over these wear heavy wool socks. Slippage occurs between the pairs of socks, rather than between the socks and your feet. Also, the heavy socks cushion your feet from pounding on hard ground and from abrasion

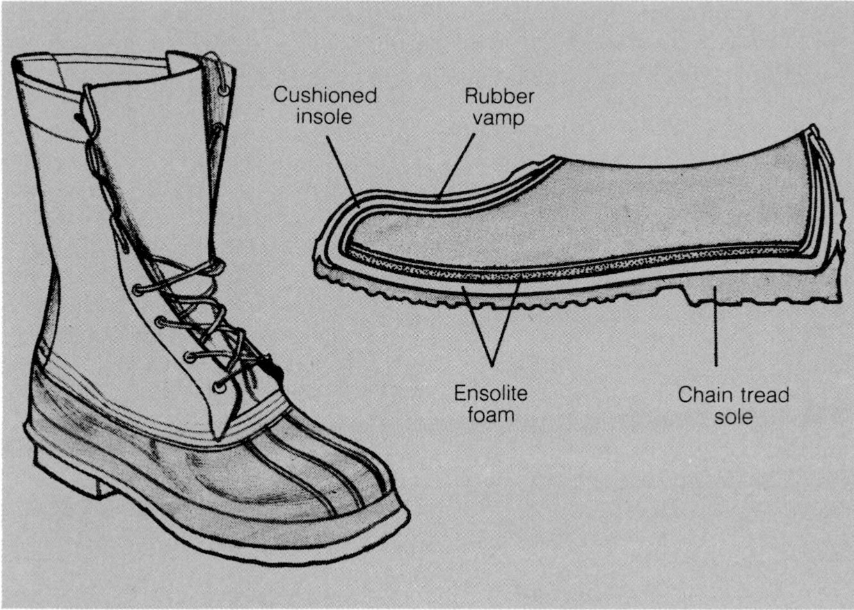

Insulated rubber and leather boots can help protect an outdoorsman's feet from cold and moisture. Two thicknesses of leather uppers give ankle support and extra protection from rocks and logs. Rubber lowers keep water out, while the leather tops allow some foot moisture to escape. In cold climates heavy socks increase the insulation capability of the boots and wick away excess foot moisture.

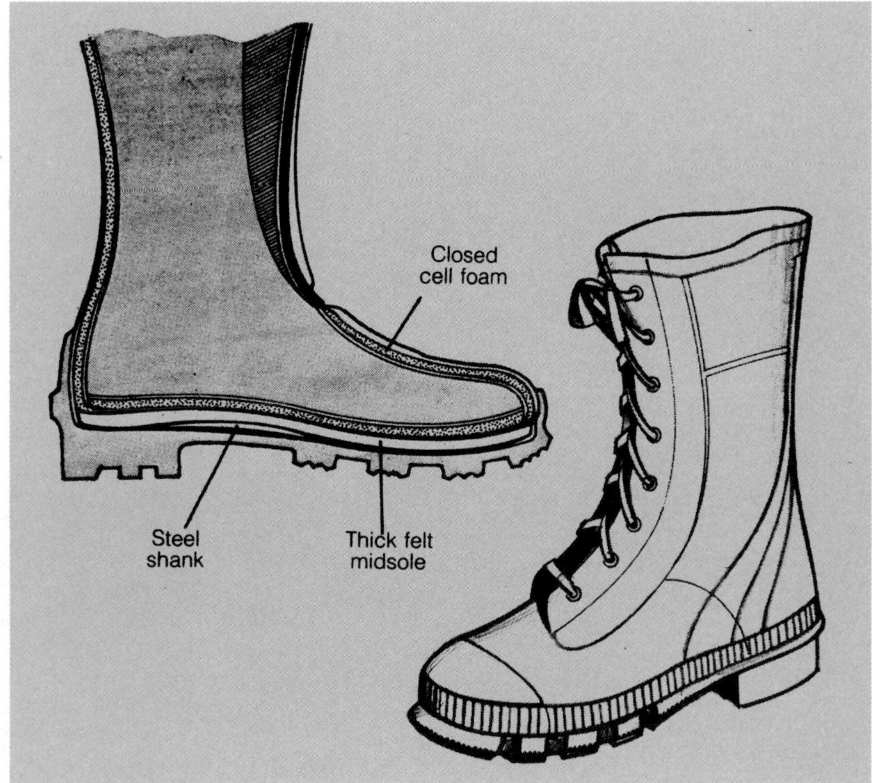

When cold weather is extreme, heavily insulated rubber boots work well. A felt midsole under the foot plus a foam padded ankle and vamp hold body heat (see cutaway). But, since rubber doesn't breathe and feet will sweat, carry along extra dry socks for periodic changing.

against rocks and logs. The thick socks also wick moisture away from your feet to keep them dry and comfortable.

Foam rubber insoles are a good addition to hiking boots. They absorb moisture, keeping feet dry and cool, and they ease the constant pounding your feet take during a hike. This is especially significant, I've found, while wearing Vibram-soled boots. I like Vibram lug soles because they ensure good footing and they wear like iron. But because they're fairly hard and stiff, they also absorb shock like iron, and they can be hard on feet without some extra padding.

For winter boots use thick felt insoles. They absorb foot moisture, and their extra half-inch of insulation between your feet and the ice or snow assures warmth.

Blisters are the most common and painful foot malady. They can weaken feet. Once, which was enough for me, I got large deep blisters on the balls and heels of my feet. They almost wiped out an elk trip for me. I learned the value of blister prevention.

The best preventive is boots that fit well. If you're buying new boots, try them on with the heavy sock you'll wear while hiking. Break them in gradually so they'll be loose and comfortable when you go on a long hike.

Damp socks also cause blisters. Carry an extra pair of socks in your pack, and change them during the day. Stopping periodically and removing boots to let socks and boots air out will also avoid dampness. If I'd done that, I would have prevented those unbearable blisters.

Moleskin, a soft adhesive material available at drugstores, also prevents blisters. If you feel hot spots or rubbed places on your feet, stop and cover them with moleskin to prevent further rubbing. It pads the sore areas, and is a hiker's best friend.

Even with the finest boots and best care, you'll still get a blister occasionally. If the blister has not popped, soak it in warm water, and with a needle or sharp knife, sterilized in direct flame, puncture the blister to drain out the fluid. Make only a small hole, and leave the skin in place over the blister to cushion and protect against contamination. Wash the blister thoroughly with soap and water, and apply a bandage.

If a blister pops, treat it like any other open wound. Wash it thoroughly with soap and water and dress it with a sterile bandage. As an added precaution, apply an antibiotic ointment to the wound before bandaging.

Athlete's foot may not be incapacitating, but it certainly can take some joy out of a trip. Here again, the culprit is moisture. And again, change socks and let feet dry. Another good idea is to dust your feet with foot powder, available at drugstores. The powder absorbs moisture and keeps feet dry.

Callouses can also cause foot pain. The safest way to reduce callouses is with a rough file made for the purpose. Do not cut too deeply, as doing so may cause infection.

Infection can be more serious in the feet than in other parts of the body. Blood circulation to the feet is poor, so healing is slow. It is important, then, to prevent contamination of blisters and callouses. The signs of infection are extreme soreness and redness. Infection may occur where toenails cut into skin, and from blisters and cuts. Treat infection by soaking the infected foot in hot water several times a day.

Poor circulation makes feet vulnerable to frostbite—another serious injury. In cold weather, lace boots loosely, and take them off at rest stops to restore full circulation to your feet. Avoid wearing clothing such as a snug belt or knickers tight at the knees that would restrict circulation to the feet.

Sore feet and joints may indicate a foot imbalance or weakness. Arch supports which often can help solve the problem, can be bought commercially. If you have a serious foot problem, you probably should see a podiatrist who will take a casting of your foot and make supports designed especially for you.

A first aid kit taken on outings should include footcare items: moleskin, foot powder, bandages, soap and antibiotic ointment.–*Dwight Schuh.*

The Knife Mystique

I read the other day that the Army is busy inventing a new knife, which is word that all knife fanciers, self included, will welcome. Most of the evolution that has brought knives to their present exalted state started out with the grim necessity for having an implement that could, well, turn off an opponent before he turned you off, and I have no doubt the new knife the Pentagon is working on will push the development of edged implements to new heights.

The account of the Army's new knife, obviously written by some whey-faced indoorsman who wouldn't know a bolster from a quillon, seemed to be trying to describe some latter-day bowie knife—broad in the blade, heavy, about 12 inches long—and it made me wonder why 150 years after the fact someone had to reinvent the famous old Arkansas toothpick that Mr. Rezin P. Bowie designed.

Now, for the benefit of deprived nonknife people in the audience, let me note that there are at least two statements in the previous paragraph that will get me in all kinds of trouble with people who know about knives or think they do. James Bowie, who fought and died at the Alamo, invented the bowie knife, they will tell me by the scores. And they also will tell me that the Arkansas toothpick and the bowie knife are two different animals; close but not identical.

I rise to defend myself. It may be a fact (and on the other hand it may not be a fact, for old Jim Bowie was a terrible liar as well as a pretty good knife fighter) that James Bowie drew up the plan for the bowie knife that an Arkansas blacksmith by the name of James Black followed in fabricating the first of the genre. That happened around 1830. But the truth seems to be that Jim pretty much copied a knife that his brother Rezin designed and had made three or four years earlier. The legend is that Rezin gave the knife to Jim, but it is my private opinion Jim swiped it, probably when Rezin was drunk. You did not give away fine handmade knives then any more than you do now. Not even to your own brother.

As to the Arkansas toothpick part of the controversy, that is a piece of esoterica that real knife freaks wrangle about incessantly, and I have no notion of getting into the middle of the argument here, except to make one mild observation: In the days when Jim Bowie was carving out his reputation, as well as his enemies' giblets, the bowie was called the Arkansas toothpick, and if it still isn't called that by purists it ought to be.

In any case, to return to the new Army knife, I was middling glad to hear about it until I got down to the fine print in the story where it said the new sticker was to be fitted with a lever-type cutter on its false edge so it could be used to cut wire. Shucks, there's no need for all that space-age nonsense. If they'd just copy the design by old Jim, or Rezin, or whoever it was who really invented the bowie, they'd have a tool that would cut wire, fell trees, split skulls, skin out deer, dig foxholes or do anything else that a real knife ought to be able to do.

What the man who designed the bowie understood was that a knife had to be heavy. A dagger, once a weapon much fancied by gamblers and perfumed ladies, can be as flimsy as a motel coathanger and still serve its sinister purpose. But a knife that doesn't have a lot of heft to it just isn't much use except for paring corns, and that's a fact. The bowie, and most of the fine knives that have followed it into American folklore, was man-size. Its weight varied with the thickness of the blade and the style of the hilt, but it always was a long knife, anywhere from around 10 inches to 16 inches and up. Rezin's original bowie was 9¼ inches long, and when Jim improved on it he stretched the blade to nearly 14 inches and broadened it from about 1½ inches to 2⅜ inches. It was an eminently useful tool for outdoorsmen, and in that simple and satisfactory world no man who wanted to see tomorrow's sunrise would venture far from his dooryard without one. Old Jim, it is said, once chopped the head off of a wretch who tried to bushwhack him, and in one stroke. He also slashed and skewered sundry frontier bullies, and we may be sure that in the final moments at the Alamo, whatever excesses the vice of braggadocio had led him into, Jim and his Arkansas toothpick gave a rousing account of themselves.

Like everyone else who spends every possible moment messing around in the woods or on the water, I feel downright undressed if I do not have an appropriate knife with me. I have had a love affair going with knives ever since my Uncle Wesley gave me my first Barlow, and I can't tell with any precision how many knives of various sorts are numbered among my chattels. The Barlow, incidentally, is a much misunderstood blade and still is one of the most useful a man can find in his armory, this despite the fact its history goes back at least as far as the Revolutionary War, and perhaps a good deal farther than that. In truth the Barlow was originally intended to be a rugged, cheap folding knife, and it served its purpose admirably. They still are made, still are well suited to the uses for which a pocketknife is intended, and, still, are often a boy's first knife. The one thing to look for in a Barlow is stout bolsters—the metal reinforcement at each end of the handle. Most authorities claim the bolsters on a Barlow should be one-third the length of the closed knife. A Barlow made by John Russell, the great American cutler, belongs as much in the folklore of this land as the bowie, and young fellows in the time of Tom Sawyer greatly prized a Russell Barlow.

There never has been a time when outdoorsmen could pick and choose between so many fine knives as they can now. You can get a lot of quality, and still not have to lie to your wife about the price, from such companies as Gerber, Buck, Kershaw, Browning, Normark, Imperial, Schrade, Camillus, Case, Ka-Bar, Boker, Queen and Timberwolf.

And any man fascinated—as I am—by knives and knife collecting could spend himself into the poorhouse nearly as fast as the guy who can't resist a new handgun or some new electronic go-devil for his bass boat. Some knives can cost as much as rifles, and be worth it. A knife is a lot more useful than any firearm (and that is another statement that will draw mail). The old deer-camp argument about picking the one survival implement you would have if you could have only one is no contest at all, for a good, heavy, well-made hunting knife is the clear winner. A rifle, or better a shotgun, would be handy in many cases, but a man who finds himself in a fix in the woods simply has to have a knife. Nobody ever started a fire or built a lean-to with a rifle, I don't care how good a shot he is.

My favorite is this U.S. Marine Corps knife of World War II vintage—a straightforward, no-frills weapon that will do anything you ask it to.

There is a mystique about knives that is probably not really understood by anyone who isn't a natural-born knife freak. An honest knife has as much personality as the best custom-honed tack driver ever to shoot bullets, and maybe more, but a lot of nonknife people don't understand this. The late Warren Page, a firearms writer of great circumstance, probably knew as much about shooting irons as any man of his time, but he was a knife illiterate. I was on a hunting trip with him once, and I had a new knife, a very nice jackknife with a four-inch blade and an amber handle, along with me. It turned into a dullish trip, with much rain and fog and little game, but I was happy because I had a fine white Arkansas hone with me, as well as a can of oil, and I had this first-class new knife to tune.

I guess I had spent a couple of days more or less full-time honing the knife when I became aware that Warren was looking a little distraught. I put it down to the fact that he had, more or less on the pain of death, quit drinking, but I found out I was wrong when he asked me, about the third day of rain and fog, how long I was going to keep honing that infernal pig sticker.

"Till it's sharp," I said.

"When will that be?" Warren asked.

"When the sun comes out and we can get out of this flaming cabin," I replied.

The knife vanished on the same trip, and I've always believed Warren pinched it and chucked it in the lake because he thought I would, in the absence of any more suitable game, dice him and our guide. I've noticed the same sort of apprehension on fellow toilers in newspaper offices, which are notorious nests of men and women who are convinced the outdoors and all the people in it are savage and dangerous. I happen to use a stylish little Finnforest sheath knife with a 3⅜-inch long blade as a letter opener, and it has earned me a reputation among the saloon-parlor set as some kind of a hell of a fellow.

It is, of course, only a question of time before the hand-wringers and losers who are terrified of firearms discover that it also is possible for people to hurt themselves and others with knives, and I suppose when that happens there will be a great hue and cry to keep gentlemen from carrying any blade more than an inch-and-a-half long. Until that happens, however, men who belong to my generation would sooner go out in society without trousers than go anywhere without a knife. I got me a very nice dress knife with a bone handle, and it usually is sharp enough to shave with if I should ever get caught short without a razor. I also have one of those knives attributed to the Swiss army, which has got eight or 10 implements attached to it, including an ivory toothpick, but if you want to know the real truth, I regard it as more a curiosity than a real knife. Mainly, of course, I seem to keep gathering knives useful in the outdoors, and with very little notice I think I could tool up to skin out anything from a gnu to a pterodactyl.

But to be perfectly honest, which is a dreadful handicap in this business, an outdoorsman doesn't actually need more than one knife, and what shape it takes is about as personal a choice as a man ever has to make. My own favorite is a U.S. Marine Corps knife of World War II vintage, and it looks like just what it is: a straightforward, no-frills weapon that will do absolutely anything you ask it to if you keep it reasonably sharp. I gather there is at least one manufacturer still making this knife, and if you can't find an original in some surplus store you could do worse than settle for a freshmade copy.

The USMC knife, however, is somewhat like the gents who once carried it in battle in various outposts, which is to say crude, tough and suitable for all manner of rugged duty. Compared to some of the handmade beauties that are available nowadays, it is as ugly as a stack of unpaid bills. But for working in the woods or on a fishing boat or, I suppose, in a mean saloon, it is totally effective. I sometimes carry fancier and newer cutlery, but that doesn't have anything to do with where my bedrock affection lies. Shucks, I sometimes drink martinis, too, even if I do consider them effete and destructive of moral fiber.

And make no mistake about it, there still are first-rate woodsmen who carry bowie knives, which like the old lady said when she kissed the cow, is all a matter of taste. But my opinion is that the bowie is mostly too much knife for what the average man is going to do with it. If handkerchief duels are your bag, well, then the bowie is probably what you need. But for shaving up kindling, skinning a whitetail or splitting a pheasant down the keel, a blade five or six inches long ought to be ample, so long as it is kept sharp.

On the subject of knives there is nearly as much misinformation as there is on the question of firearms, and this has led to some strange prejudices. For example, many jurisdictions have laws on the books limiting the length of a blade a man can tote around with him, this on the mistaken assumption that a short blade cannot inflict lethal damage. This is nonsense, and I well remember as a young reporter viewing the mortal remains of an unlucky fellow who had been done in with a tiny penknife that had a blade that could not have been longer than 1½ inches. He was just as dead as any of Col. Bowie's spectacularly gory victims, but the chap who did the vile deed had not violated the law, at least not to the extent of carrying an illegal weapon.

Another bit of legal dimbulbism that has always graveled me is the proliferation of laws against switchblade knives. Now I understand very well that the switchblade can be used for unlawful purposes, but so can a lot of other useful implements. In fact the switchblade is a very handy knife for outdoor work since it is carried closed like any ordinary jackknife but can be readied for use with one hand, which the jackknife cannot. Anyone who has ever tried holding down a flopping fish with one hand and groping for a (closed) jackknife with the other can understand how handy a switchblade can be. In Blighty they call them "flick knives" and the bobbies hate them there too. If I were of a missionary turn of mind I would print up a letterhead and launch a society to restore the switch knife to the respectability it once enjoyed.

Even more than a shotgun, if that is possible, a knife needs to fit the man for whom it is intended. Good knives, even good production-line knives, have a fair amount of hand finishing in them, which means every knife is a little bit different and deserves to be hefted and fitted to the palm before purchase. And, of course, this precaution is even more important with respect to handmade knives.

The lore of knives has made a comeback in this country, and there is a mountain of literature available on the subject, as well as a number of collectors' clubs, periodicals and the like. And if you've got the swag to indulge yourself, there are people forging custom knives in this country that have never been equalled anywhere on earth. Cheap they are not, but when you hold one of them in your hand you know you are touching the finest expression of one of mankind's most ancient crafts, and if it doesn't raise gooseflesh on you it may be that the Creator intended you to collect beer cans.–***Richard Starnes.***

Scent Trails . . . for Big Bucks

At 7:15 that morning, I heard a rustling sound to my right. I turned slowly and saw a buck walking at a fast pace toward me. He was 30 yards away, and he had his nose to the ground. The buck was following my trail like a beagle on a rabbit. I had laid a sex-scent trail about 90 minutes earlier, and the buck was coming along it step by step, precisely the way I had laid it in the predawn darkness.

I first saw the whitetail at about 30 yards, and I watched him cover about 10 yards more until he was passing my stand. Not once did he raise his nose off the ground. His nostrils were flared, engulfing every delectable whiff of the sex scent. His neck was swollen from the rut, and hair stood up on the back of his neck. Black streaks ran over his tarsal glands down to his hooves. The buck was convinced there was a doe ready to be serviced. He was going to fulfill the mating urge, and nothing was going to stop him.

I slowly rose to my feet and drew my Wing Slimline bow. I angled the arrow in behind his front shoulder, and the buck broke for heavy cover a few yards away. And then, silence! Was he down for good? I decided to wait 20 or 30 minutes before checking it out. I sat down again and started thinking about what had happened.

If you play your cards correctly, you can bring a big buck right to your stand with a sex scent, but if you use these scents incorrectly, you'll see neither hide nor horns.

At that time, I had been bowhunting for six seasons, and this was the first trophy buck that gave me an opportunity for a shot. Previously, I had gotten my share of shots at small bucks, mostly spikes and forkhorns, but the big ones had eluded me for a long while. After I started using sex scents, I started seeing bigger bucks regularly, and I have lured six bucks within bow range in the past 10 years with these scents.

These scents aren't infallible. All the bucks in the woods will not beat paths to your stand just because you are using one of them. Even with a good scent, scoring on a buck still takes a lot of planning, and you must have a thorough understanding of the whitetail in order to use a scent effectively.

I'm convinced that a $3 bottle of good sex scent is a wise investment, but there are many hunters who scoff at the idea. I think there are two reasons behind all the doubt. For one thing, the labels and printed directions (if any) of the brands I have examined do not go into detail about how to use them. Space on most labels doesn't allow it.

Second, some advertisements for these scents are misleading. One advertiser tells you to simply sprinkle a few drops around your stand and then watch out for incoming deer and get ready to see the buck of your life. Some claim that the scent will lure bucks from a mile away!

Misinformation often engenders failure, and bad news travels fast. It doesn't take long for word to get around that a particular product doesn't work. Perhaps this article will clear up some of the misinformation.

Before getting down to laying a scent trail, it is necessary to understand the buck whitetail's traits. A buck must survive at least four hunting seasons in order to reach his prime and grow an impressive set of antlers. He does so by possessing keen hearing and scenting ability and by learning that it is easier to simply avoid man than it is to escape him entirely. A big buck lives in the most rugged, out-of-the-way terrain within his territory. He knows hunters cannot move through such places without making a lot of noise. A big buck's home range includes the three basics: food, water and shelter, and he doesn't have to travel very far between the three.

Mature bucks travel well-defined routes through thick cover that expose them to the least amount of danger. They use much the same trails during the rut, but they range farther and travel more.

What does all this have to do with laying a scent trail? Even more important than knowing how to lay a scent trail is knowing where to lay one. It isn't enough to simply put a little sex scent on your boots and then walk through the woods in the hope that a rutting buck will cross your trail and follow it. You have to lay the trail on the buck's home ground, in a place where he is likely to travel during daylight hours.

As the rut approaches, bucks feel the need to establish their dominance. Big headgear often is enough. If a buck has lived four or more years and has grown a large rack and has a strong, muscular body, the smaller bucks in the area simply allow him to service the does unchallenged.

If several deer in a given range have similar racks, battles between aspiring suitors establish dominance. After a buck establishes his dominance by fending off all challengers in his area, he stakes off the perimeter of his territory.

Photograph by Gary Knepp

He makes a series of small rubs interspersed with larger ones by thrashing and beating brush and trees with his antlers. The small rubs are almost always under overhanging branches, which are often chewed as well as beaten. The buck deposits a secretion on these tree branches that is produced by the preorbital glands located at the forward corner of his eyes.

The large territorial rubs differ from the numerous small rubs made earlier in the year by bucks cleaning the velvet from their antlers. With large rubs, the bark is rubbed from the tree trunk and there will often be small holes in the wood of the tree made by the points of the antlers. A dominant buck may leave only a few of these large territorial markers or he may leave many.

A buck can fulfill the mating

urge any time during the rut. Does, however, cycle in and out of heat several times during the rut. A dominant buck in a given territory also makes scrapes that tell all the deer that he is standing at stud and is ready to service any doe in estrus. The buck urinates or even ejaculates into the scratched-out area in the ground, and the strong odor of the scrape draws does in heat from distances. Three or four fresh rubs are often near a scrape.

The buck makes several scrapes within his territory, but he rarely ventures very far from his established runs. Being the nervous creature that he is, he avoids clearings and open fields. He stays in the thickets and draws where he feels secure.

If a doe visits the scrape and the buck is not there, she often goes looking for him. But before she does, the doe leaves her own urinary calling card, walks around in the scrape to tell the buck that she was there.

The important thing here is the fact that does in heat often look for the dominant buck after they leave their calling card in one of his scrapes. Contrary to popular belief, bucks seldom roam around the woods at random hoping to come across a hot doe. This is why scent trails work only if they are placed in the proper places.

The hunter is really trying to simulate the presence of a hot doe. That is why he has to lay a scent trail on a run he knows the dominant buck is using.

If the buck returns to his scrape, which he often does during day and night to check things out, he often picks up the scent of a doe that is elsewhere looking for him. And if you play your cards correctly, it can be a scent trail that you laid down.

The dominant buck defends his territory from inferior bucks during the rut. If he is killed, however, a lesser buck establishes his dominance and continues mating with the unserviced does so that a good place to hunt with a scent trail remains a good bet from season to season.

Why go to all the trouble of laying a scent trail? Why not just find a fresh scrape, build a blind downwind and wait for the buck to return? I have hunted over quite a few scrapes without using sex scents, but I had very little success. A buck makes several scrapes in his territory, and he does not check all of them during the daylight hours. When hunting pressure is heavy, and a lot of hunters are scrambling around the woods, the wise old bucks become increasingly nocturnal. I believe a large percentage of scrapes are visited under cover of darkness. If the hunter has laid a long scent trail through the buck's domain, say 100 to 300 yards long, no matter where the buck hits the trail, he will often pick up the artificial scent and follow it to the hunter's stand.

I hunt the same areas year after year, and I have learned that scrapes and rubs will appear in almost the same places season after season. When I determine that the rut is on, I frequent these places every day to check for scrapes. If I find fresh ones, then I know it is time to start laying scent trails. I know where the best places are for blinds, and I know which direction the prevailing wind comes from.

I walk into the wind or at least across the wind, and I make sure I reach my stand at least 30 minutes before first light. It's not good to reach your stand too early. The buck may follow your trail before it is light enough to shoot. That very thing happened to me several years ago.

I had been in my tree stand only five minutes, and it was at least an hour before first light, when I heard something coming through the dry leaves toward me. It sounded like three or four deer walking close together, but I couldn't see five feet in any direction. All I could do was listen. One of the deer—it had to be a buck—eventually walked up to the base of the tree I was sitting in. I was about 12 feet off the ground.

I could hear him sniffing the air. A doe would not have been interested. Just be patient, I thought, they'll hang around until it gets light and I'll get a shot. But the deer gradually walked away and when daylight finally arrived, they were nowhere in sight. If deer could climb trees, that buck would have come right up that pine tree after me.

I usually tie either a small sponge or piece of rag onto the sides of my boots with nylon cord. If I don't have to walk through standing water or across any muddy areas, I put the rag or sponge under the arch of my boots. I squirt or pour some sex scent—it doesn't take much—on the rags or sponges. I then put a little scent on the tail of my hunting coat to mask the human odor.

I walk down a run where I located nearby fresh scrapes the day before and head for a tree stand or ground blind that I previously prepared. At the stand, I put a little more scent on a small rag and locate it nearby to mask any human odor.

During bow season, I am completely camouflaged from head to toe, including my bow and arrows. I use an olive-green mosquito head net to cover my face. I think a hunter's face, especially if he wears eyeglasses, is the first thing a deer detects, especially on a sunny day.

During gun season, I also wear complete camouflage, but, of course, I also wear a fluorescent orange vest. If it is an overcast day, I use camouflage paint on my face instead of a head net. I like to have something behind me to break up my silhouette, as well as some cover in front of me.

If a rutting buck picks up my scent trail, he will often drop his guard to some degree as he follows it to my stand. However, the buck does not become a complete fool just because he is rutting. I make sure he is looking away from me or has his head down before making a move, and even then, I move in slow motion.

I believe the best time to shoot a whitetail is when it is quartering away from you. The arrow should angle in behind the front shoulder. For that reason, I often continue my scent trail a few yards past my tree stand before climbing the tree. If I'm lucky, the buck goes beyond my stand or blind and angles away, which offers an ideal shot.

During Indiana's 1980 muzzleloader season, a big nontypical buck did exactly that. I was using a .50 Hawken and I dropped him right in his tracks. I was so sure he was down for good, I didn't bother to reload. After a few seconds he sprang to his feet and ran. All I could do was sit there.

I knew there were several hunters in the woods, and I didn't want to push the buck past anybody, so I stayed still for about 20 minutes. Then I reloaded and followed the blood trail for perhaps 30 minutes.

I found the place where my buck had been gutted out by another hunter. Steam was still rising from the gut pile. It was easy to see where he had been dragged to a nearby road. Needless to say, I never saw my buck again. I can only imagine the beautiful mount over someone else's fireplace.

The chance to take the buck that I described at the beginning of the story worked out differently. I sat and waited for only a few minutes and then followed the blood trail for about 50 yards. Luckily he went northeasterly toward the place where my pickup was parked. I found him dead about 30 yards from the road.

He was a handsome eight-pointer, but it was obvious he was past his prime. He was very gray in the face and his teeth were worn almost smooth.

He had a large gash in his left ear, probably inflicted when he battled with another buck. His 250-plus pounds probably enabled him to defend his territory effectively.

I have one closing thought about using sex scents. No buck has ever followed a scent trail I laid during a weekend or holiday when there were many hunters in the woods. Nowadays, I always try to hunt during the week. I doubt that any worthwhile buck will follow a scent trail that has been crossed by a dozen hunters.–*Bill Wilzbacher.*

Gun Care in the Cold

You've been following the tracks since daybreak, and the subzero air has turned your fingers to stinging icicles and your feet are throbbing lumps. But it was worth it. The huge buck, probably the one they call Old Bucketfoot, stands only yards away casually looking back in the direction he thinks you'll come, but you've outfoxed him all the way. The crosshairs bounce with excitement, squiggling all over his chest, but you're too close to miss and the trigger is pulled.

THULUMP is the only sound the rifle makes.

Unbelievingly, you work the action and see a loaded round eject. The buck is alert, looking dead at you, his tail flashes. Reloaded, you throw a shot at his ghost. This time the rifle bellows but the target is gone, safe in the frozen gloom.

Picking up the unfired round you see that the firing pin indent is deep and well centered, clearly the shell is a dud. And out of a fresh box too. "Well," you tell yourself, "the maker of this cartridge will sure hear from me," and you toss a fresh barrage of expletives to the swirling snowflakes.

What made the cartridge failure particularly frustrating is that you take such good care of your equipment, always heading off malfunctions before they happen. Getting ready for this hunt, for example, you gave the inside as well as outside a thorough coating of waterproofing grease, and every night of the hunt you left the rifle out in the cold so as to avoid moisture condensation. And to have a lousy bum shell ruin everything! You'll tell 'em, and you'll also tell everybody you see not to use so-and-so's lousy ammunition.

Whoa, back up for a minute. Did you say you lubed your rifle *inside* as well as outside? How much lube? What kind? And where?

"Well," you say, "the usual, around the bolt, especially the mainspring and striker, where water hides and causes rust. Used a popular brand of rust-proofing grease, wiped on plenty too, nothing's going to rust my rifle."

So there you have it, the making of a cold-weather misfire. When grease and most other petroleum-based lubricants are used at normal temperatures they are soft and free-moving. But when the thermometer drops below freezing such lubricants and rust preventatives get stiff and sluggish, so sluggish in fact that they can slow a firing pin until it can't do its job.

"But," you say, "the primer was deeply indented, it should have fired."

That is part of the problem of cold-weather gun performance, and the key to cold-weather care.

INTERNAL TROUBLE

What happened was that the heavy coating of grease on the firing-pin spring congealed when the temperature dropped, thus retarding the velocity of the striker. The firing-pin spring had sufficient pressure to indent the primer in what appeared to be normal fashion, but that was not enough. The blow has to be *fast*. The reason the second cartridge fired was because the first try had plowed enough of the thick grease out of the way to permit a snappier firing-pin fall.

Making matters worse, primer sensitivity is reduced in cold weather, and the primer metal gets stiffer as temperatures go down, reducing cartridge efficiency. If cold-weather hunting is your bag, you need to do everything possible to make sure everything works when you pull the trigger.

The first step in preparing a firearm for cold-weather use is to strip it down so that the firing mechanism, especially the mainspring is exposed. With bolt-action rifles this usually is done simply by unscrewing the bolt sleeve or shroud and sliding out the striker with mainspring and firing pin attached. The hammer mechanism of most autoloading and pump-action rifles and shotguns is easily removed from the receiver by removing a couple of large thru-pins. The hammers and mainsprings of most doubles and lever-action models are harder to get to (except, of course, doubles with detachable sidelocks), and usually call for partial disassembly or stock removal.

In any event the whole idea of getting at the mainspring is to remove any grease or heavy lubricant that may be in the spring itself or on the rest of the firing mechanism. Imported guns in general, and military surplus rifles in particular, usually have enough grease trowled over the mechanism to prevent storm and shipwreck damage.

Don't just get rid of some of the grease, take it *all* off with solvent, swabs, and a brush, and then wipe the parts bone-dry. The trigger mechanisms of autoloading and pump-action shotguns are particularly susceptible to accumulations of dust, grime, and powder particles. These stick to the oil and grease and eventually become as gummy as Irish stew. In cold temperatures it can get thick enough to really gum up the works, not only slowing the hammer but messing up the timing and locking as well. With old-style, recoil-operated shotguns, the Browning types with the heavy spring around the magazine, you should clean the recoil spring and the friction ring and wipe them dry.

When the mechanism and springs are clean and dry you have two ways to go. You can lubricate *lightly* with one of the spaceage miracle lubes that are unaffected by temperature, or you can leave the works dry and clean for the duration of the hunt. Using some lubricant is preferable, if only as rust protection, but when the temperature drops to zero or below, I prefer a dry mechanism to one lubricated with ordinary oils and greases. Remember, if the label on the lubricant container does not state that it remains thin and workable at subfreezing temperatures, it probably doesn't.

Piece of tape over the muzzle (left) keeps out snow and mud and can prevent a burst barrel. It works equally well with rifles, muzzleloaders, and shotguns. Air pressure blows tape off before projectile emerges, and accuracy is not affected. Unitized hammer mechanisms of many guns are easily removed (below) for cleaning. After all the gunk is removed, leave mechanism dry for duration of cold-weather hunt or lubricate with special lube guaranteed to remain uncongealed at very low temperature.

OUTSIDE SURFACES

Very good cold-weather (or any weather) protection for the outside surfaces of your gun are spray-on soft waxes sold under the trade names Rust Guardit (Schwab) and Cloward's Rust Proof Spray (Cloward's Gun Shop). These have no lubricating effect and should be kept off the mechanism itself, except perhaps the external surfaces of the bolt. But they are about the best proofing against ice, rain, and sleet, and they also keep your bare fingers from sticking to cold metal, which reminds me of a story.

One bitterly cold day more years ago than anyone can remember, a couple of my teenage pals and I were thrashing some brushpiles in the hopes of jumping a late-season cottontail or two. Nothing was moving so one of my pals, a budding trumpet player, announced he would toot a few notes on the barrel of his single-shot shotgun, the way old-time hunters did to call their dogs. So the muzzle of the unloaded gun went to his lips, and there it stuck fast, frozen to the tender skin. He danced around for a while, and in fact several odd notes did issue from the open breech before the muzzle became unstuck. We've called him Gabriel ever since.

MUZZLELOADERS

Blackpowder shooters are heir to a special set of cold-weather problems. A well-oiled lock that smartly strikes steel or busts caps in balmy weather is more than a little likely to become sluggish in cold weather. The traditional design of most muzzleloading locks, percussion or flint, involves considerable friction between the moving parts. The tumbler, for example, is sandwiched between lockplate and bridle and usually rubs on both. And the old-style flat mainspring may rub against the lockplate for much of its length. Though this situation prevails with most of the muzzleloaders used today, it is scarcely noticeable because most shooting is done on warm days. The trouble usually is eliminated with oil.

When the temperature drops,

the oil gets sluggish and lock parts get tight, which often results in a misfire at the worst possible time. Murphy is always out there.

Here we can take some advice from the great English gunmakers of two centuries ago, who polished the works of their locks to mirror brightness. The inside edges of the flat mainsprings (the edges that rub against the lockplate) were softly rounded and polished so that friction was reduced to a minimum. With no lubricant whatever, their locks worked with oily precision. A piece of crocus cloth wrapped around a firm, flat backer (such as an old file) will do wonders by slicking up sluggish action parts. This pays extra dividends when it's very cold.

When you go on a cold-weather muzzle-loading hunt be sure to start out with a clean, fresh nipple with a square top and good shoulders. The sensitivity of percussion caps declines with cold, so take extra steps to insure good ignition.

If I were facing the prospect of subfreezing hunting with a front-loading rifle, I would be much inclined to experiment with patch lubricants. Uncle Jess's Wonder Bear Grease may work fine on the sun-kissed practice range, but what does it do when the inside of your rifle barrel registers minus five on the thermometer? If there is any doubt about your present patch lube, put a lubed patch in the freezer for a few hours. Ideally, it should remain soft enough to ease the projectile down the barrel.

Muzzleloading rifles with their big bores and long barrels are especially susceptible to clogging with snow or mud. To make matters worse, you can't open the breech to make sure the barrel is clear. The best remedy is an ounce of prevention. Stick a piece of plastic tape across the muzzle to prevent entry of clogging materials. The same goes for modern guns. Don't worry about the tape affecting accuracy, I've tried it on several rifles, shooting from a bench-rest, and could never detect even the slightest effect.

Wood suffers in cold weather too, and the best protection is a tough, water-resistant plastic-type finish such as those used by some manufacturers and custom stockmakers. Most stocks are finished with varnish or lacquer and don't take well to temperature changes. The hairline "age" cracks you see in some stock finishes are accelerated by extreme temperature changes, and one of the best protections against this is an old-fashioned paste-type floor wax, the kind recommended for hardwood floors. A good waxing not only protects your stock from wet and cold but makes it look much better too. You'll find that a lot of those little scratches on your stock will vanish.

SCOPES

Time was when users of telescopic sights lived in endless fear of scope "fogging" and freezing on the day of the big hunt. That's one reason why quick-detachable scope mounts were all the rage three decades ago and before. Most of today's scope owners will never see it happen, but for the curious here's what took place.

Warm, moist air could and did enter the unsealed scopes of that era. Since the moisture was suspended in the air it was invisible and caused no concern, but when the scope was exposed to the cold the inside air contracted, causing the moisture to condense into a layer of water droplets. If the layer of droplets was sufficiently dense you couldn't see anything through the scope except a foggy image. If the weather was really cold the condensed moisture would freeze, creating a frosty pattern of ice crystals inside the scope. You *really* had problems.

Makers of scopes here in the U.S. now offer wonderfully waterproof, fogproof instruments and the better imports are also fogproofed. The catch is that some tinkerers can't resist screwing the eyepiece off their scopes to see how they work, thereby ruining the seals and allowing moisture to enter. Some of the latest scopes, are tamperproofed for this reason.

If you have an older scope that you think might give you problems in cold weather, the wise thing to do is retire it from big-bore shooting in cold weather. These older scopes make wonderful sights for rimfire rifles. Get yourself a new fogproof model for your big-game rifle. These newest scopes are unaffected by rain, snow, and subzero temperatures.

Even a new scope is subject to *outside* fogging. If your gun has been outside in subfreezing weather for any length of time, it becomes as cold as the surrounding atmosphere. Then, if the gun is taken inside a warm, steamy tent, cabin, or car, the cold steel and glass causes moisture in the surrounding air to condense and collect on the gun's surface and the scope, including the lenses. It's the same thing that causes eyeglasses to steam up when you've been in the cold and go into a warm room.

Sometimes this layer of moisture is surprisingly dense, enough to pretty well soak a hand towel if you wipe it off and will remain on the gun for a good while. If you take the gun back outside, into the freezing air, while it is still wet, the moisture will freeze into a thin layer of ice and stay there. A coating of this ice will put your scope out of order until it is removed from the lens, and in some cases will even freeze the action shut. The rule then is once your gun gets cold, let it stay cold until the hunt's over and then give it a good drying and a nice coat of oil. It will make you both feel better. Many old-timers simply left their guns on the porch. Nowadays, it's wiser to leave them in an unheated shed or cellar room with a good lock. *–Jim Carmichel.*

PART 6 MATTERS OF SPORTSMANSHIP

Socking It to the Poachers

Late one fall evening before the Ohio deer hunting season opened Jim Splete, a conservation officer, was cruising slowly along Beagle Club Road looking for a place to hide. He turned his car onto a farm machinery lane and drove 100 yards into a field. Then he backed into a thicket from which he could watch the country road below without being seen.

He and Bill Carper, another southern Ohio officer, settled down to wait. Hours went by, but scarcely any traffic moved along the road. Shortly after one o'clock in the morning, when Splete and Carper were about to give up, a car snaked around a bend and the beam of a flashlight quickly swept over the field.

Splete let the car pass. Then he radioed another law-enforcement car waiting on the next road to the west, thinking that he and the officers in that car might be able to trap the jacklighters between them. For a while, driving along the twisting hilly roads without lights, Splete and Carper saw no trace of the poacher's car.

"I decided I had lost him," Splete told me, "so I turned on my lights and picked up speed."

He'd no sooner topped a rise when he saw the poacher's car stop directly in front of him, its driver playing a light over the field. Suddenly the poacher's car

Photograph by Art Carter

An incredible two million deer and countless moose, elk, ducks, rabbits, and other game species are being killed every year by poachers. For years the public's attitude toward this ruthless slaughter has been largely one of indifference. But that's changing. Now many lawabiding citizens are incensed about it, and they're providing the evidence and support law-enforcement officers need to really sock it to the poachers.

rocketed forward in a cloud of dust. The mud-caked license-plate numbers were illegible. The subsequent chase lasted 45 minutes during which the officer's car went off the road several times.

"I don't want another one like that," Splete said.

The jacklighters escaped, but that was no great surprise to Splete. He was confident he knew who the poacher was. An artist at eluding capture, the man had a thick file of citizen complaints against him. The officers were sure that sooner or later they would nail not only the deer poacher but his teenage son who for years had been understudying his daddy's tricks.

A break finally came in the form of a phone call. The poacher had been seen shining a deer, and a rifle shot had been heard. This time officers were on the scene fast enough to halt the car. The poacher had two friends with him. The officers found a flashlight in the car, but no gun. That meant no case.

Early next morning while searching the fields along the road, the officers found two dead deer. Then they confronted the men who had been riding in the poacher's car, one at a time, with their evidence. They learned that two men, including the poacher's son, had jumped from the car the night before, taking the gun, and had walked home. The officers confronted the poacher with their evidence, and he and his son confessed.

Once caught, the poacher enjoyed telling how he operated. He bragged of having killed 389 deer, and by the time you read this he may be back in business. He was infuriated when the judge gave him a four-month jail sentence for killing two deer.

"You ain't seen nothin' yet," the poacher said. "Wait till I get out."

This is only one case that illustrates how our wildlife resources are being raided by criminals. In state after state poachers are cutting heavily into the game supply.

It is impossible to estimate with any precision how many deer are killed illegally, but if wildlife officials are correct, the total must be staggering. In New Mexico, where a hard-hitting campaign against poachers is under way, authorities believe wildlife thieves take 34,000 deer a year. These are valued at more than $3 million, and to that figure can be added the cost of maintaining a force of officers to combat poaching. In just this one state lawabiding hunters are taking a multi-million dollar beating at the hands of outlaws. Poaching can vary with the pressure put on the poachers, but officials in numerous states maintain that the illegal kill of deer equals or exceeds the number taken legally. The annual legal kill of whitetail and mule deer in the United States is about two million.

Commercial poaching is extensive. While sometimes a woodsman who sells a few deer in the course of the year gets picked up, conservation officers also uncover large rings of market hunters. On one Saturday morning in January 1979 some 30 federal game agents teamed with 130 Michigan wildlife officers and swept down on a market-hunting ring operating in the Detroit and Jackson areas. Within two hours 53 of the 54 suspects on whom solid evidence had been collected were arrested, and the 54th was picked up later that day. The ring was known to have sold more than 100,000 wild animals and fish, all taken illegally. Included were 300 deer, 4,400 ducks, 1,700 squirrels and 1,100 rabbits. The leader of the ring boasted that in just one year he made $200,000 by selling wild meat.

Added to the market hunters' take are individual animals killed illegally for home consumption. An unknown number of wild animals are also shot for reasons unknown. Among them are deer, elk and moose that are left to rot in the woods, eagles potted with rifles, and illegally killed ducks hidden in marshes.

One hopeful sign in this depressing picture is that public attitudes toward poachers appear to be changing. Increasingly, law-abiding citizens incensed over poaching of wildlife are giving tips and evidence to officers and agreeing to appear in court. Many who haven't wanted to get involved traditionally have passed poaching off as the game warden's problem. But there appears to be a growing realization that poaching is everyone's business, and that it is time to shed the fuzzy, time-worn excuses that have protected wildlife thieves. All of us have heard the excuses— "They're only taking an animal now and then and that's not going to hurt anything." The loss is not the single animal taken but the total impact on wildlife resources made by thousands of illegal acts that take place across the country year after year.

Another argument goes, "Those are just poor folks out there taking what they need." That's the weakest of excuses. Those poor folks often drive costly pickup trucks equipped with two-way radios that they use to warn each other of the whereabouts of the law-enforcement officers.

"My gut feeling," says Patrol Inspector James C. Wictum of California's Department of Fish and Game, "is that the effect of unemployment is minimal."

State of Minnesota figures show that when the annual average unemployment levels are compared with the number of big-game arrests from 1967 to 1977, only between 1974 and 1975 do they move in the same direction. At all other times, as unemployment increased, arrests decreased.

In any case, is poverty a legitimate excuse for stealing? John Crenshaw of the New Mexico Department of Game and Fish says, "If it is OK for him to steal wildlife as long as he eats it, it is OK for him to steal a calf as long as he eats it too."

Richard Branzell, a federal game agent who works out of Reno, Nevada, is one who sees attitudes changing. "Twenty years ago when I started out as a state wildlife officer," he says, "the pillars of the community would sic their dogs on me. It's not so anymore.

People are getting away from the feeling that it is better to protect the outlaw than be a snitch. The old days of going out on blind patrols are gone. We spend most of our time now following up on leads and complaints."

Tips often bring poachers to justice. On a September day in 1979 two young men in Ohio used rifles to kill two Canada geese. A nearby farmer heard the shots and saw the geese. He pursued the shooters as they fled the scene, leaving the geese and their rifles behind. Later a state game protector found the shooters. Each of them forfeited $700 bonds and had their rifles confiscated by the court.

In November 1979 some duck hunters crouched in blinds along Saginaw Bay near Fish Point, Michigan. Several watched a flock of seven whistling swans come in low across the bay. Then two men stood and emptied their shotguns, and two of the swans fell. Years ago the witnesses might have kept quiet, but this time several of them volunteered their evidence to the local federal game agent. The agent later sent them all personal letters thanking them for helping bring the poachers to court where they were fined $500 each.

Following a Game and Fish Department appeal for help, a citizen's tip led Arizona wildlife officers to two men who had killed six elk illegally. Their fines totaled $3,808, and they also were sentenced to 60 days in jaul.

Branzell's experience has been that people have various reasons for informing on poachers. "Some just want to do what is right," he says, "and others want to even up old scores." Officers also find that their best information often comes from those who will talk for money, and this may be why law-enforcement agencies are increasingly willing to pay for tips that lead them to poachers. As a result, poachers can never be sure who will hear about their activities.

The Michigan United Conservation Clubs believes in the reward system. MUCC maintains a standing $500 reward for information leading to the conviction of poachers for killing elk, moose, wolves, and eagles, all fully protected. In Michigan this program is known as the Poacher Patrol. The $500 reward has been given several times. Furthermore, MUCC wants the state legislature to add 25¢ to the cost of each hunting, fishing and trapping license to raise $700,000 a year for rewarding those who help nail poachers. MUCC believes this would bring fast relief to poaching problems.

In Oklahoma's Operation Game Thief rewards range from $50 to $250. This state, like some others, also maintains a toll-free telephone number for informers calling long distance. Bruce Stromp, Oklahoma's information specialist, admits that the program was copied from New Mexico's Operation Game Thief.

The origin of the plan in New Mexico is traced to citizen participation and not to a brainstorm in the state Department of Game and Fish. One day Tom Reinhardt of Albuquerque walked into the department's office. He was upset by a report that poachers were taking more deer than law-abiding hunters were, and he had detailed plans for fighting poachers.

As a result, if you spot a poacher in New Mexico you may, by simply supplying wildlife officers with the information you have, get a reward ranging anywhere from $50 to $1,100. Information leading to the arrest of a big-game poacher brings rewards starting at $250. If you want to be anonymous, the department will assign a secret number to you instead of asking your name, and it will even arrange to drop reward money at an agreed upon location.

At first, the department ran up against a block when the state didn't supply money to pay the rewards. But sportsmen clubs quickly contributed funds, and the New Mexico Wildlife Federation chipped in $4,700. People are still contributing and the plan is flourishing.

"Some of our calls are coming from characters who are crooks themselves," says Ted Burt, chief enforcement officer for the department. But Burt sees this undergoing a slow change. "Last season," he told me, "we had a lot of calls from sportsmen who saw something and called us as soon as they could get to a telephone. I think they're learning that if they call, there is going to be a case made." The department has a 99 percent conviction rate on cases they brought before the courts.

Since the New Mexico program began in June 1977 the illegal killing of 99 deer, 22 antelope, 49 elk, 7 bears, 5 cougars, 3 javelinas, 3 turkeys, 31 game birds, and 10 hawks and owls had led to 297 cases by February, 1980. Fines totaled $77,340. Officers say that 90 percent of these crimes would have gone undetected had it not been for tipsters.

Meanwhile, other states, including Florida and Alaska, are moving to get similar programs started. Arizona, one of the early ones, has a toll-free HOW-Line (Help Our Wildlife) coupled with a rewards system that has brought conviction of poachers taking deer, elk, bears, mountain lions, and small game.

During last year's Ohio deer season, wildlife officer Doug Elson followed up a complaint and visited a farm where he found three men in hunting clothes loafing by the barn. He asked if they were "Doing any good." They said "No," but Elson couldn't help wondering about the blood in their pickup truck. By the end of the day, wildlife officers had arrested six men on 10 charges that cost the camp $1,000 in fines. One hunter had failed to tag his first deer and was out looking for another one. Two illegal does were found in the barn, one hidden in the haymow and the other stuffed into a rain barrel.

"One starts something," says Elson, "and they all join in. And these were nice guys. Professional men out of Columbus. They invited me back next year."

Aircraft are especially effective on night patrols. "We can spot a person lighting a cigarette from 4,000 feet above him," one officer told me. Illinois conservation officers fly a twin-engine plane. "When our aircraft are in the air," says William Brey, "we average 10 arrests a night." Furthermore, the noise of small aircraft keeps poachers nervous and hiding when they might otherwise be shining deer.

Though a poacher may be caught in the act, he may get off with a sentence too light to curb his thieving tendencies. Wildlife officers have complained for years that some judges look upon game-law violation cases as a bad joke played on their courts. But, increasingly, courts are imposing heavy penalties on poachers.

"When you nail one of these characters for ten grand," says Branzell, "somebody took it seriously." Branzell was thinking of the conviction of a poacher who killed a desert bighorn sheep in Nevada, then compounded his troubles by transporting it back across the state line, thereby violating the 80-year-old federal Lacey Act. The poacher was ordered to pay a $10,000 fine, report monthly to his probation officer for two years, and for the same period give up all his hunting, fishing, and trapping privileges. Furthermore, his ill-gotten trophy was confiscated.

So long as we have game laws we will probably have people who will break them. But if more of us join the anti-poaching campaign we'll be helping to cut down this illegal drain on the country's wildlife. To report a game-law violator call either the toll-free number maintained by your state's fish and game department for that purpose, or your nearest conservation officer. If you don't know how to get in touch with that officer, ask the county sheriff's office for his phone number.

Before making the call, write down all the information you have. The more complete the details, the better the possibility of taking successful action against the lawbreaker. Here are the important details, although you may not be able to supply them all:

1 License number of the vehicle involved. This may be the single most important bit of information you can supply.

2 Description of the vehicle.

3 Names, addresses, ages, descriptions of suspects.

4 Kind of violation.

5 When it occurred.

6 Where it occurred.

7 Location of any contraband you know about.

The earlier you report a crime the better the chances of apprehending the suspect.

–*George Laycock.*

Terror in Our Deer Woods

Anyone who has ever encountered a pack of feral dogs can testify it is an experience that will raise his hair, a judgment I can concur in after a recent hike that ended when my companion and I realized we were sharing the woods with a number of dogs (probably four or five) gone wild. Their cry is one of the spookiest sounds to be heard in nature, ranking right up there with the howling of timber wolves on the prowl. And I, an occasional woods crawler, vow never again to risk confronting wild dogs without having some swift means of persuasion at hand.

Feral dogs are big, tough, outdoorwise and dangerous. They are the bane of stockmen, and they are rated the No. 1 problem by many game managers. Many animal behaviorists believe wild dogs actually do much of the predation that coyotes and wolves are blamed for.

Wild dogs are also somewhat of a mystery. For reasons firmly rooted in the economics of the nation's entrenched pet bureaucracy, very little unchallenged fact is known about feral dogs in the rural setting. Free-roaming dogs in urban areas have been studied to death, but expertise in the ways of feral dogs that kill deer and many other species of wildlife is hard to come by. For example, many outdoorsmen are convinced that deer killed by autos or in apparently inexplicable collisions with fences or trees are actually driven to their deaths by wild dogs, but there is little or no proof of this. There is general agreement that wild dog packs kill a significant number of deer every year (one authority suggests 7 percent), but the numbers one encounters are mostly conjecture.

Indeed, no one knows the dog population of the United States, much less the number of dogs that have become feral. But there are thousands of them, notably in the Deep South and in the mountain states, and they constitute a problem that anyone who takes to the woods would do well to become aware of.

Since my own encounter, which ended in my inglorious retreat, I have read what is available on the problem and talked with a number of recognized experts on the subject. Some of those who know the most about the subject were reluctant witnesses, for such is the sentimental mush that goes for dog wisdom in this country that any realistic appraisal of dangerous wild dogs is likely to be met by ravening hordes of little old ladies dragging tar pots and bales of chicken feathers. The truth is that many, if not most, game wardens and wildlife managers kill feral dogs on sight—as they should. But they have learned not to talk about it for fear of being drowned in the subsequent flood of sentimental outrage from badly informed dog lovers.

Self-styled dog lovers, in fact, must share a good deal of blame for the feral dog problem, since many wild dogs start life as pets (owned dogs in the argot of the experts) only to be abandoned to fend for themselves when they become too troublesome or costly to keep.

Dr. Michael W. Fox, a London-trained veterinarian who is director of the Institute for the Study of Animal Problems (an offshoot of The Humane Society of the United States), is one of the world's most respected animal behaviorists and probably knows as much as anyone about feral dogs. In an interview with Outdoor Life he was quick to note the distinction between feral and free-roaming dogs.

"A free-roaming dog is an animal with a home base someplace," he said. "He lives a part of his time with a family, and only periodically reverts to wild behavior. A true feral dog, on the other hand, is a dog that lives completely independently of man."

Fox cites one reality that often comes as a rude shock to dog owners: Perfectly respectable owned dogs often revert to feral behavior and join in wild-pack depredations.

"Many owners simply do not understand the Jekyll-Hyde nature of dogs," he said. "A dog's entire nature changes when it has the stimulus of the pack. In domesticating dogs we have not eliminated the pack and hunting instinct."

Many pet owners, he continued, "have a naturalistic ethic, that is, they feel it is best for the dog to be as free as possible. This is nonsense. It demonstrates neither ecological awareness nor social responsibility. Free-roaming dogs are frequently killed by autos, injured in steel-jawed traps, shot and poisoned."

From a standpoint of game management, feral and free-roaming dogs pose grave dangers that go beyond killing, maiming and harassment of wild animals.

"There is serious concern that feral dogs spread highly contagious viral diseases to game animals," Fox said. "Feral cats do it as well; feline distemper can wipe out whole colonies of foxes. Other diseases, heartworm and mange, for example, are spread to various wildlife species by feral dogs. And this is not to mention that competition for food between feral dogs and game animals."

Although feral dogs reproduce in the wild, most experts think litter survival rates are low, and they almost universally share the belief that unthinking, uncaring owners who lose or abandon pets are the principal source of wild packs. Fox decries what he calls "civilized ignorance" of many dog owners.

"Owners victimize themselves by impulse buying from puppy mills, or by misplaced faith in the worth of 'papers' from the American Kennel Club on purebred dogs," Fox said. "Papers are a lot of garbage. The AKC has no means of guaranteeing the quality of any dog, no matter how good the breeding. Greedy and unscrupulous breeders will mate dogs with absolutely no thought for their suitability as parents. Consequently, people often buy purebred dogs that turn out to be biters or house-wreckers. The result is more abandoned dogs, a certain percentage of which will turn feral. The only rule when buying a dog is to actually see one or both parents."

Fox, who is something of a crusader on the subject, insists that "the mass production of purebred dogs is an uncontrolled pipeline that feeds the feral dog problem."

No one, least of all Fox, who truly appreciates the wonderful strengths of dogs, has anything but admiration and compassion for dogs that make it in the wild after being all too often betrayed by their careless human owners. He speaks of the "superferal" dog that is appearing in great numbers in the West as a consequence of hybridization of feral dogs and coyotes, and he is extravagant in his praise of the dhole, a wild dog he studied in India. The dhole, which matures at 35 to 40 pounds, hunts in packs that range in size from six to 20, and routinely brings down Indian spotted deer, wild pig, and even the sambar, a large Asiatic deer.

It has been my observation that the feral dog problem exists in direct ratio to the economic distress of an era. Packs of starving curs periodically terrorized the villages of Laos, for example, and were even a dangerous nuisance at night on the streets of the capital city of Vientiane. And, of course, they are a blight all over Latin America.

Fox confirms this, and said, "I would expect that abandonment (of dogs) will increase if economic conditions worsen in this country."

An outdoorsman who has a unique first-hand knowledge of the magnitude of the feral dog problem is David Morris, who is owner and manager of the 16,000-acre Burnt Pine game plantation in Morgan County, Georgia. He also edits the *Georgia Sportsman*.

"We had just added 1,000 acres that had been fallow for a number of years," he said in an interview, "and it had an enormous number of feral dogs on it. One day I walked into an old abandoned barn on the tract—fortunately I was carrying a .308 rifle with iron sights—and kicked open the door of one of the rooms that opened off the central hallway. There were five wild dogs in the room, and one of them lunged at my face. I shot him and three of the others, but the fifth got away. It was scary, but based on my experience I'd say it wasn't typical. Over the years I've had several encounters with feral dogs, and they rarely attack human beings." (Fox confirms this, noting that the "socialized" free-roaming dog, rather than the man-shy feral dog, is the one most prone to bite.)

Morris recalls several stand-offs with feral dogs, and warns that their behavior is unpredictable.

"Two years ago I shot a doe," he said. "I knew it was a killing shot, but she didn't go down and I blood-trailed her for two or three hundred yards until I found her in a honeysuckle thicket backed up against a river. I was afraid to push her for fear she'd go into the river and I'd lose her, so I just settled down to wait until she died."

But a pack of feral dogs had picked up the blood trail and set upon the dying doe.

"There were seven or eight dogs in the pack," Morris recalled. "I shot the lead dog—a big black animal—but I must say those dogs showed very little fear of me in the presence of that blood trail."

In microcosm, Morgan County, Georgia, offers a good example of how the feral dog problem managed to reach its present magnitude. At its peak in the early 1900s, its human population was 29,000, but it is now less than a third of that.

"As families moved away to go to the cities," Morris explained, "they simply left behind their dogs. They always had several, sometimes up to 10 or 12. The dogs just went wild in order to survive, and nobody can blame the dogs."

Animal behaviorists seem to agree that almost any free-roaming dog can become feral, but it is the less human-dependent breeds that usually succeed in doing so. Some authorities think collie types and shepherds predominate in many feral packs (this is sure to get an argument from collie and shepherd fanciers). The truth is that feral dogs include in their numbers any breed of dog that's big enough and tough enough to survive in the wild—and none that aren't.

Although there is still much sentimental nonsense being batted back and forth in the animal-control business, there is also a growing awareness that handwringing and professions of love are not the answer to the problem of too many dogs. You can get a lot of guesses on the number of owned dogs in this country (the Pet Food Institute puts it at about 45 million), but there is no guesswork about the following statistic: Last year about 14 million dogs were put to death in animal shelters throughout the United States, and even that probably did not keep the dog population from increasing by 10 percent.

Like everything else, dog ownership is becoming more expensive, and as this full-time dog owner can testify, keeping a dog is a heap of trouble. It seems inevitable that the problem of abandonment is not going to go away, hence the problem of feral dogs and their depredations among wildlife is not going to go away either.

What should responsible hunters do in the presence of dogs that are plainly feral? I will catch a lot of flack for saying earlier that they should shoot them, but even The Humane Society of the United States agrees, adding only the caveat that this deed of mercy should only be undertaken by an expert marksman. It is worth noting that until recently many states urged hunters to kill feral dogs on sight. But, so far as I know, this injunction has been removed from all game department manuals in response to outraged howls from sentimental boobies who have never seen what's left of a feral dog after he's starved to death or been struck by a car.

But putting dogs to death, however humanely it is done, isn't the answer. Somehow our nation of warm-hearted, if faintly dotty, animal lovers has got to adopt sensible attitudes toward spaying and neutering pet dogs and cats. And it must demand, and pay for, the strict enforcement of laws designed to shut down puppy mills.

Many states have laws against abandoning unwanted pets, but the laws are almost universally unenforced. In Maryland, for example, a law mandating a $1,000 fine for abandoning animals has never been enforced.

Feral dogs are a menace to every species of wildlife. Deer are the most noticeable victims, but large numbers of waterfowl also fall to these voracious marauders, as do quail and other upland birds. The U.S. Department of Agriculture estimates livestock losses to feral dogs at up to $10 million a year. And, as I have found out, many a part-time countryman has begun to think in terms of a pocket gun so he can enjoy his walks safely.

"These are often super-super dogs," Dr. Fox observes, "and not a one of them became feral because he wanted to."

That's true. But admiring these resourceful brutes doesn't solve the difficult and dangerous problems they pose. America just has to buckle down and begin to get rid of its huge, heartbreaking surplus of unwanted dogs.–***Richard Starnes.***

Test of a Hunter

There was the unmistakable sound of jubilation in the voice of my friend the Inveterate Hunter that no amount of long-distance electronic witchcraft could disguise, and true to my ready skill at reading signs, I said, "There are unmistakable sounds of jubilation in your voice."

"Right," he said, "and do you know why?"

"No," I replied, "but I can't escape the feeling that you are about to tell me."

"Right again. Guess what my kid did?"

"Got struck rich? Got himself admitted to the Harvard Law School at, what is he, age 15? Poked a stick in the mean soil of your garden and tapped a gusher of high-grade crude?"

"Even better than that. He got himself a 10-point buck the first time out. The first time! That's about the best thing that can happen to a kid of 15, in my opinion."

"Or the worst."

There was an expensive pause and then, perhaps a bit downcast, my colleague in good times and bad said, "What kind of negativism is that? A kid who hits the first time he goes into the woods with his old man is going to be a persuaded hunter all his life. How long was it before you connected when you started hunting?"

"To tell the absolute truth, I can't remember. Except that it was a long time—three or four dry seasons at least."

"Bet you were plenty discouraged," he said, his tone plainly saying he thought his case proved.

"Well, yes, I was. You're right."

"And probably felt like giving up the whole game, more than once."

"That's correct. I remember coming home wet and cold and empty-handed, and feeling like maybe hunting wasn't for me. . . ."

"So it would have been better if you'd come home the first time out with a fat whitetail, right?"

I didn't want to deflate my friend, of course, and I said, well maybe he was right, and then I listened to his inch-by-inch account of his son's triumph, which if you want to know the facts, had a good-size increment of luck in it, although I made no ungracious observation to the enthusiastic father at the other end of the phone. After we'd talked about other things for a bit, he hung up, doubtless to call other hunting companions to share his triumph. But then I let my memory sift back through the years when my older son was learning the demanding, tough, occasionally heart-breaking business of becoming a hunter. There was no fat 10-pointer in his experience the first year, nor the second. As in many other matters, Chip seemed determined to be a carbon copy of his old man, mistakes and all, and it was a couple or three years before he got his first big animal.

These were discouraging times for him, and in all modesty it was probably only my born skill as a father—that kept him from turning to stamp collecting or ballet. There was one morning that will stick in my mind long after much else has fled. It was as dark and cold as it is possible to be in springtime Alaska and it took all my considerable powers of persuasion to get Chip stirring. It was unseasonably cold, the bears hadn't been moving, and Chip, who cherished sack time then as now, was disinclined to swap the comfort of his sleeping bag for the cold and the wet and the dubious prospects of a shot. I reminded him we'd started seeing a few signs, and he replied, with absolute accuracy, that we'd seen all manner of signs the year before and the year before that and he hadn't seen an animal bigger than a chipmunk either time.

Ultimately I fell back on the sort of child psychology my own old man used once in a while. "Get up off your duff, or I'll spill you out of that sleeping bag like a sack of potatoes," I growled. "This country is full of bears but you are going to have to work to get one. Where is it written that all you need to do is sit on a log and wait for a brownie as big as a streetcar to wander by and give an easy heart shot?"

Ultimately Chip got his bear, a bigger one than I have ever shot, and it is my judgment that in all the thousands of years men have been hunting there was never a prouder moment. He'd worked a week in the kind of bitter cold rain that southeastern Alaska is celebrated for, he'd waded up to his withers in streams icy enough to have frozen solid if they hadn't been running so swiftly, and he'd been looking another bleak day of discouragement in the face when finally he'd gotten a shot. The light was getting bad, the bear was spooky and Chip knew there wasn't going to be any second chance. When I got up to the scene of the action (I'd been standing waist-deep in the ice water trying to keep a skiff from beating itself to death on the rocks) Chip was standing there looking at the bear the only way a man should look at a great animal he has just killed: reverently and with tears in his eyes.

Now then, not to take anything away from the lucky son of my friend alluded to earlier, I submit that of the two tads, Chip was the more fortunate. He had learned (again like his old man—the hard way) that hunting is exactly that. Hunting. Finding, maybe. Shooting occasionally. Getting your game when all the elements come together in fortunate sequence. Chip had earned the understanding that toil, hardship, even danger, and certainly discouragement are a part of an equation that even the best of hunters cannot escape.

Contrast Chip's dose of reality with the giddy happenstance of the Inveterate Hunter's boy. Next year, or the year after or whenever, the kid is going to collide with that long dry spell that all of us have experienced, and that's when he will really begin to learn about hunting. I wonder if he'll be up to it. He is, with a 15-year-old's linear logic, entitled to think now that deer hunting consists of finding a likely spot, waiting a reasonable time until a trophy animal moseys past and presents an easy shot, and then waiting for good old Dad to come along and help with the dressing and packing out. Experienced hunters know that it doesn't work that way very often. Hunters who connect on day one every year are men or women who have paid their dues. They've walked the long, hilly miles in the cold and wet, they've come home with nothing to show for their trip but a busted bank account and incipient pneumonia and, in time, they've learned to be hunters.

One of the most successful hunters I know—one of those who seems automatically to fill out on day one year after year—once told me he'd hunted six straight seasons before he bagged his first deer, and he lived right in the middle of some of the richest deer country in Virginia.

"I think I'd have quit," I said.

"I did. Every dadblamed dry year at the end of the season I'd clean my shotgun and decide I was a natural-born bird shooter and nothing else."

"But you kept going back."

"Sure I did. I don't like anything to lick me. I got to going out long before the season started, studying the animals, staking out what looked like good stands, learning to move around in brushy spots without making noise. I tried to put myself in the frame of mind of a whitetail, which is not the smartest animal on earth by a long shot. I learned how they weren't really much smarter than people, and were by and large guided by the same instincts—the need for food, shelter, comfort, security. Finally I got to know what I was doing."

It doesn't take any great insight to know that when this man's next dry spell comes along, as it will, he is not going to conclude that the fates are against him and quit hunting. He already knows what to do in a dry spell, which is to find out what he is doing wrong and try to become a better hunter. I am convinced a great deal of the epidemic orneriness we see in the woods—the shoot-at-anything-that-moves crazies, the clowns who shoot insulators off utility poles, the vandals and the contemptible violators of game laws—are first and foremost lousy hunters. They haven't learned the patience and guile it takes to hunt; they become frustrated upon learning that it is possible to spend a whole season of back-to-back hard days in the woods without getting a shot. So they get drunk and shoot the foot off a companion, or go to the hardware store and get one of those flashlights with 18 batteries in it so they can at least shine deer if they can't learn to take one legally.

This is not to suggest that my friend's son will succumb to any of these vices. His father is a sensible man, and I have no doubt there will be counsel available when there won't be a single shot to be had.

But I think it might be easier for his old man and better for the youngster if he'd learned his discouragement at the front end, the way Chip did. Then, for the rest of his life, his expectations will be tempered with realism. He will have learned going in that there are not any guarantees in this world with respect to hunting or anything else. Sure, it is always possible that enough blank days will set a youngster against hunting for the rest of his life, and what of it? There isn't anything written on some celestial scroll that says all the sons or daughters of all hunters have to turn onto hunters themselves. Andy, three years younger than Chip and the product of identical upbringing, got the same sort of introduction to hunting that his older brother did—and turned out to be the fisherman of the family. Andy would go to the ends of the earth for a good fishing trip, and he'd know what to do when he got there. But I don't believe he'd go to the far end of the county to shoot a deer. There is nothing wrong with being a fisherman instead of a hunter; indeed, from the old man's point of view, it is ideal to have one of each in the family. If I get an invite to go on some lavish fishing trip to Central America, I know a good fishing companion is only a phone call away. And if I need someone to go hunting with, I got me a first-class son available for that as well.

And maybe more to the point, both of them are purely dedicated outdoorsmen, which means they'll hike or explore with you when the season on everything is closed. That's what it's really all about anyway; learning to deal with the outdoors at all levels and in all seasons of the year, with a hunting or fishing trip dangling off in the future as the prize for the nine months of the year you've spent climbing hills or pushing a canoe up some forgotten river.

Ha, I hear some surly fellow snort, this guy is trying to tell me it is better for a kid, or a grownup for that matter, to come back empty-handed from a hunting trip he's planned and saved for all year. Well, it won't float. Everybody knows it's better to get the game you go after, just the same as it is better to have loved and not lost, and anybody who thinks otherwise probably still believes in the tooth fairy.

Well, for the record let me note that I stopped believing in the tooth fairy about the time I met my first chief petty officer, and nothing that has happened since has restored that belief. Nor am I saying it is better to get skunked after sweating out a hunting or fishing trip all year. But what I am saying, and all sophisticated gunners and anglers will agree with me, is that inevitably there will be those dreary, discouraging days when you do not connect, and the hunter who has learned to expect them and to deal with them in a mature way is going to be a whole lot better off than the initially lucky dude who fills out the first time he takes up a rifle or a cane pole, and ever after is convinced this is his inalienable right.

There was a poet who wrote a very nice piece that contained this line: "Luck's a chance and trouble's sure," and it was a pretty good piece of philosophy. I doubt he ever laid hand to a fly rod or a fowling piece, but his advice is sound for any person who takes to the outdoors in quest of game. Learn to live with the tough days, and the good times will be that much sweeter.–*Richard Starnes.*

PART 7 BOWHUNTING: BASICS AND FINE POINTS

Bowhunting: Getting Started

THE HUNTING BOW

There are many places where you can purchase a hunting bow, including department stores, discount stores, mail-order houses and general sporting goods stores. Aside from price, the best place to buy a hunting bow is your local archery pro shop, where you'll find a good selection to choose from and an expert to help you pick out the correct equipment. Some archery shops also have shooting-range facilities so you can try several bows before buying one.

Recurve bows

Recurve bows have been around for a long time, proving themselves time and time again on game of all kinds. They're available in a variety of lengths, handle sizes, shapes, and draw weights to match any hunting situation. Recurve bows are relatively inexpensive and very simply constructed. They are extremely rugged and reliable, and many hunters use them with excellent success. Some companies offer take-down models that can be carried or stored in compact cases. These are good choices for traveling or backpacking bow-hunters.

Compound bows

Compound bows are fairly new on the hunting scene, but they are very popular. A compound bow has some basic advantages over a recurve bow. First, it "lets-off" from its "peak draw weight." This let-off will be anywhere from 15 to 50 percent of the peak weight, depending on the bow, which minimizes finger strain and muscle fatigue when an archer is at full draw. Another advantage of a

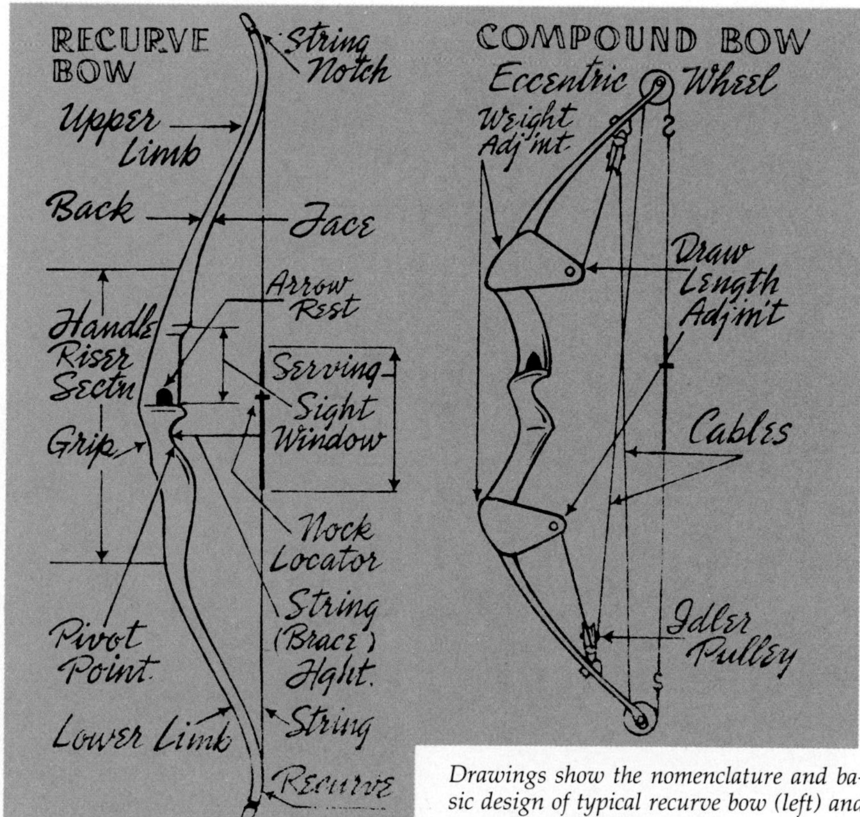

Drawings show the nomenclature and basic design of typical recurve bow (left) and a compound bow (above).

With compounds, draw weight is same as peak weight—the weight you "pull through" before bow "lets off" at full draw.

compound bow is that it can shoot a slightly lighter arrow than a recurve bow of the same draw weight, which means flatter arrow trajectory. A bow that has a relatively flat arrow trajectory allows somewhat more error in judging the distance to the target. There are many compound models available and there is bound to be one just right for you. Some models take down for easy storage and transport, and many have adjustable draw weights and draw lengths, which makes them very versatile hunting tools. On the average, compound bows cost more than recurve bows; however, a wide variety of prices are now available.

What about draw weight?

The draw weight of a bow is defined in two ways: for recurve bows it is the number of pounds it takes to draw the bowstring back to 28 inches. As a rule of thumb, for each inch of draw above or below 28 inches, you should add or subtract 2 pounds of bow weight to determine the approximate weight of your personal draw length. For compound bows draw weight is the same as peak weight—the amount of weight you "pull through" before your bow lets off in weight at full draw.

A bowhunter should use a bow with the maximum draw weight he can shoot comfortably. There are several reasons for this. For one thing, a bow with a heavy draw weight shoots an arrow faster than a light draw weight bow. This gives better penetration on game. Also, the flatter arrow trajectory will give you a better percentage of hits on game at unknown distances. Another important consideration is that the faster an arrow reaches an animal, the less chance the animal has to "jump string" (dodge the arrow).

For these reasons, you should shoot a recurve bow that has a minimum draw weight of 45 to 50 pounds, or a compound bow that has a minimum peak weight of 50 to 55 pounds. These are average weights used by bowhunters across the country. With a little practice, an average-size man can usually shoot a bow 5 or 10 pounds heavier that this with ease.

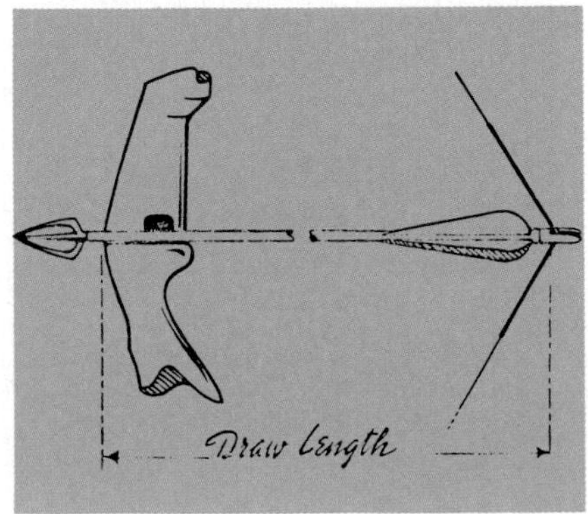

Draw length is the distance you draw your arrow back before you shoot.

You should also match your draw weight to the game you intend to hunt. Generally speaking, the bigger the game, the heavier the bow required.

Know your draw length

Draw length is defined as the distance you draw your arrow back before you shoot. This length is measured from the bottom of the string groove in the nock of the arrow to the front or far side of the bow when you pull your bow to full draw. Your own personal draw length will be determined by your physical size, where you "anchor" (where you hold your bowstring hand just before you release the string to shoot), and other peculiarities of your own bow-shooting style.

Compound bows let off in draw weight at different draw lengths. If you want to select a compound bow, you must know what your draw length is so you can get a bow that lets off at the right place to match your draw.

You can determine your draw length in one of two ways. The conventional method is to draw back a hunting bow several times to loosen up your muscles and find a consistent anchor point (the index finger in the corner of the mouth is most common for hunting). After loosening up, draw an extra-long arrow to your anchor point and have a friend mark the shaft with a lead pencil at the point even with the front of the bow. Measure the distance from this mark to the bottom of the string groove of the arrow nock, and you have your draw length.

Another method is to stand facing at 90° to a wall with the knuckles of your clenched fist against the wall, arm fully outstretched. Have a friend measure the distance from the wall to the corner of your mouth with a yardstick. This is your draw length. The "knuckles on the wall" method is preferred for beginning archers because there is no chance of "caving in" (underdrawing a bow because of muscle strain).

You can't shoot a bow without a bowstring

The bowstring is a very important part of any bow—it propels the arrow out of the bow and on its way to the target. Be sure to buy at least two bowstrings of the proper length and strength (refer to the specifications marked on your bow). Each of these new strings should be shot in your bow a dozen times or so to stretch it out properly. Each should then be installed with a nocking point so you can place your arrow in the same location every time for accuracy. There are many commercial nocking points available today, including the crimp-on and heat-shrink types available at any archery store. Actually, any slightly raised "bead" on the bowstring will serve as a nocking point. Some bowhunters prefer to make their own nocking points with several wraps of fine thread or dental floss. An arrow is generally nocked directly beneath this nocking point.

Carry at least one extra bowstring with you in the woods at all times in case the string on your bow becomes frayed, cut, or broken. This extra string should be exactly like the one on your bow, with identical nocking point, bowstring silencers, and any other shooting aids you decide to put on your string.

To make string changing safe and easy, and to prevent damage to your bow, buy a bowstringer designed specifically for your compound or recurve bow and learn how to use it. Your archery dealer should have exactly what you need. Then you'll be prepared to quickly and safely change a damaged string in the field and continue hunting.

What arrow rest should you use?

An arrow rest consists of a shelf (which a arrow rests on) and a plate (which the side of an arrow rests against). A hunting-bow rest should be made of "quiet" material to prevent game from spooking because of arrow clank or rattle; it should be sturdy so you don't have to worry about it breaking in the field; and it should attach to your bow easily and securely for convenience and trouble-free bowhunting.

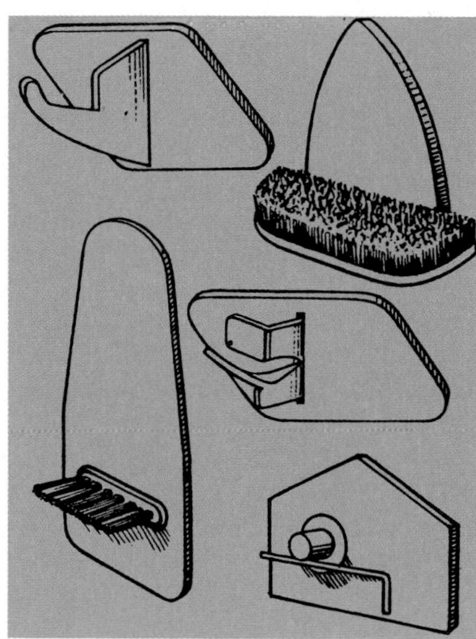

These hunting-bow rests are "quiet" and prevent arrow rattle in the woods.

THE RIGHT ARROW

After you buy your hunting bow, the next step is to match it with the right set of arrows. There are three common materials used to make arrow shafts: wood, fiberglass and aluminum.

Wood

Good wood shafts are fairly light in weight for flat arrow trajectory. Wood costs less than other shaft materials, too, a plus for the budget-minded bowhunter.

Fiberglass

Fiberglass shafts never warp in wet weather and very seldom break or shatter unless they hit rocks or other hard objects. They're the heaviest arrow shafts available, which means a more arching arrow trajectory and a little greater chance of missing game. However, this extra weight yields maximum arrow penetration when an arrow hits a game animal.

Aluminum

Aluminum shafts are light in weight for flat arrow trajectory, very consistent in weight, straightness and stiffness, and completely waterproof. They're available in a

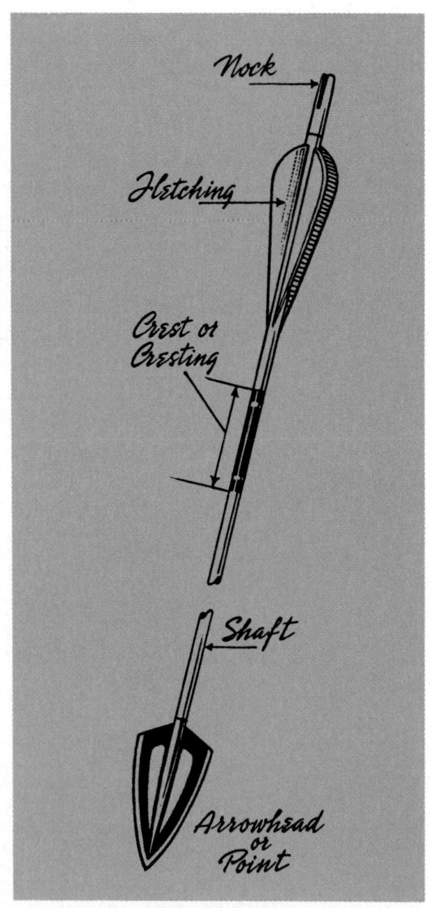

Regardless of material—wood, glass, aluminum—nomenclature is same.

greater range of weights and stiffnesses than any other kind of arrow shaft, giving a bowhunter versatility on various game animals.

Other shaft materials

Hunting shafts are sometimes made of materials besides wood, fiberglass and aluminum. Alternate materials include stainless steel, graphite and carbon glass. If your archery dealer stocks shafts made of materials other than wood, fiberglass and aluminum, ask him about the advantages and disadvantages of these special shaft materials. Then you can pick the arrow that best suits your own hunting needs.

One other kind of shaft is worth mentioning here: the bowfishing shaft. It is generally made of solid fiberglass or solid aluminum to take rough treatment like repeated impact with rocky stream bottoms. Used with a bow reel and heavy-test fishing line, such a shaft can also withstand the bending and twisting that occurs when a bowfisherman fights a large fish.

Use arrows of proper spine and length

Once you decide which arrow shaft you want to shoot, go to your local dealer and have him help you select a shaft of the proper spine (stiffness). He has charts that tell which arrow shafts will shoot best from your particular bow at your particular draw length. Careful arrow selection results in accurate arrow flight. Your arrow shafts shoud be about 3/4 of an inch longer than your draw length so a wide hunting broadhead won't bump the front (far side) of your bow when you draw back to shoot. It's much better to have an arrow a little too long than a little too short.

What about fletching?

The feathers or plastic vanes on the back of an arrow are called fletching. They stabilize an arrow as it flies. A standard hunting arrow is fletched with three feathers or vanes about 5 inches long and 9/16-inch high. Fletching smaller than this might not stabilize your arrows properly, causing wobbly arrow flight. The smaller the fletching, the faster an arrow flies. However, stabilization is much more important than slight increases in speed, resulting in more accurate arrow placement on game. Ask your archery dealer whether vanes or feathers are best for you—this depends to a large degree on the kind of bow you shoot and your individual shooting style.

The oversize flu-flu fletchings (top and bottom) and the standard fletching.

Oversized flu-flu fletching (feathers that are usually 1 inch high and longer than conventional fletching) slows an arrow down fast after shots at game in the air or in trees. If you intend to hunt squirrels or birds, buy some flu-flu arrows. You won't lose them as easily as other arrows, and they're also safe to use because they won't fly very far when shot into the air.

Match the arrowhead to the job

There are arrowheads available to do a variety of jobs. Be sure to shoot the proper head so you take game cleanly and efficiently.

Field points

These are simple, rugged steel points used for target practice, shooting at dirt clods and other natural targets, and hunting very small animals and birds.

Broadheads

These are arrowheads with two to six cutting edges used to hunt big game and some large species of varmints, small game and birds. Most bowhunters prefer broadheads with at least three edges to ensure massive tissue damage for quick, humane kills. Broadheads fall into two basic categories: unsharpened and presharpened.

Unsharpened broadheads

Many sturdy, well-designed unsharpened broadheads are available to bowhunters. A broadhead has to be shaving sharp to drop game fast, so these heads must be carefully sharpened by the bowhunter before they can be used on game. They cost less on the average than presharpened heads, but require considerable time and skill to prepare them for the field. Once sharp, however, they do an admirable job on game.

Presharpened broadheads

Factory-sharpened broadheads cost a bit more than unsharpened broadheads. However, they feature shaving-sharp blades that are ready to hunt with right out of the package. Most presharpened broadhead designs allow the bowhunter to quickly replace any blades that become dull from the normal clanks and jars an arrow receives in the field. This allows the bowhunter to keep all the edges on his broadheads sharp with a minimum of effort—which leads to quick, clean kills on game.

Blunts

These are flat-nosed arrowheads of various sorts used to stump-shoot and hunt small mammals and birds. The most common ones are made of steel or rubber. Blunts are the best points to shoot into stumps and other hard targets—they bounce off or give shallow penetration, and never wedge tightly in wood as field points and broadheads sometimes do.

Fish heads

These are long, slender arrowheads with spring-loaded or stationary barbs that penetrate and hold a fish until it is landed.

How to install arrowheads on shafts

There are two basic ways to put an arrowhead on an arrow shaft—glue it on the shaft's point taper with hot-melt ferrule cement, or attach it with one of the handy screw-in point adapter systems on the market. The screw-in systems let you conveniently change arrowheads in seconds—a real advantage if you're hunting more than one type of game during one single trip, or need to replace a dull or broken broadhead with a sharp one.

Anybody can quickly install arrowheads and various kinds of point adapters with a little practice. Hot-melt ferrule cement is generally used to install point inserts in tubular aluminum shafts. Epoxy is used to put point inserts in tubular fiberglass shafts. A small gas or alcohol flame is recommended for heating hot-melt ferrule cement to install inserts and arrowheads, although a stove burner can be used in a pinch.

Screw-in tips let you change from field tip to hunting tip in a few seconds.

Caution: Excessive heat can burn wooden shafts and ruin aluminum alloys. Use as little heat as possible when installing arrowheads and point adapters with hot-melt cement.

THE HUNTING QUIVERS

A bowhunting quiver should hold an adequate number of arrows firmly and silently. It should cover up sharp broadheads to protect you from serious cuts. It should also be easy to carry around. Here are some common designs used by bowhunters.

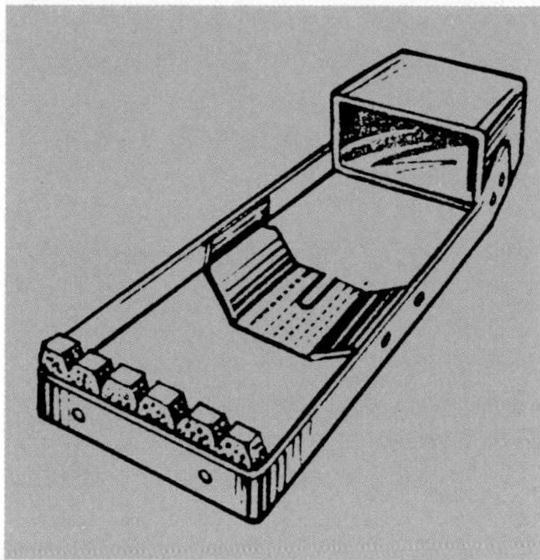

This style quiver attaches to the bow.

Back quivers

Back quivers are fine for some types of hunting. They're relatively inexpensive and simply constructed, and most designs are handy to hang in a tree stand or blind. However, most back quivers allow arrows to rattle together, which can spook game and dull broadheads. These quivers also tend to bump into low limbs when a bowhunter is walking. Another disadvantage is the fact that arrow access requires lots of game-spooking arm movement.

Hip quivers

Hip quivers with individual arrow clips provide easy arrow access and no arrow rattle. They're relatively inexpensive and compact. One disadvantage with these is that they tend to hang up and make noise when a hunter walks through heavy brush.

Bow quivers

Many bowhunters prefer this style of quiver. It attaches directly to a bow, which means easy arrow access, easy transport in thick brush and trees, and excellent maneuverability. Some bowhunters feel a bow quiver adds unnecessary weight to a bow, making it feel awkward and unbalanced. However, this is the most popular quiver in use today.

BOW-HUNTING GEAR AND CLOTHING

Other shooting equipment you'll need includes an arm guard and a finger glove or tab. The arm guard does two things: it protects your arm from the bowstring and keeps your shirt or jacket sleeve away from the bowstring to ensure accuracy and prevent noisy string slap. A long arm guard that goes above as well as below your elbow has advantages if you are shooting with loose clothing. Finger gloves and tabs protect your fingers from bruises and blisters caused by bowstring friction when you release the string. They also ensure a smooth, accurate string release.

Despite the slight improvements in arrow trajectory provided by compound bows, a bowhunter must still estimate the distance to ensure solid hits on game. Such pinpoint estimation is impossible without the help of a hand-held optical rangefinder. Such a tool instantly determines the distance to objects out to 70 yards or more with the turn of a dial, allowing a bowhunter to determine exact distances to landmarks around his stand or actually take distance readings off animals. A rangefinder allows an archer to hold his sights exactly right without guesswork.

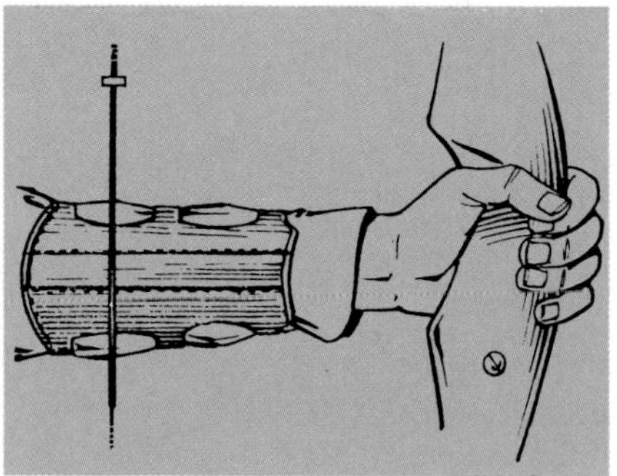

An armguard keeps loose clothing out of the way and prevents bruises.

Wear the right hunting duds

Bowhunting clothes should be chosen carefully to make your

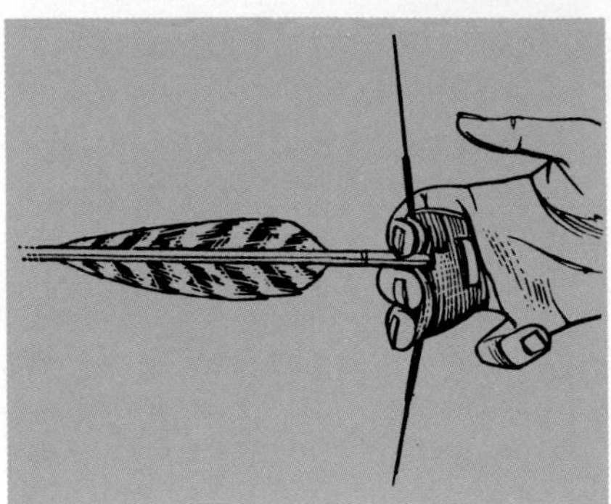

Finger tabs prevent blisters and bruises and help to ensure a smooth release.

hunt comfortable and successful. First of all, they must be soft and quiet to avoid alerting animals when you move through heavy woods. Wool and soft cotton are extremely quiet fabrics. Avoid wearing "scratchy" hard-surfaced materials—they spook game.

Clothes should blend with the environment. Leaf-print camouflage is the traditional clothing of bowhunters, and it's very good. Contrasty plaids blend well, too. Avoid wearing solid colors—these stand out against most backgrounds. Remember that game animals are colorblind: It's the tone of the clothes that makes a difference. For instance, a red-and-black plaid shirt is an excellent bowhunting color combination.

Be sure to match your clothes to the weather you intend to hunt in. Wet weather calls for either a suit of pliable, waterproof rain gear or garments made of wool. Wool stays warm even when wet and tends to be much quieter than most commercial rain suits. It is also wise to dress in layers so you can add or shed clothes if weather changes occur.

Clothing must not interfere with shooting your bow. Be sure to wear a hat that doesn't collide with the bowstring when you come to full draw. Baggy shirts or jackets can catch a bowstring and ruin accuracy.

Footwear should be soft-soled for silence and dull-colored for camouflage. Shoes or boots must also match the weather conditions. As an example, a pair of lightweight, uninsulated boots can get mighty cold in zero-degree weather.

One more tip: A light, shiny face sticks out like a sore thumb against almost any outdoor background, so be sure to camouflage your face with a headnet or camouflage makeup anytime you go bowhunting.–***Chuck Adams.***

Portions of text reproduced by permission of Archery Manufacturers Organization.

Whitetail Wizard

The taking of a whitetail buck with a bow is more than just a matter of luck. It's a skill finely honed by years of woods experience, study and observing deer habits. It often requires a hunter to know what bucks will do before they do it, and to learn how and where to find and hunt a specific animal. No hunter in North America has this art down better than Claude Pollington of Marion, Michigan.

His bowhunting skill is legendary. The credentials he's established are impressive. He has killed 35 whitetail bucks in 25 years, an enviable feat in any bowhunting circle. He's taken these deer in Michigan, although he's killed mule deer and whitetails in the West, using the same techniques. His success depends on many things, but keen study of a buck's characteristics during the fall is what hangs venison at his Buck Pole Deer Camp near home.

Claude Pollington, the hunter, is somewhat different from Claude Pollington, the successful businessman. He owns a thriving tool and die shop in Marion. He hires good men, and most of them have taken fine bucks under his tutelage.

Pollington is tall, broad-shouldered, rawboned and wiry like many of the old-time hunters in his area. He's quiet, almost shy, with strangers, and a man of few words. At 48 he's the father of seven children, but only the two boys hunt. One of the traits that endear him to beginning bowhunters is his goal to make their first hunt a success. This fails, on occasion, due to the complexity of whitetails, but many people have scored on their first day under his intense directions on where and when to sit and how to expect a buck to approach their area.

Pollington owns nearly 1,500 acres of prime deer habitat in central Michigan. He's seen deer population explosions and scarcities. Nonetheless, he kills a buck each year. He does this by knowing when, where and how a buck travels through his land, and he's a better-than-average bow shot.

Pollington shared his whitetail bowhunting expertise with me in an interview. His know-how could help you to take a buck this fall.

LOCATING DEER

The success of any deer hunt hinges on being in an area frequented by whitetails. A thorough scouting for bucks is imperative and should be done before the season opener. Whitetail bucks, before the rut begins, are susceptible to hunting as they move freely with or without does into feeding areas. The location of a feeding area, and to a lesser extent, a bedding area, is the first of many steps needed to convert a buck into a venison dinner.

I use high-powered binoculars to glass likely areas for two or three days. A tall tree or other elevated position is best, and the higher you climb the better vantage point you'll have. Begin glassing shortly before daybreak and again one hour before dusk. A hunter should be in his observation post 30 minutes before these time periods to avoid spooking deer during his approach.

If you observe deer using a specific location at dawn and dusk it should be easy to pinpoint the feeding areas. Check dirt roadsides, edges of corn or winter-wheat fields, or wherever the ground is soft enough to reveal tracks. It's important to narrow your search down to the certain areas where deer enter or leave a feeding area. This knowledge will enable you to determine where to erect a permanent or temporary tree stand.

Look for droppings which may contain clues to which crops deer are eating. Observation of deer feeding on corn or oats, winter wheat, or acorns and other mast, is the final clue. Keep in mind that deer will change feeding areas for no apparent reason. Sudden changes in feed sites may be due to human intrusion, so I always look for areas not heavily hunted.

I've noticed that bucks often feed in smaller areas than does and yearlings. I try to locate small food plots near fairly heavy cover. I've taken several bucks from one two-acre patch of field corn wedged in tight against a wall of cedars and swampy land. Does and yearlings often by-pass this spot and head for feed sites where they have more food and greater visibility. The bucks approach smaller areas with caution and feed quickly before retiring to dense cover.

THE WIND

Wind direction and velocity are two things all hunters must deal with. A whitetail's nose is as sharp as a barber's razor, and it works overtime. A hunter who knowingly places himself upwind from a buck is defeating his purpose. Unless there is no other alternative, deer just won't move upwind if they know a human is present.

You can overcome wind direction problems by locating tree stands high, overlooking approach areas. Some states specify the maximum allowable height, but I've found that a stand 20 to 30 feet above an active deer trail is best. The prevailing wind will blow the scent over approaching deer, even those coming upwind toward your stand. But for every rule there are exceptions, and one is on days when a falling barometer sends swirling or gusting winds from first one quarter and then another. A low pressure center can push scent toward the ground, where it can be picked up by approaching bucks.

My best days are bright, with a steady, moderate breeze. It's a daily habit with me to check the weather vane on my roof. Knowing the wind direction, stability and velocity enables me to choose my tree stand with some hope of success.

Cold days with moderate breezes and bright, clear weather are steady producers for me and others hunting at my deer camp. I dislike hunting in rainy or very windy weather because deer seldom travel then. Many hunters believe whitetails move daily, but it's not true. I've seen bucks lay themselves up for a day or two when the weather is nasty. Take a cue from the deer and do the same. A good time to hunt is whenever the sun breaks through a two-day or longer cloud cover and the wind and rain stop. Every deer within the area of that frontal system will be moving out to feed as the front passes.

I've observed deer on my club lands all year, and it's become a routine for me to pinpoint travel routes according to wind direction. The deer follow a basic west-to-east pattern in the evening, east-to-west in the morning. The reason for this is the prevailing wind direction. These deer, due to food and cover requirements, must travel downwind much of the time. Big bucks may try to quarter cross-wind in hopes of picking up hunter scent, but I haven't found that true in many cases.

Bucks often follow the shortest distance between two points, and this means they must move downwind morning and evening. They travel to feeding areas at night and back to bedding locations at dawn.

In the past 25 years, Claude Pollington has taken 35 whitetail bucks with a bow. His secret: hair-splitting accuracy and a thorough knowledge of whitetail habits. His thoughts on why whitetails behave as they do, and some advice for bowhunters this fall.

This movement contradicts what many hunters believe about wind direction and whitetail travel. Deer in my region are not constantly pursued by sportsmen. They move in any direction they choose, in this case, downwind.

This travel pattern is easily disturbed by too many hunters or too much noise. My tree stands are permanently placed at locations where I've seen bucks pass. Two years ago bowhunters dropped 12 bucks on my property, and every deer was following this downwind pattern. This buck movement downwind has been overlooked by many hunters because they've been indoctrinated to think bucks always travel upwind. They do only if hunter intrusion into the woods increases human odor and noise.

Food sources are the primary reason bucks in my locale travel downwind. It's the shortest distance between feeding and bedding areas. Just don't overlook the downwind approach; it can deliver a nice buck within easy bow range if you've located your tree stand properly.

TREE STAND LOCATIONS

Most of my tree stands are in or very near thick cover or known feeding sites. I choose areas where large spikes can be driven into tree trunks or where hunters can use tree limbs to climb into the stand. Most of my better areas have two or three stands nearby so I can cover any approaching deer, regardless of wind direction. This is something that few hunters think about.

Tree stand site selection is critical. Stands must be in an area frequented by bucks on their way to or from a bedding or feeding area. My stands are successful because they rely on height to prevent deer from spotting waiting hunters. Very few are in thick, bushy trees where a draw will be hampered by nearby limbs. We favor open tree stands where movements must be kept to a minimum.

It's difficult to pick a perfect site. I favor trees within 25 yards of edge areas like woodlots, or brushy spots where deer exit or enter a feeding or bedding site. Whitetails often cross fences at the same location every day. A nearby stand allows easy standing or walking shots as bucks slow down or pause before jumping a fence.

Another thing I look for when planning stand sites is acorns or other mast. Such sites are boom or bust as mast crops thrive or fail. One thing few hunters realize is that bucks will feed during daylight hours if hunting pressure is slight. This can be a good time to nail a trophy buck.

Experience is the teacher. It pays to have two or three similar stands in each location to compensate for wind changes. My criteria for a stand are height and a clear avenue for arrow flight. A common failing is to select a site that parallels a deer trail but doesn't allow for a clear shot. Consider the time invested in scouting out the area, finding a specific buck and determining the prime feeding and bedding locations. Ample time should be allotted when choosing a stand location. I often spend a day or two on each site before I finally decide whether it's good.

Backup tree stands do not require such critical selection as primary sites. They will be used only when a switch is needed. Some days I change stands two or three times as the wind changes.

RUTTING BUCKS

The best time to bowhunt whitetail bucks is during the rut. In my area this occurs from mid-October through late November, although I've seen good bucks still chasing does as late as Christmas. Many bowhunters give up on rutting bucks long before this and miss out on some fine action. Bucks customarily lose some caution, although survival and an avoidance of humans are strong instincts, too. I've read articles describing whitetail bucks as being incredibly dumb during the rut, but I have not found that to be true. They may not show too much caution at times, but dumb they're not.

Bucks in my area, due possibly to heavy hunting pressure outside my club, may make a few mistakes during the rut, but I don't count on it. It's far better to rely on common sense, visual observation and skill than on Lady Luck. That old gal will let you down just when you're counting on her. I've found that tree stand hunters stand a better chance at taking trophy bucks during the rut than bowhunters in ground blinds. Bucks follow does by scent, often with their noses to the ground. Any human odor lingering at ground level will trigger the survival instinct. A buck, lovestruck or not, will disappear like the morning mist and abandon that particular area for some time.

Buck rubs and scrapes are only an indication of where a buck travels. He may bed down in thick, heavy cover within earshot of a scrape, or he may be a mile or more away. I dislike sitting in a tree stand over a scrape because bucks, especially heavy-antlered deer, approach scrapes with utmost caution. I've learned it's better to locate the buck, determine where and how he lives and spends his time, and set up an ambush somewhere between the bedding area and his string of scrapes. Scheduling a buck's movements may require a week or two, but it's time well spent.

Scheduling a buck is just part of my strategy. Some bucks visit scrapes at daybreak, others at dusk, and some come just at night, when it's impossible to pinpoint their movements. The midday hours, between 10 a.m. and 2 p.m., can be an excellent time to waylay a big buck because some animals lie low during the hours when hunting pressure is heaviest. Bucks often move during midday, when the woods are quiet. I've taken many bucks during this period, when bucks actively feed or pursue does. A good bowhunter makes himself available whenever and wherever deer move. I'll often pack a light lunch wrapped in a cotton cloth and eat at my tree stand. This enables me to remain in one area when bucks should be moving.

Heavy cover is the key to downing a big swollen-neck buck. They usually follow heavy cover into a scraping area. A tree stand overlooking the approach area enables a hunter to spot an incoming buck.

HOW I SHOOT WHITETAIL BUCKS

A perfect tree stand, hay bale blind, pit blind, or stump set will be useless unless the hunter has nerves of steel and can outwait an approaching buck. Hair-splitting accuracy is needed to place an arrow in a killing spot. Many bowhunters just don't practice enough with bow and arrow to drop bucks with consistency.

I practice daily with my bow, from varying locations and heights. It's one thing to shoot bucks from ground level at a range of 20 feet, but it's another ball game shooting almost straight down or at an extreme angle from a stand high in a quivering aspen tree. I have a target butt that can be moved from one spot to another. My son Matt practices with me, and we take turns climbing trees and shooting or moving the target into different areas. This enables us to be proficient at delivering an arrow from different angles and heights, and allows us to take shots with some feeling of making a good hit.

My razorheads are sharp enough to slice hair from my forearm. My compound is set at 67 pounds, and I advise anyone to shoot as heavy a bow as he can comfortably pull from a sitting position. Bowhunters often find they can draw a bow with a heavy draw weight while standing but cannot do so while sitting in a tree stand or pit blind.

One mistake bowhunters often make is to hope for a standing shot at a buck. A motionless target is easier to hit, so they think. I've found it better to make my draw on a walking buck because the noise of his passage may cover some of the sounds I make while coming to full draw and releasing the arrow. A slowly moving or feeding deer isn't any more difficult to hit than a motionless animal. It involves tracking the deer smoothly and making a proper release. Try it—it can pay off with better shots and more game. *–David Richey.*

Second Choice Ain't Bad

I couldn't believe the size of the buck's antlers. I've lived in the superb mule deer country of western Colorado all my life and I've seen my share of big bucks. But the one I was looking at now was enormous, and the nontypical rack he carried was an incredible mass of points sticking out in all directions.

If this had been rifle season, the mule deer wouldn't have been much of a challenge, but I was bowhunting and had to get much closer than I was for a shot. The deer was grazing lightly on a steep hillside about 100 yards above me. It was going to be a tough stalk.

My heart sank as the buck suddenly whipped his head up and stared straight at me. He spotted me. But if I didn't move, I told myself, he might decide I was part of the woods. I was in a fairly thick mix of aspens and spruce.

Finally, he lowered his head and started feeding. I hunkered down in the undergrowth and gathered my thoughts. I needed to move out well ahead of the buck and set up an ambush. I decided there was no way to stalk him in that dense vegetation. He'd have to come to me.

I was apprehensive about getting a shot. It seemed as if everything had gone wrong today.

Just a few hours before, my companion and I had stalked into the midst of an unbelievable herd of big bull elk. We hadn't scored, and it was our own fault.

That morning was the first time I had hunted big game that season. Warren Bruton, my hunting companion, runs an outfitting business in Mesa, Colorado. I work for Warren as a guide. We had just finished a guided hunt, and had hurried over to this area after saying goodbye to our clients.

It was August 29, 1976. I was 18 years old and was feeling pretty good because I had just passed all my tests to become a licensed guide. I had worked for Warren since I was 14.

After getting our clients and their meat to the airport, Warren and I and his son, Eric, drove to a place where he knew there were big bucks. He had more hunters coming soon, and wanted to check the area out before taking them in there. Warren always tries to get his clients into the best game country, and only the rare hunter goes home without getting a shot at a big buck deer or bull elk.

We were really tired from the previous hunt. Outfitting and guiding is a tough business, what with climbing one ridge after another, packing out game and tending to all the other chores around camp.

The author poses with the mount of his nontypical mule deer, the largest ever shot by a bowhunter.

Warren parked the pickup about three miles from where we wanted to hunt in the morning. It was after midnight, so we spread a big tent on the ground and lay down in the doorway so there'd be canvas under and over us. We were too bushed to set up the big tent.

When we woke up it was already daylight, almost too late. Warren made some peanut butter sandwiches, and we took off into the woods at a trot. Eric decided to sleep late.

Because the area is steep, with treacherous lava rock-slides, hunting by horseback is out of the question. Access is by foot only, which might be the reason the area had a reputation of producing trophy game animals.

Warren and I climbed up a steep mountain and topped out. Sign was scarce, and we wondered if we'd made a bad choice.

Then we heard a clattering noise in a canyon below. Warren stopped and raised his eyebrows. That means, "Did you hear it?"

I nodded back. We knew instantly what the noise was. Big animals were rubbing the velvet off their antlers on bushes. By the sound of the clattering, the animals almost had to be elk, and a bunch of them at that.

We tested the wind and found it perfect. Warren motioned that he'd work along one side of the creek, and I'd take the other.

As we approached the bottom of the canyon, the sound of the rushing creek blotted out our footsteps. The wind was still favorable. There was plenty of brush for cover.

Presently, we reached a point where we had a good view of the drainage. The sight before us was mind-boggling. There were at least nine bull elk in the canyon. Two five-pointers were the smallest; the rest were six and seven-pointers. Breeding season was still a few weeks off, and it wasn't unusual for big bulls to herd together, but this was an elk hunter's dream.

By moving carefully and using the brush as a screen, we were able to sneak into the middle of the herd.

The biggest bulls, a pair of huge seven-pointers, were farthest away. They were up on the ridge, but slowly walking down toward us.

A five-point bull walked right by me, nibbling on bunches of grass. My mind raced as I agonized over what to do. I could see Warren; he was passing up a big six-point bull. I was learning a lot about trophy hunting in those minutes, and finally decided to hold off unless Warren shot. It was strange. Warren and I each had dandy bulls dead to rights, but we were passing them up! It was obvious he was going to hold out for the biggest bulls on the ridge. If I shot at the five-point, the rest of the elk would spook, fouling Warren's chance at one of the big ones. I had spent a lot of time tagging along behind Warren and owed all my woods knowledge to him. I wasn't about to mess up his chance at a big bull. Besides, prospects were good that we'd each get a shot at one.

Suddenly the two big bulls coming off the ridge stopped and stared in our direction. They were alert and appeared nervous. Another bull behind me quit rubbing his antlers and became quiet, but several other bulls were still thrashing at the willows around us.

I heard one of the elk make a strange grunting noise, as if he were trying to squeal. I've heard plenty of bulls squeal, but I'd never heard a noise quite like that. As soon as he sounded off, all the bulls stopped rubbing. The canyon became quiet immediately, with only the sound of the creek as it splashed down the canyon bottom. I could see three bulls, and all were straining to pick up signs of danger. Their big-racked heads swiveled about as they looked.

A moment later, one of the bulls crashed through the willows on a dead run. That's all the herd needed. They took off in unison, with some running up the hill and others down. The five-point that I had let walk by before suddenly crossed an opening in front of me. I had a good, clear, broadside shot, so I let an arrow fly. I saw it disappear over his back—the shot was too high. I kicked myself hard and almost regretted passing him up the first time.

Warren and I had a quick conference. He would follow the elk that went up, and I'd follow the others. The elk might settle down. I was disgusted. If I had taken the bull when I had the opportunity, I probably would have scored. Chances of catching up now were poor.

Twice I stalked the herd almost within bow range, but twice I failed to get a shot. The first time, the bulls winded me and took off, and the second time I fell off a log and spooked them as I crashed into the noisy underbrush.

The elk moved into a dense timbered area with thick downed logs. It was impossible to move quietly. I decided it was no use and dropped out of the timber.

I focused my attention on deer sign. Maybe I'd have a chance at one of the huge bucks that were known to be in the area. Still mad at myself over the elk foul-up, I cut cross-country and topped three low ridges. Deer sign became more plentiful, and I began thinking the day might not be a total loss after all.

Then I heard a thumping sound. I looked up the mountainside and spotted the buck I mentioned at the start of this story.

After I decided to ambush him, I eased along, keeping as low as possible, and moved only when he lowered his head. As I changed position on the mountainside, I realized that he was moving along a well-worn trail.

A thick bush offered good cover near the trail and would put me about 30 yards from the buck if he stayed on course. I decided to head for it. The wind was perfect, coming straight off the mountain toward me.

I slipped along as carefully as I could. When I got to the bush, I was pretty shaky. I saw the buck in the distance, still coming down the trail. He looked bigger than ever.

As the seconds dragged by, I got jittery and started talking quietly to myself to calm down. I had to concentrate on the shot and be absolutely ready when the deer moved into position. I had been following him for almost an hour, and I was mentally exhausted.

The buck walked slowly forward and stepped into the spot I was counting on. The shot was a perfect broadside at about 35 yards.

I drew back slowly and anchored. The buck was in the middle of a step when I let the arrow go, and he took a big lunge as the shaft hit. He pounded up the mountain with big strides.

I know I hit that buck, I said to myself. *I'm positive I hit him.* Yet I wasn't convinced.

Then, as he ran straight up the hill away from me, I saw blood on both sides of his front quarters. The arrow had penetrated completely.

The buck spun abruptly and headed back downhill toward me. I nocked an arrow and watched as he cleared the brush in great bounds, but a second shot wasn't necessary. The deer folded and slumped to the ground.

I walked up to him and stared in wide-eyed amazement. He was a gigantic animal, but I had no idea at the time just how big he really was.

After field-dressing the buck, I sat down next to him and just stared at the antlers. I still couldn't believe it. This was the first buck I'd killed with a bow, though I'd killed several with a rifle.

I left the buck in the shade and headed for camp, which was about two miles away. Eric was still in bed, and I wasted no time waking him. He had barely squinted his eyes open when I started telling him the story of my buck. Meanwhile, Warren had walked up behind me and listened. He didn't say anything, but I knew he figured I was telling a tall tale. Generally, when I spread my hands apart to show how big a buck or bull is, Warren kids around and says I always double the true measurement.

This time, though, he must have believed me, because when I took off at a dead run from camp toward the buck, he and Eric were right on my heels.

When we reached the buck, Warren took a good look and let out a gasp.

"Dean," he exclaimed, "this is the world record!"

I hadn't seen Warren so excited in a long time. In my estimation, he's the best bowhunter alive, and here he was all worked up over my buck.

We dragged the buck to a clean area, then caped and skinned it. It was tough to move. Usually Warren and I just grab hold of a deer and pull it along, but this one was so big we had to pull it in little lunges.

Camp was a long way off, so we boned the meat and put it in sacks. Warren packed half the meat, I packed the other half, and Eric carried the cape and head. By the time we got to camp, we were exhausted. It was tough going most of the way, with lava rock and timber to deal with, not to mention the steep terrain.

Driving home, we stopped at a lodge to have dinner. When we were eating, a man came in and stopped at our table.

"That's a nice elk you got out there in the truck," he said.

"Elk!" exclaimed Warren. "That's a buck deer."

At that about half the people in the dining room jumped up to go look at the buck.

After the 60-day waiting period was over, the buck was measured by various people. First it was measured locally, then I sent it to Denver where it was checked by more measurers as well as wildlife officials. They told me it should be the new bow-killed nontypical mule deer, but it wouldn't be official until it was measured by the Pope and Young committee at the spring 1979 meeting in Salt Lake City.

That day finally came, and the judges scored it at 246 6/8, the new No. 1 nontypical mule deer.

The trophy hangs on my living room wall, and I never get tired of looking at it. Sometimes I wonder what would have happened if I had killed that five-point bull elk!–***Dean Derby.***

PART 8 THE SPIRIT OF THE HUNT

Ridgeline Reunion

My younger brother Jeff was four hours overdue for dinner, and I was fighting visions of him with a flat tire and no jack along a Nevada desert road.

"Could you hold his dinner another half hour?" I asked my wife Barbara. "Throw some water on it to moisten it up."

"It's fossilized," she said, taking Jeff's dinner from the oven. "He probably just got a late start." She scraped the remains into a garbage can. They hit bottom with a final, dry rattle.

I went out onto my front porch where I could see the road. An owl hooted. Another answered. The start of Idaho's deer season was a little more than a day away, and I wondered if Jeff and I would make it. Jeff's hunting license and tags had been my gift to him. More than anything else, they represented a good excuse to spend a week together, something we hadn't done since he started high school and I finished college eight years before. I had seen him infrequently, the last time at mom's on a Thanksgiving afternoon, when we tried to fill in the blanks but couldn't. Only after dinner when we talked about deer hunting did familiarity return. Jeff confessed that for as long as he had hunted he had got only a glimpse of a distant lone buck disappearing into brush. That's when I got the idea of a hunt. If Jeff killed a buck during this hunt it would be his first, and I wanted to be in on it.

His headlights were nearly in my driveway before I recognized his truck. He stepped out, stretching to relax himself after a 13-hour ride from Sacramento.

"Sorry I'm late," he said as I took his hand and put my arm around his shoulders. "I got a late start."

The next afternoon I parked my 1960 van off a shale logging road in a sheltered draw crowded with lodgepole pine. I cautioned Jeff not to slam his door, then shouldered my small backpack and pulled my Weatherby .270 Magnum from its case. We started up an almost vertical knifeback that rose from the valley floor to a ridgeline 2,500 feet above.

"Did you ever wonder if you could pull the trigger?" Jeff said behind me. "Is it ever difficult for you?"

"Only when I 'm not sure of the shot," I replied. "Then, it's impossible. Why? Having second thoughts?"

"First thoughts," he said.

About 300 yards above the truck we reached a shale ridge that divided two big avalanche chutes. Limber pine and Engelmann spruce crowded the north-facing slope, and we edged into them for cover. The grade increased. I began to breathe hard. The smell of sage was heavy. To keep on our feet we grabbed scrubs growing between shale outcroppings. Sweat glistened on Jeff's forehead. Across the valley, a shadow cast by the main ridge above us moved slowly upward. Shadows among the sage and bitterbrush deepened, and distant shale outcroppings seemed to grow into ears and antlers.

"How about a break?" Jeff asked.

Illustration by Kip Lott

"A short one," I said. "It'll be dark soon."

A silver four-wheel-drive pickup stopped on the road below. A figure stepped from it, rested his elbows on the hood, and glassed the hills below for several minutes. Then he stepped into the truck, which continued to the road's end, turned, and then slowly came back down.

We climbed past an old mine shaft. Erosion had erased its road. Weathered timbers supported the entrance, which had filled with shale. Across the ridgeline above us a spring was hidden in a pine-choked gully. In early fall deer were high and around it. They'd beaten the earth to dust with their hoofs.

"Seems like a lot of work," Jeff said, panting. "I hope we see something tomorrow."

"We'll see something," I replied.

"We might not get a shot, but we'll see something."

"You always work this hard?"

"Always. It's never easy."

We climbed another two hours before reaching the main ridge. Except for a deep purple tint on the horizon, all was dark. My flashlight illuminated flat ground under a stand of spruce, and we pitched my two-man tent. After spreading our sleeping bags and rifles inside, we collapsed against opposite trunks. I tossed a quart bottle of pink lemonade at Jeff. He took a sip and handed it back. I handed him an apple and leaned back. A wind whistled through spruce needles above us, and a branch creaked nearby. Farther away something cracked and crashed heavily into the underbrush.

"Why didn't we see deer on those south slopes?" Jeff said.

"There's a full moon. They could be feeding all night," I replied. I looked east at the Devils Bedstead. It was barely silhouetted before a faint white glow.

"Will the moon make hunting hard tomorrow?" Jeff asked.

"It could, but the deer should cross this ridge to bed down. If those guys in the silver truck come back, they might move deer up to us."

I shined an apple and took a bite. "You know the difference between deer meat and venison?"

Jeff shook his head.

"Deer meat gets dragged downhill for five hours," I said. "Venison rolls twice and lands on a road."

"Sounds too easy," he said.

"When I heard it I didn't laugh either. Road hunting stinks."

A wind shook loose some needles, and I looked up into the tree's black interior.

"Jeff, for me 90 percent of hunting deer is work—long hikes and hours of glassing," I said to him. "If I'm lucky enough to get a shot and skilled enough to kill cleanly, then there's a long drag out and butchering."

"If I get a chance," Jeff said, "I'll like the work."

"Along with the work," I continued, aware I was making too much noise but unable to leave it half said, "a successful stalk, a clean kill, and the tension that ties it together has its own reward. A buck makes everything that comes before and after a hunt part of a memory."

A gust of wind made the nylon tent pop like a spinnaker and I shifted to tighten a guy. A harvest moon rose above the Devils Bedstead. A twig snapped uphill, but wind gusting through pine needles masked any other sounds.

We pulled off our boots and crawled into our bags. The wind rattled the tent. I thought I heard a coyote howling in the distance, but when I held my breath and listened, I couldn't tell. An owl hooted nearby.

"Hear that?" I whispered.

"Yeah," Jeff replied.

Soon his breathing had the mechanical rhythm that meant he was asleep. As kids, we'd shared the same room. Now we lived in different states and wrote and phoned rarely. Jeff devoted a lot of his time to his business. As I lay watching the moon shine through the green tent, I realized that he would leave if he shot a deer. I could prolong the hunt. I could have him follow deep trails through the forests, where his chances of surprising a buck would be slim, or we could hunt ridges above town where dogs ran the deer and made them doubly wary. But Jeff's time was valuable. Images of dead bucks and Jeff's leaving got tangled together, and the sadness for the one was sadness for both. Almost asleep, I thought I ought to pack our gear and start down the moonlit south slopes before dawn showed a buck in the open. It was a part of a dream, and I tried to secure the memory for morning.

After midnight the wind came up, snapping the nylon, tugging at the tiedowns. I came awake and saw that the tent ridge had sagged to our sleeping bags. I crawled out to tighten the tiedowns. The wind and shadows turned sage clumps into visions of feeding deer, and I sat staring across the hillside, shivering in the cold. I brushed the needles out of my socks and climbed back in the bag. An hour before sunrise the wind died. I woke and shook Jeff. He sat, staring with a false awareness that comes from trying to wake quickly.

A few minutes later Jeff was hiking up the main ridge in the faint light. I waited 10 minutes, then started across the hillside. It was covered with patches of trees and small meadows filled with bitterbrush. I followed a worn game trail, stopping every four steps, the Weatherby balanced in my right hand. Fresh droppings littered the ground.

I settled against a trunk above a game trail that entered a meadow. A blue grouse flushed from a spruce, set its wings and soared downhill. A squirrel crossed the edge of the meadow, jumped into a gnarled pine, then circled its trunk. The Weatherby lay across my knees. I waited. Soon a doe would reach the clearing. This early in the season she would be followed by a fawn. Another doe would wait in the shadows until the first crossed, then step cautiously into the open. Bringing up the rear would be the buck. Only he would know I was near. His mule ears would focus on stray noises, and he would turn uphill as I raised the rifle. A rifle blast startled me. I hoped that it was a first and last shot, that a buck was lying dead in the sage. Then another shot sounded, somehow less definite. It was followed by another, then another, and another. I ran uphill. I was still running when the next report echoed through the trees. Then three more cracked. All were steadily spaced shots that echoed, *cripple, cripple, cripple.*

When I caught up to Jeff, he was out of ammunition. He stood in a clearing holding his .270 and was looking across to a minor ridge.

"Where is he?" I asked.

"You'll have to finish him," he replied. "I'm out of ammunition. He went down after the first shot, but I couldn't hit him again."

I searched the tree line on the opposite ridge but couldn't see the buck.

"He's right below the ridge on that open grass face," Jeff said, pointing.

"I still don't see him."

"Do you see that large white rock? Now left about 15 feet."

Then I saw a buck standing against the hillside and looking our way. The shot was a long one—too long. The buck studied us, looked uphill, took a few steps, then turned and started back.

"Down!" I said, and we lowered ourselves into the grass. The buck took four steps downhill and stopped to look across at us.

"Are you sure you hit him? Did you knock him down?"

"Hard," Jeff said. "He struggled in that grass, and I lost him. When I found him again in the scope he was back up. What are you waiting for? Finish him."

"He's too far away," I said. "If you really did hit him, he'll lie down soon. No sense to start him running. We'd lose him."

I looked at the buck through my scope. His rack was small. He appeared to be a forkhorn with maybe another point on each side. We backed carefully into the trees and followed a game trail that angled downhill. When we reached a rise, we could see the buck standing with his left side toward us. He was looking at a rock outcrop above. I put the scope's cross hairs on his neck and started to squeeze. Then, just out of the scope's range, something moved, stopped, then moved again. I looked away from the scope and saw a large buck slide unsteadily down a shale slope, struggle to catch itself, and tumble, his antlers rattling as they hit rock. The small buck—we could tell that it was a three-point now—watched in confusion, trotting one way, then another. The wounded buck reached a small ledge, seemed to hang for a moment, then crashed onto a talus slope below. He rolled twice and stopped.

I steadied the cross hairs behind the left shoulder of the small buck and squeezed. The 130-grain bullet sucked the legs up underneath him, and he fell heavily in the sage.

Neither of us spoke. We crossed to the bucks. Jeff's had five points on each side, heavily muscled quarters, and a prime coat.

"You hit him in the back," I said, pointing to a small entrance wound. I was thinking it was a good deer. It would be years before he shot another as good.

"I hit it in a bad place, didn't I?" he said. "I tried for a chest shot."

"You took too long a shot, Jeff," I replied. "But it was your first. Next time you pull the trigger you'll be sure the deer will go down and stay down. Each time I stand over a dead buck I ask myself whether it was worth it. So far I've been able to answer yes. When the time comes that I don't know, I'll quit. Now, pull your deer into that shade and I'll show you how to clean it."

The cleaning went quickly. Afterward Jeff grasped one antler and dragged his buck into the open. I quickly dressed my buck and followed Jeff. The carcass slid limply, crushing the sage. I can't smell sage anymore without thinking of dragging a deer. The buck's dead weight pulled at my arm, and after 20 steps I had to stop to rest.

"Jeff," I called out, "was it worth it?"

He stopped and flexed his hand, "Yeah," he said, looking up at me and nodding. "Yeah, it was."

I shook my left arm, changed grips, and followed Jeff downhill toward the truck.–***Andrew Slough.***

Of Bucks and Boys

The Salmon River Breaks of Idaho are wild, lonesome, rugged and gut-busting steep. There are few roads and none penetrate the farthest reaches. Most men who hunt there are trophy hunters drawn by the lure of a big rack. But there are few really great racks, even in that remote country, and the hunt often becomes a personal test of tenacity and stamina. Most hunters fail the test.

The canyon walls dive from the pine and fir-mantled upper rim, their basalt walls standing in places like columnar palisades. The slopes plunge even more steeply as one descends into the canyon, scorched and seared brown by the August heat. It's inhospitable country, this River of No Return wilderness.

Mule deer thrive in this seemingly hostile environment, and that's where my son Tom and I went in the fall of 1980 to try for his first big buck. We had seen the deer two weeks previously on a scouting trip, but we caught only a glimpse of his impressive rack. We backpacked in the day before the season opened and set up camp on the rim. The Salmon River was a rumbling silver ribbon 3,500 feet below.

It was still dark when we awoke, and the stars were bright in the penetrating cold. Frost covered our sleeping bags and backpacks. The fire still smoldered, and Tom laid dry moss and toilet paper on the coals. Moments later, flames curled against the water kettle.

Breakfast was still warm inside us an hour later when we hiked down into the canyon, and sunrise found us on the rocky ridge 800 feet below the rim, where we had seen the big buck.

We edged slowly upwind around a rocky knob, following the fresh tracks of a herd. Tom pointed out a very large set of tracks clearly imprinted on top of the smaller ones. The buck was still there.

Droppings still fresh and shiny littered the sparse grass, and we moved carefully, looking over the ridge as we edged slowly forward. A doe's big ears and the top of her head came into view across the draw. Tom dropped down and snaked a shell into the chamber of his rifle. He was shaking as he crawled ahead on his hands and knees.

We bellied up to the open ridge, avoiding the cactus. Crawl and look. The doe was feeding again. Inch ahead . . . slowly. Look some more. Watch the doe. A little bit farther, and we can see into the draw.

And there they were, a dozen does and fawns followed a mo-

My son came unglued when he wounded a trophy buck, but I found out that he had the guts to put himself together again.

ment later by a high-racked three-pointer, and then there were more than 20 deer silhouetted by the growing light. We froze, trying to ignore the sharp rocks jabbing into our ribs. Ahead of me, Tom was trying to extricate his knee from a clump of needle-spined cactus. His agonized movements were too much, and a dozen pairs of ears suddenly radared in our direction. Tom's knee was still in the cactus when the big buck came up in a rush, the whipcord muscles of his hindquarters driving him up over the rocks with massive grace and incredible power. His neck was swollen huge with the rut. He paused on the opposite slope, one foreleg raised. Tom's rifle slid forward and Tom's forward hand came to rest on a rock. It was obvious that the boy needed no coaching, but it was a long shot. Then the rifle roared and kicked up a storm of dirt and grass in front of the muzzle.

It was 250-plus yards to the deer, but our canyon-and-hillside route was well over 400. A fourth of the way there I relinquished the lead to Tom and watched him leap up the rocks. I suddenly realized that Tom could no longer be led. It was time for me to follow. I slowed to a walk and reflected on the years that had brought us here.

Tom was a 15-year-old sophomore in the Grangeville, Idaho, high school. He had hunted since he was 8, often following me on his short legs.

By the time he was 10, he was carrrying his own lightweight Ithaca. I loaded his 12-gauge shells down to reduce the recoil, and he shot ineffectively for weeks before a straightaway Hungarian partridge ran afoul of his shot pattern. He had enjoyed hunting before he got that bird, but afterward he was obsessed.

Tom got a new Ruger .30/06 and his first deer tag for his 12th birthday. When the deer season opened four weeks later, he was totally familiar with the rifle. He shot a two-point mule deer the second day.

He didn't score in 1978 because he held out for a big buck and never got a shot, but the things he learned about deer and hunting were invaluable.

Tom capitalized on his burgeoning store of knowledge in 1979 and stalked his own deer while I watched from a distant ridge. He took a big whitetail with one shot.

I was hoping for another one-shot kill when we climbed the ridge where the big mule deer had stood, but the deer was gone. A trail of dislodged rocks and crushed grass marked his sliding descent. Sure that he had collapsed out of sight below, we hurried down.

The trail ended at a 100-foot-square stand of brush, and we moved slowly into it. We worked straight down the hill, but the buck didn't move. Then we worked across the patch of brush. Still nothing. Finally, we crisscrossed the brush until it was nearly flattened. Nothing. The buck was gone and so were Tom's spirits. It wasn't the cold breeze that caused his eyes to water.

"Where could he . . . ?"

I looked down into the yawning canyon at our feet, and then out across the endless maze of other canyons, rock ledges and brush-filled draws. There was no conviction behind my reassurance.

"We'll find him, Tom," I forced myself to say. "You hit him hard, and he'll have to go downhill. He's in the bottom of this draw." We sat down to glass and to drink from our canteens. It was only 7:30. It was going to be a long day.

We were glassing the slopes below, hoping to spot the deer before he could drop all the way down into the bottom of the canyon, when the herd materialized in a bowl-like basin half a mile below. The buck was at the rear of the herd and he was hobbling *uphill.*

It seemed impossible that he could have gone that far, and even more so that he was still able to go uphill. We cranked up the 60X spotting scope. Through the heat waves that were already starting to rise, we saw the dragging front leg. The muscle was shot up, but the bone was intact.

The buck lay down under a mountain mahogany bush at the lowest lip of the small basin. A few old does waggled their ears in our direction, but most of the herd had already forgotten us. We strapped on our backpacks and started a circuitous, two-mile-long stalk that would bring us out behind and above the deer. The ordeal was beginning.

An hour later we were slow-footing down the razorback ridge that formed the back rim of the basin. A noise rattled up from below, and the wounded deer raced into view 120 yards away. He was running but favored the wounded front leg. He came to a skidding stop and looked up at us. Tom's shaky offhand shot was a clear miss, and the deer lunged forward, throwing rocks and clumps of grass into the air in his plunging escape. I had no more optimistic reassurances to make.

We sat down to wait, and in a moment the deer came into view 800 yards away. He limped out of sight around the ridge.

Fifteen minutes later we stood where we had last seen the deer. In the dirt of the trail, his huge splayed tracks were plain but there was no blood. We followed the tracks out into the warm sun of the south slope. Another drink from the canteen, and we went on. It was 10:30.

At 11 o'clock we crawled out onto a rocky promontory and looked into the next canyon. Several does were moving about in the bottom, feeding. We knew the wounded buck was down there near the creek that flowed into the Salmon, but where? If we went in too high, he'd go out below us and we'd never see him. We decided that I'd go down into the bottom and Tom would stay on the ridge. From there he'd see any deer that moved out. I backtracked out of sight behind the ridge and headed down, feeling a whole lot like a tired hound.

I edged into the lower end of the draw. At that point I was only 800 feet above the Salmon River. The rim and our camp were 2,700 long, steep feet above me.

I had no more than entered the cool shade when the buck crashed out the other side of the cover, clawing up through the brush and rose tangles. I waited for the shot, but none came, and the deer climbed out of sight. I yelled at Tom and then sat down in the shade. The hound was out of steam.

And he was out of enthusiasm too. Why had we done it? There were certainly other deer, probably even bigger ones, up near the top. Why drop into this hole? I knew it would take four hours just to walk and climb back to camp, and if Tom killed the deer it would take three times that long to pack out. Suddenly my good intentions were shot. I decided to let the deer go. It was just too tough. Besides, the deer's wound wasn't a bad one. I told myself that the buck would surely recover.

The decision was barely made when self-recrimination set in. Wasn't he the biggest deer Tom had ever seen much less shot at? And wasn't there something for Tom to learn in the pursuit, even if it turned out to be unsuccessful?

With more resolve than resources, I climbed to where Tom was waiting. He had seen the deer, but only for an instant. The buck was gone before he could shoot. He saw the deer again as it went around the distant shoulder of the mountain, still moving uphill.

We had to have a break. We fought our way through the thorns and hornets to the creek and lay on our bellies to suck up the cool water. We stayed there through the hot part of the afternoon, soaking our feet and resting. At 3:30 we started up again.

By 4:30 we had hunted out the next draw. The deer wasn't there, and we were now two miles farther from camp and still 2,000 feet below it. We were both dead tired, stumbling and slipping on the loose rock. We had to head back to camp.

It was an anguished decision, and Tom was disconsolate. His enthusiasm was long gone, and now his shoulders sagged. His best and maybe his only chance to take a big buck had evaporated, and I knew he was troubled by the animal's suffering. It was going to be a long hike back up to camp.

Half a mile later we rounded the shoulder of the hill and looked into a small depression that was covered by waist-high rosebush and snowberry. I picked up a baseball-size rock and threw it down toward the brush. Tom watched it halfheartedly as it bounced down the hill. A second later he came alive.

The deer rose suddenly out of the brush like an apparition, his antlers towering over his rut-swollen neck. He quartered downhill, racing for a gap in a rock ledge.

Tom was scrambling to yank the rifle from his shoulder. He fired the first shot offhand while the barrel bounced like a leaf in a windstorm. He frantically worked the bolt and fired a second wild shot.

"Sit down! Sit down!" I yelled at him.

The deer turned slightly and went straight downhill 80 yards away. It was a moving shot like the hundreds Tom had taken at chukars on these same slopes, and it was apparent that he suddenly knew what he was about. The rifle recoiled sharply upward, and the deer folded in midstride. The heavy *thwaaack* came back to us.

Instantly Tom was running and jumping through the rose thorns. "I got him! I got him!" he yelled. Then he came tearing back uphill, shouting the same thing over again, and hugged me.

We took pictures of the buck and measured the rack. Then we caped and quartered the buck. Antlers, cape, scope and jackets went into Tom's pack and the boned-out meat into mine. His pack weighed about 65 pounds, mine about 90. Then we lay down and slid into the packs. The straps bit into our shoulders as we straightened up. It was going to be one killer of a pack.

"Dad, camp's right up there," Tom told me. I knew very well where camp was. It was almost straight up.

An hour later we had gained only 400 feet. My legs were rubber, and my lungs on fire. Waves of nausea flooded over me. The waist straps dug into our hips, pinching sciatic nerves into stabs of pain.

We released the waist straps to spare our hips, and the weight fell completely onto our shoulders, compressing our ribs and lungs. After two hours of being bent over like crabs, we ached everywhere. We had forgotten what it felt like to stand upright.

Twice ledges 20 feet high and a half a mile long barred our way. We were too tired to walk around then so we took the packs off and hauled them up with our rope. It was easier to use our arms than our legs. On one of those climbs I reached for a handhold and grasped the dry, shed skin of a rattlesnake. I recoiled in horror and almost fell backward off the ledge.

By 7 o'clock the last vestige of sunlight had disappeared over the mountains in Oregon, and the stars shone clear above us. We climbed on, almost exhausted. At 9 o'clock, 200 feet from the rim, we collapsed on the ground and rolled out from under the imprisoning weights. It was impossible to stand up.

We lay there for 30 minutes trying to recover strength.Then the coyotes opened up, and the canyon was filled with music that reverberated from the ridges.

We slid a final time into the straps and started on the last 70 yards to camp. The ordeal was almost over, and the agony was already diminishing in our minds.

Perhaps that deer hunt was only a beginning for Tom. Maybe he will go on even more demanding hunts, but every time he sees those antlers on the wall he will remember our long hunt and our long climb.–***Dewey Haeder.***

PART 9 AFTER YOUR DEER IS DOWN

Surefire Way to Field Dress Your Deer

There are several different ways to field dress a deer. The one described here is not only easy, it's excellent for beginners. The chief hazard in field dressing is piercing or cutting internal organs so that urine or intestinal fluids and contents ruin the meat or make it unpalatable. By following these steps, you keep your knife away from the organs, and you'll deposit very little hair on the meat. Of course, the first and most important step is to shoot the deer through the neck, lungs, heart, or spine so that the stomach and the intestinal tract remain undamaged.

If you hit your animal in the abdominal cavity, about all you can do is gut the carcass, wipe it out as thoroughly as possible with clean grass or cloth and hope for the best. Portions of the meat may be ruined by urine or fluids, but most of it will be alright, provided you work quickly.

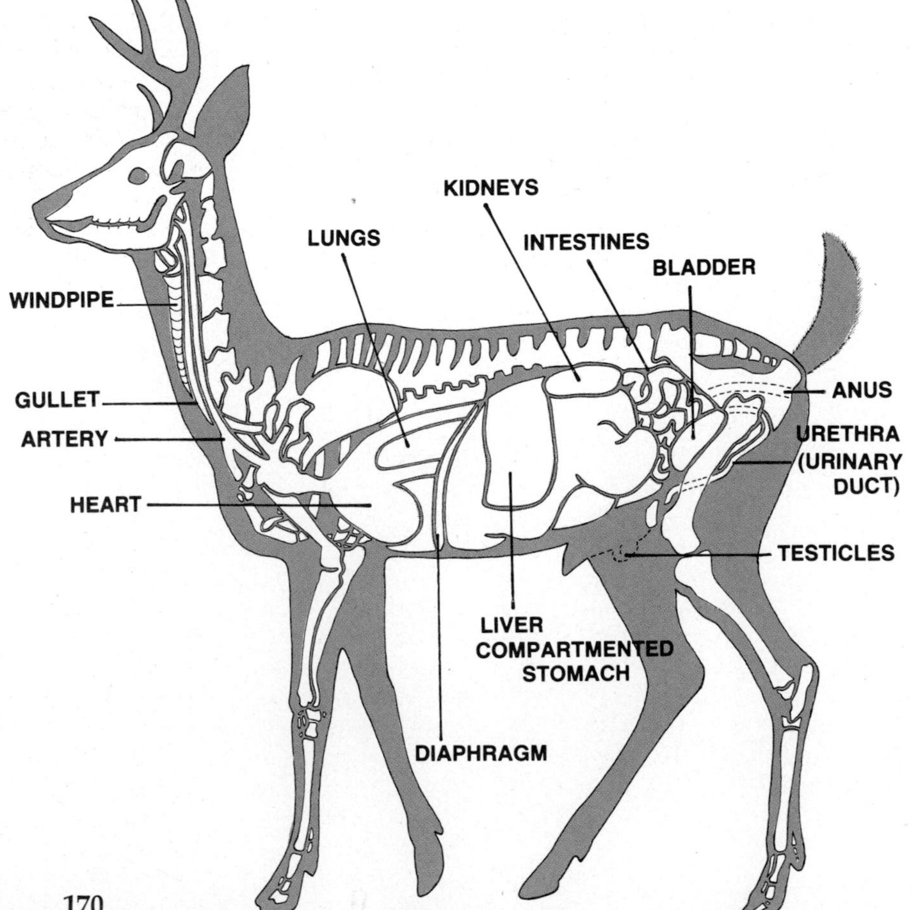

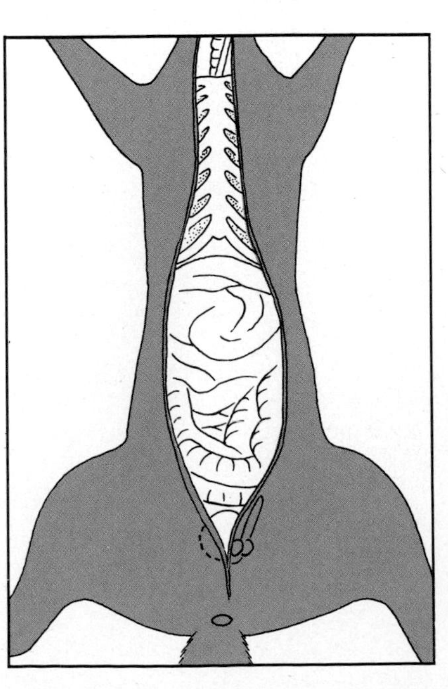

Illustrations by Gerhard Richter

1. Place the deer on its back, preferably on a slope so that the body can be easily rolled downward to spill out the body cavity's contents. If the slope is too steep, place a log or rock on the downhill side to keep the carcass steady.

2. Straddle the deer, facing toward the tail. Insert the tip of your knife, edge up, just below the sternum (triangular breastbone where the last two ribs come together). Being careful not to cut too deeply, cut toward the tail. Make a slit about three inches long. This cut must be very shallow in order not to pierce the stomach. Work carefully and make sure that you are only cutting the hide and the lining of the cavity. With the deer on its back, the stomach falls away from the breastbone, but it pays to be cautious.

3. Insert the first two fingers of your left hand in the cut with your palm up. Spread your fingers and place the knife blade between them, edge up. Extend your cut toward the tail. The fingers and then the back of your hand force internal organs downward so that the tip of your knife only cuts the hide and the lining of the cavity.

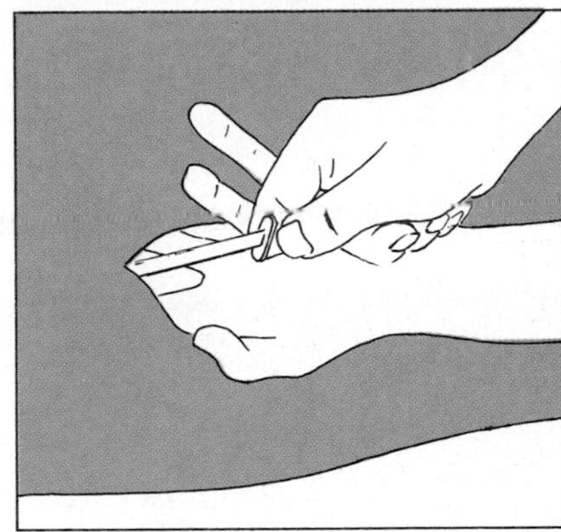

4. When you reach the penis, cut to one side of it and the testicles. Continue the cut to the anus, but do not cut into it. This is the most critical part of the cut. Force internal organs away from the knife.

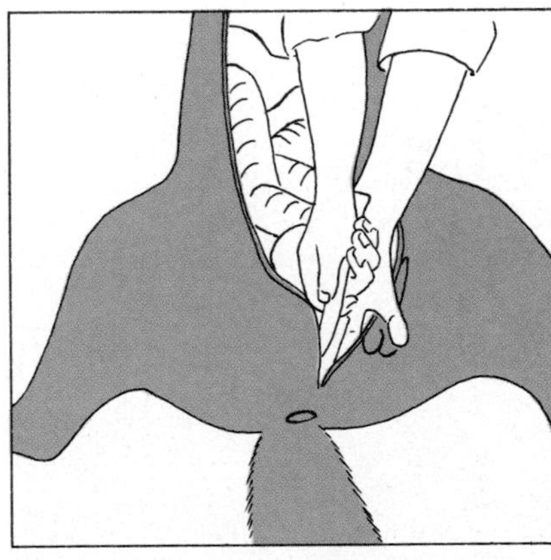

5. Turn around and face the deer's head. Insert the knife, edge up, between the hide and the sternum or breastbone. Slit the skin all the way to the base of the neck.

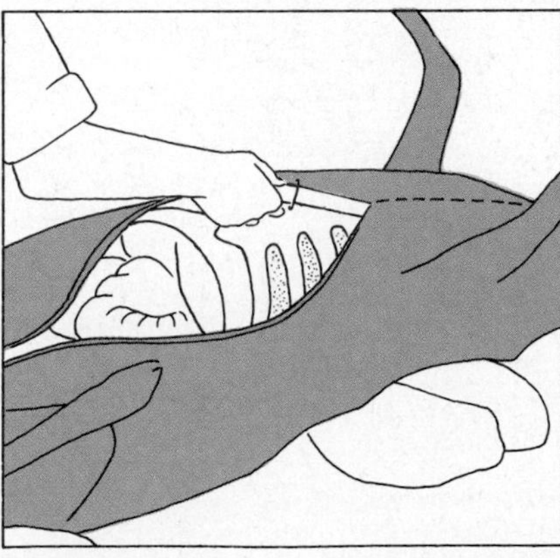

6. Next step is to open the chest cavity. The centerline of the sternum is tough and cannot be cut with a knife. Instead, cut to one side of it where the ribs join. The bone is softer there. Hold the knife haft with both hands and cut forward and upward, following the previous cut in the hide. Try not to cut into the heart, but even if you do, it does not contain anything that would spoil the meat. If you have one with you, it's easier to make this cut with a hatchet.

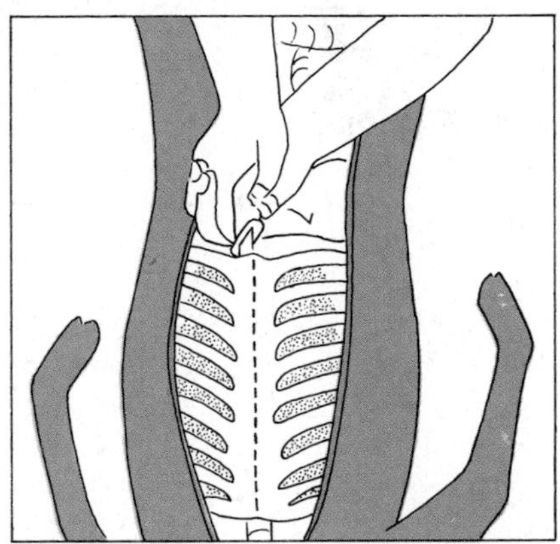

7. Spread the chest opening a bit, reach inside, and grasp the windpipe and the gullet with one hand. Pull them out of the cavity and sever at the base of the neck.

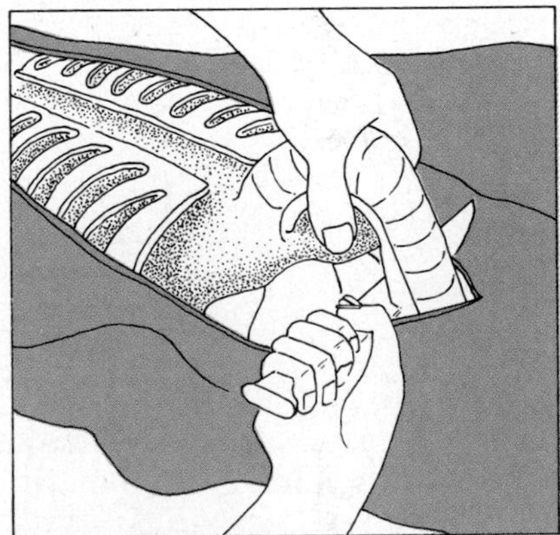

8. The forward end of the whole intestinal tract is now free, and all that remains is to work your way to the rear, lifting out internal organs and intestines and cutting only where necessary to free them. Use your knife as little as possible. Roll the deer to the left or

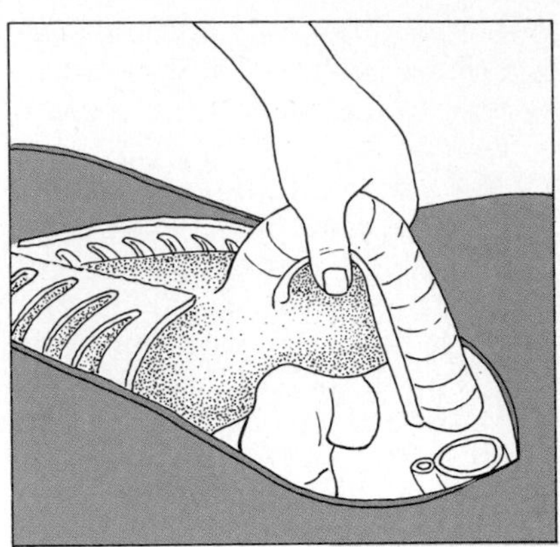

right as required to make any cuts. To begin, pull on the windpipe and gullet. This will lift the heart and lungs out of the cavity.

9. The diaphragm is a tough wall of tissue between the chest cavity and the abdominal cavity. It separates the lungs from the stomach and is attached to the wall of the cavity at the last two ribs. Roll the carcass lightly uphill and prop it so that the organs fall away from the opposite side. Cut the diaphragm free on that side all the way to the backbone. Then roll the animal in the opposite direction and cut the diaphragm free on the other side.

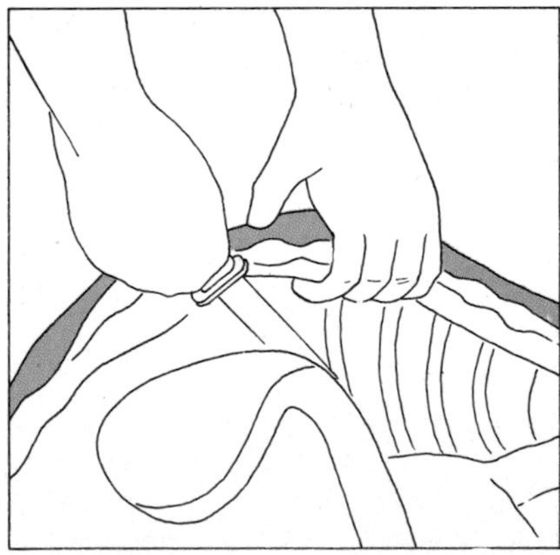

10. Roll the deer onto its side (remove prop). With the heart, lungs and diaphragm free, the stomach, liver, and intestines should roll out easily with perhaps a tug or two here and there and a touch of the knife now and then. Most often the kidneys remain attached to the fat under the backbone. If so, cut them free of the fat, but do not pierce them or cut the ducts that lead from them to the bladder. Cut liver and heart free from the rest of the organs and cool them as quickly as possible in a snowbank or flowing water. In very hot weather, they spoil quickly.

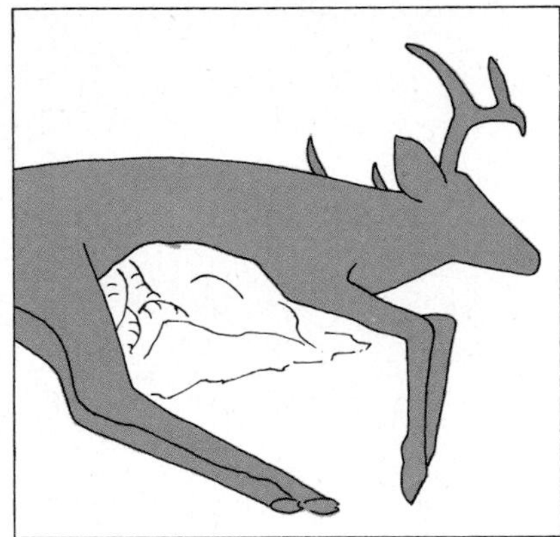

11. With all the intestines outside the carcass, it is easy to get at the bladder, anus, and testicles. The bladder lies inside the pelvic bone at the extreme rear of the deer. Working carefully, lift it so that you can tie off the urethra (urinary duct to the penis) with a piece of twine. Sever the urethra beyond the tie-off. If you are careful, no urine will spill. Discard bladder.

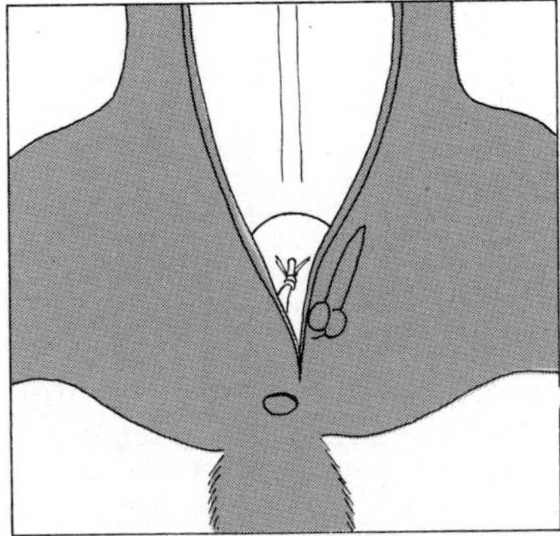

12. With the bladder gone, you can use your knife freely. From outside the deer, "ream" the anus by cutting all around it with your knife inserted as deeply as it will go. Pull the anus into the body cavity and out of the carcass. This method is better than reaming the anus with the bladder still present as many hunters do. If the bladder is still in the pelvis when you ream, it's possible to pierce it. If your state requires "proof of sex" to remain, pluck the testicles out of the scrotum from inside, using your knife to free them, if necessary. Then skin out the penis. If proof of sex is not required, cut all three organs out.

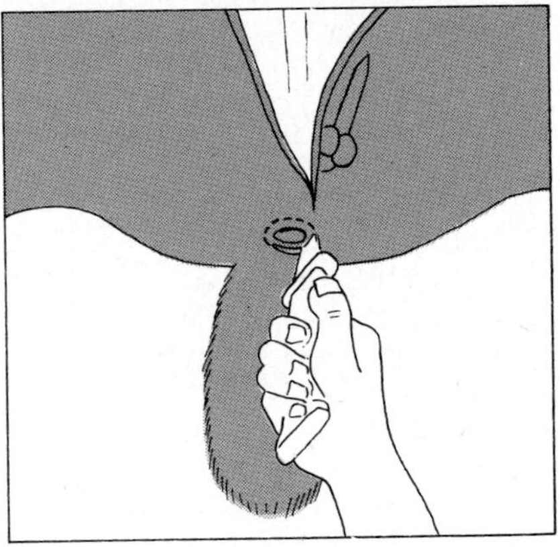

If you slip with your knife, and some feces does touch the meat, wipe it away with clean grass or a dry cloth. Spilled urine is worse and should be thoroughly wiped away as soon as possible. Move the carcass away from the gut pile and turn it belly down on clean grass or other vegetation to drain the blood, or hang the carcass by the antlers to allow blood to drain. Working with a clean cloth or dry grass and a little cool water, clean remaining blood clots from chest cavity and abdominal cavity. Get the carcass back to camp or your home and store it in a cool place until you skin out and butcher it. If it is hot and flies are present, encase the carcass in a cheesecloth bag. *–George H. Haas.*

Getting the Game Home

Transportation is the weak link between a field kill and a taste thrill. Whether game becomes a treat to the palate or a threat to the stomach depends almost entirely on carrying out an action plan that begins the moment an animal falls.

The three things we have to consider when transporting meat are temperature, humidity, and blood. The more blood left in the carcass, and the higher the temperature and humidity, the quicker the meat will spoil.

Domestic animals are hung by the heels, stunned, and stuck with a knife where the base of the neck joins the rib cage. The heart pumps blood out of the carcass before it stops beating. But in most cases, sticking a game animal is useless. It has been shot, the heart has stopped, and there is no natural way for the blood to flow from the veins. There is a strong chance, however, that the animal was shot in the chest, and that the cavity has filled with blood. Immediate field-dressing will remove most of this blood and stop spoilage from beginning in that area.

The ideal temperature for meat is 35°. But even if the temperature climbs into the low 40's, a field-dressed deer with blood washed out of its chest cavity can hang for four or five days, with the hide on or off, and not spoil. Transporting meat may be delayed for a week or more if the temperature stays under 40°.

Humidity speeds up mold growth. The higher the temperatures, the more moisture the air will hold, and the faster mold will produce spoiled meat that's slick to the touch. I have already mentioned that washing out the chest cavity is advisable in safely hanging a deer for days. However, that only applies when temperatures are low. When it's very warm, as it can be during Southern hunts, it's wise to wipe the chest cavity with a cloth carried for that purpose. The meat can then dry quickly and growth of the mold is delayed. Remember that. Wash in cool weather, wipe in warm weather. There are no proved guidelines telling us exactly when to do one or the other. But my guess would be 55° as the point separating the two practices. Above all, get that deer to a locker or cooler fast if air is warmer than 55°.

The same recommendations apply when handling other big animals and small game as well. One additional tactic—a little-known squirrel hunter's trick—could help southerners and warm-weather small-game hunters. If it will be two hours or more before fielddressed birds or animals can be got home or to an ice chest, bury them. Carry several plastic bags with you, and have a wet cloth in one. Paw a hole in cool, moist, shaded soil, place the game in a plastic bag, drop it into the hole, and cover it with dirt. Wipe your bloody fingers on the cloth. Pick up the game on the way back to your vehicle, and take it home in a cooler if you have to travel more than a few miles.

Most hunters who shoot small game close to home don't bother to carry an ice chest with them during cool or cold weather. But they'd be pleasantly surprised if they did. The worst possible way to transport small game animals or birds is to lug them around crammed in a rubberized hunting-coat pocket, and then to throw them in a pile in the trunk to be cleaned at home. It's best to field dress them immediately, skin or pluck them before going home, and transport them in a cooler. Let the meat slosh around in water and ice; it will help to wash the blood on the way home. Don't carry game in cold water for very long, however. If the trip home takes more than a few hours, it would be best to keep the meat dry.

If birds or small animals can be frozen, they'll last about 48 hours in a good cooler before beginning to thaw in moderate weather. If the game thaws a bit, don't worry too much. If the meat still has ice crystals in it, there's no danger in refreezing it. If you can't see any crystals, put a thermometer in the ice chest with the game. If it reads 40° or less, and the meat has been at that temperature for no more than two days, it's still safe to refreeze it. Do not refreeze or eat any game that smells bad or registers above 45° in a long thaw (more than a day).

Because there is some risk of spoilage if the game meat thaws and must be refrozen, don't freeze it if the weather is hot or the trip will last more than 48 hours. In such cases, it's best to transport the meat iced. Keep the meat and ice in separate plastic bags in the cooler to avoid getting the meat wet for a prolonged period of time. Check the ice and drain the water frequently.

Dry ice is less messy than ordinary ice. It evaporates instead of melting, and it absorbs almost twice as much heat as an equal weight of ordinary ice. It is an excellent refrigerant to use when transporting game. But dry ice is harder to get than water ice. The best places to get it are dairies, especially those that make ice cream. Keep the dry ice separate from the meat. Use wrapping paper or, better yet, corrugated cardboard. Otherwise the meat will be "burned."

When planning to transport small game, find out what the regulations are regarding what should be kept on the body—head, wing, feet—for species identification. U.S. Fish and Wildlife Service regulations require that either a wing or the head be kept on migratory birds whether being transported locally, interstate, or across the border from another country.

Sometimes transporting big game is complicated by conceit. Some of us like to display our animals on top of the car or on the bed of a pickup, and we even fry them on the hood above the hot engine. All but the last are acceptable if the hunting is done very near home. But exposing it to wind and sun is no way to haul a prized animal a hundred miles or more, even during cool weather.

The simplest big-game "cooler" consists of blankets or sleeping bags, sheet plastic, wrapping paper, cardboard, and dry ice. Cool air falls, so trap it by using blankets or a sleeping bag for insulation under the animal. Protect the sleeping gear with sheet plastic. Spread wrapping paper over the animal and top that with dry ice on cardboard. Again, use sheet plastic to protect the bedding, then pile on as many blankets or sleeping bags as possible to hold in the cold air. If not enough bedding is available, many layers of newspaper can be a good substitute.

If possible, transport the animal inside the vehicle. The back end of a station wagon or the inside floor of a camper can be used, but the trunk of a car is better because it's aways unheated. The back seat of a car is the last choice because it is too warm. You can minimize the heat by removing the seat.

If the animal must be carried outside, use the same insulation, dry ice, and so on, and wrap the assembly with plastic mummy style so that the wind can't easily blow the cold air out of the package. Position it on the vehicle so that the plastic overlaps like shingles on a roof. Wind or rain should blow over not into the overlaps.

If no dry ice is available for use on a long trip, and temperatures are above 45°, conventional ice will have to be used. That calls for a different approach. Nobody wants a camper or the back seat of a car full of melted ice. But it's OK to use ice in an ordinary trailer. Just pack the ice around the animal and lash down a cover. Even a cleaned-up dog trailer will do if the compartments in it are large enough or the separations can be removed. Check the ice frequently.

Here are a few suggestions for those who might want to build a trailer especially for transporting game, or to put together a large

A trophy head should be shipped to the taxidermist with the cape attached to the skull. To protect antlers, ship suspended by wires in a wood frame. Cover frame with brown paper.

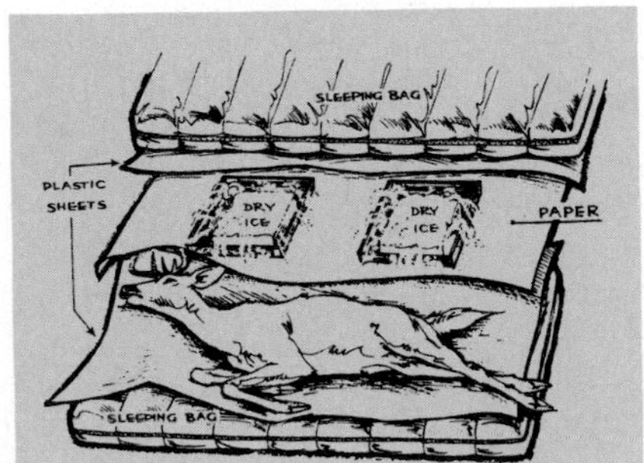

The "sandwich" method for transporting game consists of blankets or sleeping bag under the animal to hold the cold air in, plus plastic sheet to protect bedding. Lay paper over deer, and place dry ice in shallow cardboard boxes so it can't burn the meat. Another plastic sheet and more bedding for insulation top it off.

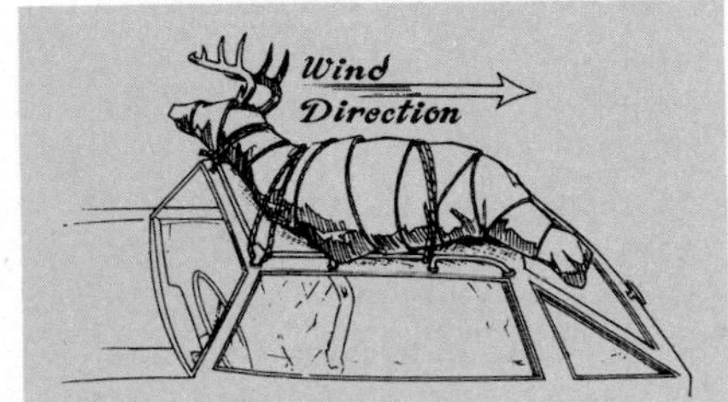

If the animal must ride outside vehicle, wrap it with insulating material such as blankets. Top it with a wrap of plastic. The spiraling wrap should shed wind as shingles shed rain on a roof.

box for the pickup bed or even a smaller box to mount on luggage carriers on top of a car.

Build the framework to allow at least four inches of insulation between the five-eighths of an inch exterior plywood shell and the galvanized sheetmetal, aluminum, or fiberglass liner. Install a small (three-eighths or half an inch) drainpipe. A larger drain might suck out too much cold air if left open while traveling.

Dimensions of the box will vary according to the game species being hunted and the number of animals expected to be transported. Sears has a trailer kit that has a 56×44-inch frame and carries an 860-pound payload. Larger kits have frames up to 96×72 inches and carry up to 1,260 pounds. Perhaps even a molded-plastic luggage carrier could carry a quartered deer on top of most cars.

Game can be shipped, of course. Greyhound has a "Next Bus Out" service that provides for carrying a cooler of frozen birds a hundred miles to certain terminals on an overnight basis.

The only carrier choice for longer distances and bigger packages is air freight. But don't assume it's available everywhere. TWA, for example, has limited service in Wyoming and Montana. A crate bigger than 38×48×40 inches couldn't be carried. Always check air freight facilities in advance. Ask if the flight is direct. A "dogleg" route that might involve transfers could cost more and might delay the package, making refrigeration a greater problem.

Air-freighting a whole animal usually is impractical because of size, shape, and refrigeration limitations. In most cases the animal must be taken to a processor to be cut up, packaged, frozen, and then shipped. If things go smoothly, you should have the meat before it thaws.

Frankly, I'd make my own arrangements with the airlines. Too often when shipping plans have been left to the processor the meat has arrived spoiled. However, if the processor is to handle the arrangements, discuss the carrier and the route with him. Tell him not to ship on Fridays, or perhaps even Thursdays, if the meat is to be taken to a locker for storage. The meat could be delayed on the way and arrive on a weekend when the locker plant is closed.

Costs of air freight vary widely. For example, one major airline charges 56¢ a pound to carry freight from Seattle to St. Louis. That's $84 to ship 150 pounds of venison.

If the package is relatively light but large—a trophy head, perhaps—the airline figures the pound charge on the basis of 194 cubic inches. Example: Take a box 48 inches on each side. Multiply 48×48×48. It comes to 110,592 cubic inches. Divide that by 194 and you get about 570 "volume pounds." Multiply that by 56¢. The result is $319.20 for shipping from Seattle to St. Louis.

If the head is to be shipped to a taxidermist, don't have it sent on Thursday or Friday. It could arrive when the taxidermist is closed for the weekend.

To prepare it for shipping, an elk or moose head should be caped. But an amateur is better off if he includes the whole hide of a deer. The entire neck should be peeled off inside out. This eliminates the tendency of the average hunter to start a straight cut from between shoulders to the base of the skull, only to find his knife wandering off the line and down the side of the neck.

Trim the excess flesh and fat and saw off the skull cap (with the antlers) on a horizontal line from the eye socket. Cool it to air temperature, and then cover it with a scrub bucket (no less) of table salt. Roll it up and let it soak for 48 hours. Then unroll it and air dry it somewhat before rolling it up again and placing it in a plastic bag for shipment.

To avoid antler breakage during shipment, use a strong wooden cubical framework. The antlers and attached hide can be suspended in the center by wires. Heavy brown paper makes an adequate outside cover.

When transporting game to the U.S. from a foreign country, plan carefully and well in advance. Each country has different regulations, as do our individual states. For example, a group of Louisiana waterfowlers who had hunted in Mexico missed their direct flight home. So they arranged a flight to Texas from which they could transfer to another plane going to Louisiana. Texas authorities arrested and fined them for importing ducks without a state permit. That wouldn't have happened if they had flown to Louisiana.

Other hunters have been arrested for making hamburger of game before bringing it home. Ask first and all regulations in every state, province, and country involved.

State game departments usually are in capital cities. Most foreign countries have consuls in major cities from whom additional addresses can be obtained. Check with the U.S. Customs Service and the nearest U.S. Fish and Wildlife Service agent in a major city, or write to the Department of the Interior, Fish and Wildlife Service, Washington, DC.

If driving from Mexico or Canada, file customs form 3315 at the border. If shipping, fill out the form and send it with the head or meat. Game can be shipped in bond without the form, but customs will check it at the destination. That causes a delay. So get the form in advance.

Planning is the key to successful game transportation. Do it well.–*Larry Mueller.*

What to Do with Your Deer Hide

One of the most valuable parts of a deer is its hide. Unfortunately, thousands of skins are discarded every year because many hunters don't know what to do with them. Lyn Schuette, president of W. B. Place Tannery in Hartford, Wisconsin, says of the more than 130,000 deer hides legally taken last year in Wisconsin, about half were commercially tanned, as many as 25 percent were home-tanned, and 25 percent were thrown away.

If you've been tossing out your deer hides, consider this: They can be made into leather garments and other goods, they can be tanned with the hair on and used as wall rugs, they can be sold to fur buyers and taxidermists, or they can be donated to veterans hospitals or centers for the handicapped.

To make use of your deer hide, the first consideration is caring for it as soon as the animal is down. Don't stick the deer's throat—a common but unnecessary procedure. Because an animal's heart stops when it dies, cutting a dead deer's throat cannot drain the body of blood.

If you intend to have the deer head mounted by a taxidermist, you must remove the cape (head and shoulder skin) correctly and protect it. That means you should keep it free of cuts and holes. Don't drag the carcass or the brittle hair will fall off.

Jack Atcheson, a taxidermist in Butte, Montana, said he pays $15 or more for a good, clean cape from a mature buck mule deer. Jim Mackrell, a Concordville, Pennsylvania, taxidermist, pays about the same for a large whitetail buck's cape.

"Many taxidermists are in the market for good capes," Mackrell said. "When a hunter brings in a shot-up or spoiled cape, the taxidermist must use another one. Many hunters don't care for capes properly—they skin them incorrectly or they cut them off too short. When that happens, we must find replacement capes."

You can sell the hide to a taxidermist, fur dealer, or a tannery. Prices depend on current market value.

Mackrell says the value of deer hides goes up if cowhide prices rise. If cowhide prices fall, so do deer-hide prices. I checked with several fur buyers in the United States while researching this article. A top-quality hide brings about $5, and as much as $8 if the market is good. A hide after the cape has been removed brings $1.50 to $2.50.

Even when market prices are high, fur buyers could cheat you. Shop around if you want to sell several hides. Game wardens are good sources of information about fur buyers.

Several years ago, while working as forester and game manager for the U.S. Military Academy at West Point, New York, I kept busy after work by skinning deer that were killed by Army officers and cadets, and I kept the hides as payment for the job. When I accumulated 40 or 50 hides, I sold them to Russ Carpenter, a well-known gun writer who owned Carpenter's Gun Shop. Russ paid top prices for the hides. My small profit kept me in shotgun shells and hunting gear for the year. You could do almost the same thing. Many hunters would welcome someone to skin their deer and use hides that otherwise would be thrown away.

You should skin a deer as soon as possible after it has been killed. Place the hide in a cool place because high temperatures hasten decay. Salt the hide immediately, but if you don't have salt, wrap the hide in burlap or cheesecloth to protect it from flies or it will soon be ridden with maggots. Never put a hide in a plastic bag. It will quickly overheat and spoil.

To salt a hide, stretch it tautly hair side down on a flat surface and remove all fat and flesh. Take care not to puncture the skin. Pour five to seven pounds of salt uniformly on the hide, rubbing it into the edges and pockets where the fur curls over.

Then roll up the hide and place it in a cool place. Because the salt will draw moisture, fluid might run from the skin. To prevent the skin from sitting in a pool of its own liquid, put a couple of small boards or bricks in a tub and put the hide on this pallet.

The next day, unroll the hide and examine it to be sure every square inch has been salted. You can usually see an area that was missed because it will be a different color than the well-salted parts. Salting every spot is essential because the hair will fall out from unsalted parts.

After the hide has drained well, resalt it, roll it up, and take it or ship it to a taxidermist or tannery. If necessary, you can freeze the hide without damaging it. Well-salted skins can be kept for weeks or months if stored in a cool, well-ventilated area.

Though most hunters have their deer hides tanned commercially, it's possible to tan them at home. The process is simple but requires much effort and time.

Here are the steps as suggested in the 135-page book *Tan Your Hide,* by Phyllis Hobson. (The book, an excellent source of tanning information, also has patterns for garments and accessories. Send $4.95 plus 75¢ for handling and postage to Garden Way Publishing Company, Charlotte, VT 05445.)

Soak the hide overnight in a solution of one-quarter cup of lye dissolved in 10 gallons of cold water. If the hair doesn't slip off easily, keep the hide in the solution until it does.

Drape the hide over a fleshing beam or round log (preferably smooth-barked or peeled), and scrape the hair off with a fleshing tool or butcher knife. (A fleshing tool can be bought from taxidermy supply houses. Check with a taxidermist for information.) Then turn the skin over and use the fleshing tool to remove fat and flesh.

Next soak the hide in a bath of enough diluted vinegar to cover it. Use two cups of vinegar to every 10 gallons of water. After the hide has soaked overnight, rinse it thoroughly in water and immerse it in the following solution:

Dissolve two bars of naphtha soap in one cup of hot water, then add this mixture to three gallons of hot water. Allow the solution to cool, and soak the hide in it for four or five days. Stir the skin around several times daily, taking care that it remains completely submerged.

Remove the hide, rinse it in clean water, and pull and stretch it until it's partly dry. Smear a generous coat of lard, bacon grease, or neat's-foot oil on the hide and once again soak it in a new solution of naphtha soap. Allow it to soak for three more days, stirring it several times daily. Rinse the skin in clean water, and pull and stretch it vigorously over a stake. (You can make a stake by jamming a broken oar or paddle deeply into the ground so it's stable. Work the hide across the rounded oar until the skin is pliable.) When the skin is well worked and partly dry, stretch it taut and tack it to a frame. Let it dry in a cool, shaded, well-ventilated place. Before the hide dries completely, once again work it over the stake until it is soft.

Smoke the hide by draping it over a framework of poles erected over a small smoky fire. Smoke until the skin turns a golden tan.

Remember that it takes a lot of work to make the buckskin supple. If it starts to stiffen, moisten it with water and give it another going-over on the stake.

If this procedure seems tedious, consider the way Indians tanned skins. They threw wood ashes into a quantity of water to make a lye solution, then soaked the hide until the hair slipped. After the skin was fleshed across a peeled log with the thigh bone of an animal, it was smeared with a mixture of the animal's brains and tallow, and cooked over an open fire. After being allowed to dry somewhat, the skin was worked over a sharpened stump and scraped with stones and shells until it was soft. Smoking completed the process.

If you decide to have your deer hides tanned commercially, you can have them returned to you until you have enough for a garment, or you can have the hides tanned and made into the garments or accessories of your choice.

Beware of outfits that offer to accept your untanned hides as part payment for garments. The difference between the value of your hides and the cost of the clothing could be outrageously high. For example, you might send five hides to a company, which would then charge you an exorbitant rate for tanning. That rate might be so high that the garment would cost more than a similar one at a retail store, and you could keep your hides.

Hides are priced by the square foot, tanned. According to W. B. Place Company, you'd have to pay about $9.50 to have a typical deer hide tanned into buckskin. If you want the hair left on the hide, you'd be charged about $15.95. There are about 9.5 feet of usable hide in a typical deerskin.

Lyn Schuette says many hunters send or take their hides in every fall and accumulate the buckskins until they have enough for the garments they want. When a hunter turns in his collection of deerskins, all are dyed in the same vat so that they are uniformly colored.

A clothing maker needs five to seven hides to make a jacket, seven to eight hides for a coat, one-and-a-half for a gun case. One average-size hide can yield as many as three pairs of moccasins or gloves. A purse takes one skin, and a small purse or wallet could be made from the trimmings.

W. B. Place sets two prices for each leather item—a "making price" and a "retail price." The making price is the one you pay if you provide the tanned hides; the retail price is what you pay if you don't supply hides. A "casual-style ladies coat," for example, costs $184.95 retail. If you provide eight tanned hides, however, your price is $59.95. Suppose you had paid $9.50 per hide for tanning and $1.75 per hide for dying. That means your total price for the coat made from your hides would be $149.95. The difference between $149.95 and $184.95 is not that great, but by providing the deerskins yourself, you could take pride in knowing that you provided the leather from your own deer.

To get the W.B. Place leather-goods catalog, which also contains information on tanning, shipping, and measuring hides, write to the company at 368 West Sumner Street, Hartford, WI 53027. Other companies around the country provide similar services, but most work only with fur dealers and taxidermists who ship hides in large volumes. Most hunters take their hides to a taxidermist, who then sends the skins in bulk quantities.

Before shipping your hides, mark them with a leather punch to identify them as yours, or tag them securely. (You can borrow a leather punch from a high-school crafts class or shoe repairman.) To ship the hides, drain them well (be sure they've been well salted), and dry them lightly with a paper towel. Roll them flesh side in, place each hide in a large grocery bag, wrap the package in newspapers, put it in a cardboard box, and seal it tightly. Include a list of instructions, and be sure to indicate if you want the hide tanned into buckskin or with the hair left on. Then send them through the U.S. mail or a commercial parcel-delivery service.

Because hide thickness varies a great deal, manufacturers often pass deerskins through a splitting machine, which slices them to thicknesses having tolerances of 1/100 of an inch. The outer side (the side that formerly held the fur) has grain and is used in clothing. The underside is used in other processes, such as suedes and other types of leathers. You will receive the uniform, grainy "split," which will be thinner than your original deerskin. A split, being thinner, is not as durable as an unsplit hide. But a split can be sewn on a regular sewing machine while heavy-duty factory machines are needed to sew a full-thickness hide. Find out your tannery's policy on splitting deerskin. Many leather-clothing makers use only splits.

Many people make their own leather garments, particularly the growing numbers of Americans who call themselves "mountain men" or muzzleloading enthusiasts.

Bob Bearor's family of Troy, New York, is a good example of the growing muzzleloader clan. His wife Holly makes buckskin clothing for the family and also has a small business making deerskin clothes.

Holly chooses garment styles after studying illustrated historical books in libraries and museums and muzzleloader catalogs that show frontier clothing.

For a pattern, Holly uses an old pullover shirt and a pair of blue jeans that have been taken apart at the seams. She traces the pattern on the buckskin, leaving a one-half-inch margin around each piece. She prefers the thick, natural deerskin to a split and sews by hand.

If you are interested in contemporary garments, look for patterns in fabric shops. The book *Tan Your Hide* has patterns for key fobs, knife sheaths, a case for glasses, belt, wallet, gun holster, mittens and vest.

Several organizations solicit deer hides from hunters. For example, the Elks have a national program of collecting raw hides, having them tanned, and distributing them to veterans hospitals around the country. As a member of the local Elks lodge told me, "Those patients wait all year for the buckskins to come in. They make all kinds of leather articles, and besides making a little money it's great therapy."

The next time you tie your tag on a deer, don't look at the animal simply as a source of meat. Remove its hide carefully and use it. –***Jim Zumbo.***

DEER-HIDE TANNERIES

These tanneries tan small quantities of deer hides for hunters. The first five companies make buckskin and the last two produce hair-on hides only:

W.B. Place Company, 368 West Sumner Street, Hartford, WI 53027; Pagano Gloves, 3-5 Church Street, Johnstown, NY 12095; Custom Coat Company, 227 North Washington, Berlin, WI 54923; Colorado Tanning and Fur Dressing Company, 1793 So. Broadway, Denver, CO 80210; Fox Valley Leather, 633 West Center Street, North Salt Lake, UT 84054; Nelson and Sons, 625 Humble Street, San Antonio, TX 78225, and Pacific Northwest Tannery, Box 485, Fort Klamath, OR 97626.

PART 10 BIG BUCKS AND THE RECORDS

The Two Trophy Scoring Programs

Most hunters know that the *Boone and Crockett Club* and *Pope and Young Club* are the two major records keepers for native North American big game. But few hunters know how to measure trophies, let alone how to submit trophy scores for official recognition. Yet, with the proper score chart and a ¼-inch-wide measuring tape, almost anyone can accurately measure a trophy to determine if it might qualify for a records book.

BOONE AND CROCKETT

Founded in 1887, the Boone and Crockett Club published its first big-game records book in 1932 and followed with a second book in 1939. The current scoring system was adopted in 1950 and was incorporated into the 1952 records book. Successive records books have been published at roughly six year intervals, with the latest in 1981 (*Records of North American Big Game*, 8th edition).

The Boone and Crockett Club deer scoring system for typical (normal, symmetrical antlers) is based on measurements of the antler beams, the normal points (with whitetails, points grow on top of the main beam; with mule deer and Columbia blacktails, points are the normal "forks"), circumferences of the main beam (and/or forks) and the inside spread. Added together, this results in a numerical score from which the lack of symmetry between matched point lengths is subtracted, along with any abnormal points (points from sides or bottom of beam or from other points) to arrive at the final score for the trophy. Nontypical (abnormal, asymmetrical) antlers are scored in separate trophy categories. Score then determines trophy rankings in the records book. Currently, the minimum entry scores for typical antlers and nontypical antlers are as follows: whitetail (170 and 195), Coues whitetail (110 and 120), mule (195 and 240), and Columbia blacktail (130 typical; no category for nontypical).

If your preliminary measurement indicates that your trophy meets the minimum score, or comes close, you should request that a measurement be made by an official measurer. Since these official measurers donate their time, offer to deliver the trophy to them at their convenience. Should the official score be over the minimum, your trophy is then eligible for entry into the records archives and for listing in the next edition of the records book. The completed score chart, signed by the official measurer, should then be forwarded along with an entry fee and other necessary documents.

The current three-year entry period for the Boone and Crockett Club ends December 31, 1982. The top trophies in each category of this awards period are eligible for invitation to the awards judging, display, and ceremonies scheduled for mid-1983. Additionally, these trophies are shown in a special awards program photo brochure that gives selected measurements and other information about the hunt.

Full information on trophy entry and the several books and other products sold by the Boone and Crockett Club can be found in a free information brochure about the records keeping. One of the more interesting items available is a specially made ring-end measuring tape, specifically designed for taking the circumferences of the measuring system. Score charts, with scoring instructions, are 25¢ each.

The Boone and Crockett Club records book shows not only trophies taken by gun, but also those by bow, and unknown methods – in which the trophies are known as *pick-ups*. These pick-ups are included for their scientific value, with several of the world records among them. Trophies taken only by bowhunting may also be entered into the Pope and Young Club records book.

POPE AND YOUNG

Begun in 1957 for bowhunters, the Pope and Young Club has a records system patterned closely after that of the Boone and Crockett Club. In fact, Pope and Young employs Boone and Crockett score charts and has only slightly different entry procedures. The Pope and Young Club published its first records book in 1975 and its second in 1981.

Entry periods are two years long, with the current period ending December 31, 1982. Awards judging, display, and ceremonies will be held in mid-1983. Current Pope and Young Club minimum entry scores for typical and nontypical deer trophies are whitetail (125 and 150), Coues whitetail (60 and 66), mule deer (145 and 160), Columbia blacktail (90), and Sitka blacktail (65). For the latter two, there is no category for nontypical heads.

Boone and Crockett Club Records

This whitetail (typical) ranks No. 2 in B&C records, scoring 205 points, with an inside spread of 24-2/8 inches. It was shot by Larry Gibson in Randolph County, Missouri, in 1971.

This mule deer (typical) ranks No. 2 in B&C records, scoring 225-6/8 points, with an inside spread of 30-6/8 inches. It was shot by Doug Burris, Jr., in the San Juan National Forest, Colorado, in 1972.

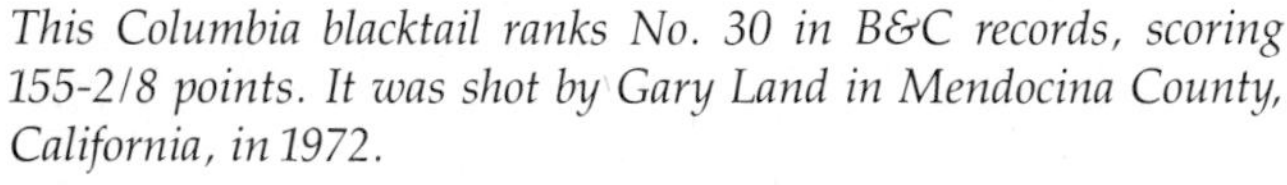

This Columbia blacktail ranks No. 30 in B&C records, scoring 155-2/8 points. It was shot by Gary Land in Mendocina County, California, in 1972.

Larry Raveling poses with the B&C No. 2 ranking nontypical whitetail he took in 1973. The head scored 282 points. Raveling took his trophy in Clay County, Iowa. Shown also are heads in various categories that were displayed at the 16th Awards Program in 1977.

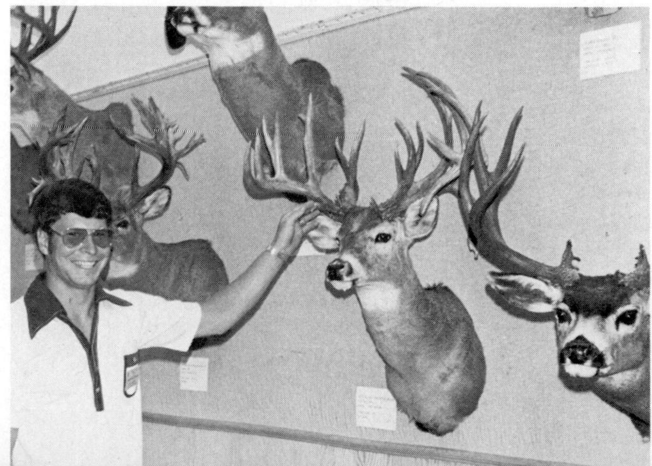

FOR MORE INFORMATION

For official score charts, special measuring tapes, records books, or further information, write

Boone and Crockett Club
205 South Patrick Street
Alexandria, VA 22314

or

Pope and Young Club
Route 1, Box 147
Salmon, ID 83467

Pope and Young Club Records

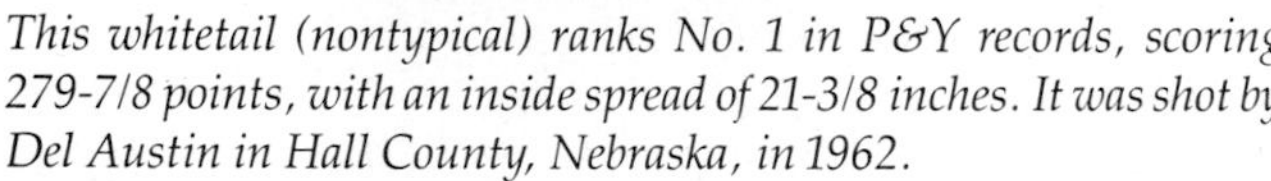

This whitetail (nontypical) ranks No. 1 in P&Y records, scoring 279-7/8 points, with an inside spread of 21-3/8 inches. It was shot by Del Austin in Hall County, Nebraska, in 1962.

This Coues deer (pronounced cows*), a diminutive whitetail subspecies with a range restricted to Mexico, Arizona, and New Mexico, ranks No. 1 in the P&Y Coues records. It has an inside spread of 15 inches and scored 104-2/8 points. It was shot by Larry Peterson near Payson, Arizona, in 1978.*

This Columbia blacktail (typical) ranks No. 1 in P&Y records. It scores 172-2/8 points, with an inside spread of 20-4/8 inches. It was shot by B.G. Shurtleff, near Silverton, Oregon, in 1969. For the full story on the hunt, see "Blacktail King," beginning on page 115.

This mule deer (nontypical) ranks No. 1 in P&Y records, scoring 246-6/8 points, with an inside spread of 24-6/8 inches. It was shot by Dean Derby II in Mesa County, Colorado, in 1976.

Index